VICTIMOLOGY

Legal, Psychological, and Social Perspectives

Harvey Wallace

California State University, Fresno

Allyn and Bacon

Boston • London • Toronto • Sydney • Tokyo • Singapore

Editor-in-Chief, Social Sciences: Karen Hanson
Editorial Assistant: Elissa V. Schaen
Marketing Manager: Susan E. Brown
Editorial-Production Service: Shepherd, Inc.
Composition and Prepress Buyer: Linda Cox
Manufacturing Buyer: Megan Cochran
Cover Administrator: Jenny Hart

Copyright © 1998 by Allyn & Bacon
A Viacom Company
160 Gould Street
Needham Heights, MA 02194

Internet: www.abacon.com
America Online: keyword:College Online

Library of Congress Cataloging-in-Publication Data
Wallace, Harvey.
    Victimology: legal , psychological, and social perspectives/Harvey Wallace.
        p.   cm.
    Includes bibliographical references and index.
    ISBN 0–205–19153–3
    1. Victims of crimes—United States. 2. Victims of crimes—Legal status, laws, etc.—United States. 3. Criminal justice, Administration of—United States. I. Title.
    HV6250.3.U5W35 1998   97–37664
    362.88'0973—dc21   CIP

Printed in the United States of America

10 9 8 7 6 5 4 3 2 1   02 01 00 99 98 97

To my wife, Randa F. Wallace

CONTENTS

Preface ix

Introduction

1. Introduction and History of Victimology 1
Introduction 2
The Development of Laws 3
Social Forces 6
Victimology Theories 9
The Rise of the Victims' Rights Movement 12

2. Measurement of Crime and Its Effects 19
Official Reports 20
Other Reports 29

3. The Criminal Justice System and Victims 35
The Criminal Court System 36
The Parties 42
Criminal Justice Procedures 47

4. The Civil Justice System and Victims 57
Civil Procedures 58
Juvenile Court Dependency Procedures 66
Restorative Justice 68

Responses to Victimization

5. The Consequences of Victimization   73
  Physical Consequences   74
  Mental Consequences   78
  Financial Consequences   82

6. Empowering Victims   90
  Introduction   91
  Media   91
  Legislation   96
  Public Speaking   100
  Fundraising   103

Special Types of Victims

7. Homicide Victims   107
  Introduction   108
  Responding to Special Needs   114

8. Females as Victims   122
  Sexual Assault   123
  Stranger Rape   128
  Acquaintance Rape   132
  Marital Rape   134
  Sexual Harassment   137

9. Spouses as Victims   146
  Introduction to Spousal Abuse   147
  Theories on Spousal Abuse   152
  The Criminal Justice Response to Spousal Abuse   156

10. Child Victims   168
  Types of Child Abuse   169
  Extent of the Problem   171
  Cycle of Violence   174
  Other Theories Regarding Child Abuse   177
  Special Types of Child Abuse   183

11. **Elder Victims**   **194**
    Elder Abuse   195
    Theories of Elder Abuse   197
    Elder Victimization   200

12. **Hate Crimes**   **206**
    Cultural Awareness   207
    Hate Crimes   211
    Cultural Awareness Case Study   218

13. **Special Victim Populations**   **222**
    HIV/AIDS Victims   223
    Disabled Victims   229
    Gay and Lesbian Victims   233

Victims' Rights

14. **Negligence and Intentional Torts**   **244**
    Introduction   245
    Negligence   247
    Wrongful Death   249
    Assault and Battery   250
    False Imprisonment   251
    Mental Distress   252
    Joint Tortfeasors   253
    Defenses to Intentional Torts   256

15. **Third-Party Liability and Insurance**   **262**
    Introduction   263
    Duty to Protect   264
    Classifications of Parties   266
    Theories of Liability   269
    Unlawful Activity   270
    Life Insurance   271
    Homeowners' Insurance   273
    Automobile Insurance   275
    Liability Insurance   277
    Workers' Compensation   278

16. Constitutional and Civil Rights of Victims   283
Section 1983 Actions   284
1983 Theories of Liability   287
Violence Against Women Act   290
Injunctions   292
Defenses   296

17. Compensation and Restitution of Victims   302
Compensation   303
Restitution   308

18. Victim Impact Statements   316
History of Victim Impact Statements   317
Use of Victim Impact Statements   322
Effect of Victim Impact Statements   325
Victim Impact Panels   328

Epilogue: Emerging Trends   332
Campus Crime   332
Stalking   333
Workplace Violence   334
Gang Violence   336
Rural Crime Victims   338
Violence and Victims   340
Technology   341
Professionalism versus Academia   341
The Study of Victimology   342

Appendix: Critical Dates in the Victims' Rights Movement   344

Index   355

PREFACE

The study of victimology is in its infancy. However, the plight of victims of crime has been discussed for centuries. In our early history, victims were an integral part of the criminal process. We then moved away from that model and the state became the representative of the victim. Finally, we are again moving toward acknowledging the rights of victims of crime. This has caused scholars to reexamine the victim–offender relationship in more detail.

Victimology as a discipline is an outgrowth of law, sociology, psychology, and criminology and as such has its distractors as well as its advocates. It will continue to grow and take on more substance with the passage of years. Any attempt to list those topics that are critical to the study of victimology is bound to generate controversy. Most texts on the market today include sections dealing with family violence issues. That may be because we have more information regarding the victim–offender interaction in these areas or because many scholars believe these are critical issues in the study of victimology. I have included a number of these same topics in this text. I drew upon my previous text, *Family Violence: Legal, Medical, and Social Perspectives,* as a source of information. Based on comments from professors using that text, I updated and changed the material when appropriate to reflect the victim's perspective.

I have also attempted to take a global perspective on the study of victimology and have divided the text into four major areas: The Introduction section includes the traditional theories regarding victimology, the measurement of crime, and both the civil and criminal process. I included the civil process because it is an important aspect of the victim–offender interaction. I have also included a brief discussion of the juvenile system, because more attention is being focused on youth violence. The second section, Responses to Victimization, includes two relatively new topics: the consequences of victimization and empowering victims. Several excellent texts already deal with the physical and mental consequences of crime; however, very few of these discuss the financial impact of crime. Chapter 6, "Empowering Victims," deals with issues that confront victim service providers as well as victims who are trying to change the system. The third section, Special Types of Victims, discusses traditional subjects such as homicide victims, family violence victims, and a discussion of special victims such as the disabled, those subjected to hate crimes, and gay and lesbian victims. The final section, Victims' Rights, includes civil remedies available to victims of crime.

This is not to say that I have covered all these topics adequately. I have attempted to present the reader with an overview of some complex and controversial subjects and to supply the reader with resources in the form of references and reading that would allow for more in-depth study and research of these areas. Simply by leaving out some topics, such as robbery, burglary, kidnapping, and others, does not mean they are unimportant. Victims of these crimes would argue that they have suffered just as much as other victims. As indicated in the epilogue, it is simply a matter of space and other priorities. There is still much to be done in this area.

Just as we are becoming more interested in the study of family violence, so are more and more universities offering classes on victim issues. These classes will become more popular as students, the general public, and the various professionals that deal with victims become aware of their availability. It is a young discipline that continues to grow, and it is exciting to be present and watch that growth.

I would like to express my appreciation to a number of individuals for their support, guidance, and advice during the time it has taken to complete this project. First and foremost, I would like to thank my editor, Karen Hanson, executive editor at Allyn & Bacon, who provided support for this project. I would also like to thank Donna Simons of Allyn & Bacon and Lora Kalb, who assisted in the preparation and copyediting of the manuscript. I thank my colleagues at California State University, Fresno, for their comments, feedback, and support. Christine Edmunds, Anne Seymour, Ellen Alexander, Skip Sigmon, Trudy Gregorie, Janice Lord, Dan Eddy, Dean G. Kilpatrick, Ph.D., Jane Burnley, Ph.D., and other friends associated with various victim organizations provided their advice and guidance regarding a number of issues. The students at California State University, Fresno, and the professionals who attended the National Victim Assistance Academies provided input and advice. Two reviewers provided me with invaluable suggestions and corrections that helped improve this text. They are Mario Gaboury, University of New Haven, and Steve Walker, Kansas Community College. Finally, I express appreciation to my family for their support during this time.

Harvey Wallace

1

INTRODUCTION AND HISTORY OF VICTIMOLOGY

Chapter Outline

Introduction

The Development of Laws
    The Code of Hammurabi
    Other Early Codes and Laws
    Modern Codes and Laws

Social Forces
    The Feminist Movement
    Development of Civil Rights Laws
    Conservatism Regarding Crime

Victimology Theories
    Mendelsohn's Theory of Victimization
    von Hentig's Theory of Victimization
    Schafer's Functional Responsibility
    Wolfgang's Study of Homicide
    Karmen's Theory of Victimology

The Rise of the Victims' Rights Movement
    The Beginning of the Movement
    Gains and Losses
    Increased Public Awareness
    Increased Professionalism
    Additional Laws

Summary

Key Terms

Discussion Questions

Suggested Readings

Learning Objectives

After reading this chapter, you should be able to:

- Distinguish between criminology and victimology
- Discuss how laws have affected victims
- Understand social forces that have impacted on the development of victimology
- Distinguish between the various victimology theories

Introduction

Although victimology as an academic discipline is a relatively new concept in the United States, the victims' movement continues to gain strength and momentum across the country.[1] States continue to enact laws giving victims of crime more opportunities to participate in the criminal justice system. Therefore, those individuals who work or interact with victims need to understand the legal, psychological, and social aspects of victimology.

Currently, few academic institutions offer courses of study in victimology. However, some universities offer courses that examine various aspects of the victim–offender relationship. These courses are typically found in sociology, criminal justice, social work, criminology, and psychology. Victimology is a discipline that combines theoretical research with practical experience. Although there is

---

FOCUS: Critical Dates in the History of Victimology

1750 B.C.—Code of Hammurabi adopted	1215 A.D.—Magna Carta signed
1200 B.C.—Mosaic Code established	1787 A.D.—U.S. Constitution created
450 B.C.—Twelve Tables written	1965—first victims' rights law passed
Roman Empire—Justinian Code drafted	1996—U.S. constitutional amendment proposed
1066 A.D.—Norman Conquest of England	
Middle Ages—Development of common law	

some interaction between these two groups or approaches, there is still much to learn from the combination.

Criminology is the science upon which victimology is founded. Criminology itself is a relatively new discipline and there are those who argue that it is not a true academic discipline or science, but rather a subspecialty of sociology.[2] However, there is an abundance of current literature and research to support the proposition that criminology is a science.

In 1947 Edwin H. Sutherland, an eminent criminologist, set forth the following definition:

> *Criminology is the body of knowledge regarding crime as a social phenomenon. It includes within its scope the process of making laws, of breaking laws. . . . The objective of criminology is the development of a body of general and verified principles and of other types of knowledge regarding this process of law, crime, treatment or prevention.*[3]

Criminology is the study of crime as a social phenomenon. Scholars have looked at several aspects of criminology and several have presented definitions of victimology which will be examined in detail later in this chapter. For purposes of clarity, however, the following definition of victimology is offered: ***Victimology*** is the study of the victim, the offender, and society. This definition can encompass both the research or scientific aspects of the discipline as well as the practical aspects of providing services to victims of crime. This combined definition allows for a wide-ranging examination of various issues affecting victims of crime.

A complete and accurate understanding of the concepts inherent in victimology can only be attained by a review of the development of law, its history, and its philosophy. Modern criminal law is the result of an evolutionary process in the development of law that has attempted to deal with deviant behavior in society.

The Development of Laws

Primitive law was a system of rules used by preliterate societies to govern the tribe, clan, or other gathering of individuals. These rules or regulations represent the foundation upon which the modern legal system is built. Primitive laws usually contained three characteristics: (1) acts that injured others were considered private wrongs; (2) the injured party was entitled to take action against the wrongdoer; and (3) this action usually amounted to in-kind retaliation. These types of laws encouraged blood feuds and revenge as the preferred methods of making the victim whole.

As society continued to evolve, we learned the art of reading and writing. One result of this evolution was the development of written codes of conduct. An example of an early written code was the Code of Ur-Nammu which dates back to the twenty-first century B.C. Many of these codes treated certain wrongs, such as theft or assault, as private wrongs with the injured party being the victim.[4]

The Code of Hammurabi

The Code of Hammurabi is considered one of the first known attempts to establish a written code of conduct. King Hammurabi ruled Babylon at approximately 2000 B.C. He was the sixth king of the First Dynasty of Babylonia and ruled for nearly fifty-five years. Babylon during that period was a commercial center for most of the known and civilized world. Because Babylon's fortune lay in trade and other business ventures, the Code of Hammurabi provided a basis for order and certainty. The code established rules regarding theft, sexual relationships, and interpersonal violence, and it was intended to replace blood feuds with a system sanctioned by the state.[5]

The Code of Hammurabi was divided into five sections:

1. A penal or code of laws
2. A manual of instruction for judges, police officers, and witnesses
3. A handbook of rights and duties of husbands, wives, and children
4. A set of regulations establishing wages and prices
5. A code of ethics for merchants, doctors, and officials[6]

The code established certain obligations and objectives for the citizens of Babylon to follow. These included:

1. An assertion of the power of the state. This was the beginning of state-administered punishment. Under the code, the blood feuds that had occurred previously between private citizens were barred.
2. Protection of the weaker from the stronger. Widows were to be protected from those who might exploit them, elder parents were to be protected from sons who would disown them, and lesser officials from higher ones.
3. Restoration of equity between the offender and the victim. The victim was to be made as whole as possible and in turn forgave vengeance against the offender.

Of noteworthy importance in the code was its concern for the rights of victims.[7] In reality, this code may have been the first "victim rights statute" in history. However, it was relatively short lived. Victims were again to be neglected in society's rush to punish the offender with the result that victims' rights would not resurface again until the present century.[8]

Other Early Codes and Laws

The Mosaic Code, which is based on the assumption that God entered into a contract or covenant with the tribes of Israel, had a long-lasting impact on our collective consciousness. According to tradition, Moses returned from a mountaintop carrying the Ten Commandments, which were inscribed on two stone tablets. These commandments subsequently became the foundation of Judeo-Christian morality. The Mosaic Code also became the basis for many of the laws in our modern society: The prohibition against murder, perjury, and theft were all present in the Mosaic Code thousands of years before the founding of the United States.[9]

Another important milestone in the development of American law was early Roman law. Roman law was derived from the Twelve Tables, which were written around 450 B.C. These laws had existed for centuries as unwritten law and applied only to the ruling patrician class of citizens. A protest by the plebeian class who were the workers and artisans of Rome caused commerce to come to a standstill. These workers wanted the law to apply to all citizens of Rome.[10] As a result, the laws were inscribed on twelve wooden tablets and prominently displayed in the forum for all to see and follow. These tables were a collection of basic rules relating to the conduct of family and religious and economic life.

In the middle of the first century, England was conquered by Roman legions. Roman law, customs, and language were forced on the English people during the next three centuries of Roman rule.

Emperor Justinian I codified the Roman laws into a set of writings. The Justinian Code, as these writings became known, distinguished between two major types of laws: public laws and private laws. Public laws dealt with the organization and administration of the Republic. Private laws addressed issues such as contracts, possessions and other property rights, the legal status of various persons such as slaves, husbands, wives, etc., and injuries to citizens. It contained elements of both our civil and criminal law and influenced Western legal theory into the Middle Ages.

Prior to the Norman Conquest of 1066, the legal system in England was very decentralized. There was little written law except for crimes against society. As a society, we had forgotten or moved away from the teaching of the Code of Hammurabi, and crimes during this period were again viewed as personal wrongs.

When an offense was committed, compensation was paid to the victim or to the victim's family. If the perpetrator failed to make payments, the victim's family could seek revenge, usually ending in a blood feud. For the most part during this period, criminal law was designed to provide equity to what was considered a private dispute.

The Norman Conquest under William the Conqueror established royal administrators who rode circuit and rendered justice. These royal judges would use local custom and rules of conduct as a guide in rendering their judgment. This system known as *stare decisis* (Latin for the phrase "to stand by the decided law") would have far-reaching effects on modern American criminal law.

The next major development in the history of law was the acknowledgment of the existence of common law. Early English common law forms the basis for much of our present-day legal system.[11] Common law is a traditional body of unwritten legal precedents created by court decisions throughout the Middle Ages in England. During this period, when cases were heard, judges would start their deliberations from past decisions that were as closely related as possible to the case under consideration. In the eleventh century, King Edward the Confessor proclaimed that common law was the law of the land and subsequently court decisions were recorded and made available to lawyers who could then use them to plead their case. This concept is one of the most important aspects of today's modern American law.

Modern Codes and Laws

The Magna Carta of England and the U.S. Constitution both stand as great documents and great moments in the history of American law. The Magna Carta was signed on June 15, 1215, and was later interpreted to grant basic liberties for all British citizens. The U.S. Constitution established certain individual rights, defined the power of the federal government, and limited punishment for violation of laws.

American law combines both common law and written statutes. Statutory laws are enacted by state legislatures and Congress and are the major source of American criminal law today. These laws are usually compiled in various codes and are subject to revision by the legislatures.

An offshoot of written law, *administrative law* is made up of rules and regulations adopted by governmental agencies at the federal, state, and local levels. Many governmental agencies are invested with the power to pass regulations that prohibit certain types of conduct. Some of these regulations provide for fines rather than imprisonment of the offender.

Constitutional law is another source of American criminal law. The Constitution does not define new crimes (the only crime defined in the Constitution is treason), rather it sets limits on other laws as they apply to individuals. An example of this principle is the U.S. Supreme Court ruling that flag burning, which was proscribed as criminal conduct by a state statute, is protected under the First Amendment right of freedom of expression.

Social Forces

A number of forces in the past several decades have contributed to the development of victims' rights. The major contributing forces have been the feminist movement, the development of civil rights laws, and a growing conservatism regarding crime.[12]

The Feminist Movement

The feminist movement alerted us to centuries of discrimination and violence directed against women. By speaking out, feminists forced us to realize that women were victims not only of violent crime on the streets of cities, but also of sexual harassment within the work environment and family violence within the home. Although men may also become victims of crime and violence, the types of crimes suffered by women are distinct from those suffered by men.

Many of these crimes, although sexual in nature, are in fact nothing more than aggressive assaults that have little to do with sex. Sexual assaults are in reality a way for the perpetrator to control, dominate, and humiliate the victim.

Three works by feminist authors and researchers set the stage for the beginning of our awareness of the sexual victimization of women. Millett's *Sexual Politics,* Griffin's article "Rape: The All American Crime," and Brownmiller's *Against Our Will* each raised our consciousness regarding the domination of women by men.[13]

Sexual Politics examines the concept of patriarchy which Millett claims is a social and political system utilized by men to control women. She argues that patriarchy is a feature of all past and present societies and exists across cultures and socioeconomic systems today. Millett concludes that power and coercion are central features of patriarchy and are used to control women's sexuality.

Griffin's short article, "Rape, The All American Crime," contains numerous themes. One important theme concerns the nature of the crime of rape. She argues that rape is not a sexual act, rather it is a violent, political act. Griffin concluded that the threat of rape is used as a method of social control and affects all women.

Brownmiller discussed the history of rape. She asserts that rape is an act used by men to maintain their dominance over women through the use of force. She expanded on both Millett's and Griffin's work and concluded that the threat of rape creates a climate of fear. It is this fear that acts as a form of social control which benefits men.

Kelly, in her book *Surviving Sexual Violence,* reviewed these early feminist approaches to sexual abuse and concluded that sexual violence is based on three concepts: power, sexuality, and social control.[14]

Power in the feminist analysis is not police or political power, rather power is defined in terms of a relationship which structures the interactions between men and women. Power therefore is not a property right, but a personal force that establishes male control and dominance over women. This power is multifaceted and thus quite complex. It is present not only in interpersonal relationships, but also extends to society's social structure and beliefs.

Sexuality has two aspects: first, male control of women's sexuality is a key factor in women's oppression; and second, sexuality is defined by men's experiences which legitimatize the use of force or coercion in intimate relationships. There is some conflict among feminists regarding the issue of sexuality and whether it has the same significance for women in all cultures.

Social control is the outcome of power and sexuality. The mere threat of sexual violence may result in women developing strategies for self-protection that will limit their mobility, work, or advancement. The reality of sexual violence not only impacts women in intimate and work relationships, but also spills over into a previously thought safe environment: the campus setting. Many colleges and universities now provide "escort services" for women who attend evening classes. This speaks volumes for the fear that exists in all areas of our lives.

These feminists laid the foundation which allows us to more fully understand the concept of sexual violence and women. The first concrete effort by feminists groups in the United States to help women who were victims of crime was the establishment of rape crisis centers in Berkeley, California, and Washington D.C., in 1972. These centers have spread rapidly and are now an integral part of the criminal justice system. In 1976 the federal government established a comprehensive research program, the National Center for the Prevention and Control of Rape, within the Department of Health, Education, and Welfare (this agency is now called Health and Human Services).

The feminist movement not only attacked society's perceptions regarding victims of sexual assault, but it also focused its efforts on educating the public regarding domestic violence. It is important to note that at the same time battered women's shelters were being established, there was a growing awareness that victims of crime, as a class of citizens, were being treated unfairly by the criminal justice system. This awareness coincided with changes within the judicial system.

Development of Civil Rights Laws

During the 1960s and 1970s, a series of U.S. Supreme Court decisions established certain principles regarding the constitutional rights of individuals. These decisions were in the areas of both criminal procedure and civil rights. The Supreme Court established constitutional safeguards for those accused of crime. By interpreting the Constitution as applying to each and every individual, the court required that society afford those accused of crime certain procedural and substantive rights. These rights embraced the entire spectrum of liberties, including freedom from unreasonable search and seizures, the right to an attorney, and fundamental fairness during a criminal trial. By adopting a philosophy that individuals carried with them certain inalienable rights, the court was posed to expand this concept in the area of civil rights.

The Supreme Court acted to enforce both statutory and constitutional provisions during the 1960s and 1970s in the area of civil rights. These decisions allowed a black man to attend a previously all-white university, maintained that police officers could be held liable for use of excessive force, and required that all persons be treated equally under the law. As a result of these and other decisions, cases such as *Thurman v. City of Torrington*[15] (discussed in Chapter 9) were decided in favor of victims of family violence.

Conservatism Regarding Crime

Another factor that contributed to the awareness of the plight of victims arose as a result of a change in attitude in America. In the 1980s and 1990s, society became more conservative and concerned about crime in general. This law and order movement was a result of citizens becoming more fearful of violent crime, and many groups consequently calling for more stringent punishment of those who violate the law. In addition, the victims' rights movement was gaining momentum. Imprisoning offenders was viewed as a way of vindicating victims of crime. Victim organizations began lobbying for changes in the criminal justice system.

These changes were aimed at making the system more victim oriented. The rights of victims of family violence began to grow and expand as our society became more aware of this type of violence.

These forces focused an awareness on the plight and the dilemma of victims of crime.[16] As a result, victims began to realize that they could have an effect on sentencing in criminal cases and could pursue civil litigation to recover for damages they suffered as a result of the perpetrator's actions.

Victimology Theories

As with any new profession, many of victimology's early thinkers proposed theories or concepts that, on further study, were revealed as incorrect. However, by examining these early efforts we can better understand the growth and present status of victimology. From its inception in the 1940s to the present day, victimology, like family violence, has been an interdisciplinary approach to violence and its effect on victims.

Mendelsohn's Theory of Victimization

Benjamin Mendelsohn was a practicing attorney. In the course of preparing a case for trial, he would conduct in-depth interviews of victims, witnesses, and bystanders.[17] He would use a questionnaire that was couched in simple language and contained more than 300 questions concerning the branches of criminology and associated sciences. The questionnaire was given to the accused and all others who had knowledge of the crime. Based on these studies, Mendelsohn came to the conclusion that there was usually a strong interpersonal relationship between the offender and the victim. In an effort to clarify these relationships further, he developed a typology of victims and their contribution to the criminal act.[18] This classification ranged from the completely innocent victim to the imaginary victim. Mendelsohn classified victims into six distinct categories:

1. *The Completely Innocent Victim.* This victim may be a child or a completely unconscious person.
2. *The Victim with Minor Guilt.* This victim might be a woman who induces a miscarriage and dies as a result.
3. *The Victim Who Is as Guilty as the Offender.* Those who assist others in committing crimes fall within this classification.
4. *The Victim More Guilty Than the Offender.* These are persons who provoke others to commit a crime.
5. *The Most Guilty Victim.* This occurs when the perpetrator (victim) acts aggressively and is killed by another person who is acting in self-defense.
6. *The Imaginary Victim.* These are persons suffering from mental disorders such as paranoia who believe they are victims.

Many scholars credit Mendelsohn with coining the term "victimology" and still others consider him the father of victimology.[19] His typology was one of the first attempts to focus on victims of crimes rather than to simply examine the perpetrator. However, Mendelsohn was only one of two early scholars who explored the relationship between victims and offenders. The other noted early researcher in victimology was Hans von Hentig.

von Hentig's Theory of Victimization

In an early classical text, *The Criminal and His Victim,* von Hentig explored the relationship between the 'doer' or criminal and the 'sufferer' or victim.[20] Von Hentig also established a typology of victims.[21] This classification was based on psychological, social, and biological factors. Von Hentig established three general classes of victims: the general classes of victims, the psychological types of victims, and the activating sufferer. His classification identified victims by examining various risk factors. The typology includes:

- The General Classes of Victims

  1. *The Young.* They are weak and the most likely to be a victim of an attack. Youth is the most dangerous period of life.[22]
  2. *The Female.* The female sex is another form of weakness recognized by the law, because numerous rules of law embody the legal fiction of a weaker (female) and stronger (male) sex.[23]
  3. *The Old.* The elder generation holds most positions of accumulated wealth and wealth-giving power, and at the same time is physically weak and mentally feeble.[24]
  4. *The Mentally Defective.* The feeble-minded, the insane, the drug addict, and the alcoholic form another large class of victims.[25]
  5. *Immigrants, Minorities, and Dull Normals.* Immigration means more than a change in country. It causes a temporary feeling of helplessness in vital human relations. The inexperienced, poor, and sometimes dull immigrant, minority, or other are easy prey to all kinds of swindlers.[26]

- The Psychological Types of Victims

  6. *The Depressed.* These victims may suffer from a disturbance of the instinct of self-preservation. Without such an instinct, the individual may be easily overwhelmed or surprised by dangers or enemies.[27]
  7. *The Acquisitive.* This type of person makes an excellent victim. The excessive desire for gain eclipses intelligence, business experience, and inner impediments.[28]
  8. *The Wanton.* Often a sensual or wanton disposition requires other concurrent factors to become activated. Loneliness, alcohol, and certain critical phases are "process-accelerators" of this type of victim.[29]

9. *The Lonesome and the Heartbroken.* Loneliness causes critical mental facilities to be weakened. These individuals become easy prey for criminals.[30] The heartbroken victims are dazed by their loss and therefore become easy targets for a variety of "death rackets" that might, for example, charge a widow an outlandish fee for a picture of her late husband to be included in his biography.[31]

10. *The Tormentor.* This victim becomes a perpetrator. This is the psychotic father who may abuse the wife and children for a number of years until one of the children grows up and under extreme provocation kills him.[32]

11. *The Blocked, Exempted, and Fighting.* The blocked victim is so enmeshed in such a losing situation that defensive moves become impossible. This is a self-imposed form of helplessness and an ideal condition for a victim from the point of view of the criminal.[33]

- The Activating Sufferer

12. *The Activating Sufferer.* This occurs when the victim is transformed into a perpetrator. A number of factors operate as activators on the victim: certain predispositions, age, alcohol, and loss of self-confidence.[34]

Von Hentig theorized that a large percentage of victims, because of their acts or behavior, were responsible for their victimization.[35] This concept has since been repudiated by modern studies which have more closely examined and defined the relationship between the victim and the offender.

Schafer's Functional Responsibility

Using von Hentig's approach, a third scholar has also been instrumental in establishing another classification of victims. Stephen Schafer examined both Mendelsohn's and von Hentig's work in his text, *The Victim and His Criminal*, and attempted to classify victims on a basis of responsibility instead of risk factors.[36] Schafer believed that the study of the criminal–victim relationship indicated an increasing recognition that the criminal justice system must consider the dynamics of crime and treat both criminals and victims.

Schafer went on to state that "the study of criminal–victim relationships emphasizes the need to recognize the role and responsibility of the victim, who is not simply the cause of, and reason for, the criminal procedure, but has a major part to play in the search for an objective criminal justice [system] and a function solution to the crime problem."[37] He stated that responsibility is not an isolated factor in society, rather it is an instrument of social control used at all times by all societies to maintain themselves.[38] Schafer believed responsibility was a critical issue in the problem of crime.

According to Schafer, crime was not only an individual act, but also a social phenomenon. He believed that not all crimes simply "happen" to be committed, but that victims often contribute to crime by their acts of negligence, precipitative actions, or provocations. Schafer concluded that the functional role of a victim is to do nothing to provoke others from attempting to injure him and at the same time to actively prevent such attempts. In other words, this is the victim's functional responsibility.[39]

Wolfgang's Study of Homicide

From 1948 to 1952 in Philadelphia, Marvin E. Wolfgang conducted the first major study of victim precipitation.[40] He focused on homicides, studying both the victim and the offender as separate entities and as "mutual participants in the homicide."[41] Wolfgang evaluated 588 homicides and found that 26 percent (150) of all the homicides studied in Philadelphia involved situations in which the victim was a direct positive precipitator in the crime—the first to use force during the acts leading to the homicide.[42] Wolfgang's study and other theories of homicide will be addressed in Chapter 7.

Karmen's Theory of Victimology

Scholars have continued to expand their scope of inquiry and explore other aspects of the victim's role in society. Karmen discusses the development of victimology and points out that those who study this relatively new discipline have three main areas of concentration:

1. Victimologists study the reasons (if any) of why or how the victim entered a dangerous situation. This approach does not attempt to fix blame on the victim, rather it examines the dynamics that resulted in the victim being in the risky situation.
2. Victimology evaluates how police, prosecutors, courts, and related agencies interact with the victim. How was the victim treated at each stage in the criminal justice system?
3. Victimologists evaluate the effectiveness of efforts to reimburse victims for their losses and meet the victim's personal and emotional needs.[43]

Karmen correctly points out that victimologists view the dynamics of the victim's role in society from a multidisciplinary perspective. There is still debate among scholars, however, regarding the correct or predominate role for the victimologist. Similar to the development and study of criminology, a number of different perspectives regarding victimology have also developed throughout the years.

The Rise of the Victims' Rights Movement

As the various social forces were developing, a series of events took place that began to raise the consciousness of the victims themselves regarding their impact on the criminal justice system.

The Beginning of the Movement

During the late 1960s, victims of crime began volunteering to serve within various victim assistance programs. As these crime victims continued to speak out, states and the federal government reacted by establishing commissions to study crime and its consequences.

There were two federal responses to crime victimization during this period. One was the establishment of the National Crime Survey which will be discussed in more detail in Chapter 2. The second major action on the part of the federal government was the establishment of the Law Enforcement Assistance Administration (LEAA). This agency provided funds to law enforcement agencies for a variety of purposes including the establishment of victim-witness programs.[44] LEAA's role in fundraising will be discussed in Chapter 6.

In 1975, the LEAA called a meeting in Washington, D.C., of various victim advocates to discuss methods of increasing victims' rights. One consequence of this meeting was the formation of the National Organization for Victim Assistance (NOVA). NOVA is considered by many to be one of the leading victim rights organizations in the world.

Gains and Losses

During the late 1970s and early 1980s, the movement foundered. Lack of funding by the federal government caused many community-based victim organizations and service providers to cease operations. Additionally, within the movement issues such as professionalism and training caused increasing divisiveness. The movement began to separate into specialized groups that focused on specific issues. Several sexual assault and domestic violence organizations, such as the National Coalition Against Sexual Assault, were established to address the specific needs of those victims.[45]

Although there was tension between various service providers because of diminishing funding and disagreement regarding specific goals, there was also progress in other areas of the victims' movement during this time period. Parents of Murdered Children (POMC) was founded by Robert and Charlotte Hullinger in 1978, and Mothers Against Drunk Driving (MADD) was founded by Candy Lighter in 1980. Both of these organizations continue to have an impact on victims' rights and the victims' movement. Additionally, Congress passed a federal Victims' Bill of Rights. By 1990, two-thirds of the states had enacted similar types of laws protecting victims.

In what may become one of the most critical dates in the history of victim rights, on June 25, 1996, President Clinton proposed a Victims' Rights Constitutional Amendment to the U.S. Constitution. In a speech made in the Rose Garden announcing the Victims' Rights Constitutional Amendment, President Clinton stated:

> *Having carefully studied all of the alternatives, I am now convinced that the only way to fully safeguard the rights of victims in America is to amend our*

Constitution and guarantee these basic rights—to be told about public court pro-
ceedings and to attend them; to make a statement to the court about bail, about
sentencing, about accepting a plea if the victim is present, to be told about parole
hearings to attend and to speak; notice when the defendant or convict escapes or
is released, restitution from the defendant, reasonable protection from the defen-
dant and notice of these rights.[46]

The Victims' Rights Constitutional Amendment faces a long and complex
process before it becomes law. It must be approved by Congress and then adopted
by three-quarters of the states to become part of the Constitution. It is not something that will happen in a few weeks or months and there are those who already
claim that the proposed amendment is too detailed and should be made broader.
No matter what the outcome, the simple fact that such an amendment has actually been proposed is a significant acknowledgment of the plight of victims of
crime.

Increased Public Awareness

During 1982 through 1986, victims' organizations began to use the media to
increase public awareness of crime victim issues. President Ronald Reagan, and
Congress, responded to this heightened awareness with actions that would eventually have long-term consequences for the victims' movement. In 1982, President
Reagan appointed a Task Force on Victims of Crime. This task force published a
report that has since become a foundational platform for victims' rights.[47] The
Office for Victims of Crime (OVC) was created in the Department of Justice to
implement the task force's recommendations.

Victims' Rights Constitutional Amendment

Section 1. To ensure that the victim is treated with fairness, dignity, and respect, from the occurrence of a crime of violence and other crimes as may be defined by law pursuant to section two of this article, and throughout the criminal, military, and juvenile justice process, as a matter of fundamental rights to liberty, justice and due process, the victim shall have the following rights: to be informed of and given the opportunity to be present at every proceeding in which those rights are extended to the accused or convicted offender; to be heard at any proceeding involving sentencing, including the right to object to a previously negotiated plea, or to a release from custody; to be informed of any release or escape; and to a speedy trial, a final conclusion free from unreasonable delay, full restitution from the convicted offender, reasonable measures to protect the victim from violence or intimidation by the accused or convicted offender, and notice of the victim's rights.

Section 2. The several States, with respect to a proceeding in a State forum, and the Congress with respect to a proceeding in a United States forum, shall have the power to implement further the rights established in this article by appropriate legislation.

Source: OVC, U.S. Department of Justice, Washington, D.C., 1996.

In 1984, another key event took place when Congress passed the Victims of Crime Act (VOCA).[48] This act established the OVC in the Office of Justice Programs, Department of Justice. OVC provides grants to states for programs with direct services for victims of all crimes. VOCA also established the Crime Victims Fund to provide money to local victim assistance programs and state victim compensation programs. The fund receives money from federal criminal fines, penalties, and bond forfeitures. VOCA's operation is further examined in Chapter 16.

Increased Professionalism

From 1984 to the present, the victims' movement has been characterized by an increase in the professionalism of the victims service advocates and providers. In previous times, the victims' movement was heightened by strong dynamic leaders with vision and determination. At present, the movement has expanded beyond the ability of any one person being able to influence its direction. It is now a national movement with a tremendous influence on local, state, and national politics.

Universities are expanding their victim-related courses. Various victim oganizations are offering increased training opportunities and in 1995, the U.S. Department of Justice sponsored the first National Victim Assistance Academy in Washington, D.C. This academy was repeated in 1996 and 1997 using distance learning technology to link other universities in a joint academic effort.

The public awareness of victim issues continues to grow, and victim advocates have become an acknowledged force in modern politics. Victim service providers are realizing that their profession requires training that is multidisciplinary in nature. There is a growing awareness that to be accepted by other professionals requires continuing education, certifications, or other acknowledged credentials. This increased professionalism should translate into more sophisticated interventions and a faster rate of progress within the victims' movement.

Additional Laws

Increased professionalism also means increased knowledge and insight into the problems of victims. In 1994, Congress enacted the Violent Crime Control and Law Enforcement Act. Title IV of that law is entitled the Violence Against Women Act (VAWA). Congress mandated that various professions form partnerships and work together to respond to all forms of violence against women.

The attorney general is required to make a report to Congress annually on the grants that are awarded under the act and ensure that research examining violence against women is encouraged. The report must include the number of grants, funds distributed, and other statistical information. Additionally, the report must assess the effectiveness of any programs which are funded under VAWA.

The act provides funding for a variety of research-based studies. It also requires that federal agencies engage in research regarding violence against women. For example, the National Institute of Justice is mandated to conduct four important projects: (1) the development of a research agenda that will address violence with particular emphasis on underserved populations; (2) the assessment of establishing state databases to record the number of sexual and domestic violence incidents; (3) a study to determine how abusive partners obtain addresses of their victims; and (4) the examination with other agencies of the battered woman syndrome.[49]

Summary

The history of victimology is in many ways the history of our world. As long as there has been crime, there have been victims who have suffered. Early law viewed crime as a personal act that required response by the victim or the victim's family. The Code of Hammurabi, although harsh and violent, recognized victims as injured parties and may have been the first victims' rights law. Other codes and laws evolved throughout history to shape our modern concept of justice.

A number of social forces affected the development of victimology. The feminist movement raised our awareness of the plight of women. The civil rights movement resulted in a number of laws being passed which afforded individuals certain rights. As crime increased, our society became increasingly conservative and became more aware of the trauma suffered by victims of crime.

The victims' rights movement began as a small group of volunteers who themselves were crime victims and who had been victimized a second time as a result of their involvement with the criminal justice system. This small group of volunteers has grown and become a powerful force in America that continues to expand and change the way we view victimology.

Key Terms

Criminology is the study of crime as a social phenomenon.

Victimology is the study of the victim, the offender, and society.

Primitive law was a system of rules in preliterate societies.

Stare decisis means to stand by the decided law.

Administrative law is made up of rules and regulations adopted by governmental agencies at the federal, state, and local levels.

Discussion Questions

1. Explain why some authorities call the Hammurabi Code the first victims' rights law.

2. What was the most significant event in the development of law that has affected the victims' movement?

3. Is the feminist movement still important to the victims' movement? Why?

4. Compare and contrast von Hentig's and Mendelsohn's theories of victimology.

5. Why is Schafer's theory of functional responsibility important?

6. Wolfgang studied homicide, how does this relate to the study of victimology?

7. Has the victims' movement reached its full potential? Name three specific goals that the movement should strive for in the next ten years.

Suggested Readings

G. B. Vold & T. J. Bernard, *Theoretical Criminology*, 3rd ed. (Oxford University Press, New York) 1986.

Sir Henry Summer Maine, *Ancient Law*, 10th ed. (John Murray, London) 1905.

S. Schafer, *The Victim and His Criminal*, (Random House, New York) 1968.

Masters & Roberson, *Inside Criminology*, (Prentice-Hall, Englewood Cliffs, N.J.) 1985.

I. Drapkin & E. Viano, Eds., *Victimology: A New Focus*, vol. 2 (D.C. Heath, Lexington, Mass.) 1974.

S. A. Cook, *The Laws of Moses and the Code of Hammurabi*, (Adam and Charles Black, London) 1903.

S. T. Reed, *Criminal Justice*, 3rd ed. (Macmillan Publishing Company, New York) 1993.

A. Karmen, *Crime Victims: An Introduction to Victimology*, 2nd ed. (Wadsworth, Belmont, Calif.) 1995.

L. Kelly, *Surviving Sexual Violence*, (University of Minnesota Press, Minneapolis, Minn.) 1988.

N. A. Weiner & M. E. Wolfgang, Eds., *Pathways to Criminal Violence*, (Sage, Newbury Park, Calif.) 1989.

Emilio C. Viano, *Victim/Witness Services: A Review of the Model*, (GPO, Washington, D.C.) 1979.

President's Task Force on Victims of Crime, (Final Report, GPO, Washington, D.C.) December 1982.

Endnotes

1. California State University at Fresno is the only academic institution in the United States that offers a B.S. in criminology with a victimology option.

2. For an excellent discussion of criminology as a science, see G. B. Vold and T. J. Bernard, *Theoretical Criminology*, 3rd ed. (Oxford University Press, New York) 1986.

3. Edwin H. Sutherland, *Principles of Criminology*, 4th ed. (Lippincott, Philadelphia) 1947.

4. Sir Henry Summer Maine, *Ancient Law*, 10th ed. (John Murray, London) 1905.

5. S. Schafer, *The Victim and His Criminal*, (Random House, New York) 1968.

6. Masters & Roberson, *Inside Criminology*, (Prentice-Hall, Englewood Cliffs, N.J.) 1985.

7. H. Gordon, *Hammurabi's Code: Quaint or Forward Looking*, (Rinehart, New York) 1957.

8. G. O. Mueller & H. H. A. Cooper, "Society and the Victim: Alternative Responses," in I. Drapkin & E. Viano, Eds., *Victimology: A New Focus*, vol. 2 (D. C. Heath, Lexington, Mass.) 1974, pp. 85–102.

9. S. A. Cook, *The Laws of Moses and the Code of Hammurabi*, (Adam and Charles Black, London) 1903.

10. O. W. Mueller, "Tort, Crime and the Primitive," 43 *Journal of Criminal Law, Criminology, and Police Science*, 303, 1955.

11. S. T. Reed, *Criminal Justice*, 3rd ed. (Macmillan Publishing Company, New York) 1993.

12. A. Karmen, *Crime Victims: An Introduction to Victimology*, 2nd ed. (Brooks/Cole, Pacific Grove, Calif.) 1985.

13. K. Millett, *Sexual Politics*, (Abacus, London) 1972, S. Griffin, "Rape: The All American

Crime, *"Ramparts* 10(3), pp. 26–35, 1971, and S. Brownmiller, *Against Our Will: Men, Women and Rape*, (Penguin Books, New York) 1975.

14. L. Kelly, *Surviving Sexual Violence*, (University of Minnesota Press, Minneapolis, Minn.) 1988.

15. 595 F. Supp. 1521 (Conn. 1984).

16. G. D. Gottfredson, "The Experiences of Violent and Serious Victimization," in N. A. Weiner & M. E. Wolfgang, Eds., *Pathways to Criminal Violence*, (Sage, Newbury Park, Calif.) 1989, pp. 202–234.

17. B. Mendelsohn, "The Origin and Doctrine of Victimology," 3 *Excerpta Criminologica*, June 1963, pp. 239–244.

18. S. Schafer, *The Victim and His Criminal*, (Random House, New York) 1968.

19. B. Mendelsohn, "Rape in Criminology," *Giustizia Penale*, 1940.

20. Hans von Hentig, *The Criminal and His Victim*, (first published by Schocken Books, New York 1979, republished by Yale University Press 1984) (Hereafter *The Criminal and His Victim*).

21. Some scholars have subdivided von Hentig's original typology (probably for ease of understanding). See, for example, Doerner and Lab, *Victimology*, (West Publishing, St. Paul, Minn. 1994) where the authors list thirteen classifications. They arrive at this number by listing immigrants, minorities, and dull normals as separate categories instead of one subdivision as von Hentig did.

22. *The Criminal and His Victim*, p. 404.

23. Id. at p. 406.

24. Id. at p. 410.

25. Id. at p. 411.

26. Id. at p. 415.

27. Id. at p. 420.

28. Id. at p. 422.

29. Id. at p. 427.

30. Id. at p. 428.

31. Id. at p. 431.

32. Id. at p. 431.

33. *The Criminal and His Victim*, p. 433.

34. Id. at p. 445.

35. H. von Hentig, *The Criminal and His Victim*, (Yale University Press, New Haven, Conn.) 1948.

36. S. Schafer, *The Victim and His Criminal*, (Random House, New York) 1968.

37. Id. at p. 5.

38. Id. at p. 139.

39. Id. at p. 152.

40. M. E. Wolfgang, *Patterns of Criminal Homicide*, (University of Pennsylvania Press, Philadelphia, Penn.) 1958.

41. M. E. Wolfgang, *Analytical Categories for Research in Victimization*, (Kriminologische Wegzeichen, Munich, Germany) 1967, p. 17.

42. Id. at pp. 24, 72.

43. Andrew Karmen, *Crime Victims, An Introduction to Victimology*, 2nd ed. (Brooks/Cole, Pacific Grove, Calif.) 1995.

44. Emilio C. Viano, *Victim/Witness Services: A Review of the Model*, (GPO, Washington, D.C.) 1979.

45. M. Largen, "Grassroots Centers and National Task Forces: A Herstory of the Anti-Rape Movement," 32 *Aegis*, Autumn 1981, pp. 46–52.

46. "Remarks by the President at Announcement of Victims Constitutional Amendment," *Press Release*, The White House, Office of the Press Secretary. Washington, D.C. June 25, 1996, p. 2.

47. *President's Task Force on Victims of Crime*, (Final Report, GPO, Washington, D.C.) December 1982.

48. Victims of Crime Act of 1984, 42 U.S.C. Section 10601 (1984).

49. Jeremy Travis, "Violence Against Women: Reflections on NIJ's Research Agenda," *National Institute of Justice Journal*, February 1996.

2

MEASUREMENT OF CRIME AND ITS EFFECTS

Chapter Outline

Official Reports
   Uniform Crime Reports
   National Incident-Based Reporting System
   National Crime Victimization Survey
   National Assessment Program

Other Reports
   National Family Violence Surveys
   Other Sources of Data on Violence
   Other Types of Crime Research

Summary

Key Terms

Discussion Questions

Suggested Readings

Learning Objectives

After reading this chapter, you should be able to:

- Explain the differences between the various types of official reports
- Distinguish between the other types of reports that provide information regarding the commission of crimes

- Understand the advantages and disadvantages of each of the various mechanisms that are used to measure crime

Official Reports

There are many different types of official reports which are compiled by private or public agencies in the form of statistical data. These provide a much needed resource for further research into the extent of crime and victimization. Those most commonly relied on are reports by local law enforcement agencies, the Uniform Crime Reports, and the National Crime Victimization Surveys.

Uniform Crime Reports

During the 1920s, the International Association of Chiefs of Police (IACP) formed the Commission on Uniform Crime Reports to develop a uniform system of reporting criminal statistics. The committee evaluated various crimes based on their seriousness, frequency of occurrence, commonality across the nation, and likelihood of being reported to the police. In 1929, the committee finished its study

---

BOX 2.1   The Extent of Crime

More than 49 million victimizations and attempted victimizations occurred each year for the period of 1987 to 1990. Specific categories included the following figures:

- **Fatal crimes.** These crimes, which include criminal and vehicle homicide, arson, and child abuse, claimed some 31,000 lives in 1990.
- **Child abuse.** A conservative estimate of the number of children sexually, physically, or emotionally abused was 794,000 in 1990.
- **Rape.** The number of rape and sexual assault victims in 1992 was estimated at 1.1 million.

- **Assault.** The number of nonfatal assaults against children under 12 comes to approximately 450,000 each year. This study estimates the number of domestic assaults at 2 million annually.
- **Drunk Driving.** Tentative estimates put the number of injuries from drunk driving at about 500,000.
- **Arson.** There were 137,000 arson victimizations, including 15,000 that resulted in injuries.

Source: Adapted from "The Extent and Costs of Crime Victimization: A New Look." *Research Preview.* (National Institute of Justice, Washington D.C.) January 1996.

and recommended a plan for crime reporting that became the foundation of the Uniform Crime Reports (UCR) program.

Seven crimes were chosen to serve as an index for determining fluctuations in the overall rate of crime. These seven offenses became known as the "crime index" and included the following crimes: murder and manslaughter, forcible rape, robbery, aggravated assault, burglary, larceny-theft, and motor vehicle theft. In 1979, Congress mandated that an eighth crime, arson, be added to the index. During the study phase of the project, members recognized that differences in state criminal codes would cause the same act to be reported in various methods and categories. To avoid this problem, they made no distinction between felony and misdemeanor crimes and established a standardized set of definitions to allow law enforcement agencies to submit data without regard for local statutes. In 1930, Congress enacted federal law that authorized the attorney general to gather crime information.[1] The attorney general designated the FBI as the national clearinghouse for all data and since that time data based on this system have been obtained from the nation's law enforcement agencies.

The Uniform Crime Reports (UCR) program is a nationwide statistical computation involving over 1600 cities, counties, and state law enforcement agencies who voluntarily provide data on reported crimes. During 1993, law enforcement agencies in the UCR program represented over 245 million inhabitants or approximately 95 percent of the total population of the United States. The program is administrated by the Federal Bureau of Investigation which issues assessments on the nature and type of crime. The program's primary objective is to generate a set of reliable criminal statistics for use in law enforcement administration, operation, and management.[2]

The Federal Bureau of Investigation is tasked with administering the UCR program and issues periodic reports addressing the nature and type of crime in the United States. Although the UCR's primary objective is the issuance of reliable statistics for use by law enforcement agencies, it has also become an important social indicator of deviance in our society.

The UCR prepares an annual crime index. This index is composed of selected offenses used to gauge changes in the overall rate of crime reported to law enforcement agencies. The crime index is composed of those specific crimes previously discussed. Therefore, the index is a combination of violent and property crimes. In 1993, for example, 14 percent of the index offenses were violent crimes and 86 percent were property crimes.

The UCR is an annual report that includes the number of crimes reported by citizens to local police departments, and the number of arrests made by law enforcement agencies in a given year. This information is of somewhat limited value, because the data are based on instances of violence that are classified as criminal, and are reported to the local law enforcement agencies. Many serious acts of violence are not reported to the police and therefore do not become part of the UCR.

A number of factors influence the reporting or non-reporting of crimes to local law enforcement. The Bureau of Justice Statistics reports that the most common reason victims give for reporting crimes to the police is to prevent further crimes from being committed against them by the same offender.[3] For both household crimes and other theft-related crimes, the most common reason given by victims in reporting the offenses is to assist in the recovery of the property.

Violent crimes are the most likely to be reported to the police. Household crimes are the next highest reported form of crime. Personal thefts are the least likely crimes to be reported to the police.

The most common reason given for not reporting violent crimes to the police is that the crime was considered by the victim to be a private or personal matter. The second most common reason for not reporting violent crimes is that the offender was unsuccessful in his attempt to commit the crime. The most common reason for not reporting household crime or other theft-related crime is that the object was recovered.

Victims gave different reasons for not reporting crimes to the police when the offender was a stranger instead of an acquaintance. Victims of crimes committed by strangers gave the following reasons for not reporting:

- The offender was unsuccessful.
- The victim considered the police inefficient.
- The victim felt the police did not want to be bothered.
- It was not important enough to the victim to report the crime.

Victims of crimes committed by acquaintances gave the following reasons for not reporting:

- The victim considered the crime a private or personal matter.
- The victim had reported the crime to another official.

The Hate Crime Statistics Act was passed by Congress in 1990 and mandates that a database of crimes motivated by religion, ethnic, racial, or sexual orientation be collected. On January 1, 1991, the UCR program distributed guidelines for reporting hate crimes, and the first report was published in 1992. Participation in reporting hate crimes continues to grow and as of 1993, 6840 law enforcement agencies representing 56 percent of the U.S. population were reporting hate crime data.

With the exception of the hate crime category as noted, the UCR remained virtually unchanged for fifty years. Eventually, various law enforcement agencies began to call for an evaluation and redesign of the program. Because the UCR only lists crimes that are reported to it, this presents a serious problem as not all police agencies report crimes to the FBI and the Department of Justice. Because the UCR relies on law enforcement agencies to voluntarily report crimes, there is the possibility of underreporting by some agencies based on political reasons.[4] The UCR generally provides only tabular summaries of crime and does not provide crime analysts with more meaningful information. Additionally, the method of counting crimes causes problems. For example, only the most serious crime is reported. If a person is robbed and his car stolen, police agencies are instructed to report only the robbery. Finally, some crimes, such as white-collar crime, are excluded from the UCR system. After several years of study, the FBI began to institute various modifications to the UCR program. These changes established a new, more effective crime reporting system.

National Incident-Based Reporting System

The newly redesigned UCR program is called the National Incident-Based Reporting System (NIBRS). In 1989, the FBI began accepting data, and nine states started supplying information in the new format. NIBRS collects data on each single incident and arrest within twenty-two crime categories. Incident, victim, property, offender, and arrestee information is gathered for each offense known to the local agency. The goal of the redesigned system is to modernize crime reporting information by collecting data presently maintained in law enforcement records. The enhanced UCR program is a by-product of modern law enforcement records systems that have the capability to store and collate more information regarding criminal offenses.

National Crime Victimization Survey

The *National Crime Victimization Survey (NCVS)* is a nationwide sample of interviews of citizens regarding victimization. It attempts to correct the problems of non-reporting inherent in the UCR. The report was originally entitled the National Crime Survey (NCS) but was renamed to more clearly reflect its emphasis on the measurement of victimizations experienced by citizens. The NCVS began in 1972 and collects detailed information about certain criminal offenses, both attempted and completed, that concern the general public and law enforcement (see Figure 2.1). These offenses include the frequency and nature of rape, robbery, assault, household burglary, personal and household theft, and motor vehicle theft.[5] The NCVS does not measure homicide or commercial crime.

A single crime may have more than one victim; for example, a bank robbery may involve several bank tellers. Thus, a single incident may have more than one victimization. A victimization, the basic measure of the occurrence of crime, is a specific criminal act because it affects a specific victim. The number of victimizations, however, is determined by the number of victims of each specific criminal act.

NCVS is an annual survey of citizens which is collected by the U.S. Bureau of Census in cooperation with the Bureau of Justice Statistics of the U.S. Department of Justice. Census Bureau personnel conduct interviews with all household members over the age of twelve. These households stay in the sample for three years

OMB No. 1121-0111: Approval Expires December 31, 1987

NOTICE — Your report to the Census Bureau is **confidential** by law (U.S. Code 42, Sections 3789g and 3735). All identifiable information will be used only by persons engaged in and for the purposes of the survey, and may not be disclosed or released to others for any purpose.	FORM NCS-1 and NCS-2 (4-10-88)

U.S. DEPARTMENT OF COMMERCE
BUREAU OF THE CENSUS

ACTING AS COLLECTING AGENT FOR THE
BUREAU OF JUSTICE STATISTICS
U.S. DEPARTMENT OF JUSTICE

NATIONAL CRIME SURVEY

NCS-1 BASIC SCREEN QUESTIONNAIRE

NCS-2 CRIME INCIDENT REPORT

N C S 1 and 2

PGM 2

Sample	Control number				HH No.
	PSU	Segment	CK.	Serial	
J ____					

ITEMS FILLED AT START OF INTERVIEW

1. Interviewer identification
Code ! Name
201

2. Unit Status
202 1 ☐ Unit in sample the previous enumeration period — *Fill 3*
2 ☐ Unit in sample first time this period — *SKIP to 4*

3. Household Status — *Mark first box that applies*
203 1 ☐ Same household <u>interviewed</u> the previous enumeration
2 ☐ Replacement household since the previous enumeration
3 ☐ Noninterview the previous enumeration
4 ☐ Other — *Specify* ⌐

4. Line number of household respondent
204 _____ Go to page 2

TRANSCRIPTION ITEMS FROM CONTROL CARD

5. Special Place type code
205 _____

6. Tenure
206 1 ☐ Owned or being bought 2 ☐ Rented for cash 3 ☐ No cash rent

7. Land Use
207 1 ☐ Urban 2 ☐ Rural

8. Farm Sales
208 x ☐ Item blank 1 ☐ $1,000 or more 2 ☐ Less than $1,000

9. Type of living quarters
Housing unit
209 1 ☐ House, apartment, flat
2 ☐ HU in nontransient hotel, motel, etc.
3 ☐ HU permanent in transient hotel, motel, etc.
4 ☐ HU in rooming house
5 ☐ Mobile home or trailer with no permanent room added
6 ☐ Mobile home or trailer with one or more permanent rooms added
7 ☐ HU not specified above — *Describe* ⌐

OTHER unit
8 ☐ Quarters not HU in rooming or boarding house
9 ☐ Unit not permanent in transient hotel, motel, etc.
10 ☐ Unoccupied site for mobile home, trailer, or tent
11 ☐ Student quarters in college dormitory
12 ☐ OTHER unit not specified above - *Describe* ⌐

Use of telephone
10a. Location of phone — *Mark first box that applies.*
210 1 ☐ Phone in unit . . . .
2 ☐ Phone in common area (hallway, etc.) . . . .
3 ☐ Phone in another unit (neighbor, friend, etc.) . .
4 ☐ Work/office phone . . . . .
5 ☐ No phone -- *SKIP to 11a*
} *Fill 10b*

10b. Is phone interview acceptable?
211 1 ☐ Yes 2 ☐ No 3 ☐ Refused to give number

TRANS. ITEMS FROM CONTROL CARD — Cont.

11a. Number of housing units in structure
212 1 ☐ 1-*SKIP to 12* 4 ☐ 4 7 ☐ Mobile home or trailer - *SKIP to 12*
2 ☐ 2 5 ☐ 5-9 8 ☐ Only OTHER units
3 ☐ 3 6 ☐ 10 +

11b. Direct outside access
213 1 ☐ Yes 3 ☐ Don't know
2 ☐ No x ☐ Item blank

12. Family income
214 1 ☐ (a) Less than $5,000 8 ☐ (h) 20,000-24,999
2 ☐ (b) $5,000- 7,499 9 ☐ (i) 25,000-29,999
3 ☐ (c) 7,500- 9,999 10 ☐ (j) 30,000-34,999
4 ☐ (d) 10,000-12,499 11 ☐ (k) 35,000-39,999
5 ☐ (e) 12,500-14,999 12 ☐ (l) 40,000-49,999
6 ☐ (f) 15,000-17,499 13 ☐ (m) 50,000-74,999
7 ☐ (g) 17,500-19,999 14 ☐ (n) 75,000 and over

PGM 3 **ITEMS FILLED AFTER INTERVIEW**

13. Proxy information — *Fill for all proxy interviews*

a. Proxy interview obtained for Line No.	b. Proxy respondent		c. Reason (Enter code)
	Name	Line No.	
301 ____		302 ____	303 ____
304 ____		305 ____	306 ____
307 ____		308 ____	309 ____
310 ____		311 ____	312 ____

Codes for item 13c
1 – 12 – 13 years old and parent refused permission for self interview
2 – Physically/mentally unable to answer } *FILL INTER-COMM*
3 – TA and won't return before closeout

14. Type Z noninterview

a. Interview not obtained for Line No.	b. Reason (Enter code)	Codes for item 14b
313 ____	314 ____	1 – Never available . . . .
315 ____	316 ____	2 – Refused . . . .
317 ____	318 ____	3 – Physically/mentally unable to answer – no proxy available . . . . .
319 ____	320 ____	4 – TA and no proxy available . . . . } *FILL INTER-COMM*
		5 – Other . . . .
		6 – Office use only

▶ *Complete 17 – 28 for each Line No. in 14a.*

15a. Household members 12 years of age and OVER
321 _____ Total number

15b. Household members UNDER 12 years of age
322 _____ Total number
0 ☐ None

16. Crime Incident Reports filled
323 _____ Total number — *Fill BOUNDING INFORMATION*
0 ☐ None

Notes

FIGURE 2.1   National Crime Victimization Survey Questionnaire

PERSONAL CHARACTERISTICS

17. NAME (of household respondent)

Last

First

18. Type of interview
PGM 4

`401`
1 ☐ Per. — Self-respondent
2 ☐ Tel. — Self-respondent
3 ☐ Per. — Proxy ⎫ Fill 13 on cover page
4 ☐ Tel. — Proxy ⎭
5 ☐ Noninterview - Fill 19-28 and 14 on cover page

19. Line No.
`402`

Line No.

20. Relationship to reference person	**21.** Age last birthday	**22a.** Marital status THIS survey period	**22b.** Marital status LAST survey period	**23.** Sex	**24.** Armed Forces member	**25.** Education — highest grade	**26.** Education -complete that year?	**27.** Race	**28.** Hispanic origin
`403` 1 ☐ Reference person 2 ☐ Husband 3 ☐ Wife 4 ☐ Own child 5 ☐ Parent 6 ☐ Brother/Sister 7 ☐ Other relative 8 ☐ Non-relative	`404` Age	`405` 1 ☐ Married 2 ☐ Widowed 3 ☐ Divorced 4 ☐ Separated 5 ☐ Never married	`406` 1 ☐ Married 2 ☐ Widowed 3 ☐ Divorced 4 ☐ Separated 5 ☐ Never married 6 ☐ Not inter-viewed last survey period	`407` 1 ☐ M 2 ☐ F	`408` 1 ☐ Yes 2 ☐ No	`409` Grade	`410` 1 ☐ Yes 2 ☐ No	`411` 1 ☐ White 2 ☐ Black 3 ☐ Amer. Indian, Aleut, Eskimo 4 ☐ Asian, Pacific Islander 5 ☐ Other	`412` 1 ☐ Yes 2 ☐ No

`PGM 5`

29. Date of interview
`501` [ ] [ ] [ ]
Month Day Year

30. Before we get to the crime questions, I have some questions that are helpful in studying where and why crimes occur.

How long have you lived at this address?
Enter number of months OR number of years. If more than 11 months, enter number of years and leave months blank.

`502` _____ Months (1–11) — **SKIP** to 31
OR
`503` _____ Years (Round to nearest whole year) — Fill Check Item A

CHECK ITEM A How many years are entered in 30?
☐ 5 years or more — **SKIP** to Check Item B
☐ 1–5 years — **SKIP** to 32

31. How many people 12 years of age or older were living in your previous household, including you?

`504` _____ Number of people 12 +

32. Altogether, how many times have you moved in the last 5 years, that is, since _____, 19_____?
(Mo. of Int.)   (5 yrs. ago)

`505` _____ Number of times

CHECK ITEM B Is the respondent 16 years or older?
☐ Yes — Ask 33
☐ No — **SKIP** to 35a

33. Did you work at a job or business LAST WEEK? (Do not include volunteer work or work around the house)
INTERVIEWER — If farm or business operator in the household, ask about unpaid work.
`506` 1 ☐ Yes – **SKIP** to 35a
2 ☐ No

34a. Did you work at a job or business DURING THE LAST 6 MONTHS?
`507` 1 ☐ Yes – Ask 34b
2 ☐ No – **SKIP** to 35a

34b. Did that job/work last 2 consecutive weeks or more?
`508` 1 ☐ Yes
2 ☐ No

35a. Does anyone in this household operate a business from this address?
`509` 1 ☐ Yes – Ask 35b
2 ☐ No – **SKIP** to 36

35b. PERSONAL — Fill by observation.
TELEPHONE — Ask.
Is there a sign on the premises or some other indication to the general public that a business is operated from this address?
`510` 1 ☐ Yes
2 ☐ No

Notes

Page 2

FORM NCS-1 (4-10-86)

FIGURE 2.1 (Continued)   *Continued*

HOUSEHOLD SCREEN QUESTIONS

36. Now I'd like to ask some questions about crime. They refer only to the last 6 months —
between _____ 1, 19___ and _____, 19___. During the last 6 months, did anyone break into or somehow illegally get into your (apartment/home), garage, or another building on your property?

☐ Yes — How many times?
☐ No

37. (Other than the incident(s) just mentioned) Did you find a door jimmied, a lock forced, or any other signs of an ATTEMPTED break in?

☐ Yes — How many times?
☐ No

38. Was anything at all stolen that is kept outside your home, or happened to be left out, such as a bicycle, a garden hose, or lawn furniture? (other than any incidents already mentioned)

☐ Yes — How many times?
☐ No

39. Did anyone take something belonging to you or to any member of this household, from a place where you or they were temporarily staying, such as a friend's or relative's home, a hotel or motel, or a vacation home?

☐ Yes — How many times?
☐ No

40. What was the TOTAL number of motor vehicles (cars, trucks, motorcycles, etc.) owned by you or any other member of this household during the last 6 months? Include those you no longer own.

511
0 ☐ None — SKIP to 43
1 ☐ 1
2 ☐ 2
3 ☐ 3
4 ☐ 4 or more

41. Did anyone steal, TRY to steal, or use (it/any of them) without permission?

☐ Yes — How many times?
☐ No

42. Did anyone steal, or TRY to steal parts attached to (it/any of them), such as a battery, hubcaps, tape-deck, etc.?

☐ Yes — How many times?
☐ No

INDIVIDUAL SCREEN QUESTIONS

43. The following questions refer only to things that happened to YOU during the last 6 months —
between _____ 1, 19___ and _____, 19___. Did you have your (pocket picked/ purse snatched)?

☐ Yes — How many times?
☐ No

44. Did anyone take something (else) directly from you by using force, such as by a stickup, mugging or threat?

☐ Yes — How many times?
☐ No

45. Did anyone TRY to rob you by using force or threatening to harm you? (other than any incidents already mentioned)

☐ Yes — How many times?
☐ No

46. Did anyone beat you up, attack you or hit you with something, such as a rock or bottle? (other than any incidents already mentioned)

☐ Yes — How many times?
☐ No

47. Were you knifed, shot at, or attacked with some other weapon by anyone at all? (other than any incidents already mentioned)

☐ Yes — How many times?
☐ No

48. Did anyone THREATEN to beat you up or THREATEN you with a knife, gun, or some other weapon, NOT including telephone threats? (other than any incidents already mentioned)

☐ Yes — How many times?
☐ No

49. Did anyone TRY to attack you in some other way? (other than any incidents already mentioned)

☐ Yes — How many times?
☐ No

50. During the last 6 months, did anyone steal things that belonged to you from inside ANY car or truck, such as packages or clothing?

☐ Yes — How many times?
☐ No

51. Was anything stolen from you while you were away from home, for instance at work, in a theater or restaurant, or while traveling?

☐ Yes — How many times?
☐ No

52. (Other than any incidents you've already mentioned) was anything (else) at all stolen from you during the last 6 months?

☐ Yes — How many times?
☐ No

53. Did you find any evidence that someone ATTEMPTED to steal something that belonged to you? (other than any incidents already mentioned)

☐ Yes — How many times?
☐ No

54. Did you call the police during the last 6 months to report something that happened to YOU which you thought was a crime? (Do not count any calls made to the police concerning the incidents you have just told me about.)

512

☐ No – SKIP to 55
☐ Yes — What happened?
_____

CHECK ITEM C Look at 54. Was HHLD member 12 + attacked or threatened, or was something stolen or an attempt made to steal something that belonged to him/her?

☐ Yes — How many times?
☐ No

55. Did anything happen to YOU during the last 6 months which you thought was a crime, but did NOT report to the police? (other than any incidents already mentioned)

513

☐ No – SKIP to Check Item E
☐ Yes — What happened?
_____

CHECK ITEM D Look at 55. Was HHLD member 12 + attacked or threatened, or was something stolen or an attempt made to steal something that belonged to him/her?

☐ Yes — How many times?
☐ No

CHECK ITEM E Who besides the respondent was present when screen questions were asked? (If telephone interview, mark box 1 only.)

514
1 ☐ Telephone interview — Go to Check Item F
Personal interview— Mark all that apply.
2 ☐ No one besides respondent present
3 ☐ Respondent's spouse
4 ☐ HHLD member(s) 12 +, not spouse
5 ☐ HHLD member(s) under 12
6 ☐ Nonhousehold member(s)
7 ☐ Someone was present — Can't say who
8 ☐ Don't know if someone else present

CHECK ITEM F If self-response interview, SKIP to Check Item G
Did the person for whom this interview was taken help the proxy respondent answer any screen questions?

515
1 ☐ Yes
2 ☐ No
3 ☐ Person for whom interview taken not present

CHECK ITEM G Do any of the screen questions contain any entries for "How many times?"

☐ Yes -- Fill Crime Incident Reports.
☐ No — Interview next HHLD member. End interview if last respondent.

FORM NCS-1 (4-10-86)

FIGURE 2.1 (Continued)

and are interviewed every six months. The total sample size of this survey is approximately 66,000 households with 101,000 individuals.[6]

The NCVS provides data regarding the victims of crime which include age, sex, race, ethnicity, marital status, income, and educational level, as well as information about the offender. Questions covering the victim's experience with the justice system, details regarding any self-protective measures used by the victims, and possible substance abuse by offenders are included in the survey. There are periodic supplemental questionnaires that address specific issues such as school crime.

However, the NCVS suffers from problems that mitigate its validity, such as respondents underreporting or overreporting crimes. The NCVS is based on an extensive scientific sample of American households. Therefore every crime measure presented in the NCVS report is an estimate based on results of the sample. Because it is only an estimate, it will have a sampling variation or margin of error associated with each sample. Additionally, it is only an estimate of criminal activity and does not mean that the crime actually occurred.

Each method of collecting data on violence presents a different perspective and has its own validity problems. What is certain is that violence occurs on all social and economic levels in our nation. Its toll on victims is severe and long lasting. No matter which statistic or sample one uses, all agree further research is necessary. Other researchers have gathered data regarding specific forms of violence.

National Assessment Program

The National Institute of Justice conducts the *National Assessment Program (NAP)* survey approximately every three years that seeks to determine the needs and problems of state and local criminal justice agencies. Although not technically a measurement of crime, it identifies the day-to-day issues affecting professionals in the criminal justice system. It therefore provides a valuable insight into concerns that are raised by the professional whose job it is to fight crime.

The 1994 NAP survey contacted over 2500 directors of criminal justice agencies including police chiefs and sheriffs, prosecutors, judges, probation and parole agency directors, commissioners of corrections, state court administrators, prison wardens, and other criminal justice professionals. The samples covered all fifty states and the District of Columbia. Both urban (populations greater than 250,000) and rural (populations of 50,000 to 250,000) counties were included in the survey. Respondents were asked a variety of questions dealing with workload problems, staffing, and operations and procedures.

The results of the survey indicate a great concern about the impact that violence, drugs, firearms, and troubled youth are having on society and an overburdened criminal justice system. Overall, the survey indicates that cases involving violence caused problems with agencies' workloads. Police chiefs and sheriffs indicated that domestic violence was primary among crimes of violence causing them increased workload problems. Prosecutors ranked child abuse and domestic violence as significantly increasing their workload.[7] In the opinion of police

---

BOX 2.2   Uniform Crime Reports (UCR) and the National Crime Survey (NCS) Are the Main Sources of National Crime Statistics

How do UCR and NCS compare?

	Uniform Crime Reports	National Crime Survey
Offenses measured	Homicide	
	Rape	Rape
	Robbery (personal and commercial)	Robbery (personal)
	Assault (aggravated)	Assault (aggravated and simple)
	Burglary (commercial and household)	Household burglary
	Larceny (commercial and household)	Larceny (personal and household)
	Motor vehicle theft	Motor vehicle theft
	Arson	
Scope	Crimes reported to the police in most jurisdictions; considerable flexibility in developing small-area data	Crimes both reported and not reported to police; all data are available for a few large geographic areas
Collection method	Police department reports to FBI or to centralized State agencies that then report to FBI	Survey interviews; periodically measures the total number of crimes committed by asking a national sample of 49,000 households encompassing 101,000 persons age 12 and over about their experiences as victims of crime during a specified period
Kinds of information	In addition to offense courts, provides information on crime clearances, persons arrested, persons charged, law enforcement officers killed and assaulted, and characteristics of homicide victims	Provides details about victims (such as age, race, sex, education, income, and whether the victim and offender were related to each other) and about crimes (such as time and place of occurrence, whether or not reported to police, use of weapons, occurrence of injury, and economic consequences)
Sponsor	Department of Justice Federal Bureau of Investigation	Department of Justice Bureau of Justice Statistics

Source: *Report to the Nation on Crime and Justice*, 2nd ed. Bureau of Justice Statistics, U.S. Department of Justice, Washington, D.C., March 1988, p. 11.

chiefs and sheriffs, programs that prevent young people from obtaining guns is one of their greatest needs. In essence, it appears that law enforcement views the problem of juvenile crime in large part as a result of firearms.

Interest in community policing continues to grow. Although the controversy around the effectiveness of community policing still exists, most law enforcement officials express a desire to implement all or portions of a community policing program in their jurisdiction. This approach recognizes the importance of involving the community in addressing the crime problem.

The program points out that we continue as a nation to become more culturally diverse. Law enforcement officials acknowledge this trend in a variety of ways. Sheriffs and police chiefs state that they are aware of the need to respond to culturally diverse populations in the wake of changing national demographics.

These findings will assist policymakers in establishing research priorities for the near future. Professionals in the field have the same concerns that researchers and citizens display—the need for an end to violence in our society. These official reports provide insight into the problem, but they do not offer any concrete solutions.

Other Reports

National Family Violence Surveys

Two of the most comprehensive studies of family violence were carried out by Murray Straus and Richard J. Gelles in 1975 and 1985.[8] Both surveys involved interviews with a nationally representative sample of 2143 respondents in 1975 and 6014 respondents in 1985. The results of these landmark surveys continue to provide information and data for study in the area of family violence. They are continually cited as authority in numerous texts, articles, and research projects.

In both surveys, violence was defined as an act carried out with the intention, or perceived intention, of causing physical pain or injury to another person. Acts of violence that had a high probability of causing injury were included even if injury did not occur as a result. Violence was measured by using the Conflict Tactics Scale (CTS). This tool was developed at the University of New Hampshire in 1971 and is still used in many studies of family violence. The CTS measures three variables: (1) use of rational discussion and agreement, (2) use of verbal and non-verbal expressions of hostility, and (3) use of physical force or violence. Respondents were asked how many times within the last year they used certain responses that fell within one of the three classifications when they had a disagreement or were angry with family members.

Both studies were judged to be reliable because of the sampling procedure, the large number of respondents, and the validity of the conflict tactics scale as a measuring instrument. The studies surveyed families from all fifty states and assessed several different relationships: parent to child, child to parent, wife to husband, husband to wife, and sibling interactions. Interviews were conducted by trained investigators and lasted approximately one hour in the 1975 study and thirty minutes in the 1985 survey.

A comparison of the results of these studies indicated that physical child abuse declined from 1975 to 1985. Straus points out that there are several explanations for such a result. First is the increased awareness of child abuse from 1975 to 1985. During that ten-year period, child abuse became a common media topic.

This knowledge, on the part of the respondents, may have lessened the likelihood of their reporting such acts of violence. Second, different data collection techniques were used in the two surveys: the 1975 data was obtained via the telephone, and the 1985 results were collected by means of personal interviews. Finally, there may have actually been a decline in child abuse incidents from 1975 to 1985. Even if the last explanation is correct, as Straus points out, this still translates into the fact that one of every thirty-three children, three to seven years old and living with their parents are victims of child abuse.

Other Sources of Data on Violence

Clinical studies are another source of information regarding violence. These studies are carried out by practitioners in the field—medical professionals, psychiatrists, psychologists, and counselors—all of whom use samples gathered from actual cases of family violence. These researchers collect information from hospitals, clinics, and therapy sessions. Clinical studies normally have small sample sizes and therefore caution must be used when drawing any conclusions. However, these studies provide valuable data on the nature of abuse and assist in evaluating the different types of interventions utilized in family violence as well as pointing out areas for further research.

Women are not the only victims of violent crime. Researchers and professionals have attempted to study violent crime from a variety of perspectives including both the offender's and the victim's. In 1989, Weiner conducted a review of the major research dealing with individual violent crime.[21] He reviewed over forty major studies conducted by scholars between 1978 and 1987. He concluded that the further an offender advances into the sequence of violent crime, the greater the risk that the offender will continue his violent behavior.[22]

There are also other violent acts that have only recently become criminalized. Stalking is the crime of the nineties.[23] It is a newly emerging area of criminal law that is being studied by several experts in the field of human behavior. Zona and his associates are using the files of the Threat Management Unit of the Los Angeles Police Department in an effort to study stalkers.[24] Meloy has published several articles and texts that examine the nature and extent of stalkers and violence.

Other Types of Crime Research

Violent crime receives most of the publicity in our society; however, it is only one of many crimes suffered by citizens. Property crime, fraud, and white-collar crime take a tremendous toll on their victims. There is a number of reasons for this lack of attention regarding nonviolent crime: the victims' movement initially focused on serious violent crime, a lack of understanding regarding the psychological and financial consequences of property or economic crimes, and a traditional under-reporting of the nature and extent of this type of crime.

Sutherland's classic definition of white-collar crime is one way of viewing this offense. He defined white-collar crime as an offense committed by a person of respectability and high social status in the course of his occupation.[25] The FBI on the other hand, defines white-collar crime as those illegal acts characterized by deceit, concealment, violation of trust, and nondependence on the application or threat of physical force or violence. They are committed to obtain money, property, or services; or to avoid the payment or loss of money, property, or services; or to secure personal or business advantage.[26] Both of these definitions deal with economic crimes, or crimes that have the gathering of assets from the victim as their objective.

Several prominent researchers have called for more information about economic crime.[27] Understanding the nature and extent of economic crime is necessary if we are to attempt to respond to its consequences. One of the most common forms of economic crime is fraud. A nationwide survey of fraud revealed that a sizable portion of the adult population in the United States is affected.[28] Fraud was defined as a deliberate intent, targeted against individuals, to deceive for the purpose of illegal financial gain.[29] Included in this definition were various forms of telemarketing frauds, frauds involving consumer goods and services, deceptive financial advice, and insurance scams.

The survey used a random sample of the adult population of the United States. The respondents were asked about twenty-one types of fraud plus a catch-all category and were asked if they had ever been victimized or if an attempt had been made to victimize them. Fraud crosses all sociological barriers and victimization occurs in all ages, genders, races, or incomes.

More than half of those surveyed indicated that they experienced victimization, or an attempted victimization at some time in their past. Approximately one in every three respondents were potential victims of fraud within the year preceding the survey. The attempt to defraud these victims was successful 50 percent of the time.

Economic crime is a serious form of victimization that is often overlooked by those tasked with, or interested in, studying the effects of crime on individuals. The consequences of fraud will be addressed in more detail later in this text. At this stage, it is important to acknowledge that there are other forms of victimization than violence-related crimes.

Summary

It is important in the study of any discipline to know how to measure the variables that affect that discipline. Because of a number of factors, which will be discussed in more detail later in this text, the measurement of crime can never be completely accurate.

Official reports are those measurements of crime conducted by federal agencies. The most well-known official report is the Uniform Crime Report. This report, prepared annually by the FBI, acts as a barometer of our society. Because of several inherent shortcomings in the UCR, the National Crime

Victimization Survey was developed. This survey relies on self-reporting in an attempt to determine a more accurate accounting of the nature and extent of crimes in our society.

Other reports include the National Family Violence Survey and a variety of other sources of information regarding acts of violence. Researchers are paying significant attention to economic crimes and their effects on victims. Recent studies indicate that economic crimes, such as fraud, are widespread and occur at all socioeconomic levels within our society.

We continue to modify our measurement tools in the hopes of perfecting a valid and true method of measuring crime. Understanding the nature and extent of criminal victimization is only the beginning in understanding the process of victimization itself. However, it is a critical phase in the study of victimology and one that all professionals in the field should understand.

Key Terms

Uniform Crime Reports (UCR) program is a nationwide statistical computation involving over 1600 cities, counties, and state law enforcement agencies who voluntarily provide data on reported crimes.

National Crime Victimization Survey (NCVS) is a nationwide sample of interviews of citizens regarding victimization.

National Assessment Program (NAP) seeks to determine the needs and problems of state and local criminal justice agencies.

Discussion Questions

1. Explain the problems in using the UCR. If you were in charge of preparing it, what changes would you suggest to make it more reliable?

2. How would you improve the NCVS?

3. How does the NAP information benefit victim service professionals?

4. The National Family Violence Surveys were conducted over ten years ago. Why are data from the surveys still important?

5. Compare and contrast the other types of crime research. Can you think of another method to collect information about crime and victims?

Suggested Readings

M. A. Straus, R. J. Gelles & S. K. Steinmetz, *Behind Closed Doors: Violence in the American Family*, (Anchor/Doubleday, New York) 1980.

M. A. Straus, "Is Violence Toward Children Increasing? A Comparison of the 1975 and 1985 National Survey Rates," R. J. Gelles, ed.,

Family Violence, (Sage, Newbury Park, Calif.) 1987.

D. G. Kilpatrick, C. N. Edmunds & A. K. Seymour, *Rape in America: A Report to the Nation,* (National Victim Center, Arlington, Va.) 1992.

D. E. H. Russell, *Sexual Exploitation,* (Sage, Beverly Hills, Calif.) 1984.

N. A. Weiner and M. E. Wolfgang, eds. *Violent Crime, Violent Criminals,* (Sage, Newbury Park, Calif.) 1989.

E. H. Sutherland, *White Collar Crime, The Uncut Version,* (Yale University Press, New Haven, Conn.) 1983.

Report of the Attorney General, *National Practices for the Investigation and Prosecution of White Collar Crime,* U.S. Department of Justice, (Office of the Attorney General, Washington, D.C.) 1990.

Geis, Gilbert & R. A. Stotland, *White Collar Crime: Theory and Research,* (Sage, Newbury Park, Calif.) 1980.

Endnotes

1. 28 USC 534 (1930).
2. "Crime in the United States, 1994," *Uniform Crime Reports,* (Superintendent of Documents, Washington, D.C.) 1994.
3. Bureau of Justice Statistics, *Criminal Victimization in the United States, 1992,* (U.S. Department of Justice, Washington, D.C.) 1994, p. 100.
4. M. E. Milakovich & Kurt Weis, "Politics and the Measure of Success in the War on Crime," 21 *Crime and Delinquency,* 1–10 (January 1975).
5. The UCR states that the NCVS started in 1973. See "Crime in the United States, 1994," *Uniform Crime Reports,* (Superintendent of Documents, Washington, D.C.) 1994.
6. The UCR presents a different estimate of households than the NCVS. See "Crime in the United States, 1994," *Uniform Crime Reports,* (Superintendent of Documents, Washington, D.C.) 1994.
7. Tom McEwen, "National Assessment Program: 1994 Survey Results," *Research in Brief,* National Institute of Justice, (May 1995) p. 2.
8. See M. A. Straus, R. J. Gelles & S. K. Steinmetz, *Behind Closed Doors: Violence in the American Family,* (Anchor/Doubleday, New York 1980) for an in-depth discussion of the 1975 survey; and M. A. Straus, "Is Violence Toward Children Increasing? A Comparison of the 1975 and 1985 National Survey Rates," R. J. Gelles, ed., *Family Violence,* (Sage, Newbury Park, Calif. 1987) for an analysis of the 1985 survey.

9. Personal communication with Christine N. Edmunds, co-author and project director, National Victims Center, Washington, D.C.
10. M. P. Koss, "Detecting the Scope of Rape," 8/2 *Journal of Interpersonal Violence,* 200–203 (June 1993).
11. For an excellent in-depth discussion of these issues, see M. P. Koss, "Detecting the Scope of Rape," 8/2 *Journal of Interpersonal Violence,* 198–222 (June 1993).
12. M. R. Burt, "Attitudes Supportive of Rape in American Culture (Final Report, Grant #ROIMH29023). (National Institute of Mental Health, National Center for the Prevention and Control of Rape, Washington, D.C.) 1979.
13. S. M. Essock-Vitale & M. T. McGuire, "Women's Lives Viewed from an Evolutionary Perspective," I. Sexual Histories, Reproductive Success, and Demographic Characteristics of a Random Sample of American Women, 6 *Ethnology and Sociobiology,* 137–154 (1985).
14. D. G. Kilpatrick, C. L. Best, L. J. Veronen, A. E. Amick, L. A. Villeponteaux & G. A. Ruff, "Mental Health Correlates of Criminal Victimization: A Random Community Survey," 53 *Journal of Consulting and Clinical Psychology,* 866–873 (1985).
15. S. Riger & M. T. Gordon, "The Fear of Rape; A Study in Social Control," 37 *Journal of Social Issues,* 71–92 (1981).
16. D. G. Kilpatrick, C. N. Edmunds & A. K. Seymour, *Rape in America: A Report to the Nation,*

(National Victims Center, Arlington, Va.) 1992.

17. D. E. H. Russell, *Sexual Exploitation*, (Sage, Beverly Hills, Calif.) 1984.

18. S. B. Sorenson, J. A. Stein, J. M. Siegel, J. M. Golding & M. A. Burnam, "Prevalence of Adult Sexual Assault: The Los Angeles Epidemiologic Catchment Area Study," 126 *American Journal of Epidemiology*, 1154–1164 (1987).

19. I. Winfield, L. K. George, M. Swartz & D. G. Blazer, "Sexual Assault and Psychiatric Disorders Among a Community Sample of Women," 147 *American Journal of Psychiatry*, 335–341 (1990).

20. G. E. Wyatt, "The Sociocultural Context of African American and White American Women's Rape," 48 *Journal of Social Issues*, 77–92 (1992).

21. Neil Alan Weiner, "Violent Criminal Careers and 'Violent Career Criminals,'" *Violent Crime, Violent Criminals*, N. A. Weiner and M. E. Wolfgang, eds. (Sage, Newbury Park, Calif.) 1989.

22. Id. at p. 127.

23. See for example, H. Wallace, "Stalkers, The Constitution's and Victims' Remedies," vol. 10/1 ABA *Criminal Justice*, 16 (Spring 1995).

24. Michael A. Zona, et al., "A Comparative Study of Erotomonic and Obsessional Subjects in a Forensic Sample," 38 *Journal of Forensic Science*, 894 (July 1993).

25. E. H. Sutherland, *White Collar Crime, The Uncut Version*, (Yale University Press, New Haven, Conn.) 1983.

26. Report of the Attorney Gerneral, *National Practices for the Investigation and Prosecution of White Collar Crime*, U.S. Department of Justice, (Office of the Attorney General, Washington, D.C.) 1990.

27. Geis, Gilbert & R. A. Stotland, *White Collar Crime: Theory and Research*, (Sage, Newbury Park, Calif.) 1980.

28. Much of the material presented in this section dealing with fraud comes from Richard Titus, Fred Heinzelmann & John M. Boyle, "The Anatomy of Fraud: Report of a Nationwide Survey," Research in Action, *National Institute of Justice Journal*, 28 (August 1995).

29. Id.

3

THE CRIMINAL JUSTICE SYSTEM AND VICTIMS

Chapter Outline

The Criminal Court System
  Introduction
  State Court System
  Federal Court System
  Juvenile Court System

The Parties
  The Victim
  The Perpetrator
  Law Enforcement
  The Prosecutor
  The Defense Attorney
  The Courts
  The Correctional System

Criminal Justice Procedures
  Pretrial Activities
  The First Appearance
  Preliminary Hearing or Grand Jury Hearing
  Arraignment
  Jury Selection
  Opening Statement
  Case-in-Chief
  Defendant's Evidence
  Closing Argument
  Deliberation and Verdict
  Sentencing

Summary

Key Terms

Discussion Questions

Suggested Readings

Learning Objectives

After reading this chapter, you should be able to:

- Understand the principle of federalism and how it affected the structure of our court system
- Discuss how the dual system of state and federal courts functions
- Describe the characteristics of the American court system
- Discuss how the juvenile court system functions
- Understand the roles and responsibilities of each party in the criminal justice system
- Describe the various steps in the criminal justice process
- Explain the differences between the various types of pleas a defendant may enter

The Criminal Court System[1]

Introduction

Understanding the role and functions of the various court systems in the United States provides professionals with a solid foundation for understanding the dynamics of the law. It is a complex aspect of our legal system that can be confusing and frustrating to victims when they are first exposed to it. Understanding the rationale behind its present-day structure may help victims understand more clearly the manner in which laws operate and interact.

To comprehend the role of federal and state law, it is essential to have a firm grasp of the principles of how the American criminal justice system functions. For a victim of crime, it is the most confusing, frustrating, and complex environment to navigate. This section will provide a brief overview of the criminal court system in the United States.

The court system in the United States is based on the principle of federalism. The first Congress established a federal court system, and the individual states were permitted to continue their own judicial structure. There was general agreement among our nation's founders that individual states needed to retain significant autonomy from federal control. Under this concept of federalism, the United States developed as a loose confederation of semi-independent states having their own courts, with the federal court system acting in a very limited manner. In the early history of our nation, most cases were tried in state courts. It was only later that the federal government and the federal judiciary began to exercise jurisdiction over crimes and civil matters. *Jurisdiction* in this context simply means the ability of the court to enforce laws and punish individuals who violate those laws.

As a result of this historical evolution, a dual system of state and federal courts exists today. Therefore, federal and state courts may have concurrent jurisdiction over specific crimes. For example, a person who robs a bank may be tried and convicted in state court for robbery, then tried and convicted in federal court for the federal offense of robbery of a federally chartered savings institution.

Another characteristic of the American court system is that it performs its duties with little or no supervision. A Supreme Court justice does not exercise supervision over lower court judges in the same way that a government supervisor or manager exercises control over employees. The U.S. Supreme Court and the various state supreme courts exercise supervision only in the sense that they hear appellate cases from lower courts and establish certain procedures for these courts.

A third feature of the U.S. court system is one of specialization and occurs primarily at the state and local level. In many states, courts of limited jurisdiction hear misdemeanor cases. Other state courts of general jurisdiction try felonies. Still other courts may be designated as juvenile courts and hear only matters involving juveniles. This process also occurs in certain civil courts that hear only family law matters, probate matters, or civil cases involving damages. At the federal level, there are courts such as bankruptcy that hear only cases dealing with specific matters.

The fourth characteristic of the American court system is its geographic organization. State and federal courts are organized into geographic areas. In many jurisdictions these are called judicial districts and contain various levels of courts. For example, on the federal level, the Ninth Circuit Court of Appeals has district (trial) courts that hear matters within certain specific boundaries; and an appellate court that hears all appeals from cases within that area. Several studies have been conducted regarding the differences in sentences for the same type of crime in geographic distinct courts. For example, in Iowa the average sentence for motor vehicle theft is forty-seven months whereas the average sentence for the same offense in New York is fourteen months.[2] This shouldn't be taken as a criticism; rather it may reflect different social values and attitudes within specific geographic areas.

State Court System

Historically, each of the thirteen original states had their own unique court structure. This independence continued after the American Revolution and resulted in widespread differences among the various states, some of which still exist today. Because each state adopted its own system of courts, the consequence was a poorly planned and confusing judicial structure. As a result, there have been several reform movements whose purpose has been to streamline and modernize this system.

Many state courts can be divided into three levels:

- Trial courts
- Appellate courts
- State supreme courts

Trial Courts

Trial courts are courts where criminal cases start and finish. The trial court conducts an entire series of acts that culminate in either the defendant's release or sentencing. State trial courts can be further divided into courts of limited or special jurisdiction and courts of general jurisdiction. The nature and type of case determines which court will have jurisdiction.

Courts that only hear and decide certain limited legal issues are courts of **limited jurisdiction.** These courts hear and decide issues such as traffic tickets or set bail for criminal defendants. Typically, these courts hear certain types of minor civil or criminal cases. There are approximately 13,000 local courts in the United States. They are called county, magistrate, justice, or municipal courts. Judges in these courts may be either appointed or elected. In many jurisdictions these are part-time positions and the incumbent may have another job or position in addition to serving as a judge. However, simply because they handle minor civil and criminal matters does not negate the fact that these courts perform important duties. Often, the only contact the average citizen will have with the judicial system occurs at this level.

In addition, courts of limited jurisdiction may hear certain types of specialized matters such as probate of wills and estates, divorces, child custody matters, and juvenile hearings. These types of courts may be local courts or, depending on the state, courts of general jurisdiction that are designated by statute to hear and decide specific types of cases. For example, in California, a superior court is considered a court of general jurisdiction; however, certain superior courts are designated to hear only juvenile matters, thereby becoming a court of limited jurisdiction when sitting as a juvenile court.

Courts of *general jurisdiction* are granted authority to hear and decide all issues that are brought before them. These courts normally hear all major civil or criminal cases. They are also known by a variety of names, such as superior courts, circuit courts, district courts, or courts of common pleas. Because they are courts of general jurisdiction, they have authority to decide issues that occur anywhere within the state. Some larger jurisdictions such as Los Angeles or New York may have hundreds of courts of general jurisdiction within the city limits. These courts also hear the most serious forms of criminal matters including death penalty cases.

Courts of general jurisdiction traditionally have the power to order individuals to do, or refrain from doing, certain acts. These courts may issue injunctions that prohibit persons from performing certain acts, or they may require individuals to do certain functions or duties. This authority is derived from the equity power that resides in courts of general jurisdiction.

Equity is the concept that justice is administered according to fairness, as contrasted with the strict rules of law. In early English common law, such separate courts of equity were known as courts of Chancery. These early courts were not concerned with technical legal issues; rather they focused on rendering decisions or orders that were fair or equitable. In modern times the power of these courts has been merged with courts of general jurisdiction, allowing them to rule on matters that require fairness as well as the strict application of the law. The power to issue temporary restraining orders (TROs) in spousal abuse cases comes from the equitable powers of the court.

Appellate jurisdiction is reserved for courts that hear appeals from both limited and general jurisdiction courts. These courts do not hold trials or hear evidence. They decide matters of law and issue formal written decisions or "opinions." There are two classes of appellate courts: intermediate, or courts of appeals and final, or supreme courts.

Courts of Appeals

The intermediate appellate courts are known as courts of appeals. Approximately half the states have designated intermediate appellate courts. These courts may be divided into judicial districts and will hear all appeals within their jurisdiction. They will hear and decide all issues of law that are raised on appeal in both civil and criminal cases. Because these courts deal strictly with legal or equitable issues, there is no jury to decide factual disputes. These courts accept the facts as determined by the trial courts. Intermediate appellate courts have the authority to reverse the decision of the lower courts, and to send the matter back with instructions to retry the case in accordance with their opinion. They may also uphold the decision of the lower court. In either situation, the party who loses the appeal at this level may file an appeal with the next higher appellate court.

Supreme Courts

Final appellate courts are the highest state appellate courts. They may be known as supreme courts or courts of last resort. There may be five, seven, or nine justices sitting on this court depending on the state. Final appellate courts have jurisdiction to hear and decide issues dealing with all matters decided by lower courts, including ruling on state constitutional or statutory issues. Their decision is binding on all other courts within the state. Once this court has decided an issue, the only appeal left is to file in the federal court system.

Federal Court System

Whereas state courts have their origin in historical accident and custom, federal courts were created by the U.S. Constitution. Section 1 of Article 3 established the federal court system with the words providing for "one Supreme Court, and . . . such inferior Courts as the Congress may from time to time ordain and establish." From this beginning, Congress has engaged in a series of acts that has resulted in today's federal court system. The Judiciary Act of 1789 created the U.S. Supreme Court and established district courts and circuit courts of appeals.

Federal District Courts

Federal district courts are the lowest level of the federal court system. These courts have original jurisdiction over all cases involving a violation of federal statutes. District courts handle thousands of criminal cases per year.

Federal Circuit Courts

Federal circuit courts of appeals are the intermediate appellate level courts within the federal system. These courts are called circuit courts because the federal system is divided into eleven circuits. A Twelfth Circuit Court of Appeals serves the Washington, D.C., area. These courts hear all criminal appeals from the district courts and habeas corpus appeals from state court convictions. These appeals are usually heard by panels of three appellate court judges rather than by all the judges of each circuit.

U.S. Supreme Court

The United States Supreme Court is the highest court in the land. It has the capacity for judicial review of all lower court decisions, as well as state and federal statutes. By exercising this power the Supreme Court determines what laws and lower court decisions conform to the mandates set forth in the U.S. Constitution. The concept of judicial review was first referred to by Alexander Hamilton in the *Federalist Papers,* in which he described the Supreme Court as ensuring that the will of the people will be supreme over the will of the legislature.[3] This concept was firmly and finally established in our system when the Supreme Court asserted its power of judicial review in the 1803 case of *Marbury v. Madison.*[4]

Although it is primarily an appellate court, the Supreme Court has original jurisdiction in the following cases: cases between the United States and a state; cases between states; cases involving foreign ambassadors, ministers, and consuls; and cases between a state and a citizen of another state or country.

The Court hears appeals from lower courts including the various state supreme courts. If four justices of the U.S. Supreme Court vote to hear a case, the court will issue a *Writ of Certiorari*—an order sent to a lower court requiring the records of the case to be sent to the Supreme Court for review. The Court meets on the first Monday of October and usually remains in session until June. The Court may review any case it deems worthy but in actuality hears very few of the cases filed. Of approximately 5000 appeals each year, the Court agrees to review about 200; however, it may not issue an opinion on each case.

Juvenile Court System

Because of the significant increase in importance of juvenile crime in our society, an overview of juvenile courts within the state and federal court system is warranted. Although there are some differences, both federal and state systems were initially founded on the concept of rehabilitating young offenders. Additionally, both systems wanted to shield juveniles from public scrutiny; therefore, each contained provisions for keeping matters confidential.

The Federal Court Juvenile System

When Congress addressed the issue of juvenile offenders it established two alternatives for their prosecution:

- The juvenile can waive personal rights to be treated as a juvenile; or
- The juvenile can have the matter treated as a civil proceeding called *juvenile adjudication.*

If the court finds that the juvenile committed the offense, that individual faces a series of federal sanctions including incarceration. There is a federal preference for state prosecution of juveniles, because there is no separate federal juvenile court judge or juvenile detention system. If adjudicated to be a delinquent, the juvenile is placed in a state juvenile facility. The federal government contracts with states for this service.

Until the passage of the Crime Control Act of 1990, the federal government only prosecuted juveniles who committed crimes on federal reservations, where the states had no jurisdiction. The Crime Control Act added two other categories of juveniles who fall under federal juvenile court jurisdiction: juveniles who commit felony crimes of violence and/or those juveniles involved in certain drug felonies. Similar to most state court systems, federal law allows for the transfer or certification of a juvenile to "adult status." This procedure allows juveniles to be tried as adults in either the state or the federal court system.

Under federal law, juveniles are those persons under twenty-one who commit a federal offense before their eighteenth birthday. A federal judge acts as the federal equivalent of the state juvenile court judge. The proceedings are confidential with no member of the public or press in attendance. Federal jurisdiction in juvenile matters is established when:

- The state does not have jurisdiction;
- The state does not have programs or services available for juveniles; or
- The offense charged is a violent felony or drug offense and there is a substantial federal interest in the case.

A juvenile proceeding is initiated by the filing of an "information." In most cases, the U.S. attorney must file a certification stating there are grounds for federal jurisdiction. The hearing in federal court is very similar to a court trial.

The State Court Juvenile System

The present-day American state court system of dealing with children involved in crimes began in 1899 when the state of Illinois passed the Illinois Juvenile Court Act. It was at that time that the juvenile court system as we know it today came into existence.[5] This statute separated the juvenile court system from the adult criminal system. It labeled minors who violated the law as "delinquents" rather than criminals, and required that juvenile court judges determine what "is in the best interests of the minor" in rendering their decision.

The juvenile court system is guided by five basic principles:

1. The state is the ultimate parent of all children within its jurisdiction, the doctrine of *parens patrea.*
2. Children are worth saving and the state should utilize nonpunitive measures to do so.
3. Children should be nurtured and not stigmatized by the court process.
4. Each child is different and justice should be tailored to meet individual needs and requirements.
5. The use of noncriminal sanctions is necessary to give primary consideration to the needs of the child.[6]

It is important to note that each state determines its own jurisdictional age of minors who are handled by its juvenile system. Most involve children who are under eighteen years of age. A few states use higher ages, up to twenty-one. Three states cover children up to fifteen years of age and adjudicate sixteen year olds in adult criminal courts.

Although these principles were originally adopted for delinquents or minors who committed criminal acts, they have been broadly applied to proceedings involving children who are victims of abuse. This aspect of the juvenile court system will be examined in the next chapter.

Understanding the criminal court system is only the beginning of appreciating the complexity of the American criminal justice system. Professionals working in this area must also understand the parties involved in the criminal justice system. The different parties that comprise our system will be reviewed in the following sections.

The Parties

There are seven parties involved in the criminal justice process: the victim, the perpetrator, law enforcement, the prosecutor, the defense attorney, the courts, and the correctional system. Each of these parties or organizations has different goals and needs. Not all emotions or objectives are the same for all the parties. It is obvious, for example, that the prosecutor and defense attorney will have different perspectives on the outcome of the trial. Those who work in this area must be familiar with the various responsibilities of each of these parties and be able to explain their functions to those who are involved in the criminal justice system.

The Victim

The victim of any crime is often the forgotten party in the criminal justice system. For many years, victims were perceived as simply another witness to the crime. The prevailing attitude was that the real victim was the "People of the State" in which the crime was committed. Families of murder victims could not obtain information regarding the case, and were often ignored by overworked and understaffed criminal justice personnel. Within the last twenty years this attitude has begun to change as we become more aware of the needs and desires of crime victims.

Professionals dealing with crime victims must understand that they may be suffering emotional and/or physical trauma as a result of the offense.[7] Care must be taken to ensure that victims understand how the process works and what their rights are. It is also important to realize that there are individuals other than the original victim who have an interest in the process. These parties include the victim's family and friends, and in some situations the victim's employer. All appropriate parties should be notified of every significant event within the criminal justice process. Victim service providers must also respect and protect the victim's right to privacy if that is the victim's desire.

Victims of crime will normally have a number of questions and concerns regarding the court system and their involvement in it. One frustrating aspect of this process is the fact that victims oftentimes perceive that the defendant has more rights and faster access to the courts than they do. Other chapters of this text will examine in detail the rights of victims of crime during the criminal justice process.

The Perpetrator

The perpetrator of a crime is guaranteed certain rights within our form of government. Many aspects of the criminal procedure process are controlled by the U.S. Constitution, specifically the Bill of Rights (the original ten amendments to the Constitution). These federal constitutional protections concerning individual rights are, for the most part, binding on state courts.[8]

These rights attach to the perpetrator early in the criminal procedure process and violation of these rights may result in the case being dismissed. For example, if the perpetrator confesses to the crime of murder, and that confession is obtained in violation of the person's constitutional rights, it may be suppressed.[9] If the confession is the only link connecting the defendant to the crime, the case may have to be dismissed. When these types of incidents occur, it is difficult for the victim to understand why the defendant goes free when there has been a confession. If this happens, professionals working with victims must attempt to offer other alternatives such as availability of filing civil lawsuits against the perpetrator.

Law Enforcement

One law enforcement role in the criminal process is to apprehend the perpetrator.[10] Although this may seem to be a simple concept, understanding the organization and function of law enforcement agencies in the United States can be an exercise in frustration. American law enforcement activities take place on three independent levels: federal, state, and local. There is little uniformity among these entities. Additionally, each of these agencies may enforce different criminal laws based on different jurisdictional authority. For example, the U.S. Customs Service may arrest individuals who violate federal laws regarding the importation of goods into the United States, the state highway patrol may be tasked with enforcing traffic laws on highways and streets, and the local police department may be engaged in tracking down a serial rapist.

To confuse the issue further, there is another emerging form of law enforcement activity in the United States whose activities are expanding. Private protective services have been defined as "those self-employed individuals and privately funded business entities and organizations providing security-related services to specific clientele for a fee . . . in order to protect their persons, private property, or interests from various hazards."[11] Normally these firms are employed by corporate clients to protect private interests. They act as private citizens and may make arrests for violations of crimes committed in their presence.

The Prosecutor

The prosecuting attorney is a familiar individual in the criminal justice process. The office of the prosecuting attorney is known by a variety of names including district attorney, county attorney, commonwealth attorney, and, at the federal level, the U.S. attorney. The prosecutor plays a critical role in the criminal process for a variety of reasons. That person is the go-between for law enforcement and the courts and decides what type of charges to file, whether to plea bargain a particular case, and how to present the case to the court or jury.

One hotly debated issue surrounding the prosecutor's function concerns plea bargaining.[12] From a criminal justice perspective, a plea bargain serves several purposes: a defendant may receive the opportunity to plead guilty to a lessor charge which will reduce the time spent in jail or prison; or the prosecutor may have a weak case and a plea bargain may ensure that the defendant is convicted of something rather than walking free after an acquittal. Also from the judge's perspective a plea bargain eliminates one more case.[13] A plea bargain may also benefit a victim in several ways: a plea to a lessor offense eliminates the requirement that the victim relive the crime by testifying in court and, similar to the prosecutor's position, a plea bargain guarantees that the defendant is convicted of some crime. Conversely, many victims resent plea bargains because they believe that a jury should decide the case and that if the perpetrator is guilty he should be punished to the maximum extent allowed by the law.

Another controversial aspect of plea bargaining is that some prosecutors fail to notify the victim of their intent to reduce or dismiss some of the charges in exchange for a plea of guilty. There are victims who have found out about the plea bargain at the time the prosecutor called to inquire about the status of the case. If plea bargaining is to occur, the preferred method is to fully involve the victim in the decision-making process. If the victim is adamantly opposed to the reduction or dismissal of charges, the prosecutor should seriously consider not going forward with the plea bargain.

The prosecuting attorney is the representative of the people of the state or of the United States. This person is not the crime victim's personal attorney. This aspect of our criminal justice system is very troubling to many victims. However, a prosecutor who is sensitive to the needs and concerns of victims of crime can help reduce these concerns and many of the other traumas suffered by these individuals.

The Defense Attorney

The defense attorney represents the rights and interests of the perpetrator. Unlike the prosecutor who is concerned with justice and fairness, the defense attorney's obligation as established by the American Bar Association's General Standards of Conduct is to use all available courage, devotion, and skills to protect the rights of the accused. Many defense attorneys interpret this obligation as requiring that they do everything possible to obtain an acquittal even if they know that the defendant in fact committed the offense.

The Sixth Amendment to the U.S. Constitution requires that those who are accused of crimes have a right to be represented by an attorney. The Supreme Court in the landmark case of *Gideon v. Wainwright* established the principle that all defendants have a right to counsel in all felony cases even if they could not afford to hire their own attorney.[14] The court extended this concept to misdemeanor cases in *Argersinger v. Hamilin* holding that absent a waiver no person may be imprisoned for any offense, either misdemeanor or felony, unless represented by an attorney.[15]

There are basically four types of defense attorneys: public defenders, contract defense services, assigned defense counsel, and private defense counsel. Public defenders are hired and paid for by the government and are appointed to represent those persons charged with crimes who cannot afford to hire an attorney for representation. Many counties have public defender's offices that are staffed by very able, aggressive attorneys. However, there are instances when, for a variety of reasons, the public defender's office has a conflict of interest in a case. For example, this may occur if there were two defendants in one case. In this situation, the court may appoint an attorney from the contract defense services to represent one of the two defendants. Contract defense services are normally composed of a group of attorneys who have entered into an agreement with the county to represent indigent defendants for a specified amount of money.

Assigned defense counsel exist in the majority of the counties in the United States.[16] Many of these counties are small and cannot afford the cost of maintaining a public defender's office. Under the assigned defense counsel format, the court maintains a list of attorneys who are willing to be appointed to represent indigent criminal defendants. When a defendant appears in court, the judge appoints the next attorney on the list to represent the perpetrator.

The last form of defense attorney is the private defense counsel. These attorneys usually represent those defendants who are capable of paying for their services. Well-known examples of private defense counsel include attorneys such as

Johnny Cochran, F. Lee Bailey, and Alan Dershowitz of the "Dream Team" who represented O. J. Simpson.

Not only do perpetrators have a right to an attorney, the courts have held that the attorney must be competent.[17] Although the Constitution requires competent counsel who will vigorously defend the perpetrator, there is no requirement or right to have an attorney who will knowingly present perjured testimony. In *Nix v. Whiteside,* the defense attorney, upon learning that his client was going to take the stand and commit perjury, informed the client that he could not permit such testimony and if the client insisted on going forward and giving this testimony, the attorney would disclose the perjury and withdraw from the case. The perpetrator testified and did not commit perjury; however, he did file an appeal claiming ineffective counsel. The court disagreed holding that attorneys who follow their state's rules of professional (ethical) conduct do not violate the Sixth Amendment right to counsel.[18]

The Courts

Both the structure and organization of the court system were explained earlier in this chapter. Here it is only necessary to explain that the courts play a critical role in the criminal justice process. They bring an impartiality and formality to the system that provides it with balance, and hopefully justice.

The Correctional System

One of the least discussed entities in the criminal justice process is the correctional system. Victims' involvement with perpetrators does not end at the conviction and sentencing phase. Many victims must appear each year and offer evidence as to why a certain perpetrator should not be released from custody. Therefore, it is necessary for any professional involved with victims to understand the role and responsibilities of the various correctional institutions.

There are two basic types of penal facilities: jails and prisons. *Jails* are operated by local agencies such as cities or counties. Jails are used for pretrial detention, holding after sentencing, and for incarceration of those persons who are not being sentenced to prison. Normally these are individuals who have been convicted of misdemeanors and will serve up to one year of imprisonment. Some jurisdictions are experimenting with jail "boot camps" where the inmates undergo rigorous mental and physical training during their incarceration. *Prisons* are administered by states or the federal government and are reserved for the more serious offenders. There are various types of prisons that range from minimum security institutions to those that house the most violent predators in society.

There are three types of persons involved in the corrections field: probation officers, parole officers, and correctional officers. Probation is a distinctly American institution. It began with John Augustus, who in 1841 asked a Boston judge to permit him to sponsor an offender. The court agreed to his request and the perpetrator was sentenced to Augustus's custody instead of jail. (Augustus is considered the father of probation.) **Probation** is a conditional release of the offender after having been found guilty. It is traditionally used on misdemeanor or other low-level crimes. It allows the perpetrator to remain free so long as that person meets certain conditions. Probation officers are those persons employed by the local jurisdictions to supervise these offenders. Many different forms of probation services are offered in the United States, and there is a continuing debate on which one is the most effective.

Parole is the conditional release of an inmate back into the community from a prison or other form of correctional institution. Many jurisdictions allow for the parole of offenders. This normally occurs after a board or commission has made a determination that the prisoner would benefit from early release. Many victims who appear at these hearings and oppose the release of those predators have been sexually assaulted themselves or had their loved ones killed. These hearings are held every year in many jurisdictions with the result that the victim must relive the crime annually in an attempt to keep the perpetrator incarcerated.

Correctional officers are those persons who are hired to maintain security in jails or prisons. Many of these positions require only a high school education and a clean criminal background. Some states are beginning to impose more educational requirements on applicants and several states have upgraded their training for correctional officers.

The court system and the parties involved are only a small part of the entire criminal justice system. Victim advocates must also be familiar with the criminal justice process. The next section examines the various steps in this system.

Criminal Justice Procedures

A criminal proceeding involves many steps. *Adjudication* includes all the formal and informal decisions and steps within the criminal proceeding process. It is important to remember that in criminal cases the government has the burden of proof. At each stage in the proceedings, the accused is afforded certain rights which are guaranteed by both federal and state constitutions. These constitutional protections have shaped the way in which our criminal process functions. From the first encounter, to the execution of an inmate, certain constitutional protections mandate that law enforcement officers and those representing the government carry out their duties in certain ways. These constitutional mandates have resulted in a complex series of hearings and/or actions that must occur during any criminal proceeding. The examination of this process starts with the first formal court activity, that is, those pretrial activities associated with bringing an accused into the system.

Pretrial Activities

Pretrial activities include a variety of acts including the arrest, the booking, and the filing of a complaint. An *arrest* is taking a suspect into custody in a manner prescribed by law. An arrest usually occurs in one of two ways: when a warrant of arrest has been issued by a magistrate, or when an officer has probable cause to believe that the suspect has committed a crime. Arrest usually involves transporting the suspect to jail so charges regarding the offense can be filed. In misdemeanor or infraction cases, instead of taking the suspect to jail, the officer may simply issue a citation to the suspect. A *citation* is an order to appear before a judge at a later time. An example of a citation is a traffic ticket issued by an officer to a person who violates the vehicle code laws.

When the officer transports the offender to the local police station, the booking process begins. *Booking* involves entering the suspect's name, offense, and other information into the police records. The suspect is also fingerprinted and photographed at this time. The suspect is usually allowed to make a phone call during this process. For certain types of offenses, a bail schedule is established and made available at the police department. If the suspect can pay the amount listed on the bail schedule, he is freed and ordered to report to a judge at a predetermined time. In more serious cases, the suspect is taken before a judge for a bail hearing. This type of hearing will be discussed in more detail later in this chapter.

In many jurisdictions, pretrial activities include filing a complaint by the local prosecutor's office. However, prior to filing the complaint, the prosecutor will review the facts of the case and decide what charge to file. This process takes place with both felonies and misdemeanors.

The First Appearance

Once the suspect is in custody, the suspect (who is now called the defendant) must be brought before a judge without unnecessary delay. In *County of Riverside v. McLaughlin* the Supreme Court held that defendants must be brought before a judge within forty-eight hours.[19] The court further held that weekends and holidays could not be excluded from the forty-eight-hour rule, and in some cases delays of less than two days may still be considered unreasonable.

At this first hearing the defendant is informed of the charges and the fact that he has a right to counsel. If the defendant is indigent, the judge begins the process of appointing an attorney for him. It is during this first appearance that bail is set.

Historically, the right to bail was considered so important that the drafters of the U.S. Constitution included it in the Bill of Rights. The Eighth Amendment states that excessive bail shall not be required; however, this does not mean that all defendants have a right to bail for all crimes. The right to bail requires that the judge consider the defendant's individualized circumstances in setting bail.[20] These factors include the nature and circumstances of the offense, the weight of evidence against the defendant, the financial ability of the defendant to pay the bail, and the character of the defendant.

In recent years, the defendant's dangerousness has also come under scrutiny in establishing bail. Preventive detention allows the court to deny bail based on a finding that the defendant may commit further crimes if released. The most elaborate preventive detention scheme in existence is found in the Federal Bail Reform Act of 1984 which makes the safety of any other person, or the community, a relevant consideration in setting bail.[21] This aspect of bail is especially important in family violence situations and every effort must be made by professionals who work in this field to gather all pertinent information and forward it to the prosecutor in a timely manner so that it can be presented to the judge during the bail hearing.

Preliminary Hearing or Grand Jury Hearing

In felony cases, the next step is the preliminary hearing or grand jury hearing. The preliminary hearing is similar to the first appearance in that it occurs before a judge of a lower or municipal court. The purpose of the preliminary hearing is for the judge to make an impartial determination of whether there is probable cause to believe a crime has been committed, and that the defendant committed it. The defendant is present during this hearing and is represented by counsel who has the right to cross-examine any witnesses that are called to testify by the prosecutor. At the end of the presentation of evidence the judge must determine if there is sufficient evidence to "bind over" or forward the case to the superior court for further proceedings and/or trial.

The grand jury hearing is conducted in secret. The grand jurors are citizens selected to serve for one year. They decide by majority vote whether to issue an indictment. The prosecuting attorney presents the evidence and neither the defendant nor the defendant's attorney is present. If the grand jury finds there is sufficient evidence, it files a "true bill" with the superior court. This is an indictment charging the defendant with the crime or crimes.

The Constitution does not require that states use a grand jury.[22] In about one-half of the states a grand jury indictment is used for at least some of the felony cases. Grand juries are used in federal courts and in those states that mandate the use of grand juries. In many states if the prosecutor has a sensitive case such as one dealing with a young child who has been molested, that prosecutor may decide to use a grand jury even if not mandated to do so by state statute. If a grand jury indictment is not used, the preliminary hearing is held and any information is filed by the prosecutor with the trial court. Similar to an indictment, the information sets forth all charges against the defendant.

Arraignment

Once the indictment or information is filed, the defendant is brought before the court and "arraigned." In this hearing the charges are formally read and the defendant is asked to enter a plea. This is not a trial, and other than reading the charges, the court does not examine any of the evidence against the defendant at this time.

It is during this hearing that the defendant may enter one of three basic pleas: guilty, not guilty, or nolo contendere. In a guilty plea the defendant admits to committing the offenses charged. If the defendant is entering a guilty plea the court will normally inquire if he understands the nature and consequences of the plea and if the plea is being entered voluntarily. Many courts will read all the consequences of a plea into the record to prevent appeals by the defendant at a later time.

A not-guilty plea requires that the matter be set for trial, and mandates that the prosecutor prove every element of the crimes charged and prove that the defendant committed the crime. Once the defendant enters a not-guilty plea the judge will then inform him of his right to a court or jury trial and set the case for further proceedings. Another form of not-guilty plea that may be entered at the arraignment is not guilty by reason of insanity. This type of plea is used when the defense attorney has reason to believe that her client may not be responsible for his actions as a result of a mental disorder or disease.

Nolo contendere pleas literally mean "no contest." The defendant is not contesting the charges. In essence, it is a guilty plea and carries the same criminal sanctions as a guilty plea but, significantly for victims, it cannot be used in any subsequent civil action to establish liability against the defendant.

Jury Selection

The right to a jury trial is one of our most fundamental constitutional guarantees. The use of twelve jurors in criminal cases is common, but not constitutionally mandated. It is more an historical tradition than a legal requirement. In *Williams v. Florida,* the U.S. Supreme Court held that the individual states may decide how many jurors should hear a noncapital criminal case, and as long as the number is large enough to ensure a cross section of the community, it will be considered constitutionally sound.[23]

Prospective jurors are selected based on the various states' legislative schemes. Many states use a combination of property tax roles, Department of Motor Vehicles listings, and voter registration records. When these jurors report for duty, a panel is sent to the courtroom for further selection. Twelve jurors are initially called to take their seats in the jury box and the voir dire examination of prospective jurors begins. *Voir dire* means to "seek the truth." While this process may vary by jurisdiction, it normally involves the judge questioning jurors about details in their past, or about present beliefs that might uncover possible bias or prejudice. Once the judge has finished with the questioning, the defense attorney and the prosecutor each have an opportunity to question jurors. Either side may challenge a juror for cause, meaning that the juror has disclosed something that will not allow him to be fair during the trial. Once all the challenges for cause are finished, each side may use what is called peremptory challenges to remove other prospective jurors from the panel. A *peremptory challenge* does not require an explanation and is used by either side to excuse a prospective juror without stating the reason for the dismissal. There are a limited number of peremptory challenges available and once they are exhausted, or the prosecutor or defense attorney is satisfied with the panel, the remaining jurors will sit as the jury.

Opening Statement

The opening statement is the first opportunity for the attorneys to tell the jury about the detailed facts in the case. Many trial lawyers believe that the opening statement is like the table of contents of a book. It points out the important facts and acts as a guide for the jury. Opening statements may be brief summaries or detailed accounts of the crime. The nature and scope of the opening statement depend on the preferences of the attorney who is presenting. Opening statements are not evidence, rather they are the attorney's beliefs of what evidence will be introduced during the trial. The prosecutor is allowed to make the first opening statement. The defense may make a statement at that time, or wait until the prosecution has rested and make the opening statement prior to putting on any defense evidence.

Case-in-Chief

Once the opening statements have been made, the prosecution presents its evidence dealing with the guilt of the defendant. It is during this phase that the victim of the crime will be called to testify. The prosecution must prove each element of every crime and that the defendant committed those crimes.

After a witness has testified, the defense has the right to cross-examine. After the defense has finished with its cross-examination, the prosecution has a right to question the witness again on matters raised on cross-examination. This is called *redirect examination.* After the prosecution finishes with redirect, the defense may engage in recross examination. As anyone who watched the O.J. Simpson trial observed, this process can take hours or even days. Once all witnesses for the prosecution have testified and all physical evidence has been admitted by the judge, the prosecution rests it case.

The Defendant's Evidence

It is at this time that the defense must decide what, if any, evidence it will present. The defense does not have to call any witnesses. It can rely on the presumption of innocence and argue to the jury that the prosecution has failed to meet its burden. There have been a number of cases in which the defense has elected to not call any witnesses, and the trial then moves to the next step. In the event the defense elects to put on any evidence, it will follow the same process previously described.

Once the defense has finished presenting its evidence, the prosecution has the opportunity to present rebuttal evidence. The defense is then entitled to surrebuttal and it alternates back and forth until both sides are finished. When both sides have finished presenting their evidence the trial moves on to what many attorneys consider to be the most dramatic stage.

Closing Argument

Closing argument is the final opportunity for the attorneys to address the jury. The prosecution presents its closing argument followed by the defense argument. The prosecution has the right to a final summation after the defense argument because it bears the burden of proof in criminal cases.

Closing arguments are not evidence, rather they are the attorney's attempt to persuade the jury to accept the position regarding the guilt or innocence of the defendant. Many attorneys believe that oral argument is more an art than an science. Clarence Darrow was the defense attorney in the famous case dealing with Darwin's theory of evolution, the Scopes Trial. Darrow is considered by many legal scholars and practitioners to be one of the most outstanding trial attorneys in the history of the United States, and his final summations are required readings for many young trial attorneys.

Deliberation and Verdict

Once both sides have rested, the judge reads the instructions to the jury. These instructions are the law that the jury must follow in its deliberations. The jury then retires to a jury room and selects one member to be the foreperson. The jury will then review all the evidence and reach a verdict regarding whether the defendant is guilty of the crimes charged. In the event the jury cannot reach a verdict, it informs the judge. This is called a "hung jury" and the judge may declare a mistrial. If the jury reaches a verdict, it notifies the judge and all parties reassemble in the courtroom. The judge's clerk reads the verdict. If found not guilty, the defendant is free to go. In the event the defendant is found guilty of all or some of the charges, the next step in the criminal process begins.

Sentencing

A review of our history demonstrates that various views and beliefs regarding punishment have evolved over time.[24] At one point in ancient Rome, punishment was viewed as a right of the victim's family. Eventually, we began to accept the concept of the sovereign as the dispenser of justice and punishment.

The four basic purposes for sentencing are: deterrence, rehabilitation, retribution, and incapacitation. *Deterrence* involves the concept that criminal sanctions, such as imprisonment, deter the public and convince them that they should not commit crimes. *Rehabilitation* focuses on reducing the offender's criminal propensities by counseling, therapy, and vocational training while incarcerated. *Retribution* is based on the biblical theme of "an eye for an eye, a tooth for a tooth." K. G. Armstrong has argued that retribution is not based on vengeance, but rather is the lawful act of the state to protect its members from further injury.[25] Another theory regarding retribution involves the concept of "just desserts." This rationale for punishment is based on Von Hirsh's classic work, *Doing Justice,* where he argues that those who commit crimes deserve to be punished.[26] *Incapacitation* removes offenders from society by keeping them incarcerated. The "Three Strikes and You're Out" law is an example of incapacitation of offenders.

Before imposing a sentence the court usually receives a presentence report. This report is generally prepared by the probation department and normally begins with a recitation of the crime. It will then present the prosecution's version of the case followed by the defendant's version. It may present information about the background of the offender, including the parents and siblings, marital history, education, health, financial condition, and previous employment. The report will also include the nature and extent of previous criminal activities and discuss the victim's desires and needs. It will make a recommendation regarding what the probation department considers to be the most appropriate sentence for this particular defendant.

Once the presentencing report is complete, the defendant is returned to court for sentencing. At this time the prosecution will have an opportunity to argue for whatever sentence it feels is appropriate. The defense can also present any evidence it chooses to convince the judge to sentence the offender according to its desires. In many jurisdictions victims have a right to appear and tell the judge of their own wishes and how the crime has impacted on their lives. This victim impact statement will be addressed in more detail later in this text.

Summary

Understanding the criminal justice system is a critical aspect in the study of victimology. Many people are victimized or feel victimized for a second time when they become involved in the judicial process. Long delays, complex procedures, and technical arguments by both prosecutors and defense attorneys can lead to a renewed feeling of helplessness on the part of a victim who only wants to see justice carried out.

The American criminal court system is a combination of historical accident and thoughtful planning by our founding fathers. Criminal courts function at both the federal and state level. The nature of the crime may determine where the offender is prosecuted.

Concern regarding the increasing role of juveniles in the commission of crime has lead to a renewed interest in the juvenile justice system. This system operates out of the general public's view most of the time because of the fundamental principle of confidentially. This concept was instituted to protect the identity of the juvenile offender and thereby avoid stigmatizing the offender as a criminal. It was believed that this would assist in the juvenile's rehabilitation; however, this concept has recently come under a great deal of criticism.

Each party in the criminal justice system has a distinct role to play which makes it adversarial in nature. Understanding the roles and responsibilities of each party is a necessary aspect of the duties of any victim service provider.

In many instances, criminal justice procedures are based on constitutional protections set forth in the Bill of Rights and in other amendments to the

Constitution. The process can be very confusing to the victim who, many times, must navigate it alone. Because conviction of crime may result in restricting the freedom of the accused, the criminal is afforded a number of rights. These rights may cause the victims of crime much frustration and anger.

It is important to remember that the criminal justice system is only a small part of the entire spectrum of victimology; however, this process is critically important to any victim. Professionals in this area must maintain the proper perspective when dealing with all parties involved in the criminal justice system.

Key Terms

Jurisdiction means the ability of the court to enforce laws and punish individuals who violate those laws.

Trial courts are courts where criminal cases start and finish.

Limited jurisdiction courts are those that only hear and decide certain limited legal issues.

General jurisdiction courts are granted authority to hear and decide all issues that are brought before them.

Equity is the concept that justice is administered according to fairness, as contrasted with the strict rules of law.

Writ of certiorari is an order sent to a lower court requiring the records of the case to be sent the Supreme Court for review.

Jails are operated by local agencies such as cities or counties. Jails are used for pretrial detention, holding after sentencing, and for incarceration of those persons who are not being sentenced to prison.

Prisons are administrated by states or the federal government and are for the more serious offenders.

Probation is a conditional release of the offender after having been found guilty. It is traditionally used on misdemeanor or other low-level crimes. It allows the perpetrator to remain free so long as that person meets certain conditions.

Parole is the conditional release of an inmate back into the community from a prison or other form of correctional institution.

Correctional officers are those persons who are hired to maintain security in jails or prisons.

Adjudication includes all the formal and informal decisions and steps within the criminal proceeding process.

Arrest is taking a suspect into custody in a manner prescribed by law.

Citation is an order to appear before a judge at a later time.

Booking involves entering the suspect's name, offense, and other information into the police records.

Nolo contendere pleas literally mean "no contest." The defendant is not contesting the charges. In essence, it is a guilty plea and carries the same criminal sanctions as a guilty plea but, significantly for victims, it cannot be used in any subsequent civil action to establish liability against the defendant.

Voir dire means to "seek the truth." While this process may vary by jurisdiction, it normally involves questioning jurors about details in their past, or about present beliefs that might uncover possible bias or prejudice.

Peremptory challenge does not require explanation and is used by either side to excuse a prospective juror without stating the reason for the dismissal.

Deterrence involves the concept that criminal sanctions, such as imprisonment deter the public and convince them that they should not commit crimes.

Rehabilitation focuses on reducing the offender's criminal propensities by counseling, therapy, and vocational training while the criminal is incarcerated.

Retribution is based on the biblical theme of "an eye for an eye, a tooth for a tooth."

Incapacitation removes offenders from society by keeping them incarcerated.

Discussion Questions

1. Why is it important for victim service providers to understand the criminal justice system? Doesn't anyone who watches television already have a basic understanding of how courts work?

2. Should we continue to have separate state and federal courts? Wouldn't one unified court system make more sense and be more efficient?

3. Should we treat juveniles as adults once they commit a violent crime? What crimes would apply and how old would the minor have to be to be tried as an adult?

4. Should the victim have the same constitutional rights as the defendant?

5. Should victims have the right to veto any proposed plea bargain? Why? Why not?

6. Should all child sex abuse cases go to the grand jury?

7. Which justification for punishment is the most popular in today's climate of violent crime? Is it the most effective use of our resources?

Suggested Readings

American Bar Association, *Law and the Courts: A Handbook about United States Law and Court Procedures*, (American Bar Association, Chicago) 1987.

Territo, Halsted, & T. Bromley, *Crime and Justice in America: A Human Perspective*, (West Publishing Company, St. Paul, Minn.) 1992.

Siegal, L. & T. Senna, *Juvenile Justice*, (West Publishing Company, St. Paul, Minn.) 1994.

Endnotes

1. This section has been adapted from the author's previous work published in the *National Victim Assistance Academy Text* (1995) which was supported by Grant No. 95-MU-GX-K002 awarded by the Office for Victims of Crimes, Office of Justice Programs, U.S. Department of Justice.

2. Robert Pursley, *Introduction to Criminal Justice*, 6th ed. (MacMillan Publishing Company, New York) 1994.

3. *The Supreme Court of the United States.* (Government Printing Office, Washington, D.C.)

4. 1 Cranch 137 (1803).

5. S. Fox, *Modern Juvenile Justice: Cases and Materials*, (West Publishing Company, St. Paul, Minn.) 1972.

6. R. Cadwell, "The Juvenile Court: Its Development and Some Major Problems." *Juvenile Delinquency: A Book of Readings.* (John Wiley & Sons, New York) 1996, p. 358.

7. M. Randell & L. Haskell, "Sexual Violence in Women's Lives," 1/1 *Violence against Women*, 6 (1995).

8. The Fifth Amendment's right to grand jury indictment and the Eight Amendment's right regarding excessive bail have not been applied to the states. See *Hurtado v. California*, 110 U.S. 516 (1884).

9. If the confession was obtained by coercion, it may not be admitted even for impeachment purposes. See *Mincey v. Arizona*, 437 U.S. 385 (1978).

10. H. Wallace, C. Roberson & C. Steckler, *Fundamentals of Police Administration,* (Prentice-Hall, Englewood Cliffs, N.J.) 1994.

11. *Private Security: Report of the Task Force on Private Security,* (U.S. Government Printing Office, Washington, D.C.) 1976, p. 4.

12. See H. Wallace & C. Roberson, *Principles of Criminal Law,* (Longman, White Plains, N.Y.) 1996.

13. See P. W. Lewis & K. D. Peoples, *The Supreme Court and the Criminal Process,* (W.B. Saunders, Philadelphia) 1978, p. 974–975.

14. 372 U.S. 335 (1963).

15. 407 U.S. 25 (1972). See also *Scott v. Illinois,* 440 U.S. 367 (1979) where the U.S. Supreme Court held that the right to counsel only applies when imprisonment is actually imposed rather than merely authorized by statute.

16. Bureau of Justice Statistics Bulletin, *Criminal Defense Systems* (U.S. Department of Justice, Washington, D.C.) August 1984, p. 6.

17. *Strickland v. Washington,* 466 U.S. 668 (1984).

18. 475 U.S. 157 (1986).

19. 500 U.S. 44 (1991).

20. *Stack v. Boyle,* 342 U.S. 1 (1951).

21. 18 U.S.C. Section 3141 et seq. (1984).

22. *Hurtado v. California,* 110 U.S. 516 (1884).

23. 399 U.S. 78 (1970). However, in *Ballew v. Georgia,* 435 U.S. 223 (1978) the court held a five-person jury was a violation of the Fifth Amendment. More recently, a statute authorizing a vote of five of six jurors was struck down in *Burch v. Louisiana* 441 U.S. 130 (1970).

24. For more information on the various aspects of sentencing, see H. Wallace & C. Roberson, *Principles of Criminal Law.*

25. K. G. Armstrong, "The Retributionist Hits Back," 70 *Mind,* 471 (1969).

26. Andrew von Hirsh, *Doing Justice,* (Hill and Wang, New York) 1976.

4

THE CIVIL JUSTICE SYSTEM AND VICTIMS

Chapter Outline

Civil Procedures
    Introduction
    Jurisdiction
    Filing a Complaint
    Filing a Response
    Pretrial Activities
    Trial
    Verdict
    Judgment

Juvenile Court Dependency Procedures
    Detention Hearing
    Adjudicatory or Jurisdictional Hearing
    The Dispositional Hearing

Restorative Justice
    Introduction
    Functioning of a Restorative Justice Program
    Victim–Offender Mediation

Summary

Key Terms

Discussion Questions

Suggested Readings

Learning Objectives

After reading this chapter, you should be able to:

- Explain the basic differences between a criminal and a civil trial
- Understand the concepts of negligence and intentional torts
- Describe the various stages of a civil trial
- Discuss the phases of a juvenile dependency hearing

Civil Procedures

Introduction

The preceding chapter discussed various aspects of the criminal justice system and its effect on victims. This chapter will briefly explore the second aspect of the legal system to impact victims: the civil law system. A criminal action punishes a person for committing a public wrong, whereas a civil action punishes a person for committing a private wrong or injury.[1] Civil law includes all actions that are not deemed criminal in nature.[2] Understanding the civil law system is important to those studying victimology because many victims of crime turn to civil law in an effort to obtain redress for injuries not compensated by the criminal law system.[3]

Victims file civil actions against their perpetrators for various reasons. One reason may be that they do not believe they received appropriate satisfaction as a result of any criminal proceedings. The defendant may have been acquitted or convicted of a lesser charge than the victim believes is proper. Victims may also feel mistreated by the criminal justice system and have a desire to be in control of the proceedings instead of being treated as merely a witness in a case. They may also want to receive more compensation for injuries than is available in the criminal justice system.

Civil law includes a wide variety of subjects including the following:

- *Torts:* Injury that does not involve a contract.
- *Contracts:* Violation of an agreement.
- *Property:* Disputes relating to real or personal property.
- *Estates:* Issues relating to inheritance and probate.
- *Family*: Issues regarding marriage, children, and divorce.
- *Civil rights:* Injury to another in violation of certain statutory rights.

Some of these common legal concepts that affect victims will be examined in more detail in other chapters. When a victim suffers a civil injury, it is necessary to begin the civil process. This process starts with an examination of whether the courts have jurisdiction over the parties and the cause of action. The next section will examine the concept of jurisdiction.

Jurisdiction

Jurisdiction is the ability of a court to hear and decide issues of law and fact. If a court does not have jurisdiction, it is without power to act. Courts must have both jurisdiction over the parties and the subject matter of the complaint.[4]

Jurisdiction over the parties or personal jurisdiction requires that the court be able to bring the party before it. Personal jurisdiction is of two types: in personam and in rem. **In personam** personal jurisdiction refers to the court's powers to bind the parties to the court's judgment. **In rem** personal jurisdiction is one that involves property that is located in the state where the court is located, and in which the parties have their dispute. Jurisdiction of the person is normally obtained by serving upon the individual a copy of the complaint. This process will be discussed later in this section.

Jurisdiction of the subject matter requires that the court have authority to hear and decide the issue of law involved in the dispute. For example, some courts require that a minimum level of damages be requested before the matter can be heard in their court.[5] Other courts hear only certain types of matters and cannot rule on any issues. For example, probate courts cannot hear family law issues and vice versa.

Due process is a constitutional mandate that requires fairness in judicial proceedings. Occasionally one raises a question as to whether a person or organization that does not live or is headquartered in a state can be forced to appear in that state and defend a lawsuit which has been filed there. The doctrine of due process may prevent the out-of-state defendant from having to appear and defend lawsuits unless the defendant has some sort of minimum contacts in the state. This doctrine is based on the concept that it would be unfair to require a person or business to travel to a state and defend a lawsuit where that defendant has had no other contact with that state. In the leading case of *International Shoe Co. v. State of Washington,* the U.S. Supreme Court held that certain activities engaged in by a corporation in a state will allow it to be sued in that state.[6] These activities must involve some minimum contacts in the forum state of such character that being forced to defend a suit in that state would not offend traditional notions of fair play and substantial justice.

The concept of venue is closely associated with jurisdiction, but is a separate and distinct aspect of civil litigation. Lawsuits must be filed in the proper location. Venue statutes determine the geographic districts in which the case can be heard. Once the question of jurisdiction and venue is determined, the plaintiff can evaluate the possibility of filing a complaint for damages.

Filing a Complaint

Filing a complaint is the first concrete step in the civil process. Unlike the criminal law process in which the prosecutor determines the nature and type of charges to file, the victim and the victims' attorney have complete control over the causes of action that are filed against the perpetrator. Additionally, as mentioned previously, the victim as the plaintiff has control over the location where the complaint is filed.

The *complaint* is a written document, called a "pleading," that contains three essential components: (1) it establishes the subject matter jurisdiction, (2) it sets forth facts constituting various causes of action, and (3) it asks for certain types of relief. (see Figure 4.1). Causes of action are legal theories that if proved, entitle the plaintiff to recover for any injuries suffered. Many victims will allege alternative, and sometimes conflicting, causes of actions in the complaint and after discovery dismiss those that cannot be proved.

UNITED STATES DISTRICT COURT FOR THE CENTRAL DISTRICT OF CALIFORNIA

Judy Jones
v.   No. _____
Dan Defendant   Civil Action

COMPLAINT

Plaintiff Judy Jones complains against Dan Defendant as follows:

1. Jurisdiction in this case is based on diversity of citizenship and the amount in controversy. Plaintiff is a citizen of the State of California and defendant is a citizen of the State of Oregon. The amount in controversy exceeds, exclusive of interests and costs, the sum of fifty thousand ($50,000) dollars.

2. On September 30, 1996, at approximately 10:00 P.M., plaintiff Judy Jones (Jones) was standing near the intersection of First Street and Thomas Road in Fresno, California. Defendant Dan Defendant (Defendant) was driving a vehicle eastbound on Thomas Road at that intersection.

3. Defendant intentionally fired a handgun at Jones which resulted in a bullet entering Jones's left arm.

4. As a direct and proximate result of Defendant's actions, Jones suffered injuries to her arm and shoulder and other body parts, received other physical injuries, suffered physical and mental pain and suffering, incurred medical expenses and lost income in the future.

WHEREFORE, plaintiff Judy Jones demands judgment against defendant Dan Defendant for the sum of $1,000,000 with interest and costs.

Dated:

_____
John Smith
Attorney for Plaintiff

FIGURE 4.1   Sample Complaint

A variety of relief is available in civil proceedings. The first and most common form of relief is monetary damage. Monetary damages may be either compensatory or punitive in nature. ***Compensatory damages*** are awarded to plaintiffs to make them whole financially for any injuries they suffered as a result of the defendant's actions. ***Punitive damages*** are awarded to punish the defendant and to send a message to other similarly situated persons that if they commit the same or similar type of action they could face a similar fate.

Other forms of relief available in civil courts are *injunctions,* or orders that prohibit a person from doing certain acts. This form of relief is possible because of the courts equity power. This power authorizes the court to issue orders preventing injustice or wrongs from occurring. This power resides with the court, and juries do not decide issues of equity.

These orders are issued by judges after they receive evidence regarding the facts surrounding the necessity for the issuance of an injunction. A specific form of injunction, the temporary restraining order (TRO) or protective order is used in domestic violence or stalking cases and will be discussed in more detail in Chapter 16, which will examine constitutional and civil rights of victims.

The complaint is filed in a court which has jurisdiction over the parties and the subject matter. For example, a case dealing with the commission of intentional torts on federal land would be filed in federal court, because only that court has jurisdiction. The same acts if committed elsewhere would be filed in state court.

The complaint lists the parties and is known by the name of the plaintiff and the defendant. For example, if Laura Leonard was suing John Jones for striking her, the lawsuit would be entitled *Leonard v. Jones.* After identifying the parties and stating that the court has jurisdiction, the complaint sets forth the various causes of actions and asks for relief. This relief is contained in what is known as the "prayer." The prayer sometimes asks for a specific amount of money or may include language stating "damages according to proof." This allows the plaintiff extra time to fully assess the nature and extent of any damages.

The complaint is usually filed by the plaintiff's attorney. All courts require parties filing a lawsuit to pay a filing fee. Depending on the jurisdiction, this can range from a nominal fee in small claims courts to several hundreds of dollars in superior courts. Once the complaint is filed, the defendant must be served with a copy. Normally, the plaintiff pays the county to serve the complaint using deputy sheriffs. Sometimes, private process servers are used to serve defendants that are hard to contact or who are evading service of the complaint. There are several other methods of serving the defendant including using registered mail, posting a copy of the complaint on the defendant's property, or publishing the complaint in a newspaper. It is not necessary that the defendant have actual notice of the complaint so long as the method of service is likely to provide notice.[7] Once the defendant is served with a copy of the complaint or has received notice of the lawsuit, a response is required within thirty days or a default judgment may be entered for the plaintiff. A default judgment is an order granting the plaintiff the relief asked for in the complaint. Because of the drastic nature of default judgments, most defendants respond to complaints.

Filing a Response

Once the defendant is served with a copy of the complaint there are a number of alternative responses available. The defendant may file any of the following responses: an answer with or without affirmative defenses, a demurrer, a motion to strike, or a cross-complaint or counterclaim. Each response has a definite purpose and is commonly used in many civil cases.

Answer

The defendant may file a response that is known as an *answer,* which is a response to the complaint and may admit or deny the allegations. Answers are pleadings and may contain detailed responses or be a general denial of everything contained in the complaint. An answer, like the complaint, is filed with the court and served on the plaintiff.

Affirmative Defenses

The defendant may assert *affirmative defenses,* which are certain defenses that, if proved, negate any legal responsibility for the injuries suffered by the plaintiff. Affirmative defenses include such common theories as accord and satisfaction, assumption of the risk, contributory negligence, duress, estoppel, fraud, illegality, laches, license, statute of frauds, statute of limitations, and any other matter constituting an avoidance. The affirmative defenses are usually listed at the end of the answer before the prayer.

Demurrer

A *demurrer* is a response that in essence admits all the allegations of the complaint as true but goes on to state that even if they are true the plaintiff has not pled any theories that would allow for recovery of damages.[8] The demurrer is filed instead of the answer because if the court grants the demurrer the case is over. Most courts allow the plaintiff to amend the complaint to overcome the defects raised in the demurrer.

Motion to Strike

A motion to strike is a response that requests the court to strike out certain language in the complaint. Motions to strike are often used in conjunction with demurrers in an attempt to get the case dismissed.

Cross-Complaint or Counterclaim

If the defendant answers the complaint, but claims that another party caused the plaintiff's injuries, the defendant may file a lawsuit against that party at the time the answer is filed. This lawsuit, which is made a part of the original action, is known as a cross-complaint or counterclaim. The defendant may also file a cross-complaint or counterclaim against the plaintiff alleging that the plaintiff injured the defendant.

Once the initial pleadings have been filed, the lawsuit moves into the pretrial stage. In some jurisdictions this occurs very quickly because of a court procedure known as fast-tracking of civil cases. In other jurisdictions, the case can take several years before anything further occurs.

Pretrial Activities

Pretrial activities include a wide range of legal maneuvers designed to clarify the issues and/or reach settlement regarding liability. Much of the criticism aimed at the legal profession has centered around some of the activities that occur during this stage of a civil lawsuit.[9] Pretrial activities include filing motions, discovery, and settlement conferences.

Motions

There are a number of motions that may be filed during the pretrial stage of a civil case. The most important motion is called a "summary judgment." This motion can be used to dismiss the entire case or strike portions of the complaint. A summary judgment motion is a pleading that alleges there is no triable issue of fact established by the pleadings or discovery and therefore the undisputed portions of the case should be dismissed. If these portions are essential to the plaintiff's case, this motion may result in dismissal of the entire complaint.

For instance, if the plaintiff is alleging that he was battered by the defendant and during discovery it is established that the plaintiff and the defendant both agree that the incident occurred during a sporting event, the defendant could file a summary judgment motion which would be granted by the court. The court would hold that when one is injured during a sporting event or game, no cause of action for battery is available because the law presumes the injured party consented to the actions of the other person while they were on the playing field. Conversely, if the plaintiff alleges that the defendant struck him after the game was over and the defendant contends the injury occurred during the game, there is a triable issue of fact for the jury to decide (when and how the injury occurred) and the summary judgment motion will not be granted.

Discovery

The discovery process in civil lawsuits can be both time consuming and expensive. "Discovery" is the legal term that includes a number of devises which allow each party to learn the facts and theories that the other side is claiming will allow them to prevail. Both the plaintiff and defendant engage in discovery during the pretrial period. In fact, a television drama showing a civil attorney being surprised during trial is a myth and has little basis in modern courtroom procedures. It is more the exception than the rule that surprises occur in civil cases. By the time a case goes to trial, attorneys representing each side know exactly what each witness will testify and what the theories of recovery or defense are.

There are a number of discovery techniques used in civil cases. The more complex cases use all, or most, of these discovery tools. They include depositions, interrogatories, and requests for production of documents. Each of these discovery techniques has specific goals and purposes.

Depositions. *Depositions* are formal, out-of-court procedures in which one party questions others regarding the facts surrounding the case. The questioning occurs under oath and is recorded by a court reporter. Either the plaintiff or the defendant may conduct a deposition and both parties are usually deposed by the other. Witnesses, experts, and other persons that may have information regarding the lawsuit may be deposed. The rules of evidence are relaxed during depositions and the parties are allowed to ask questions that may lead to other information. Once a party has given its deposition, if they change the statement during trial, the deposition may be introduced to impeach the party's credibility.[10]

Interrogatories. *Interrogatories* are written inquiries to the other side asking specific questions. Interrogatories may ask for a party to state the theory behind a cause of action and all the facts supporting that theory. Interrogatories may also ask parties to admit or deny certain specific issues.

Production of Documents. In many cases, one party will ask the other to produce all the records surrounding the occurrence that is the basis for the lawsuit. Some defendants are reluctant to produce these records absent a court order. A motion to produce can be enforced by the court and if the party fails to bring or send all the records to the other party, a court may order sanctions.

Conferences

Once the discovery phase of the civil action is complete, many jurisdictions require the parties to meet and discuss the possibility of settling the case or narrowing the issues.[11] This conference may result in the parties entering into agreements or stipulations about issues that are not in conflict such as the date of events, who took which pictures, and other items that move the trial along without undue time being spent on mundane matters.

Oftentimes the parties will enter into serious settlement discussions at these pretrial conferences.[12] After the discovery phase ends, the attorneys representing each side and the settlement judge have a fairly accurate idea of how the trial is going to go and what the probable outcome will be. The judge as a disinterested third party may facilitate these discussions by separating the parties and talking to each one individually. The judge may make recommendations regarding the value of the case and discuss the credibility of certain witnesses. Some judges will move back and forth between the two parties, communicating offers and counter-offers until the parties agree to settle. Many attorneys believe a good settlement judge can dispose of most, if not all, civil lawsuits. In the event the case cannot be settled, the next phase is the trial.

Trial

The trial of a civil case is conducted in much the same manner as a criminal case. The jury selection, including the voir dire, is very similar to a criminal case.

Opening statements are conducted with the plaintiff's attorney going first, followed by the defendant's attorney. The plaintiff's attorney presents that side's evidence and then the defendant presents evidence if desired. Closing arguments and rebuttal follow the same pattern as a criminal case, the jury receives its instructions, and then retires to deliberate.

However, there are some significant differences between a criminal trial and a civil trial. These differences include constitutional issues, the burden of proof, and the number of jurors who must agree on a verdict. The Fifth Amendment prohibition against self-incrimination does not apply and therefore the plaintiff may call the defendant to the stand to testify during the plaintiff's case-in-chief. As indicated earlier in this text, civil cases only require a preponderance of the evidence whereas criminal cases require proof beyond a reasonable doubt. Finally, in civil cases, only nine of twelve jurors must agree for a verdict to be reached. In criminal cases, the great majority of states require a unanimous verdict.

Verdict

Unlike a criminal case in which the jury renders a verdict of guilty or not guilty, civil cases may require juries to evaluate complex facts and legal theories. Some cases require juries to apportion fault among the parties. For example, juries may be asked to determine if the plaintiff contributed to his or her own injuries. In these cases the jury may return a verdict finding the defendant 80 percent at fault and the plaintiff 20 percent at fault. If the jury had determined that the plaintiff had suffered injuries in the amount of $100,000, the award based on this division of fault would then be reduced by 20 percent leaving the plaintiff with a final award of damages in the amount of $80,000.

In complex civil cases, judges may use what is known as a special verdict form. Instead of simply ruling for either the plaintiff or the defendant, the jury is given a series of questions regarding factual issues. Based on its response, the judge determines the outcome of the case.

Judgment

There is no sentence in a civil case. If the jury finds for the defendant, the case is over. However, if the jury returns a verdict for the plaintiff, the court must enter a judgment. Once a judgment is recorded, the plaintiff can request the sheriff or marshall to execute the judgment and seize and sell most of the defendant's real and personal property to pay the amount listed in the judgment. However, many persons are judgment-proof in that they have very little if any assets which can be used to pay the judgment. Others, such as O. J. Simpson, have assets such as pensions that cannot be attached. When this situation occurs, plaintiffs must look at other options for recovery. These alternatives will be discussed in more detail in the sections dealing with victims' rights.

Juvenile Court Dependency Procedures[13]

The previous chapter discussed juvenile courts and those minors classified as either delinquents or status offenders. This section will discuss dependant children, as these proceedings are normally considered civil rather than criminal in nature. Dependant children are defined as those children who are in need of state intervention because of abuse or neglect by their caretakers.

Although the procedure is basically the same for delinquents and dependent minors, the juvenile court process dealing with children who are victims of abuse or neglect is of particular importance to professionals who work in the criminal justice field. This process is normally initiated by filing a petition with the court. A petition is a formal pleading that alleges that the parents or custodians endangered the health or welfare of the child. The petition may allege neglect or physical, emotional, or sexual abuse of the child and it gives the juvenile court the authority to act.

Detention Hearing

Once the petition is filed, many jurisdictions hold a show cause or detention hearing. This hearing is usually conducted within twenty-four to forty-eight hours after filing the petition or the emergency removal of the child. The *detention hearing* requires child protective services or police to produce evidence justifying the emergency removal of the child, or to present evidence that would allow the court to order the removal of the child if the child is still in the custody of the parents. The parents may also admit or deny the allegations contained in the petition at this hearing.

If they admit the allegations, the court orders child protective services to conduct an investigation to determine where the child should be placed as a result of the admissions by the parents. If the parents deny the allegations, the court sets a date for an adjudicatory or jurisdictional hearing. Pending this hearing, the court may order the child temporarily placed in a living arrangement outside the home.

Adjudicatory or Jurisdictional Hearing

An *adjudicatory* or *jurisdictional hearing* is used to determine if there is sufficient evidence to determine that the allegations in the petition are true. At the conclusion of this hearing, the court will render its decision. If the petition is upheld, the court sets a date for a dispositional hearing. If the petition is not upheld, the child is returned to the parents and the case is dismissed.

During the adjudicatory hearing, the state presents evidence to support its claim that the child has been abused. This may take the form of having the child testify to the incident, or experts employed by the state may render their opinion regarding the facts surrounding the case. The state is represented by a juvenile prosecutor, state's advocate, county counsel, or other governmental attorney. The parents have a right to cross-examine witnesses and present any evidence they desire in rebuttal to the state's evidence. At the end of the hearing, both parties may present arguments in favor of their position. The burden of proof to uphold the petition is the same as a civil case. In civil trials, the plaintiff has the burden of proving the case by a preponderance of the evidence. This is normally defined as slightly more than 50 percent. A criminal case requires proof beyond a reasonable doubt. This is not proof beyond all doubt, because all things are subject to some doubt, but it is proof beyond a reasonable doubt to a moral certainty that all the material facts did occur.

In juvenile dependency cases, to remove the child from the custody of the parents, some jurisdictions require proof by clear and convincing evidence. This is more than a preponderance of the evidence, but less than beyond a reasonable doubt.[14]

The Dispositional Hearing

Once the adjudicatory or jurisdictional hearing is concluded, the next hearing to occur is the *dispositional hearing.* This hearing is to determine where the child should be placed. The court will decide whether the child should be immediately returned to the parents or placed in an out-of-home environment for a specific time. The guiding principle in this hearing is "the best interests of the child." If the court orders the child placed outside the home, it may schedule periodic reviews to determine if or when the child will be reunited with the parents. Typically, a specific plan regarding placement is established and monitored.

From the beginning of the intervention process until the final dispositional hearing and beyond, every party in the action has certain rights. The parents and the child each have distinct rights which must be observed and protected. These rights include:

- Notice
- An opportunity to be heard and to present evidence
- The right to confront and cross-examine witnesses
- Effective representation by an attorney

In a dependency hearing, the rights of a child include appointing an attorney who will speak on behalf of the child. This attorney must represent what is believed to be in the best interests of the child regardless of what CPS or the parents' advocate believes is appropriate. In some jurisdictions this is a government-funded attorney; in others, it is a private attorney appointed by the court to represent the child. Depending on the case, the attorney may side with the parents and argue for return of the child to their care, or the attorney may take the position that it is in the best interests of the child to be removed from the custody of the parents. Even if the child is removed temporarily from the custody of the parents, the child has a right to reunification efforts after a reasonable time.

Many jurisdictions additionally engage court-appointed special advocates (CASAS), or similarly trained (typically non-attorney) individuals. The role of these child advocates is to present to the court an independent analysis of what is best for the child. This is particularly important; as the child's legal representative, the court-appointed lawyer must forward the child's wishes when an objective view would be to the contrary. For example, the lawyer may decide to vigorously advocate a juvenile's wish to return home, when an independent child advocate may determine that this is not actually in the child's best interest.

During dependency hearings, parents have a right to notice of the hearing, an opportunity to be present at that hearing, and to be represented by an attorney. They may present any evidence they desire to rebut the charges. If the child is removed from their custody they have the right in most jurisdictions to a reunification plan that will allow them to regain custody of the child once they have finished treatment or counseling.

Juvenile courts that hear dependency cases oftentimes face a conflict: protection of the child versus the trauma of removing a child from the parents. Courts will normally err on the side of removing the child if there is any substantial evidence to support the allegations that the child is in danger. The juvenile court dependency process is a civil action that must always stay focused on the best interests of the child.

Restorative Justice

Introduction

More and more researchers are suggesting an alternative to the traditional criminal sanctions imposed on perpetrators by the state. These scholars are examining the concept of restorative justice as a new vision for dealing with both offenders and victims.[15] The topic of restorative justice is included in a discussion of the civil justice system because it is more similar to that philosophy than the current philosophy of criminal sanctions.

Some believe the United States is the most punitive nation in the Western world and that this country outstrips all other nations in prison-building programs. A common refrain in almost all elections is that one's opponent is too soft on crime. Therefore, American politicians must be tough on crime to get elected. This has resulted in harsher criminal sanctions in an effort to stop or deter future criminal activity.

The general public is frightened of crime and its consequences. The media feed this fear by showing drive-by shootings and all the grisly details on television daily. Americans are demanding a stop to this violence. At the same time, the public is asking that victims of crime be included in the process. Society is not only interested in including victims in the process, the public wants to make them whole emotionally and financially. This section deals with some methods of making victims whole financially by using the civil justice system. Restorative justice is also a method of healing victims.

Restorative justice promotes maximum involvement of the victim, the offender, and the community in the justice process and presents a clear alternative to sanctions based on retribution and punishment.[16] Restorative justice is based on three principles: (1) all parties (offender, victim, and the community) should be included in the response to crime; (2) government and local communities' actions should complement each other; and (3) accountability is based on the offender's understanding of the harm that has been inflicted.

The restorative justice philosophy gives meaning to sanctions such as restitution and community service. Without an understanding of the restorative justice philosophy these sanctions appear to be simply bureaucratic and punitive in nature. Restorative justice also links different programs such as restitution, community services, and victim–offender mediation together with the goal of accomplishing its mission.

Functioning of a Restorative Justice Program

There are three roles in any restorative justice program: accountability, competency, and community protection. No single role or principle is more important than another. Each role is intertwined with the others in an effort to present a balanced approach to justice.[17]

The accountability role or principle holds that when a crime occurs, a debt incurs and justice requires that every effort be made by the offender to restore any losses suffered by the victim. Accountability requires that offenders become aware of the harmful consequences of their action and make every effort to make amends to the victim and the community. The competency development role or principle requires that offenders leave the criminal justice system more capable of participation in society than when they entered the system. Competency involves work experience, active learning, and opportunities for offenders to develop productive skills. The community protection role or principle holds that the public has a right to a safe environment and the criminal justice system should use a progressive response system to ensure offender control in the community. Community-based control and surveillance can channel the offender's energy into productive activities during nonschool or nonworking hours.

Restorative justice programs focus on repairing the harm inflicted on the victim and the community using a process of negotiation, mediation, victim empowerment, and reparation. Restorative justice believes that victims are central to the process of resolving a crime and offers direct involvement of the participants in the process. One common strategy used in restorative justice programs is victim–offender mediation.

Victim–Offender Mediation

Victim–offender mediation has its roots in the Victim–Offender Reconciliation Program (VORP) started in Canada in the mid-1970s.[18] The purposes of the original VORP project were to provide an alternative method of dealing with crime, to allow the victim and offender to mutually agree on restitution, to use third parties to facilitate reconciliation, and to resolve the conflict caused by crime.[19]

These programs involve both the offender and the victim agreeing to certain actions. Some of these programs focus on making the victim whole with both parties agreeing to a contract involving restitution. Most programs strive to hold offenders accountable for their actions. Many mediation programs are sprouting up across the country and appear to be functioning quite well. They are usually supported by private or nonprofit organizations. The satisfaction with victim–offender mediation appears to be high and it should be evaluated as an alternative to the traditional sanctions imposed by courts.

Summary

The civil system is an important aspect of the study of victimology. Oftentimes victims do not feel that they received justice in the criminal justice system. Victims become plaintiffs and engage in civil lawsuits for a variety of reasons. These victims turn to the civil system in an effort to obtain redress for injuries suffered that could not be addressed in the criminal justice process. They may also believe that the defendant did not receive just punishment in the criminal justice system. Civil lawsuits allow victims to control the proceedings—something they are denied in criminal actions. They hire their own attorney and have the right to participate in all phases of the lawsuit. They sit at the counsel table during the trial and they can direct the proceedings by ordering or asking their attorney to carry out certain acts in certain ways.

The juvenile justice system provides civil remedies for children that are abused or neglected. The system is based on the premise of doing whatever is in the best interest of the child. The dependency process is very powerful, and children can be removed from the care and custody of their parents if the court finds they are in danger.

The civil law process is complex, time consuming, and expensive. It can also be frustrating to victims of crime. Professionals must exercise care before advising any victim to pursue civil remedies. The consequences and benefits of filing a civil lawsuit should be fully explained and victims must make this decision with their head, not their emotions.

Key Terms

Jurisdiction is the ability of a court to hear and decide issues of law and fact.

In personam jurisdiction refers to the court's powers to bind the parties to the court's judgment.

In rem jurisdiction is one that involves property that is located in the state where the court is located, and in which the parties have their dispute.

Due process is a constitutional mandate that requires fairness in judicial proceedings.

Complaint is a written document, called a "pleading," that contains three essential components: (1) it establishes the subject matter jurisdiction, (2) it sets forth facts constituting various causes of action, and (3) it asks for certain types of relief.

Compensatory damages are awarded to the plaintiff to make them whole financially for any injuries they suffered as a result of the defendant's actions.

Punitive damages are awarded to punish the defendant and to send a message to other similarly situated persons that if they commit the same or similar type of action they could face a similar fate.

Answer is a response to the complaint and may admit or deny the allegations.

Affirmative defenses are certain defenses that, if proved, negate any legal responsibility for the injuries suffered by the plaintiff.

Demurrer is a response that in essence admits all the allegations of the complaint as true but goes on to state that even if they are true the plaintiff has not pled any theories that would allow for recovery of damages.

Depositions are formal, out-of-court procedures in which one party questions others regarding the facts surrounding the case.

Interrogatories are written inquiries to the other side asking specific questions.

Detention hearing requires child protective services or police to produce evidence justifying the emergency removal of the child, or to present evidence that would allow the court to order the removal of the child if the child is still in the custody of the parents.

Adjudicatory or *jurisdictional hearing* is used to determine if there is sufficient evidence to determine that the allegations in the petition are true.

Dispositional hearing is to determine where the child should be placed.

Discussion Questions

1. List all the reasons victims may desire to sue perpetrators. Which reason is the most important?

2. Why should victim service providers understand the civil justice system?

3. Compare and contrast the criminal justice procedures and the civil justice procedures? List those areas that empower victims.

4. Why are juvenile court dependency procedures important for victims to understand?

5. If there was one thing you could change about the civil justice system that would help victims what would it be?

Suggested Readings

H. J. Berman & W.R. Greiner, *The Nature and Functions of Law*, 4th ed. (Foundation Press, Mineola, N.Y.) 1980.

R. Grutman & B. Thomas, *Lawyers and Thieves*, (Simon and Schuster, New York) 1990.

G. C. Hazard, Jr. & M. Taruffo, *American Civil Procedure: An Introduction*, (Yale University Press, New Haven, Conn.) 1993.

M. S. Umbreit, *Victim Meets Offender: The Impact of Restorative Justice and Mediation* (Willow Tree Press, Inc., Monsey, N.Y.) 1994.

Endnotes

1. See *Leatherman v. Tarrant County Narcotics Intelligence & Coordination Unit,* 113 S. Ct. 1160 (1993).

2. Linda S. Mullenix, "The Influence of History on Procedure: Volumes of Logic, Scant Pages of History," 50 *Ohio Law Journal,* 803 (1989).

3. F. Carrington & G. Nicholson,"Victims' Rights: An Idea Whose Time Has Come— Five Years Later: The Maturing of an Idea," 17 *Pepperdine L. Rev.,* 1 (1987).

4. Lawrence W. Moore, "Federal Jurisdiction and Procedure," 41 *Loyola Law Review,* 469 (Fall 1995).

5. See *DeAguilar v. Boeing Co.,* 47 F.3d 1404 (5th Cir. 1995) for a discussion regarding the amount in controversy requirement in federal courts.

6. 326 U.S. 310 (1945). More recently, the U.S. Supreme Court has narrowed the scope of such contacts. See *Asahi Metal Industry Co. v. Superior Court,* 480 U.S. 102 (1987) where the court held that merely placing a product in the stream of commerce is not an act that will subject a party to the forum state jurisdiction. Minimum contacts require some action directed toward the forum state.

7. H. J. Berman & W.R. Greiner, *The Nature and Functions of Law,* 4th ed. (Foundation Press, Mineola, N.Y.) 1980.

8. Mark D. Robins,"The Resurgence and Limits of the Demurrer," 27 *Suffolk University Law Review,* 637 (Fall 1993).

9. R. Grutman & B. Thomas, *Lawyers and Thieves,* (Simon and Schuster, New York) 1990.

10. Kevin A. Moore, "Simple Answers to Common Problems During Depositions," 68 *Florida Bar Journal,* 111 (June 1994).

11. G. C. Hazard, Jr. & M. Taruffo, *American Civil Procedure: An Introduction,* (Yale University Press, New Haven, Conn.) 1993.

12. William L. Adams, "Let's Make a Deal: Effective Utilization of Judicial Settlements in State and Federal Courts," 72 *Oregon Law Review,* 427 (Summer 1993).

13. Portions of this section have been adapted from the author's previous work published in the *National Victim Assistance Academy Text* (1995) which was supported by Grant No. 95-MU-GX-K002 awarded by the Office for Victims of Crimes, Office of Justice Programs, U.S. Department of Justice.

14. D. V. Otterson, "Dependency and Termination Proceedings in California—Standards of Proof," 30 *Hastings Law Journal,* 1815–1845 (1979).

15. M. S. Umbreit, *Victim Meets Offender: The Impact of Restorative Justice and Mediation* (Willow Tree Press, Inc. Monsey, New York 1994) hereinafter cited as *Victim Meets Offender.*

16. Paul McCold, "Restorative Justice: The Role of the Community," paper presented at the Academy of Criminal Justice Sciences Annual Conferences, Boston, Mass. (March 1995).

17. G. Bazemore and M. S. Umbreit, *Balanced and Restorative Justice,* (Office of Justice Programs, Washington, D.C.) October 1994.

18. *Victim Meets Offender.*

19. S. P. Hughes & A. L. Schneider, *Victim–Offender Mediation in the Juvenile Justice System,* (Office of Justice Program, Washington, D.C.) September, 1990.

THE CONSEQUENCES OF VICTIMIZATION

Chapter Outline

Physical Consequences
  Types of Injuries
  Medical Aspects

Mental Consequences
  Crisis
  Acute Stress Disorder
  Posttraumatic Stress Disorder
  Long-Term Crisis Reaction
  Other Mental Disorders
  Other Effects

Financial Consequences
  Introduction
  Tangible Losses
  Intangible Losses

Summary

Key Terms

Discussion Questions

Suggested Readings

Learning Objectives

After reading this chapter, you should be able to:

- Explain the types of physical injuries suffered by victims
- Understand from a nonmedical perspective the extent and nature of the various physical injuries inflicted on victims of crime
- Discuss the three stages of crisis
- List the effects on victims suffering from posttraumatic stress disorder
- Explain the symptoms of acute stress disorder
- Distinguish between posttraumatic stress disorder and long-term crisis reaction
- Understand the other types of mental consequences suffered by victims
- Explain the financial consequences of crime victimization

Physical Consequences

One obvious consequence of victimization is the physical injuries suffered by victims. These injuries are easy to observe and treat. They are also the ones we are most knowledgeable about, because the majority of us know someone who has suffered a broken arm, leg, or other injury.

Types of Injuries

There are four general classifications of physical injuries inflicted on victims during the commission of a crime. These physical traumas include immediate injuries that heal leaving no trace, injuries that leave visible scars, unknown long-term physical injuries, and long-term catastrophic injuries.

FOCUS: Physical Injuries: Gunshot Wounds

In 1991, gunshot wounds killed over 38,077 people and resulted in the hospitalization of an additional 31,500 people under the age of twenty-five as well as other medical treatment of another 44,500 victims. The following facts and figures point out the extent and nature of injuries and deaths suffered as a result of gunshot wounds:

- More people between the ages of fifteen and twenty-four die from gunshot wounds than any other cause of death.

- Three of four homicide victims under the age of twenty-five die from gunshot wounds.

- More than half of all gunshot victims are under the age of twenty-five.

Source: Adapted from *Childhood Injury: Cost & Prevention Facts,* (Children's Safety Network Economics and Insurance Resource Center, Landover, Maryland).

Immediate injuries include bruises, contusions, cuts, and broken bones. These injuries generally heal quickly and are not perceived as serious by most people. In fact, many of us have suffered these same types of injuries on a vacation trip. However, some victims face more serious consequences as a result of these types of injuries. An elderly person who suffers a broken hip as a result of a purse snatch may have significant complications during the healing process that could lead to death. A diabetic suffering from a stab wound may take two to three times as long to heal as another person.

Injuries that leave visible scars include those that result in facial scars; loss of teeth; loss of fingers or toes; scars on the neck, arms, or legs; and loss of mobility due to incomplete healing. The injuries are not considered catastrophic in nature, but can cause changes in life activities. For example, facial scaring may result in a model being unable to pursue her career.

Unknown long-term physical injuries can include a potential exposure to HIV and AIDS. These types of diseases can result in loss of life or a complete change in life activities. There are other sexually transmitted diseases that may occur as a result of a sexual attack including but not limited to gonorrhea, syphilis, and the herpes simplex viruses.

Long-term catastrophic injuries include those that restrict a victim's physical movements. For example, a person struck by a drunk driver may become a paraplegic or may lose an arm or a leg. These severe injuries often result in family members having to alter their lifestyles to care for the victim, while others may result in a reduction in the life span of the victim, change in identity, and change in the quality of life.

Medical Aspects

The types of physical injuries suffered by victims of crime can cover the entire spectrum of illness, from simple bruises to deadly gunshot wounds to the head. Although victim service providers are not expected to be physicians, they should have a basic understanding of the various types of injuries that victims may suffer. The next section will briefly examine the medical aspects of some of the more common traumatic injuries.[1]

Gunshot Wounds

The United States civilian population is the most heavily armed in history.[2] More than 850,000 civilians have been killed by bullets in this century.[3] The science of ballistics is complex, but a few basic rules will assist in understanding the nature of injuries that result from gunshot wounds. The magnitude of the injury is proportional to the amount of kinetic energy impacted by the bullet striking the victim. This kinetic energy is determined by a variety of factors including the distance between the assailant and the victim, the muzzle velocity, and the various characteristics of the bullet. At medium velocity, the missile has an explosive impact and creates a temporary passage in the tissue along its course. Bone and tissue may be fractured and torn without being directly struck by the missile.

High-velocity missiles cause additional problems including the possibility of fragmentation which will cause additional multiple trajectories and injuries. Medical personnel are interested in obtaining information regarding the type of weapon used, the distance from the assailant when the victim was shot, the suspected number of shots, the blood lost at the scene, and any type of fluids administered before arrival at the hospital.

Shotgun wounds present special types of problems. The shotgun was designed to strike a small, fast-moving target at close range. Because of the design of the pebbles inside the round, the shotgun is not an effective weapon at long range. However, when used at close range, a shotgun is extremely lethal. Shotgun wounds have been classified into three groups according to the range, the pattern of the pellets, and the depth of penetration. Type I wounds involve long range (greater than seven yards) and basically result in a penetration of subcutaneous tissue and deep fascia only. Type II wounds involve medium range (between three and four yards) and may create a large number of perforated wounds. Type III wounds involve short or point-blank range (less than three yards) and involve a massive destruction of tissue. Type III wounds are lethal in nature carrying a mortality rate of 39 percent to 65 percent.

Stabbing Wounds

Knives are not the only instrument used in stabbings. Ice picks, pens, coat hangers, screwdrivers, broken bottles, and other sharp objects have all been used as weapons by assailants. Stabbing wounds usually result in lacerations or punctures. These injuries may be only a minor inconvenience or they may be life threatening, depending on the location and depth of the wound. Frequently, more than one stab wound is sustained. Medical personnel are interested in obtaining information regarding the type and size of the weapon, the estimated blood loss at the scene of the crime, the time of injury, and whether the victim had ingested any drugs or alcohol.

Burns

Burns are one of the most painful and devastating types of physical injuries. They are classified into first, second, or third degree according to the depth of the burned area. First-degree burns involve the epidermis tissue and may exhibit red or pink skin accompanied by hyperesthesia and tingling. The more common causes of first-degree burns are sunburn and brief contact with hot liquids. Second-degree burns involve the epidermis and dermis tissues and may exhibit red or mottled skin with blisters, considerable swelling, wet surfaces, pain, and sensitivity to cold air. The most frequent causes include scalds and flash flames. Third-degree burns involve the dermis or deeper tissues and may exhibit pale white or charred appearance with a dry surface, body fat may be exposed, and systemic symptoms include shock, hematuria, and hemolysis. The most common causes include fire, contact with hot objects, and electrical and chemical burns.

The severity of burns is based on both the extent and type of burn. The American Burn Association classifies burns as major, moderate, or minor in nature.

Major burns include second-degree burns over more than 25 percent of an adult's body and 20 percent of a child's body; third-degree burns involving 10 percent of the body surface; all burns involving hands, eyes, face, ears, and feet, and all inhalation injuries and burns complicated by other injuries. Moderate burns include second-degree burns over 15 to 25 percent of an adult's body and 10 to 20 percent of a child's body and all third-degree burns of 2 to 10 percent not involving eyes, ears, face, hands, or feet. Minor burns include second-degree burns over less than 15 percent of an adult's body and less than 10 percent of a child's body and third-degree burns of 2 percent or less not involving eyes, ears, face, hands, or feet.

Trauma to the Head

A significant portion of all emergency department work involves the care of people suffering from trauma to the head. Vehicle accidents, including drunk driving incidents, account for a significant percentage of this form of injury. Other criminal acts such as muggings and batteries also constitute another important cause of head trauma. Oftentimes, people who sustain head injuries have other associated major traumatic injuries which they received at the same time.

One effect of trauma to the head may be the inducement of a coma. Comas may be the result of a subdural hematoma, epidural hematoma, traumatic intracerebral hemorrhage, contusion, or concussion. Defining a coma is difficult, but for the purposes here, it is an altered state that exists in a person manifesting inappropriate responses to external stimuli and who maintains eye closure throughout the stimuli.

The victim's ability to relate the course of events leading to the injury may be compromised by injury, alcohol, drugs, hysteria, or any number of factors. Medical personnel will want to know if the victim was struck on the head by the assailant, and what type of object was used. Police and firefighters will be questioned about whether the victim was awake on their arrival, and any changes in consciousness between the incident and arrival at the emergency room should be noted.

Other Medical Concerns

In addition to the different types of physical injuries suffered by victims of violent crime, victims of sexual assault endure a specific trauma that results in specialized medical issues. Rape victims will undergo a particular type of examination intended to assist in the prosecution of the perpetrator. In the recent past, these medical examinations were conducted by hospital staff with little or no specialized training regarding the effects of rape on the victim. Additionally, there were times when a male police officer remained in the examination room to conduct questioning of the victim during the examination. Fortunately, there has been progression in the medical treatment of sexual assault victims, and in many jurisdictions, rape crisis counselors are available and present during this examination. They have been trained to provide support to the victim during this and other phases of the criminal justice process.

The rape victim should discuss the issue of pregnancy with hospital staff. If she was pregnant prior to the assault, the possible effects on the fetus should be discussed. If she was not pregnant, the possibility that the assailant impregnated her should be evaluated. The victim should discuss all aspects of this issue at the earliest possible time with the medical staff at the hospital, or her own physician.

The possibility of contracting a sexually transmitted disease (STD) must be evaluated. Many of these diseases can be successfully avoided if treated immediately after the assault; however, many STDs will not show up during the physical examination, so rape victims should be tested several weeks following the attack. It is therefore critical that victims discuss this possibility with medical personnel.

With the threat of AIDS and HIV so much a part of our lives today, the possibility of contracting the disease is perhaps one of the most frightening aspects of sexual assaults. Human immunodeficiency virus (HIV) causes acquired immunodeficiency syndrome (AIDS). AIDS is a disease that attacks the body's immune system rendering the person vulnerable to infections and diseases and ultimately resulting in death. A victim may contract HIV in various ways. Victims should be tested immediately for HIV and request appropriate periodic follow-up testing. Chapter 13 discusses HIV/AIDS victimization in more detail.

Mental Consequences

Crisis

Eric Lindemann is considered by many scholars to be a leading pioneer in the study of the effects of crisis on the mental health or emotional well-being of humans.[4] Lindemann offered both a new understanding of the dynamics of crisis and a systematic approach to treating those suffering from it.[5] His study dealing with the grieving process of the survivors in the Coconut Grove fire in Boston in 1942 has become the foundation on which much of the knowledge concerning the grief process has been built. Lindemann believed that acute grief was a natural and necessary reaction to significant loss. Another scholar, Gerald Caplin, extended Lindemann's theories to include all human reactions to traumatic events and not only the grieving process as a result of loss.[6]

Individuals react differently to different situations and what may be a crisis to one person may only be a minor annoyance to another. As a result the term *crisis* has many valid meanings. In medicine crisis has one meaning, whereas in psychiatry the term is used in a different context. A number of scholars have defined the term *crisis*. Rather than adopt a sociological, medical, psychological, or legal definition of the term, it will be viewed from the perspective of a victim's reaction to crime. *Crisis* is therefore defined as a specific set of temporary circumstances that results in a state of upset and disequilibrium, characterized by an individual's inability to cope with a particular situation using customary methods of problem solving.[7]

Although some authorities may differ regarding the number of steps in the crisis reaction, one common analysis describes this process as involving three stages: impact, recoil, and reorganization.

The Impact Stage

The impact phase occurs immediately after the crime. Victims feel as if they are in shock. Some victims cannot eat or sleep, others may express disbelief that the crime actually occurred. Statements such as "I can't believe this happened to me!" are common during this stage. Many victims feel exposed and vulnerable or express feelings of helplessness.

The impact phase may last for several hours to several days after the crime and is often punctuated by episodes of severe mood swings. One moment the victim may appear to be in control and the next moment exhibit disorganized and uncontrolled emotions. A crime victim is especially vulnerable at this time and susceptible to the influence of others. What may appear to be innocent statements offered by friends may be interpreted by the victim as blame for being the victim.

The Recoil Stage

During the recoil phase, victims attempt to accept or adapt to the crime and begin to reintegrate their personalities. Victims commonly experience a variety of emotions including guilt, fear, anger, self-pity, and sadness. Some victims struggle to accept the painful feelings caused by the crime; at other times they will deny experiencing any of these feelings at all. Caplin explained this process as involving victims who need opportunities to rest from wrestling with their situation, but who must eventually awake and return to consideration of the problem.[8] In essence, after trying to cope with their feelings regarding the crime, victims become emotionally exhausted and put these feelings aside so that they can rest, recover, and begin the healing process. Later, they are able to examine their feelings regarding the crime with renewed emotional resources.

Many victims will be in denial during this phase. This emotional detachment can be an extension of the shock of the impact phase. Such detachment allows victims to develop a gradual immunity to the feelings that would overwhelm them if they faced them all at once. Victims may believe that they must seal off any feelings in order to get on with their lives. Some victims defend against any feeling during this phase by emerging themselves in work or other projects. Other victims accomplish the same objective by becoming almost obsessional with the criminal justice system—-learning about the procedures, criminal laws, parties, etcetera.

It is during this phase that victims begin to deal with their feelings about the crime. Some victims will reexamine every detail of the crime in their minds. They may want to talk about it endlessly, others will dream about the crime. As victims confront the reality of the criminal act, they may reexperience the fear. Some victims only allow themselves to feel the full intensity of emotions after the immediate threat of the crime has passed. This feeling of fear can be immobilizing. Victims must verbalize their fears and other intense emotions associated with the criminal act to begin the healing process. With time, most of the traumatic impact associated with these feelings will lessen.

Another common feeling during the recoil stage is anger toward the criminal. Victims may experience rage but be unable to vent this feeling. Some victims may spend hours thinking about revenge, especially those who have suffered from a violent attack. Victims must understand that the desire for revenge is natural and a normal part of the healing process. Many victims want to construct a reason for their victimization. These victims will search for the answer to the question,"Why me?"

The Reorganization Stage

After a period of time, the recoil stage will give way to the reorganization stage. The victim becomes more normal as feelings of fear and rage diminish in intensity and the victim has energy left over to confront life's daily activities. The victim becomes more normalized as the need to deny the victimization lessens. Victims are gradually able to put their experience in perspective and commit their energies to the task of living in the present.

Victims will never forget the experience and as indicated earlier, they will respond in a variety of ways. This discussion has focused on one method or approach to victimization. Other victims may experience different feelings. Acute stress disorder is another reaction that victims of crime may experience.

Acute Stress Disorder

Acute stress disorder (ASD) is acute stress that is experienced in the immediate aftermath of a traumatic event. This is a newly categorized disorder that was first listed in the *Diagnostic and Statistical Manual of Mental Disorders*, 4th edition (DSM-IV) in 1994.[9] The characteristics of acute stress disorder are the development of anxiety, dissociative symptoms, and other manifestations that occur within one month after exposure to the traumatic event. To receive a diagnosis of ASD, the victim must have experienced, witnessed, or been confronted with an event that involved actual or threatened death, serious injury, or a threat to the physical safety of the victim or others. Additionally, the victim's response to such a condition must involve intense fear, helplessness, or horror. This diagnosis requires that the victim experience several symptoms of posttraumatic stress disorder (PTSD), and that the victim must experience three of five PTSD dissociative symptoms during or immediately after the traumatic incident. These symptoms must persist for at least two days, but last no more than thirty days. The dissociative symptoms are derealization, depersonalization, dissociative amnesia, subjective sense of numbing, and reduction in awareness of surroundings. In the event these symptoms last longer than thirty days, the victim may be suffering from posttraumatic stress disorder.

Posttraumatic Stress Disorder

Posttraumatic stress disorder was first identified when some Vietnam veterans began experiencing flashbacks of events that occurred during combat. *Posttraumatic stress disorder* is defined as the development of characteristic symptoms following a psychologically distressing event that is outside the range of usual human experience.[10] Traumatic events include, but are not limited to, military combat, violent personal assault, terrorist attack, torture, incarceration as a prisoner of war, natural or man-made disasters, severe automobile accidents, being kidnapped or taken hostage, or being diagnosed with a life-threatening illness. The characteristic symptoms require that the person experience, witness, or be confronted with an event or events that involve actual or threatened death or serious injury, or a threat to the physical integrity of self or others, and that the person's response involve intense fear, helplessness, or horror. The symptoms that the victim may experience include reexperiencing the traumatic event, avoidance of stimuli associated with the event, or numbing of general responsiveness, and increased agitation.[11]

Victims of any type of crime can experience posttraumatic stress disorder. However, several scholars have researched the effect of rape on victims.[12] Victims of rape have reported or been diagnosed as suffering from posttraumatic stress disorder. Rothbaum's study found that 94 percent of rape victims displayed classic symptoms of PTSD one week after the assault. This figure dropped to 47 percent twelve weeks after the incident.[13] Kilpatrick's study, *Rape in America*, reported that 11 percent of all women raped still suffer from PTSD and the authors estimated that 1.3 million women in the United States are currently suffering from posttraumatic stress disorder as a result of a rape or multiple rapes.[14]

Long-Term Crisis Reaction

Long-term crisis reaction is the name of a condition identified by the National Organization for Victim Assistance (NOVA). As discussed in Chapter 1, NOVA is considered one of the early leaders in the victims' rights movement. Organization members have responded to a number of crises throughout the world. Professionals from NOVA working with crisis victims have observed this reaction on a number of occasions. *Long-term crisis reaction* is a condition that occurs when victims do not suffer from PTSD, but may reexperience feelings of the crisis reaction when certain events trigger the recollection of the trauma in their lives.[15] The trigger event may be a number of situations including the anniversaries of the crisis, birthdays, or holidays of loved ones lost during the trauma; significant life events such as marriage, divorces, births, and graduations; media events that broadcast similar types of incidents; and involvement in the criminal justice system.

The intensity and frequency of long-term crisis reactions usually diminish with the passage of time. As the victim develops coping mechanisms to deal with the trauma, these resources may lessen the victim's reaction to triggering events. The victim must learn to continue to function despite these reactions.

Other Mental Disorders

Victims of crime may suffer a wide variety of mental disorders as a result of their victimization. They are going through a process of attempting to regain their mental equilibrium that is off center as a result of the traumatic event. Following is a brief discussion of two common mental problems faced by victims of crime.

Depression

Depression is described as a major depressive episode lasting at least two weeks during which there is either a depressed mood or the loss of interest, or pleasure, in nearly all activities. Possible symptoms include changes in appetite or weight, sleep and psychomotor activity; decreased energy; feelings of worthlessness or guilt; difficulty thinking, concentrating, or making decisions; or recurrent thoughts of death or suicide. The victim must experience clinically significant distress or impairment in social, occupational, or other important areas of functioning.

Substance Abuse

The essential feature of substance abuse is a maladaptive pattern of substance use leading to significant adverse consequences related to the repeated use of substances. Normally, these substances are drugs or alcohol. The victim may suffer repeated failure in fulfilling major role obligations, repeated use of substances in situations in which it is physically dangerous, legal problems related to the use of the substance, and social and interpersonal problems.

Other Effects

Different victims of the same crime suffer different reactions to that crime, and conversely, victims of different crimes may suffer similar reactions. There is no "clear bright line" that professionals can look to and determine which symptoms victims will suffer. However, researchers have attempted to establish general categories of problems suffered by victims of certain crimes. In Susman and Vittert's text, *Building a Solution: A Practical Guide for Establishing Crime Victim Service Agencies*, they listed certain crimes and typical reactions.[16] Although individual crime victims' reactions will vary depending on a number of factors, Table 5.1 summarizes these findings.

With the passage of time and other intervention techniques, the mental and emotional consequences associated with the trauma of a criminal act may lessen or be alleviated, but the victim may never be the same person as before the crime. In addition to the mental effects victims endure as a result of the crime, they also suffer fiscal consequences.

Financial Consequences

In 1996, the National Institute of Justice released *Victim Costs and Consequences: A New Look*, an in-depth study of the costs of victimization.[17] This study raises serious questions regarding previous estimates of the costs of crime. Using the data

TABLE 5.1   Victim Reactions to Various Crimes

Burglary	Robbery	Assault	Sexual Assault
Home is no longer a safe haven	Fear of walking alone on the streets	Anger and/or bitterness	Embarrassment
Reluctant to leave home	Relief at survival	Realization of mortality	Difficulty in describing the incident
Reluctant to stay home	Realization of mortality	Physical injury	Concern about STD/pregnancy
Express lots of "I shoulds"	Frustration at loss of personal effects	Medical bills	Bills for the medical exam
Heavy financial loss	Fear of intimidation	Time loss from work	Fear of telling family members
Sorrow at loss of sentimental items	For commercial robberies, fear of loss of job	Fear of reprisals	Fear the neighbors will find out
Disgust with destruction that occurred during the burglary		If assailant is a family member, feelings of betrayal	Fear of media publicity
Realization of isolation		If a result of a traffic incident, fear of driving	Recurring nightmares, changes in sleeping patterns, loss of appetite
Frustration with police who don't investigate thoroughly		If a result of jealousy, feeling of vulnerability	Decision to prosecute
Expense of securing home		For male victims, shame at losing a "fight"	Fear that they will have to testify about prior sexual history
			Bitterness against the offender
			Sexual dysfunction

Battered Women	Homicide—Survivor Victims	Child Victims	Elderly Victims
Decision to stay	Acceptance of death	Parents' reaction	Fear of crime
Decision to leave	Funeral arrangements	Signs of emotional distress	Acute financial loss
Financial worries	Financial problems when breadwinner is killed	Guilt	Change in lifestyle
Decision to prosecute	Delayed emotional reaction	Parents' unconcern	Loneliness
Desire counseling for batterer and/or themselves	Reaction of children	Difficulty in describing incident	Family reactions
For separated couples, visitation offers opportunities for further attacks	Need for information on the criminal case	Fears about testifying	Reluctance to get involved in the criminal justice system
Isolation	Media publicity	Incest—decision about family's future	

Continued

TABLE 5.1   **Victim Reactions to Various Crimes** (Continued)

Battered Women	Homicide—Survivor Victims	Child Victims	Elderly Victims
Helplessness	Feelings of powerlessness in the criminal justice system	Incest—mixed reaction by mother	
Psychological dependence		Reaction of other children	
Fear of recurrence	Ordeal during trial	Fear of intimidation	
Feeling of personal failure	Loneliness		
Fear for safety of any children	Can't stop ruminating		
	Desire for revenge		

from the Bureau of Justice Statistics and including "quality of life" or intangible losses, this study concludes that the cost of crime is higher than previously suggested. The following sections examine the results of this study.

Introduction

It is fairly easy to establish the tangible costs of crime. These costs include a number of fairly easy-to-measure items such as medical care, police services, and other items that have a specific monetary value. However, it is not as easy to value the loss of "quality of life" or intangible losses suffered by victims of crime. How much is a murder victim's life worth? What is the cost for the pain and suffering experienced by a rape victim? Additionally, costs associated with society's response to crime are difficult, if not impossible to measure. Table 5.2 lists the major tangible, intangible, and society's costs associated with crime:

As Table 5.2 indicates, society's response to crime includes a variety of items that are not normally considered when discussing costs of crime. Measuring our actions and resulting costs based on our fear of crime is difficult. On the other hand, measuring items such as alarms for cars and homes, which are typical of the precautionary expenditures associated with protecting ourselves from criminal activity, is relatively easy. Additionally, everyone understands the costs associated with running the criminal justice system and keeping offenders incarcerated. Thus, it can be observed that society's response to crime includes both tangible and intangible costs. The costs of crime section also includes tangible and intangible losses suffered as a result of criminal acts. These costs include tangible items such as medical and mental health treatment cost. The intangible costs include quality of life and loss of companionship. Table 5.3 examines both tangible and intangible costs of crime.

TABLE 5.2 Major Costs Associated with Crime

Cost of Crime	Cost of Society's Response to Crime
Direct property losses	Precautionary expenditures
Medical and mental health care	Fear of crime
Victim services	Criminal justice system
Lost workdays	Victim service organizations and volunteer time
Lost school days	Other noncriminal programs
Lost housework	Incarcerated offender costs
Pain and suffering/Quality of life	Overdeterrence costs
Loss of affection/enjoyment	Justice costs
Death	
Legal costs associated with tort claims	
Second generation costs	

Source: Adapted from *Victim Costs and Consequences: A New Look* (U.S. Department of Justice) 1996, p. 11.

Table 5.3 indicates that costs of crime show quality of life losses generally exceed all tangible losses combined. By multiplying the costs of crime by the annual crime incidence, you can obtain the aggregate figures. The tangible losses amounted to $105 billion each year and the intangible losses were more than three times that amount at an annual cost of $345 billion. The next section will examine the tangible costs of victimization.

Tangible Losses

Personal crime costs taxpayers, businesses, and victims approximately $105 billion per year in medical costs, lost earnings, and public programs related to victim assistance. These tangible losses do not account for the full impact of crime on victims because they ignore pain and suffering and the reduced quality of life that many victims suffer as a result of a crime. These costs are estimated at $450 billion annually. Violent crime including drunk driving and arson accounts for $426 billion of this total and property crime costs $24 billion.

TABLE 5.3 Tangible and Intangible Costs of Crime

Crime	Tangible Costs	Intangible Costs	Total Costs
Murder	$1,030,000	$1,910,000	$2,940,000
Rape/Sexual assault	$5,100	$81,400	$86,500
Robbery/Attempt with injury	$5,200	$13,800	$19,000
Assault or attempt	$1,500	$7,800	$9,350
Burglary or attempt	$1,100	$300	$1,400

Source: Adapted from *Victim Costs and Consequences: A New Look* (U.S. Department of Justice) 1996, p. 11.

The following figures put these sums into perspective to help understand the true magnitude of the costs of crime to victims:

- Violent crime and its resulting injuries account for 3 percent of all U.S. medical spending;
- Violent crime results in wage losses equal to 1 percent of all American earnings;
- Violent crime causes 10 to 20 percent of mental health expenditures in the United States;
- Personal crime reduces the average American's quality of life by 1.8 percent.

Victims usually suffer three types of losses: (1) out-of-pocket expenses such as medical costs and property loss, (2) reduced productivity at work because of sick days, attending trial, etc., and (3) nonmonetary losses such as pain and suffering and loss of quality of life. Some of these losses are easily quantified, but even the intangible losses may be valued in dollars. Tangible losses include property damage and loss, medical care, mental health care, police and fire services, victim services, and productivity. Each of these losses are explained in the following paragraphs.

Property damage and loss includes the value of the property damaged during the crime, or property taken and not recovered. It also includes insurance claims administration costs that arise as a result of compensating the victim under an insurance policy.

Medical care includes payments for hospital and physician care, emergency medical transportation, rehabilitation, prescriptions, allied health services, medical devices, and related insurance claim processing costs. Managed care systems are changing health care payments and are not reflected in these costs. More study is necessary in this area as medical costs adapt to changing circumstances.

Mental health care provides funding for services to crime victims by psychiatrists, psychologists, social workers, and counselors. This cost has been one of the least researched areas in crime victimization.

Police and fire services cover initial police and fire responses and follow-up investigations. The costs of other components of the criminal justice system are not included in this element. Generally speaking, police and fire costs are a relatively small portion of the cost of crime averaging $100 per case.

Victim services costs include victim service agencies and child protective service agencies as well as foster care for maltreated children removed from their homes.

Productivity costs include lost wages, fringe benefits, housework, and lost school days suffered by victims and their families. This category includes lost productivity of co-workers and supervisors recruiting and training victims who are disabled as a result of a crime. It also includes processing costs for insurance claims and legal expenses associated with recovering productivity from drunk drivers and their insurers.

Intangible Losses

Intangible losses are hard to quantify; however, scholars have begun to place monetary values on certain aspects of a victim's quality of life. Researchers such as Ted R. Miller and others have divided intangible losses into two categories: fatal and nonfatal injuries. The monetary value for fatalities is based on the amount people routinely spend to reduce their risk of death. For example, this amount would include the cost of smoke detectors, alarm systems, and bars on house windows. As Table 5.3 illustrates, the approximate monetary value of a fatality was $2.9 million with the intangible value of $1.9 million of that amount.

The intangible value for nonfatal injuries was established by analyzing jury verdicts for pain, suffering, fear, and loss of quality of life. As discussed in other chapters of this text, violent perpetrators rarely have sufficient funds to pay these awards, but third-party codefendants such as insurance companies or businesses that were negligent can be held liable for injuries to the victim.

There is no doubt that attempting to establish a monetary value on intangible aspects of victimization is a relatively recent development in the field of victimology. For example, in 1994 a Bureau of Justice Statistics publication, *The Costs of Crime to the Victim*, specifically did not examine the intangible costs of crime.[18] Because this is a new aspect of victimization, it will continue to be controversial. However, we cannot truly appreciate the consequences of crime and victimization until we begin to accept the reality of intangible costs to victims and their families. This is an area of victimology that will continue to generate more study and debate in the future.

Summary

We have known for centuries that victims of crime suffer from specific types of physical injuries as a result of their victimization. These are for the most part easy to recognize and treat. The broken arm or jaw may be repaired and hopefully the victim will regain full use of such physical faculties.

More recently, society has acknowledged that victims of crime may also suffer mental problems as a consequence of their victimization. They may experience a wide variety of mental problems including acute stress disorder, posttraumatic stress disorder, long-term crisis reaction, or other mental disorders. These reactions do not mean that the victims are insane or crazy. Rather, these are normal reactions to an abnormal event. Victim service providers and professionals who deal with victims must understand these dynamics in order to work with and assist victims of crimes.

In addition to the physical and mental injuries, victims also experience financial consequences of most crimes. Determining the amount of money taken from a robbery victim is relatively easy; however, it is harder to place a value on the intangible costs suffered by that victim. Recent studies have begun to address this long overlooked aspect of crime victimization. The consequences of crime are multifaceted and, like a stone dropped in a calm pool of water, move out in ever-widening circles affecting victims, their families, and society as a whole. Professionals in the field must understand all the consequences of victimization to be able to function effectively.

Key Terms

Crisis is a specific set of temporary circumstances that result in a state of upset and disequilibrium, characterized by an individual's inability to cope with a particular situation using customary methods of problem solving.

Acute stress disorder is acute stress that is experienced in the immediate aftermath of a traumatic event.

Posttraumatic stress disorder is defined as the development of characteristic symptoms following a psychologically distressing event that is outside the range of usual human experience.

Long-term crisis reaction is a condition that occurs when victims do not suffer from PTSD, but may reexperience feelings of the crisis reaction when certain events trigger the recollection of the trauma in their lives.

Discussion Questions

1. What are the four stages of physical injury? How do they differ from each other?

2. Describe the various types of physical injuries that victims may suffer.

3. List and discuss the three stages of crisis. In your opinion which stage is the most critical for the victim? Justify your answer.

4. What is acute stress disorder? How is it different from a crisis reaction?

5. Explain the symptoms of posttraumatic stress disorder.

6. Define long-term crisis reaction and explain a trigger event.

7. Compare and contrast PTSD with long-term crisis reaction.

8. List other mental effects of crime on victims. Which one in your opinion is the most serious? Justify your answer.

Suggested Readings

Albert J. Reiss, Jr. & Jeffery A. Roth, eds., *Understanding and Preventing Violence*, (National Academy Press, Washington, D.C.) 1993.

Albert R. Roberts, ed., *Crisis Intervention and Time-Limited Cognitive Treatment*, (Sage, Thousand Oaks, Calif.) 1995.

C. P. Wing, *Crisis Intervention as Psychotherapy*, (Oxford, New York) 1978.

Gerald Caplin, *Principles of Preventive Psychiatry*, (Basic Books, New York) 1964.

Morton Bard & Dawn Sangrey, *The Crime Victim's Book*, 2nd ed. (Brunner/Mazel, New York) 1986.

Endnotes

1. Much of this information was gathered from interviewing members of the Fresno Valley Medical Center emergency room staff. Barbara Miller, RN and Albert Velaseo, MD were of significant assistance in providing guidance for material in this section.
2. J. D. Wright, "The Demography of Gun Control," *The Nation*, (Sept. 20, 1976), p. 241.
3. L. Adelson, "The Gun and the Sanctity of Human Life: or the Bullet as a Pathogen," *The Phasos*, (Summer 1980), p. 15.
4. Albert R. Roberts & Sophia F. Dziegielewski, "Foundation Skills and Applications of Crisis Intervention and Cognitive Therapy," in *Crisis Intervention and Time-Limited Cognitive Treatment*, Albert R. Roberts, Ed. (Sage, Thousand Oaks, Calif.) 1995.
5. E. Lindemann, "Symptomatology and Management of Acute Grief," 101 *American Journal of Psychiatry*, 141–148 (1944).
6. C. P. Wing, *Crisis Intervention as Psychotherapy*, (Oxford, New York) 1978 and Gerald Caplin, *Principles of Preventive Psychiatry*, (Basic Books, New York) 1964.
7. See Albert R. Roberts, *Crisis Intervention Handbook: Assessment, Treatment and Research*, (Wadsworth, Belmont, Calif.) 1990 and Morton Bard & Dawn Sangrey, *The Crime Victim's Book*, 2nd ed. (Brunner/Mazel, New York) 1986.
8. Caplin, *Principles of Psychiatry*, p. 46.
9. *Diagnostic and Statistical Manual of Mental Disorders*, 4th ed. (American Psychiatric Association, Washington, D.C.) 1994.
10. *Diagnostic and Statistical Manual of Mental Disorders*, 4th ed. (American Psychiatric Association, Washington, D.C.) 1994, pp. 427–429.
11. DSM-IV, pp. 427–429.
12. For an excellent discussion of the effects of rape on victims, see Bruce Taylor, "The Role of Significant Others in a Rape Victim's Recovery: People Who Are More Likely to Be Harmful Than Helpful," paper presented at the 1996 ACJS Annual Meeting, Las Vegas, Nevada, March 1996.
13. B. O. Rothbaum, E. B. Foa, T. Murdock, D. S. Riggs & W. Walsh, "A Prospective Examination of Post-Traumatic Stress Disorder in Rape Victims," 5 *Journal of Traumatic Stress*, 455–475 (1992).
14. D. G. Kilpatrick, C. N. Edmunds & A. K. Seymour, *Rape in America: A Report to the Nation*, (National Victim Center, Arlington, Va.) 1992.
15. Marlene A. Young, "Crisis Response Teams in the Aftermath of Disasters," in *Crisis Intervention and Time-Limited Cognitive Treatment*, Albert R. Roberts, ed. (Sage, Thousand Oaks, Calif.) 1995.
16. Jarjorie Susman & Carol Holt Vittert, *Building a Solution: A Practical Guide for Establishing Crime Victim Service Agencies*, (National Council of Jewish Women, St. Louis Section) 1980.
17. Ted R. Miller, Mark A. Cohen & Brian Wiersema, *Victim Costs and Consequences: A New Look*, National Institute of Justice, (U.S. Department of Justice, Washington, D.C.) February 1996. This section is adapted from the material presented in this study.
18. Patsy A. Klaus, "The Cost of Crime to Victims," *Crime Data Brief*, (Bureau of Justice Statistics, Washington, D.C.) February 1994.

6

EMPOWERING VICTIMS

Chapter Outline

Introduction

Media
    Relations with the Media
    Preparing for and Conducting the Interview

Legislation
    The Legislative Process
    Advocacy

Public Speaking
    Preparing for the Speech
    Drafting the Speech
    Some Do's and Don'ts of Public Speaking

Fundraising
    Introduction
    Types of Fundraisers

Summary

Key Terms

Discussion Questions

Suggested Readings

Learning Objectives

After reading this chapter, you should be able to:

- Distinguish between the different types of media and their objectives
- Explain the legislative process and how special interests affect the drafting of laws
- Understand how to draft a speech
- Make a presentation in public
- Understand the use of volunteers in victim service programs
- Understand the role of fundraising in victim service programs

Introduction

One common feeling experienced by victims of crime when they become involved in the criminal justice system is helplessness. Many victims want and need to do more than simply testify in a criminal trial regarding the facts of the incident. Victim service providers can assist victims in this endeavor by providing them with advice regarding the different ways that they may become involved in the system. Additionally, professionals in this field need to understand how they can work within the system to make it more responsive to the needs of the victim.

Media

The media have the ability to bring crime directly into our living rooms. It is therefore critical for victim service providers to understand how the media works and

---

FOCUS: Empowerment

Mike Reynolds–One Man's Journey

Mike Reynolds began his journey when he learned that his daughter, Kimber, had been shot and killed by an ex-felon. Mike was a professional photographer and had never been involved in politics or the victims' movement up to this point in his life. He decided one person can make a difference and set out to strengthen California's sentencing laws.

Mike Reynolds became the driving force behind the state's tough "Three Strikes and You're Out" initiative that was overwhelmingly passed by the voters. A similar law was adopted by Congress. Both statutes increased penalties for felons who committed second or third offenses or "strikes."

Although some authorities may argue that the "Three Strikes" law is reactive and imposes harsh penalties without addressing the causes of crime, it stands as a shining example of what one person can accomplish within the area of victims' rights.

how to effectively communicate with them. The media can help or hinder the victim's recovery and subsequent attitude toward life. It is therefore important that professionals develop a working relationship with the media. These relationships will help bridge the gap between the media and victims.

Many victims, police officers, and criminal justice professionals view news reporters with distrust.[1] Just as the police have a mission to accomplish, so do the media. The Constitution of the United States prohibits federal and state governments from passing any law that abridges the freedom of the press. The media call this "the people's right to know." The media's attempts to inform the public occasionally conflict with a law enforcement agency's desire to keep certain information confidential. Only by understanding the media and their role in society can victims deal effectively with the media to present their side of the story.

Relations with the Media

Understanding the media must begin with a clarification of the different types of media. The victim service provider must understand that there are certain basic fundamental principles that apply to the media in general. In addition, there are distinct rules, goals, and standards that pertain to each different type of communication system.

There are three basic types of media with which criminal justice agencies interact: newspapers, radio, and television.

FOCUS: A Code of Ethics for Victim Advocates in the Media

1. Never give a reporter a victim's name and address without prior authorization from the victim.

2. Provide your clients with knowledge of their rights in the media.

3. Always inform clients that they have the right to refuse an interview.

4. When possible, accompany a victim to an interview.

5. Review with reporters, producers, and talk show hosts exactly what questions they can and cannot ask your client.

6. Reserve the right to end an interview if the client shows signs of trauma during the course of the interview.

7. Never force a client into an interview. Graciously accept the first "no" without making your client feel guilty.

8. Never provide "off the record" information about the victim, respect the victim's right to privacy at all times.

9. For victims who wish to speak to the media, obtain a signature on a media release form.

10. Discourage the participation of children in any interview or talk shows.

Source: *Crime Victims and the Media*, A Publication of the Victim's Rights: Opportunities for Action Series. (National Victims Center, Arlington, Va.)

Newspapers

Newspapers usually provide more in-depth coverage than the electronic media. They have the ability to print charts and graphs using statistics that allow the reader to place the current story in visual perspective. In addition, many newspapers are interested in the human aspect of the story. Newspapers may run a major story, coupled with a sidebar story that touches on another aspect of the main story. A *sidebar* story is usually an article that is placed in a column next to the main article. Many newspapers will assign a reporter full time as either the police or court reporter. This reporter will know the officers, the language of the streets, and the law nearly as well as any police officer.

Different types of newspapers exist and victim service providers need to know about the ones in their area. Some publishers print a daily newspaper and others only go to press once a week. Knowing the type of newspaper assists in understanding the time constraints or deadlines that the reporter is facing. Most often when dealing with dailies the reporter must have the information right away, whereas weeklies usually allow several days before the item must be turned in to the editor. In addition to local or regional newspapers, there are news or wire services such as United Press International (UPI) and Associated Press (AP). These provide up-to-date coverage of local, state, national, and international events that are sent across the nation and the world on a news line.

Radio

A radio broadcast carries only the voice of the speaker so the news broadcaster must paint a verbal picture of the situation for the listeners. Because radio reporters do not capture the scene with live pictures, many of the interviews with the victim or a victim service provider are conducted over the telephone.

There are a variety of radio formats and anyone who has driven in a car and "surfed" the channels can vouch for the many different types of programs that are broadcast on the radio at any given moment. These programs include rock music, easy listening, classical, ethnic, educational, religious, all news, and talk shows. Each of these programs appeals to different audiences.

Many radio stations have hourly newscasts, and they can therefore update the public more effectively than the newspapers which are published daily, or the television which has evening or nightly newscasts. In this day of visual media, an effective victim service provider should not overlook the radio as an additional source by which the public may be informed of the activities of their program.

Television

Television is the most familiar medium. It brings the action directly into our living room as it occurs. Many of us have watched hostage scenes and riots as they are happening from the comfort of our easy chairs.

There are basically three forms of television: networks, independents, and cable companies. Network television includes the major corporations such as the American Broadcasting Corporation (ABC), National Broadcasting Corporation (NBC), the Turner System, and others. Independent stations may contract with the networks for some of their shows or they may buy programs that are syndicated by private companies. Cable television combines both national and independent broadcasts and many times provides a news channel for local activities or community programming.

Television by its very nature is visual. A simple news release does not satisfy the television director, who wants and needs pictures and action: a uniformed officer speaking, a suspect being placed in a patrol vehicle, the front of a shot-up building. These graphic scenes are what television is searching for on a daily basis. In addition, television news is short and to the point. Normally, a story on the evening news is twenty to thirty seconds long. No matter how long the television reporter interviews a victim or other service provider, the final broadcast usually will run no longer than one minute.

Understanding the distinctions between the different types of media allows victims and professionals to deal with them in an effective manner. It is also important that victims understand how law enforcement agencies respond to requests for information from the media.

Some criminal justice agencies have codified the rules for these contacts by distributing a standard operating procedure (SOP) on media relations. This procedure has several advantages. First, it assures the media and the administrator of the agency that there is uniformity in dealing with the press. Secondly, it establishes procedures that both parties can follow. If media representatives are consulted when the document is being drafted they will be more understanding of its purpose and will follow the procedures more readily. Lastly, the SOP informs the officer on the street how to respond to an unexpected contact with a news reporter. Understanding the process that law enforcement agencies use to release information will allow a victim service provider to interact more effectively with both the criminal justice agency and the media.

Using a public affairs officer (PAO) is becoming more common in law enforcement agencies.[2] A PAO is the department's official point of contact with the media. There are several different approaches to utilizing a PAO. One approach is to make the public affairs officer the official spokesperson for the department. All interviews are conducted by this person. While this approach may provide continuity, it is not the most effective method of dealing with either the public or the media. Any top-level administrator should be able to conduct a live interview with the media if he has above-average communications skills. A second approach is to establish the position as an official assignment and rotate officers through it based on their experience, intelligence, and abilities. This alternative allows the public and media to "talk" to a sworn officer. The disadvantage to this approach is that depending on the length of the assignment, the media will have to readjust to a new officer with every rotation. Victim service providers should become acquainted with the department's PAO. This affords them the opportunity to hold joint press releases in which both law enforcement and the victim's representative may present their views to the public.

Occasionally, members of the media will report information regarding private aspects of the victim's life. Some of this information is a matter of public record whereas other sources of data may have been obtained through leaks from criminal justice agencies that have access to what is normally viewed as confidential information. News reporters are ethically bound to not reveal the identity of their sources. Just as police officers refuse to reveal the names of their confidential reliable informants, so do news reporters carefully guard the identity of their sources. Some states have "shield" laws which prevent a news reporter from being held in contempt of court for refusing to comply with a court order to reveal the name of a source. In addition, there have been numerous incidents of reporters going to jail rather than give up the identity of their sources.

Victim service providers should accept the fact that there may be leaks to the media concerning information that the victim wishes to remain confidential. By accepting the fact that there will be occasional leaks to the media, the effective victim service provider can attempt to work out a relationship with the press to minimize the impact of such a leak. One technique is to appeal to the integrity of the reporter and inform the reporter of the consequences of releasing the story. It is fruitless to get angry at the reporter, or the unnamed source. Human nature being what it is, leaks will continue for as long as there is a reporter who is willing to listen.

Effective media relations should include occasional conferences between either the victim services provider and the news director of the television, or radio stations, and the editor or publisher of the newspaper. These periodic conferences allow each party to understand the others' points of view. This relationship is especially helpful when adverse or derogatory information is disseminated about the victim. Media representatives should always attempt to contact the victim or the victim's representative for that side of the story before it is run. In the event the reporter "neglects" to reach the victim, the victim service provider should call the editor. This will usually provide the opportunity for a follow-up story giving the victim's position.

Establishing an ongoing relationship with the media is a necessary function of any victim service provider. It must always be based on trust and mutual respect. Once such a relationship has been created, it will be of great benefit to all victims.

Preparing for and Conducting the Interview

Understanding the goal of the media assists the victim service provider and the victim in preparing for and conducting an interview. Most people talk with friends and colleagues on a daily basis and although this is a form of communication there is a distinct difference between this type of interaction and being interviewed by the local television station. This section will examine some techniques that can facilitate a victim service provider's ability to effectively communicate in public situations. The first few times a victim service provider participates in a media interview can be frightening. When a person begins to speak and the newspaper reporter begins to take notes, or the radio or television reporter thrusts a microphone in the provider's face, it can be an overpowering experience.

Preparation before the interview can help relieve some of the anxiety. Being knowledgeable about the facts of the incident and the agency's position can enhance the communication. If photo opportunities are available, the media should know about them. One should never, never lie or distort the truth. The victim service provider's credibility is on the line.

Once the professional has reviewed the facts and has had preliminary discussions with the media, the actual interview will take place. By this time it may seem anticlimactic. The provider should remember to speak clearly in everyday language and avoid the use of jargon.

If the victim service provider is anxious about talking to a reporter because her picture will be on the nightly news which is seen by thousands of citizens, she should remember that this is a one-on-one conversation. The camera person only records what is being said between the professional and the reporter. On occasion a victim service provider will be called on to give an interview "live" instead of having it taped, edited, and replayed at a later time. The person should approach this situation in the same manner as with a taped interview. She must be professional and clearly communicate with the reporter, not the unseen public.

Relations with the media have traditionally been tense. By understanding their purpose and working conditions, and trying to assist them when possible, a victim service provider may become an effective spokesperson for the victim.

Legislation

One emotional issue within the victims' rights movement is the passage of the Victims' Rights Constitutional Amendment. As indicated in Chapter 1, President Clinton has proposed such an amendment. NOVA and other victims' rights organizations have made this a priority on their agendas. In the meantime, a number of other state and federal laws can be revoked, amended, or passed that will assist victims. The purpose of this section is to provide a brief summary of legislative efforts and lobbying activities in which victims and their advocates can engage. These efforts can be very satisfying and empowering to victims or they can be very frustrating, causing victims to feel like they have been victimized one more time.

The Legislative Process[3]

Victim advocates must understand how the legislature works and what is possible from a political perspective. The fact that a proposed law may solve a problem from the victim's perspective does not mean it will be acceptable to other interest groups. We only have to turn on the evening news to hear about political gridlock at both the state and national levels to understand how politics affect our daily lives.

One of the first decisions that must be made when attempting to obtain passage of a victims' rights bill is choosing an author. The role of the author, or

---

FOCUS: How a Bill Becomes a Law

A citizen, organization, special interest group, or elected official proposes potential legislation.

↓

A legislator authors the bill. Many times this is a simple, nonlegal statement of the concept.

↓

The legislative counsel drafts the bill.

↓

The drafted bill is returned to the legislator.

↓

The bill goes to the legislative desk, where it is introduced, assigned a bill number, and "read" for the first time.

↓

The bill is printed.

↓

The bill is sent to the rules committee where it is assigned to a standing committee.

↓

After a certain number of days, the bill is heard in that committee.

↓

The committee acts upon the bill in one of three ways: It may pass the bill "as is," it may amend the bill, or it may hold the bill in committee. The later course of action effectively kills the bill.

↓

If the bill involves the expenditure of state funds, it is sent to an appropriations committee.

↓

The bill is then sent to the legislative floor for a second "reading."

↓

Bills that survive the second reading are again sent to the legislative floor for a third and final reading.

↓

Bills are then forwarded to the governor for signature.

↓

After signature by the governor, the bill is the law.

"sponsor," is critical to the successful passage of the bill. The author must be committed to the proposed legislation. The legislator should have a record of supporting other victims' issues. Additionally, the potential author should not be so controversial to alienate other legislative members. If the author is the chairperson of a key committee or serves in other leadership positions within the legislature, this assists in moving the bill through the process. The reality of modern-day politics is that victim advocates will deal with the elected officials staff more often than the actual author. It is therefore important to maintain a cordial working relationship with these staffers. Many times these staff persons will assist in identifying other cosponsors for the bill. Although obtaining an author or sponsor is critical, the addition of cosponsors, especially from both parties, indicates widespread support for any proposed legislation and dramatically improves the chances that it will become law.

The legislature has established the committee process to screen the thousands of bills that are introduced each year. Each proposed legislation is subject to review by a policy committee and if the bill involves appropriation of funds, it must also be reviewed by a fiscal committee. A major portion of the committee's time is spent holding hearings on the proposed legislation. Private citizens, victims organizations, and other special interest groups may appear and testify at these hearings. The following are four key committees with which victim advocates must be familiar:

Rules Committee: *Rules committees* act as housekeepers or gatekeepers and control the assignment of bills to other committees. A rules committee will normally assign bills to certain standing committees. It is an extremely powerful and important group.

Appropriations Committee: An *appropriations committee* may be known by a variety of names including "ways and means committee" or simply "finance committee." Any bill requiring the expenditure of state funds will normally require a vote by this committee.

Standing Committee: *Standing committees* (also known as "policy committees") as discussed consist of a group of legislators who hear testimony from interested parties. Each standing committee is responsible for a specific policy area such as criminal justice, education, or health and welfare. This committee may either pass the bill or kill it.

Select Committee: A *select committee* functions much like a standing committee except that it reports or makes recommendations to a standing committee. Sometimes bills are so complex that they need specialized hearing and select committees to serve this purpose. The select committee may propose passage of the legislation, offer amendments to the bill, or recommend that it be defeated.

Once a bill reaches a committee, victims and their advocates may testify on behalf of their bill. This is one of the most exciting aspects of the U.S. legislative process and some would consider it to be democracy in action. It is important to coordinate the efforts of everyone who will be testifying in support of the bill. This allows for a united front to be presented to the committee members.

Individual citizens, including victims, have a right to testify at committee hearings. Many law enforcement professionals believe that the dramatic testimony from a stalking victim in front of a standing committee was a critical ingredient in the passage of the California's stalking law, which was the first one of its kind in the nation.[4] Additionally, a representative from a state or local victims organization, or coalition, should offer testimony. Whoever is selected to make the presentation should be eloquent, capable of quick thinking, and knowledgeable not only about the pending bill but also about victims' rights legislation in general.

Victim advocates should always check with the bill's sponsor prior to testifying. The author may want certain points emphasized or explained in more detail.

The sponsor may want other committee members contacted before the hearing. In many jurisdictions, decisions regarding particular bills are made before the actual hearing.

The testimony should be clear and succinct. A rambling, disjointed, or boring presentation can go a long way toward killing the bill in committee. Testimony should never be read by those who are making their presentations. It should simply be discussed with the committee in a conversational tone as one would address another person. The victim service provider should know the names and districts of each committee member, and if asked a question should try to respond to that member by name and explain how the bill affects that member's district. Victims who testify should not focus on their victimization, rather they should emphasize their concern as a victim who is representing all other similarly situated actual or potential victims.

The victim advocate should write the presentation and give a copy to each member of the committee. The written document should be clear, concise, and error-free. It should be double-spaced with large (inch and one-half inch) margins. The advocate's name, the committee's name, bill number, and date should be on the upper corner of each page.

None of these suggestions ensure passage of a bill. The legislative process is complex, confusing, and at times defies logic. Because of the number of special interests that compete for a legislator's time, victim advocates must understand the principles involved in lobbying. The next section will address this highly controversial activity.

Advocacy

Advocating for victims in the legislative arena can take many forms. One of the most common forms of advocacy is lobbying. The purpose of *lobbying* is to inform, educate, and persuade elected officials to support certain legislative goals. Lobbyists can be individuals, local groups, national corporations, or coalitions of any of these entities.

Today, political action committees, the high cost of running for reelection, high-powered lobbyists, and long-term planning have turned lobbying into a professional business. There are a number of firms located in most state capitals and in Washington, D.C., whose sole income is derived from lobbying elected officials. In some of these firms, former elected officials now represent business interests and are not reluctant to call in favors rendered during their tenure in office. However, not all lobbying involves the trading of favors or the purchasing of lunches. There are many organizations and individuals that strive to influence by use of information only. These groups or persons rely on their expertise and their reputation to carry the day with elected officials.

The Internal Revenue Service monitors nonprofit organizations to ensure that they comply with all legal requirements. An effective program should carefully observe any restraints imposed by the Internal Revenue Service regarding activities by nonprofit organizations. If lobbying becomes a substantial part of the organization's activities, it stands the chance of losing its nonprofit status.

Victim advocacy is more effective if a large number of paid or volunteer individuals work to support the legislative efforts. The following is a short list of activities that can be delegated to citizens who support this work:

Selection of a Bill Manager.   The bill manager is a person who tracks the bill and coordinates all the activities involved in presenting testimony at hearings. This person will be able to answer any questions regarding the status of the bill.

Coordinator of Support Letters.   This coordinator gathers supporters from both organizations and individuals and assists them in writing letters of support for the legislation to the appropriate elected official. These letters should be more than simple form postcards. They should indicate the organization and person and why they are supporting the bill.

Coordinator of Telephone Calls.   The coordinator of phone calls can be the same person who is coordinating support letters because the purpose is the same. Persons should call the elected officials and inform them of their name, organization, and the fact that they are supporting the bill. They will not talk directly to the legislator, but the fact that they called will be noted by the staff member handling the bill.

Press Liaison.   The press liaison is in charge of drafting press releases regarding the proposed bill and attempts to get media coverage of its progress and its impact on the field. Sometimes calling a press conference with the sponsor of the bill, victims, their organizations, and other community leaders will create an impact on undecided legislators.

It is obvious that there are no clear guidelines in the area of lobbying. A small organization may combine the above mentioned functions into one volunteer position, whereas a national organization may have paid staffers working on each activity. It is important to remember the long-range goal of serving victims and not get discouraged at defeats.

Public Speaking[5]

Most victim service providers will be called on sometime in their careers to make presentations to the general public. This may be an informal gathering of citizens at a Neighborhood Watch meeting or a formal presentation to the city council. However, many people suffer from stage fright when speaking to groups. As with any other skill, practice makes perfect. This is not to say all of us will become dynamic and forceful speakers. Some people are better than others at appearing and communicating in public. However, by mastering certain basic and simple procedures, any victim service provider can make a creditable presentation.

Preparing for the Speech

Some of the most outgoing professionals become quivering masses of insecurity at the thought of facing a group of citizens and explaining the victim's perspective on crime. Although we may talk to other people all the time, we do so on an individual basis, not in front of a collective body. Even though public speaking can be viewed as simply talking to more than one person, the rules of communication change when we move into a group setting. Feedback may be delayed or never received or there may be physical barriers such as a nonworking microphone that prevent those in the back of the room from hearing adequately. Add to this the typical worry of making a mistake or looking unprofessional and many people dread speaking in public.

Drafting the Speech

Having to stand and present a speech to a room full of people can be an intimidating experience, and writing a speech can be an agonizing task for many victim service providers. However, a speech should be prepared differently than a term paper or an agency position paper. The following are some simple rules for speech writing:

1. *Prepare an outline of the topics to be discussed.* Start with the main objective or theme. The first thing to write is what the audience should be motivated to do as result of the speech. Keep this objective in mind while writing the rest of the speech.
2. *Draft an outline of the main points of discussion.* There should only be three or four major items on the list. If the list looks like a laundry list, consider combining some items or reconsider the desired goals of the speech.
3. *Revise the outline several times.* Then begin to add additional information to the main points. Think about each new piece of information. Does it explain the main point?
4. *Remember, we write differently than we speak.* Practice the speech by speaking it out loud. Based upon several rehearsals, the presentation may require revision.
5. *Prepare an outline and deliver the speech based on the outline.* Know the subject matter well enough beforehand to be able to refer only to the outline instead of the typewritten speech. The delivery will be more natural.
6. *When writing a speech, start at the middle or end.* The most difficult part of a speech is the opening. This should be done last.

Once the speech is written, the next step is delivery. The following section will briefly examine some simple principles that can make public presentations more professional for victim providers.

Some Do's and Don'ts of Public Speaking

There are as many rules to effective public speaking as there are dynamic speakers.[6] No one approach will work for all persons. This is not a text on public speaking, nor is it the intent of the author to include a great deal of detail on the various techniques of effective speaking. However, there are several simple methods that are easily mastered that will allow most professionals to make a clear and meaningful presentation. The following are some rules that will assist you, as a victim service provider, in making oral presentations.

1. *Understand the topic of the speech.* What does the group expect to hear? If they want to be informed about the concept of restitution, do not deliver a speech regarding sentencing and victim impact statements.
2. *Know the audience and direct the speech to their interests and knowledge level.* Nothing is more boring than a speech full of technical jargon that the audience does not understand. Talk on their level and the reward will be an interested audience.
3. *Humor is excellent, but it can backfire.* If you are comfortable, humor can break the ice and relax the audience for the speech. However, a long, drawn out joke that does not go over with the audience leaves a bad taste with everyone.
4. *Always be on time and dress appropriately.* Common courtesy requires that you do not keep the audience waiting for your arrival. Know the exact starting time and show up a few minutes early.
5. *Do not read the speech verbatim.* We have all sat through public speeches where the speaker droned on and on reading from prepared notes.
6. *Understand how long the speech is to last and stay within that time limit.* Even if the audience is cooperative, do not prolong the speech. Remember, the group may have other business, and if you are that good, they will ask you to return.
7. *When possible, use visual aids to assist in making your points.* Nothing makes points as well as visual aids. Businesses have known this for years. We in the public sector should take the hint and use visual aids when possible.
8. *Rehearse as often as possible.* Rehearse, rehearse, rehearse. Especially during the beginning of your public speaking career.
9. *Ask for honest feedback from the person that requested the speech.* Don't simply say, "How was I?" This will lead to the standard response, "You were great." Politely press the person to offer comments on ways to make the presentation better the next time. It's amazing that, once encouraged to give feedback, many people will provide helpful suggestions on how to make a presentation more effective.

Public speaking is really more of an art than a science, but by following these rules any victim advocate can become a better public speaker. Addressing a group of citizens or elected officials requires certain techniques. These techniques can only become more refined with practice. With the passage of time and more frequent speaking experience, you may find yourself actually enjoying this aspect of victim advocacy.

Fundraising

Introduction

In this age of tightening governmental budgets, professionals in the area of victim services must be knowledgeable regarding fundraising techniques and opportunities. Some victim assistance programs are fortunate to receive a steady supply of funds that allows them to properly administer their programs. However, most victim service organizations must always be on the lookout for additional funding sources. Fundraising is more an art than a science, but any professional who works with victims should have a basic understanding of how the process works, and its pitfalls.

Many victim-related programs were originally funded by the Law Enforcement Assistance Administration. From 1974 until 1981, Congress authorized spending of funds on a variety of law enforcement–related activities. Victim assistance was included under this definition and as a result, many prosecutors' offices established such programs. In 1981, Congress ended funding for these activities and many victim assistance programs were subsequently downsized or abolished. From 1981 until 1984, victim assistance programs had to rely on other sources of funding. In 1982, President Reagan's Task Force on Victims of Crimes made a series of recommendations addressing a variety of crime victim issues. One recommendation was the passage of a federal law addressing the plight of crime victims. In 1984, Congress passed the Victims of Crime Act (VOCA) which established a federal Crime Victims Fund. This fund received federal criminal fines, penalty assessments, and forfeited bail which is used to fund local victim assistance programs and state compensation programs. The original fund was capped at $100 million, but in 1992 the cap was removed. VOCA helps pass these funds to each state which in turn provides financial assistance to a number of victim programs. As a condition of receiving these funds, each state is required to certify that it is giving priority in funding to local programs that are assisting victims of spousal abuse, sexual assault, or child abuse.

Types of Fundraisers

Although VOCA funds may provide assistance to some organizations, there are a number of other victims' groups that do not receive VOCA funding. These groups must look elsewhere for funding. There are a number of methods used to raise funds for local victims' programs. The most common fundraising activities include government and private grants, and local fundraising events.

Grants are cash donations, by either the federal or state government, or private foundations, for specific projects. During the period of 1986 through 1991, 410 foundations gave grants totaling $150.9 million to criminal justice projects. Unfortunately, less than 2 percent of all foundation grants are for criminal justice projects including victim-related programs. Taken as a whole, the nation's foundations have not gotten the word that the public considers crime a major issue.[7]

Federal and state grants are normally a one-time source of funding for very specific projects. However, these governmental grants have decreased dramatically since the late 1970s.

The federal government continues to award grants each year. Some of the more common grants are awarded for research, others study "best practices" in the field, and still others provide funding to train professionals that serve in the field. A number of different governmental agencies and departments award grants. These grants vary from year to year and from agency to agency. The first step in obtaining a grant is to find out which state or federal department is awarding them. The local library is an excellent place to start the search for government funds. Victim service providers should not overlook their local elected officials. Many state and congressional staff persons have information regarding the availability of government grants. Finally, victim service providers should make contact with the local university. Many universities have offices that specialize in obtaining grants and some offer extension classes to the public on how to write a grant proposal. These universities are not only a source of information, but they also may lead to contacts which will result in joint grant writing endeavors involving faculty members and victim service providers.

Grants are handed out selectively. Most grants are very competitive and therefore victim service providers should be prepared for a series of rejections when they first attempt to obtain grants. Grant writing is a time-consuming and very technical process.

In the event that there are insufficient funds available in state or federal government for a specific program, victim service providers should consider private corporation or foundation grants. These funding opportunities are even more limited than federal grants, but they should not be overlooked. The same sources that provided information regarding federal grants can be contacted about private grants or awards.

There are disadvantages to government or private grants or awards. A victim service provider should not automatically apply for every grant that is available. Often grants contain hidden costs. They may require local objectives to be reevaluated and/or reprioritized, or impose burdensome paperwork. Some grants require matching funds that take money from other programs, and some grants build in expectations for ongoing future activities. All grants should be evaluated for any strings that are attached as well as the long-term commitments for the continued funding of the project. If possible, grants should be used for individual, one-time projects, rather than ongoing projects. Finally, those grants that require an extraordinary amount of funds in the form of matching dollars should be critically evaluated.

The final method to obtain funding involves local fundraising events. These events can be as varied as the mind of the organizer. They are not guaranteed to turn a profit and many times they take a great deal of volunteer and staff time to organize and execute. Typical fundraisers include dinners, banquets, auctions, house or garden tours, and sporting events. If the first fundraiser is a success, organizers should consider making it an annual event. Additionally, victim service providers should always consider asking local businesses to cosponsor these events. Their support may include monetary donations and many times will add visibility to the event.

Victim service providers must be knowledgeable regarding the various types of fundraising. With our constantly changing economic situation, no one source of funding is ever 100 percent safe. Victim service providers should consider having a variety of funding mechanisms available to them. This will allow them to more effectively service their clients.

Summary

The media are not an enemy to be attacked or avoided. Certain issues require that victims be involved with the media. These might include an appeal to a kidnapper to release a victim, an assistance call to search areas where a child was last seen, or a statement to stir up public opinion regarding the release of an offender back into the community. The efficient victim service provider will become familiar with the different types of media and their specific needs.

All victim service providers need to understand the legislative process, its complexities, and its strengths and weaknesses to understand the process by which the laws that affect victims are drafted, amended, and passed.

Public speaking like any other skill requires practice and the knowledge that speeches are most effective when tailored to the different types of audiences. An effective victim service provider can enhance a program by knowing how to present that information to members of the community.

Fundraising is a necessary activity of most victim programs. Various types of funds are available to these programs; however, the competition for this money is fierce. Oftentimes the best way to become proficient in this area is to work with people that already have established a successful track record of raising money. By watching and learning their techniques, victim providers can adapt those techniques to their individual programs.

Key Terms

Sidebar story is usually an article that is placed in a column next to the main article.

Rules committees act as housekeepers or gatekeepers and control the assignment of bills to other committees.

Appropriations committee may be known by a variety of names including "ways and means committee" or simply "finance committee."

Standing committees (also known as "policy committees") consist of a group of legislators who hear testimony from interested parties. Each standing committee is responsible for a specific policy area such as criminal justice, education, or health and welfare.

Select committees function much like standing committees except that they report or make recommendations to a standing committee.

Lobbying is to inform, educate, and persuade elected officials to support certain legislative goals.

Grants are cash donations, by either the federal or state government or private foundations, for specific projects.

Discussion Questions

1. Is there any occasion that you can think of when a victim service provider should become a "source" for a news reporter?

2. What is the most important hearing in the legislative process?

3. Should victim advocates compromise on amendments to their bills? What if failure to compromise means that the bill will be killed in a committee?

4. What is the most difficult aspect of public speaking?

5. What makes one speaker more dynamic than another? List specific characteristics that you believe are essential to effective public speaking.

6. How would you secure a steady form of money for a victims' program?

Suggested Readings

H. Wallace, C. Robinson & C. Steckler, *Written and Interpersonal Communication Methods for Law Enforcement*, (Prentice Hall, N.Y.) 1997.

B. Wurman, *Information Anxiety*, (Bantam Books, New York) 1990.

Endnotes

1. Some of this mistrust is based on law enforcement's perception of how the media report crime, see, Steven M. Chermak, "Body Count News: How Crime Is Presented in the News Media," 11/4 *Justice Quarterly*, 561 (December 1994).

2. See Craig A. Sullivan, "Police Public Relations," *Law and Order*, 94 (October 1993), for a discussion of how one agency interacts with the media.

3. The material in this section and the diagram is based on the author's discussions with leaders of several victims' rights organizations that monitor legislation in California. The actual format and process may differ slightly in other jurisdictions.

4. Presentation by Lt. John Lane, LAPD Threat Management Unit, (Threat Assessment Conference, Los Angeles, Calif.) July 1995.

5. This section has been adapted from Wallace, Robinson & Steckler, *Written and Interpersonal Communication Methods for Law Enforcement*, (Prentice Hall, New York) 1997.

6. For an excellent discussion of public speaking, see Steven N. Bowman, "The Practical Local Government Manager," *Public Administration*, 22–23 (December 1991).

7. See Ordway P. Burden, "Big-Game Hunting: Foundations' CJ Bucks Are a Rare Quarry," *Law Enforcement News*, 9 (April 30, 1991).

7

HOMICIDE VICTIMS

Chapter Outline

Introduction
   Nature and Extent of the Problem
   Theories, Types, and Characteristics of Homicide
   Drinking, Driving, and Homicide

Responding to Special Needs
   Family Relationships
   Mental and Emotional Responses
   Notification

Summary

Key Terms

Discussion Questions

Suggested Readings

Learning Objectives

After reading this chapter, you should be able to:

- Know who are the survivors of homicide victims
- Describe the extent of homicide in the United States
- Describe the typical homicide victim
- Understand the different types of homicides
- Understand the dynamics involved in the death of a family member

- Explain the mental and emotional consequences suffered by homicide survivors
- Understand how death notification adds to the trauma suffered by homicide victims

Introduction

Criminal acts take many forms and shapes. However, one particular crime has a drastic and long-lasting impact on society. Homicide affects not only the immediate victim whose life is cut short, but it has a lifelong impact on the victim's family and friends. Tens of thousands of survivors of homicide victims suffer shock, grief, and an overwhelming sense of helplessness at the loss of a loved one, friend, or acquaintance. *Survivors of homicide victims* are those individuals who had special ties of kinship with the person murdered, and who were, thereafter, victimized not only by the loss of someone close to them but also by the horrific circumstances of that untimely death.[1] Because of the special nature of homicide, it is included as a separate chapter in this text.

Nature and Extent of the Problem

In its annual report, *Crime in the United States, 1995,* the FBI reported 21,597 murders and nonnegligent manslaughters in the United States.[2] The FBI defines *murder* as the willful (nonnegligent) killing of one human being by another. This definition does not include deaths caused by negligence, suicide, or accident, nor does it include justifiable homicides or attempted homicides.

The rate or incidence of murder varies by region in the United States. The South account for 42 percent of all homicides. The Western States reported 24 percent. The Midwest has a homicide rate of 20 percent and the Northeast with 15 percent of all homicides.

The typical homicide victim was a black male over the age of eighteen. The FBI survey indicated that 77 percent of the victims were males and 88 percent were persons eighteen years of age or older. On the average, 49 of every 100 victims were black, 48 were white, and the remainder were persons of other races. Forty-five percent of the murder victims were related to (11 percent) or acquainted with (34 percent) their assailants. A survey of murder cases that occurred in 1988 was recently reevaluated to determine the nature and extent of spousal homicide.[3] This survey indicates that victims were killed by someone they knew 80 percent of the time.

One study indicated that an estimated 6.7 million adult Americans had lost a family member, other relative, or close friend to criminal homicide. Of this number, 2.8 million had lost an immediate family member to homicide.[4] A 1988 survey found that 16 percent of murder victims in large urban counties were members of the defendant's family.[5]

Firearms were used in seven of ten murders committed in the United States. The use of firearms in crimes has recently received renewed interest with the Department of Justice's decision to publish a series on firearms and crime.[6] Eighty-two percent of all victims of firearm homicides were killed with a handgun. Of these firearm homicide victims, 29 percent were killed because of an argument, 21 percent were killed during the commission of another crime, and 6 percent died as a result of a juvenile gang killing.[7]

The clearance rate for murder continued to be higher than any other crime index offense. Eighty percent of murders in rural counties and 65 percent of those in suburban counties and cities were cleared. Of the city population groups, those with populations under 10,000 reported the most successful clearance rate.

Theories, Types, and Characteristics of Homicide

As indicated in Chapter 1, Wolfgang conducted the first major study of victim precipitation.[8] He focused on homicides and studied both the victim and the offender as separate entities and as "mutual participants in the homicide."[9] Wolfgang found that 26 percent of all homicides studied in Philadelphia involved situations in which the victim was the first to use force during the acts leading to the homicide.[10]

Wolfgang identified several factors that he associated with victim participation in homicides: (1) the victim and perpetrator usually had some sort of prior relationship—spouse, family members, or close acquaintances; (2) the events leading up to the homicide started as a small disagreement that escalated into a burst of anger that resulted in a killing; and (3) alcohol was used or consumed by many of the victims prior to the incident.[11]

FOCUS: Murderers

Do You Know a Killer When You See One?

Wouldn't life be simpler and much safer if all murderers resembled large, ugly, and deformed Neanderthals? Unfortunately, this is not the case even though our fears may conjure up such images. In reality a murderer may be any good-looking, all-American male standing on a college campus parking lot with a cast on his arm asking young co-eds if they could help him put his bike up on his car's bike rack. This is how Ted Bundy, convicted of three murders and implicated in as many as thirty more acted in order to lure some of his victims.

Although no specific physical types can be classified as murderers, statistical facts drawn from arrest records may shed some light on the average characteristics of those who kill.

Age . . . . 30 years
Sex . . . . 88% male
                                                  12% female
Race . . . . 50% white
                                                  48% black
On drugs or alcohol . . . . 30+%

Source: U.S. Department of Justice, BJS, *Report to the Nation on Crime and Justice*, 2nd ed. (Washington, D.C., U.S. Government Printing Office) 1988.

Spousal homicide involves the killing of one's legally married partner. This definition does not require that the parties be cohabitating at the time of the killing; however, it does preclude same-sex living arrangements or situations. This is not to diminish the seriousness of those killings that occur in a homosexual relationship, rather it is an acknowledgment that as discussed in Chapter 6, there is very little information or statistics dealing with this type of violence.

Segall and Wilson conducted an eight-year study involving spousal homicides which established certain characteristics associated with these types of cases.[12] Most of the homicides in this study occurred in major urban locations and involved single-victim–offender killings. Spousal homicide victims tended to be older than other homicide victims. Spousal homicide victims were typically female in contrast to male victims in most other homicides.

In a classic study of family violence, David Finkelhor established characteristics that can lead to spousal homicide.[13] According to Finkelhor, these characteristics which are present in family violence situations can also lead to homicide. These factors include power differentials between the parties, perceived powerlessness on the part of the abuser, and ambiguity which exists regarding acceptable discipline and punishment.

One type of homicide that is most difficult to understand is *parricide*, which is defined as the killing of one's parents. The trials of the Menendez brothers brought the specter of children killing their parents into our living rooms via television. Recent statistics indicate that 1.97 percent of all murder victims in the United States were killed by their children.[14] Parricide usually does not occur as a result of a single episode, rather it is a manifestation of a culmination of unresolved conflicts.

Heide researched adolescents who killed their parents and found certain characteristics to be present in these events.[15] There was a history of family violence, the adolescent's attempt to get help or escape from the situation failed, the children experienced isolation, and the family situation became increasing desperate immediately prior to the killings. The youths felt helpless in coping with their stressful situations and ultimately experienced a loss of control. Most of the murderers had no prior criminal history; however, they did have easy access to guns. Recognizing and intervening in family violence situations may prevent parricide, a particularly devastating form of murder.

Considered particularly violent are the mass murderers, and until the relatively recent emergence and research into the serial killers, they were considered society's most dangerous of predators. *Mass murderers* are those who kill several people at one time in the same location. One of the most famous mass murderers is James O. Huberty who is believed to have committed the worst one-day massacre in the United States. Huberty was an unemployed security guard who told friends that he would kill others if he could not find a job and support his family. On July 18, 1984, he walked into a McDonald's restaurant in San Ysidro, California, and opened fire, killing twenty-one persons and wounding another twenty. In 1989, a deranged welder by the name of Patrick Edward Purdy entered a Stockton, California, school yard armed with an AK-47 assault rifle and began a killing rampage that ended with five dead children and thirty other wounded victims. The Stockton School Yard Massacre is another chilling example of mass murder.

A variation on the mass murderer is the spree murderer. A *spree killer* kills several persons at two or more locations with very little or any time break between the killings. Some experts would call the former Eagle Scout leader and college honor student Charles Whitman a spree killer. In 1966, Whitman murdered his wife and mother, and then armed with a variety of weapons and ammunition, climbed to the top of a tower at the University of Texas. Whitman continued his killing spree and as a result sixteen persons died and another thirty were wounded before the police shot and killed him. He subsequently became known as the Texas Tower Killer.

One of the most deadly and fearsome murderers is the serial killer. With the chilling film *The Silence of the Lambs,* our collective consciousness was raised to acknowledge that killers similar to Hannibal the Cannibal exist and indeed, may have sat next to us on a bus, train, or plane. The serial killer is the night stalker of murders. Although debate continues over a comprehensive definition, most authorities agree that a *serial murderer* is one who kills several persons over a period of time which can range from weeks to years.[16]

One of the best known and notorious of serial murderers is Jack the Ripper who killed several women in London over a period of time during the 1800s. He was never caught and these crimes were never solved, although speculation continues as to his identity and theories and articles are still written about his grievous acts. Other well-known serial murderers are the Green River Killer who is believed to have killed over fifty female hitchhikers, transients, and prostitutes near the Seattle area; the "Witch," Sarah Aldrete, who sacrificed victims to provide an aura of protection for members of a Mexican drug smuggling ring; Dorothea Puente who poisoned renters at her boardinghouse and then cashed their social security checks, and the infamous Hillside Strangler in Los Angeles.

In an effort to understand crime and criminals, researchers create typologies. These are classifications based on certain characteristics. By studying these characteristics, scholars, researchers, law enforcement officials, and others hope to understand why particular individuals commit certain types of crimes. Several noteworthy typologies of serial murders have been developed. Holmes and DeBurger identified four types of serial killers:[17]

Visionary type: These type of serial killers murder in response to commands or directions from a voice or vision. Many of these killers are suffering from some form of psychosis.

Mission-oriented type: These serial killers believe their mission or goal in life is to rid society of certain types of people such as prostitutes.

Hedonistic type: These serial killers are perhaps the most chilling of the lot in that they seek thrills during the murder. Many of these killers become sexually involved with their victims either prior to or after killing them. They may also engage in sexual mutilation of their victims.

Power/control-oriented type: These serial killers seek power over their victims. They report enjoyment from watching their victims plead, beg and cower before them.

Eric Hickey has conducted several studies on serial killers and is considered a nationally recognized expert in this area. In an early work, he classified serial killers into three distinct groups based on mobility:[18]

Traveling serial killers: These serial killers often travel to different locations seeking victims to kill.

Local serial killers: This type of serial killer stays in one area and conducts crimes in this location.

Serial killers who never leave their home or place of employment: These serial killers lure their victims into their residence or place of employment and the killing takes place within these areas.

The study of serial killers continues today and more typologies are certain to emerge as knowledge of the psychology of these killers and profiling techniques become more sophisticated. Those professionals who study this type of behavior admit that there is both a repulsion and attraction inherent in their research; however, the suffering of the survivors of these types of homicides must not be allowed to recede into the background.

Although these crimes are committed by only a marginal percentage of society, the number of their victims is not insignificant. Hickey pointed out that between 1975 and 1988 there were thirty-four female and sixty-nine male serial killers who were responsible for a minimum of 1483 deaths and a maximum of 2161 deaths![19] The toll in human tragedy and the resulting trauma visited on the survivors requires extraordinary skill and compassion on the part of today's victim service providers.

Drinking, Driving, and Homicide

Many vehicular homicides happen as a result of a person drinking and then getting behind the wheel of a car. This behavior used to be called "drunk driving," and although most people still use this term as a shorthand way of describing a behavior, it is not considered a legal term. A person does not have to be drunk to be convicted under most "driving under the influence" laws. These laws simply require that the driver's ability to operate a motor vehicle be impaired. In fact, many statutes define "under the influence" in a variety of ways. One example states that the defendant is under the influence if it can be proved that the alcohol, or alcohol and drugs, have affected the nervous system, brain, or muscles to the degree so as to impair, to an appreciable degree, the ability to operate a motor

---

FOCUS: Mothers Against Drunk Driving

In November 1979, five-month-old Laura Lamb was riding in a carseat next to her mother as they drove to the store. They were hit head-on by a drunk driver going in excess of 120 miles per hour. The perpetrator had no driver's license, no insurance, and thirty-seven previous traffic violations including three prior drunk driving arrests. Laura became one of America's youngest quadriplegics.

In May 1980, thirteen-year-old Cari Lightner was walking to a church carnival with her friend when she was hit and killed by a man who had been out of jail for only two days for another hit-and-run drunk driving crash.

As a result of these incidents in 1980 Mothers Against Drunk Driving (MADD) was formed. Since then thousands of volunteers and other victims have joined this organization in its fight against death on the highway. MADD has become one of the most notable victim organizations in the nation with chapters in every state.

---

vehicle in a manner like that of an ordinary, prudent, and cautious person in full possession of his faculties using reasonable care and under like circumstances.

In 1983, in an effort to address drinking and driving, some states began raising the minimum drinking age to twenty-one. By 1989, all states had twenty-one as the minimum age that a person could drink. Additionally, a majority of the states adopted laws that require administrative sanctions for all persons, who when asked, refuse to take a test measuring the presence and concentration of alcohol. Many of these states now permit the law enforcement officer on the scene to immediately confiscate the driver's license of a person arrested for driving under the influence (DUI) who refuse such tests.[20]

Unfortunately, despite increased penalties at the state and federal level, the death on our roadways continues. An estimated 16,884 persons died in alcohol-related traffic crashes in 1994. This is an average of one victim every thirty-two minutes. These deaths constituted 40 percent of the 40,676 total traffic fatalities that occurred in 1994.[21] As staggering as these figures are, they represent a decrease in the total number of alcohol-related deaths in the last decade. In 1980, there were approximately 28,000 alcohol-related fatalities, by 1994, that number had been reduced to 16,884.[22]

"Blood alcohol level" is a legal and medical term that is expressed in milligrams of alcohol per milliliters of blood. This level has been translated into the ability or fitness to operate a motor vehicle based on several broad categories, or zones of impairment. Tables 7.1 and 7.2 indicate the blood alcohol level of an individual who has consumed an alcoholic beverage. Table 7.1 is based on weight and amount of alcohol consumed, Table 7.2 indicates the effects on the individual based upon the blood alcohol level.

Some states have enacted presumptions that shift the burden of proving this element. If the driver of the vehicle has tested for a certain blood alcohol level and it can be shown that this level existed during the operation of the vehicle, the offender must prove he was not under the influence. This level varies from state

TABLE 7.1   Blood Alcohol Level and Impairment

Two Drinks	Four Drinks			Six Drinks			Eight Drinks			Ten Drinks		
Hours Spent Drinking	**Body Weight**			**Body Weight**			**Body Weight**			**Body Weight**		
	120	150	180	120	150	180	120	150	180	120	150	180
1 hour	0.05	0.04	0.03	0.11	0.09	0.07	0.16	0.13	0.11	0.21	0.17	0.14
2 hours	0.02	0.01	—	0.08	0.05	0.04	0.14	0.10	0.08	0.20	0.15	0.12
3 hours	—	—	—	0.06	0.04	0.02	0.12	0.08	0.06	0.18	0.13	0.10
4 hours	—	—	—	0.05	0.02	0.01	0.11	0.07	0.04	0.17	0.12	0.09

TABLE 7.2   Blood Alcohol Level and Behavioral Effects

Present Blood Alcohol Level	Behavioral Effects
0.02	Pleasant feelings including a sense of warmth and well-being
0.04	Relaxed, energetic, and happy; flushed skin and slight impairment of motor skills
0.06	Light headed, giddiness, lowered inhibitions, impairment of judgment
0.08	Definite muscle coordination impairment, reaction time slowed, heavy pulse and slow breathing, numbness in checks, lips, and extremities may occur
0.10	Clear deterioration of coordination and reaction time, staggering and slurring of speech, judgment and memory further affected
0.20	Increased depression of motor and sensory skills, pronounced slurred speech, double vision, difficulty in standing and walking
0.30	Stuporous and confused, individuals may lose consciousness
0.40	Unconscious, skin is sweaty and clammy, circulation and respiration is depressed
0.50	Near death or dead

to state, but many statutes establish the range with the 0.08 to 0.10 blood alcohol level as a presumptive indication that the defendant was under the influence of alcohol and/or drugs at the time of the operation of the motor vehicle.

Homicide in any form has a devastating effect. Family members, friends, and others within the community are left in a state of shock as a result. The next section will briefly examine the impact of homicide on the survivors.

Responding to Special Needs

Family Relationships

Grief, sorrow, and emotional pain are the hallmarks of suffering experienced by the homicide victim's surviving relatives, friends, and acquaintances. The level of grief that is experienced can generally be measured by the intensity of the relationship that existed between the survivor and the victim before death. The following section will briefly examine several relationships within a family unit and how those relationships are affected by the homicide of one of its members.

The murder a child is one of the least expected incidents in life.[23] In the normal order of things, parents expect to die before their children. Parents serve as protectors, healers, and givers of life. These duties or obligations can, in turn, promote a sense of guilt in the parents of a murdered child, even if the child was an adult when the murder occurred.

This is, in part, due to the amount of time parents invest in planning for their child's future. They want their child to accomplish more and hopefully transcend their own circumstances. Many parents link their own immortality to their child, hoping and believing that they themselves will continue to live on in some form, even after their own death. Therefore, the grief suffered over the loss of a child is increased by the perception of the loss of the parents' own immortality.

Today many families are intermixed, or "blended," with stepparents and stepchildren as a result of second or even third marriages. Because many stepparents love their stepchildren as much as their own natural children, they may also suffer guilt at the loss of the child and their grief should not be ignored by victim service providers.

Also, parents must deal not only with their own sorrow or grief, but at the same time attempt to comfort any other siblings and/or relatives who are feeling the pain of loss. Some parents may idealize the deceased child, bestowing on the victim qualities that are longed for rather than real, thereby magnifying the grief.

The murder of a spouse will affect the surviving husband or wife in a variety of ways. The reaction to the death of a spouse will depend on the nature and quality of the relationship prior to the homicide. If there was discord, anger, or bitterness in the marriage, the survivor may feel intense guilt at not trying harder to make the relationship better while the deceased was alive. If the relationship was a loving, close, supportive one, the loss may be overwhelming to the survivor.

The age of the surviving spouse also plays a critical role in the grief process. In some instances older survivors do not recover as quickly and as easily as their younger counterparts. They may be displaced from their home either because they can no longer care for themselves alone, or because their financial situation has changed as the result of the loss of one income or pension. The surviving spouse, no matter what age, may also experience feelings of anger and bitterness at being left with responsibilities he or she now has to face alone. These responsibilities may include raising children as a single parent, attempting to make ends meet financially, or caring for relatives of the deceased spouse.

The murder of a parent may leave young children worrying about their own life and stability.[24] They may see the death as a form of desertion by the parent. They may also blame the parent and question why the parent didn't fight back. Children will certainly feel an overwhelming sense of loss and abandonment that can affect them for the rest of their lives. Older children may feel guilt because they did not pay enough attention to their parent prior to the murder, or they may blame themselves if the parent–child relationship was strained prior to death.

Murder of a sibling may leave the other brothers and sisters neglected by the professional caregivers. Many agencies concentrate on assisting the parents of murdered children and occasionally overlook the fact that the other children are suffering as a result of the loss of a cherished brother or sister. Siblings may also experience extreme guilt that they are left alive and their brother or sister is dead. They may experience anger at the parents' preoccupation with the dead sibling. They may feel vulnerable and experience anxiety at being left alone. They may wonder if they also will be murdered.

If the siblings are young, this may be their first encounter with death and they may not understand why their brother or sister will not be coming home. Additionally, the victim may also have been the surviving siblings' best friend, playmate, and confidant. This loss can leave them feeling isolated and alone and increase their sense of sorrow and grief.

Although many families share emotional responses to the death of a family member and appear to be mutually supportive of one another, victim service providers must be aware of the special needs of each one of them and respond accordingly. The loss of a loved one is traumatic and long-lasting. In the event that the perpetrator was a family member, the grief and suffering endured by the survivors can be immeasurable.

Mental and Emotional Responses

Chapter 5 has already examined the consequences of victimization; however, homicide by its very nature is a unique type of crime that presents special needs and responses. Parents of Murdered Children, Inc. has examined a number of mental and emotional problem areas for survivors of homicide.[25]

There are *unexpected financial consequences*. Funeral, medical expenses, and psychiatric care for family members are all unanticipated expenses. These are serious consequences that contribute to the continuing distress that survivors of homicide suffer.

As discussed in previous chapters, *the criminal justice system* adds to the stress suffered by survivors of homicide. These survivors must learn to cope with body bags, crime scene pictures, autopsies, and other stressors inherent in a homicide trial. One of the most comforting acts a victim service provider can do in assisting the survivor of a homicide is to obtain information from the participants within the criminal justice system regarding the facts surrounding the killing.

Survivors of homicide often report that there is *an impact on their ability to function at their job or work*. Motivation may be altered, and what was considered important at work before the homicide is no longer viewed as critical. Some survivors may experience emotional outbreaks of crying or shouting during work, and having to apologize for these outbreaks at a later time contributes to their stress. Other survivors use work as an excuse or an escape to avoid working through their grief.

It is not uncommon for marriages to break up when a child of that marriage is murdered. Each partner grieves and may blame the other for the loss. They may also find it painful to be with their partner because of the memories evoked by that person. Some parents are unable to help each other, because their grief is so terrible that they cannot help themselves.

Children within the family of survivors of homicide also are affected by the killing. Children who actually witness the murder suffer a special mental and emotional upheaval, and this will be discussed in more detail later in this section. However, children who don't witness the murder are also impacted. If the murdered victim was a child, the other children in the family may be ignored by the parents as they attempt to deal with their own grief. The children will sense the parents' suffering and simply withdraw into themselves. Additionally, children suffer the same psychological reactions as other survivors of homicide.

Many survivors report that their *religious faith has been weakened* as a result of homicide. Some will express anger and frustration or question their deity regarding the reason for the death of their loved one. Others attempt to seek answers from unorthodox sources such as spiritual advisors and those that claim to talk to the dead.

Homicide survivors are often subjected to the *scrutiny of an insensitive press.* The quest for news may cause members of the media to televise a survivor's anguish on the evening news. Survivors may be subjected to views of the crime scene or other painful memories during the homicide trial as the press attempts to re-create the killing for its audience.

Finally, survivors of homicide may be *revictimized by professionals within the criminal justice system.* Many survivors report that some of these professionals do not fully understand the impact of a death by homicide on the remaining members of the family. This is an area that victim service providers can contribute to by continuing to educate these professionals regarding the effect of crime on victims.

As indicated, children who witness homicide suffer a terrible experience.[26] Many of them will suffer posttraumatic stress disorder. Children who witness killings must many times perform other tasks associated with homicides such as calling 9-1-1, trying to assist the dying victim, telling police what occurred, and testifying in court. These additional tasks can present intense conflicts or dilemmas for children. They may blame themselves for not protecting the victim or not responding to the killing in other more acceptable ways. Depending on the age of the child and the circumstances surrounding the homicide, witnessing a murder can have long-range serious mental health consequences for the child.

In some situations a child who could also have been killed is spared for no apparent reason. This can create both terror and extraordinary guilt. Any witnesses, but especially children, may be afraid that the killer will retaliate against them at another time. This is especially true if a child witnesses a continuing history of spousal abuse against the mother that finally ends in her death. The child may then endow the perpetrator with imagined superhuman powers and feel extremely threatened that the offender will return to kill him.

Survivors of sudden death sometimes have unusual experiences. Mothers Against Drunk Driving is only one organization studying this phenomenon.[27] Mystical experiences as they are known can take a variety of forms both before and after death. These experiences include premonitions of death, visitations from loved ones at the time of death or shortly following, unusual dreams or nighttime visitations, or the presence of the loved one sensed through sound, smell, touch, or taste.

Professionals who work with survivors of homicide victims should not discount these experiences. When the issue of mystical experiences is raised in support groups around the country, more than half of those in attendance indicate that they have experienced some sort of unusual episode. The vast majority of those surveyed indicate that the experience was both positive and concrete.[28] These were not ghostly sightings; rather they involved explicit, physical incidents with the loved one. Mystical experiences occur across all socioeconomic, race, and gender lines. Because mystical experiences appear to be common and comforting to survivors of homicide victims, it is important to normalize the experience and allow the survivors the opportunity to express their feelings.

Notification

One of the most traumatic moments in a survivor's life is receiving notification of their loved one's death.[29] The notification by itself is a devastating event, but it can become even more traumatic if it is carried out in an insensitive manner.[30] Some authorities believe that death notification should be given by a uniformed officer because that person is generally perceived by most citizens as an authority figure. However, some communities are training crisis intervention workers. These are usually members of the local victim assistance staff. These persons accompany the officer on the notification call. This procedure allows for a notification team that can work together to ease the pain of the survivor.

Whoever makes the notification call should have as much information regarding the death as possible. The team should be able to tell the survivor what happened, when it occurred, how the victim died, and the source used to identify the victim. The notification team should never, if at all possible, make a death notification by telephone. The team should never take personal items with them on the call—these items will only add to the suffering of the victim. However, at a later time, the victim service provider should offer to retrieve and return all property of the deceased.

When making a call, the notification team should ask to enter the home and indicate that they have important medical information but would rather talk inside the house. Once inside the home, the team should ensure that they are talking to the appropriate relative. If a child has been murdered, the team should ask to speak to both parents at the same time if at all possible. A team member should ask the survivors to take a seat and then sit down next to them. The message should be clear, direct, and simple. For example, the team may tell the parents, "I have some very bad news for you. Your son, John, was shot during an armed robbery, he died immediately." They should not use terms such as "expired" or "passed on," as they can confuse the message and leave room for doubt or false hope.

Members of the notification team should not be shocked by a variety of responses their news might elicit from the survivors. The survivors may cry, faint, laugh, or simply withdraw. The notification team should attempt to focus on the immediate needs of the survivors and help them get in touch with close relatives or friends if they want assistance. As indicated elsewhere in this chapter, one of the most important aspects of the notification process is furnishing all available information to the survivors. This simple detail may alleviate some of the suffering and allow them to understand exactly how and why the death occurred. This process is one of the hardest duties a victim service provider will have to perform. Notification is not something that gets easier with the passage of time, but it can provide survivors with the information they need to begin the healing process.

Summary

Homicide forever affects the lives of the survivors. It is a serious crime that has long-term effects for anyone close to the victim including family, friends, neighbors, and possibly even the community where the victim lived.

There are a number of different types of homicide including, but not limited to, spousal homicide, mass murder, serial murder, and vehicular homicide. Any murder represents a special problem for the victim service provider who becomes involved. These individuals should be as knowledgeable as possible regarding the different types of homicide and their effects on the survivors.

Murder affects the whole family. When a child is murdered, the effect on the parents and remaining siblings can be devastating. Professionals should ensure that in their desire to provide assistance to the parents, they do not overlook the siblings or other family members who may also be suffering shock, despair, and tremendous loss.

Just as professionals should take the lead in training law enforcement agencies regarding cultural sensitivity, so should they ensure that death notification procedures do not traumatize the survivor. Law enforcement personnel should consider including victim service providers on all notification calls. This allows for immediate contact with the survivor and provides the professional with the opportunity to coordinate details and activities with the survivor from the very beginning of the process. This technique may help some survivors to begin the grieving process.

Key Terms

Survivors of homicide victims are those individuals who had special ties of kinship with the person murdered, and who were, thereafter, victimized not only by the loss of someone close to them but also by the horrific circumstances of that untimely death.

Murder is the willful (nonnegligent) killing of one human being by another.

Spousal homicide involves the killing of one's legally married partner.

Parricide is the killings of one's parent.

Mass murderers are those who kill several people at one time in the same location.

Spree killer kills several persons at two or more locations with very little if any time break between the killings.

Serial murderer is one who kills several persons over a period of time which can range from weeks to years.

Discussion Questions

1. Is homicide on the rise in your community? What can your local elected officials do to solve this problem?

2. What type of homicide is the most dangerous? Justify your answer from a law enforcement perspective, a victim service provider's perspective, and a prosecutor's point of view.

3. Who suffers the most when a family member is killed? Parents, children, sibling, or others?

4. How would you notify parents that their child has been murdered? Would the notification process be any different if the child was the perpetrator in a crime and was killed by the intended victim during a shootout?

Suggested Readings

M. E. Wolfgang, *Patterns of Criminal Homicide*, (University of Pennsylvania Press, Philadelphia, Penn.) 1958.

A. Y. Wilson (ed.), *Homicide: The Victim–Offender Connection*, (Anderson, Cincinnati) 1993.

D. Finkelhor, R. J. Gelles, G. T. Hotaling & M. A. Strauss (eds.), *The Dark Side of Families: Current Family Violence Research*, (Sage, Beverly Hills, Calif.) 1983.

Eric W. Hickey, *Serial Murderers and Their Victims*, 2nd. ed., (Brooks/Cole Publishing Company, Pacific Grove, Calif.) 1996.

R. M. Holmes & J. DeBurger, *Serial Murder*, (Sage, Newbury Park, Calif.) 1988.

T. A. Rando, *Parental Loss of a Child*, (Research Press Company, Champaign, Ill.) 1986.

E. Furmann, *A Child's Parent Dies*, (Yale University Press, New Haven, Conn.) 1974.

Lula M. Redmond, *Surviving When Someone You Love Was Murdered*, (Consultation and Education Services, Inc., Clearwater, Florida) 1989.

Endnotes

1. "Survivors of Homicide Victims," 2/3 *NOVA Network Information Bulletin*, 1 (Washington, D.C.), October 1985.

2. *Crime in the United States, 1995*, (Federal Bureau of Investigation, U.S. Department of Justice, Washington, D.C.) 1996.

3. Patrick A. Langan & John M. Dawson, *Spouse Murder Defendants in Large Urban Counties*, Bureau of Justice Statistics, (U.S. Department of Justice, Washington, D.C.) September 1995.

4. A. Amick-McMullen, D. G. Kilpatrick, & H. S. Resnick, "Homicide as a Risk Factor for PTSD Among Surviving Family Members," 15/4 *Behavioral Modifications*, 545 (1987).

5. John M. Dawson & Patrick A. Langan, *Murder in Families*, Bureau of Justice Statistics, (U.S. Department of Justice, Washington, D.C.) 1994.

6. Marianne W. Zawitz, *Firearm Injury from Crime*, Bureau of Justice Statistics, Selected Findings, (U.S. Department of Justice, Washington, D.C.) April 1996.

7. Id. at p. 2

8. M. E. Wolfgang, *Patterns of Criminal Homicide,* (University of Pennsylvania Press, Philadelphia, Penn.) 1958.

9. M. E. Wolfgang, *Analytical Categories for Research in Victimization,* (Kriminologische Wegzeichen, Munich, Germany) 1967, p. 17.

10. Id at 24, 72.

11. Wolfgang, *Patterns in Homicide,* 265.

12. W. Segall & A. Y. Wilson, "Who Is at Greatest Risk in Homicides?: A Comparison of Victimization Rates by Geographic Region." in A. Y. Wilson (ed.), *Homicide: The Victim–Offender Connection,* (Anderson, Cincinnati) 1993.

13. D. Finkelhor, R. J. Gelles, G. T. Hotaling & M. A. Strauss (eds.), *The Dark Side of Families: Current Family Violence Research,* (Sage, Beverly Hills. Calif.) 1983.

14. J. M. Dawson & P. A. Langan, *Murder in Families,* Bureau of Justice Statistics, (Department of Justice, Washington, D.C.) 1994.

15. Kathleen Heide, "Adolescent Parricide Offenders: Synthesis, Illustration and Future Directions," in A. Y. Wilson (ed.), *Homicide: The Victim-Offender Connection,* (Anderson, Cincinnati) 1993.

16. See Eric W. Hickey, *Serial Murderers and Their Victims,* (Brooks/Cole Publishing Company, Pacific Grove, Calif.) 1991, p. 8.

17. R. M. Holmes & J. DeBurger, *Serial Murder,* (Sage, Newbury Park, Calif.) 1988, p. 55–60.

18. E. Hickey, "The Female Serial Murder," 2 *Journal of Police and Criminal Psychology,* 72–81 (October 1986).

19. Hickey, *Serial Murders and Their Victims,* 18–19.

20. Robyn L. Cohen, "Drunk Driving," Bureau of Justice Statistics, (U.S. Department of Justice, Washington, D.C.) September 1992.

21. "Fatal Accident Reporting System, 1995" *National Highway Traffic Safety Administration,* (Washington, D.C.) August 1995.

22. Id.

23. T. A. Rando, *Parental Loss of a Child,* (Research Press Company, Champaign, Ill.) 1986.

24. E. Furmann, *A Child's Parent Dies,* (Yale University Press, New Haven, Conn.) 1974.

25. "Additional Problems of Survivors of a Homicide," *Report on Families of Homicide Victims Project* (Parents of Murdered Children, Inc., Victim Service Agency, New York) 1989.

26. This section is based on information provided by the Family Bereavement Center, 1441 St. Antoine Street, Detroit, Mich.

27. Stephanie Frogge, "Mystical Experiences," Paper presented at 1995 NOVA Conference, Maui, Hawaii (August 1995).

28. Id.

29. For an excellent in-depth discussion of this process, see "Survivors of Homicide Victims," 2/3 *NOVA Network Information Bulletin,* (October 1985).

30. Lula M. Redmond, *Surviving When Someone You Love Was Murdered,* (Consultation and Education Services, Inc., Clearwater, Florida) 1989.

8

FEMALES AS VICTIMS

Chapter Outline

Sexual Assault
  Definition
  Theories of Sexual Violence
  Rape Typologies
  Extent of the Problem

Stranger Rape
  Definitions
  Legal Aspects
  Victim Selection

Acquaintance Rape
  Introduction
  Definition

Marital Rape
  Historical Perspective
  Factors Contributing to Marital Rape

Sexual Harassment
  Introduction
  Definitions

Summary

Key Terms

Discussion Questions

Suggested Readings

Learning Objectives

After reading this chapter, you should be able to:

- Understand the various theories regarding sexual violence
- Distinguish between the various types of rape typologies
- Explain the historical resistance to acknowledging the existence of acquaintance and marital rape
- Recognize a hostile working environment

Sexual Assault

Definition

Exactly what do the terms *rape, marital rape, acquaintance rape,* and *sexual violence* mean? Should we define sexual violence strictly from a legal perspective, a medical view, a psychological view, or a combination of these views? Each discipline has valid reasons for defining sexual violence in a certain manner.

A review of history indicates that the use of aggression and violence against women has existed since the beginning of recorded history. Sexual violence against women traditionally has been viewed as stranger rape—a violent, forceful sexual assault on a woman. Only recently have we recognized other forms of sexual violence. We now acknowledge that spouses may be raped, and acquaintance rape has become a common term in our vocabulary. In addition, there are other forms of sexual violence that are more subtle but just as damaging—sexual

---

FOCUS: Some Startling Facts about Rape

- Ninety-eight percent of rape victims will never see their attacker apprehended, convicted, or incarcerated.
- Over half (54 percent) of all rape prosecutions result in either a dismissal or an acquittal.
- A rape prosecution is more than twice as likely as a murder prosecution to be dismissed and 30 percent more likely to be dismissed than a robbery.
- Approximately 1 in 10 rapes reported to the police results in time served in prison; 1 in 100 rapes (including those that go

unreported) is sentenced to more than one year in prison.
- Almost one-quarter of convicted rapists are not sentenced to prison but, instead, are released on probation.
- Nearly one-quarter of convicted rapists receive a sentence to a local jail for only 11 months (according to national estimates).
- Adding the convicted rapists sentenced to probation and those sentenced to local jails, almost half of all convicted rapists are sentenced to less than one year behind bars.

Source: *Violence Against Women: The Response to Rape: Detours on the Road to Equal Justice,* (Prepared by the Majority Staff of the Senate Judiciary Committee), May 1993, p. 11.

harassment and sexual discrimination are still rampant in the United States. To define sexual violence by any one of these acts is to do injustice to the whole concept that women are equal to men. A legal definition of sexual violence focuses on certain conduct that is prohibited and strictly defined. A medical definition views sexual violence as injury to the body. A psychological evaluation of sexual violence examines the effect on the mind and emotions of the victim. Each of these approaches has certain strengths and weaknesses.

Sexual violence can take the form of a single act or a long and protracted series of incidents. It can also involve aggression and/or discrimination against women. For purposes of this discussion, *sexual violence* is any intentional act or omission that results in physical, emotional, or financial injury to a woman. The phrase "financial injury" is included to cover sexual harassment situations in which women have been terminated from employment for refusing to engage in sexual acts with their supervisors. Sexual violence does not include the termination of a romantic relationship. The ritual of courting, dating, and marriage in America commonly results in one person being hurt or heartbroken when the relationship terminates. Although this may not be appropriate, it does not rise to the level of sexual violence. Although some may argue that this definition is too comprehensive, to narrow it would be to exclude certain types of acts that result in harm to women.

Theories of Sexual Violence

As with other forms of violence, a number of theories regarding this form of aggression exist, but the exact cause of sexual violence is undetermined. No single factor can be highlighted as the cause of rape. Just as there are many forms of sexual violence, so are there a multitude of theories on the cause or causes of sexual aggression toward women. Some of the more common theories on the causes of rape include the following: sexual motivation, socialization, machoism, biological factors, psychological forces, and our culture of violence.

Sexual Motivation.   Most current research dismisses the sexual motivation theory of rape. It is not viewed as a sexual act, rather as an act of violence, aggression, and power by the male.

Socialization.   The socialization concept holds that in our society young boys are taught to be aggressive, forceful, tough, and a winner in any sport or activity. This socialization creates aggressors and can spill over into the sexual area where men are taught to sexually conquer as many women as possible. This aggressive attitude encourages, if not gives consent, for men to engage in rape.[1]

Machoism.   The machoism theory holds that men who believe in male machoism will be more aggressive toward women. Machoism is a set of beliefs that include a view of women as objects simply to be added to a numerical list of sexual conquests. These conquests may include the act of rape.[2]

Biological Factors.   The view of biological factors argues that rape is a male instinctive reaction, which is a drive to perpetuate the species. Symons believes that men still have a genetic holdover that impels them to have sex with as many women as possible and he argues that rape is closely linked to sexuality and violence.[3]

Psychological Forces.   The theory of psychological forces holds that men rape because they suffer from some sort of personality disorder or mental illness. Studies have attempted to define the dynamics of convicted sex offenders and determine exactly what type of people rape and what mental condition causes them to rape. To date, there is no conclusive profile of a rapist.

Culture of Violence.   The culture of violence theory states that our society is a violent environment which encourages some men to use violence to obtain sex. The use of violence and aggression is expected, and these individuals view women as legitimate targets of sexual aggression. These men believe that women want to be dominated and overpowered by an aggressive male.[4]

Rape Typologies

Although there are many causes of rape and sexual violence, past studies have failed to define clearly or predict who will rape. Researchers have now developed different typologies of rapists in an effort to streamline and to define this type of personality. One authority states there are over fifty different types of rapists.[5]

Groth and his associates conducted a study in Massachusetts of 133 convicted rapists and 92 victims. This classic study, "Rape: Power, Anger and Sexuality," established that issues of power, anger, and sexuality are important concepts in understanding the various types of rape. Additionally, this was one of the first research efforts to recognize that rape is a crime of violence and not a sexual act.[6] Groth and his associates classified rape types into two major categories: power and anger.

Power rapes involve the offender seeking power and control over his victim by use of force or threats. The sexual assault is evidence of conquest and domination. The perpetrator will plan and fantasize about the rape believing that the victim will respond to his advances after initially resisting. Power rapes may be further classified as power-assertive rapes or power-reassurance rapes. The power-assertive rapist views the assault as an expression of his virility, mastery, and dominance. The power-reassurance rapist, on the other hand, commits rapes to resolve doubts about his masculinity and sexual adequacy.

Anger rapes involve the expression of anger, rage, contempt, or hatred toward the victim. The objective of this type of rapist is to vent his rage on the victim and retaliate for rejections or perceived wrongs he has suffered in the past by other women. Anger rapes may be categorized as anger-retaliation or anger-excitation rapes. In anger-retaliation rapes, the rape is an expression of hostility and rage toward women. Anger-excitation rape occurs as a result of the offender's desire to obtain pleasure, thrills, and arousal secondary to the suffering of the victim during the assault.

Two years after their initial publication, Groth and Birnbaum established a more refined version of the original typology. In *Men Who Rape,* they established three categories of rapists and determined three types of rape offenses: anger rapes, power rapes, and sadism rapes.[7]

The anger and power rapes are very similar to those in the earlier study, and the sadistic rapist is obsessed with ritual during the rape. He may tie up his victim, torture her, or humiliate her and may become intensely excited during the act. This type of rape is very traumatic, and Groth found that victims of this type of rape needed long-term psychiatric counseling.

Sexual violence will continue to be researched and perhaps one day rapists will be identified by a series of tests or events. However, until that time, sexual violence continues to be a serious problem that must be evaluated and treated.

Extent of the Problem

How many women are raped each year? Exactly what is involved in the act of rape? Is sexual assault the same as rape? Should we determine if a woman has been raped once in a lifetime or just attempt to determine how many rapes occur each year? These are legitimate questions that surface when the study and research of sexual violence is undertaken. Determining the exact nature and extent of sexual violence is a complex and difficult process.

One major problem in the area of women and sexual violence is the lack of agreement among scholars, researchers, and professionals on definitions and research methodology. Depending on which article, paper, or text one reads, the estimates regarding the incident of rape will vary. This disparity has caused problems and confusion within the professions ever since the study of women and violence began. There are a number of reasons for the different figures and definitions within this area of family violence. The following is a summary of some of the more common problems encountered when this phenomenon is studied.

Definitional Issues.   Some scholars use the term *rape,* others use *sexual assault,* and still others define each of the foregoing terms differently. For example, one researcher may define rape as vaginal intercourse accomplished by use of force or fear whereas other researchers may define rape as vaginal, oral, or rectal intercourse accomplished by force or fear. The simple addition of two terms changes the entire results of any study.

Professional Issues.   Various professionals approach rape from different perspectives. Attorneys view rape in a certain legalistic way, physicians treat it as a medical problem, and psychologists approach it from a mental health point of view.

Gathering of Information.   Problems in the screening techniques, formation of questions, context of questioning, and issues of confidentiality all impact on the validity and type of response which the researcher will receive.[8]

Koss compiled many of the various studies on rape and her work illustrates the different approaches various researchers have used when attempting to determine the incidence of sexual violence against women in America.[9]

As Table 8.1 indicates, there is a wide discrepancy between the various studies as to the type and prevalence of sexual violence committed in the United States.

One recent study was conducted by the National Victims Center, entitled *Rape in America: A Report to the Nation,* and it caused an uproar across America when it was released in April 1992.[19] The National Victims Center relied on a comprehensive study entitled "The National Women's Study" to gather their information. This report was based on a national sample of 4008 women who were interviewed regarding their experience with rape. The report indicated that rape occurred at a much higher incidence than previously accepted.

Using the 1990 U.S. census figures, which indicate there are approximately 96.8 million women in America, the center estimates that one in eight women have been raped at some time in their life. This translates into an incredible 12.1 million women in the United States who have been raped! In reviewing the figures and percentages of those women, Table 8.2 illustrates the number of times women have been raped.

The information gathered from this survey indicates that 0.07 percent of all women were raped within the last year. Again using the U.S. census figures, this translates into approximately 683,000 women who are raped each year! These figures are higher than reported in either the Uniform Crime Report or the National Crime Survey. The FBI's annual Uniform Crime Report has estimated that

TABLE 8.1   Sexual Violence and Women

Study	Sample	Collection Method	Measured Phenomena and Prevalence Rate
Burt[10]	328	Interview	Completed rape 24 percent lifetime
Essock-Vitlae & McGuire[11]	300	Interview	Rape—8 percent since age eighteen
Kilpatrick and associates[12]	2004	Telephone	Forcible rape including attempts 8.8 percent lifetime
Riger & Gordon[13]	693	Telephone	Rape or sexual assault 2 percent of telephone sample
National Victims Center[14]	4008	Telephone	rape—14 percent lifetime
Russell[15]	930	Interview	Completed rape 24 percent
Sorenson and associates[16]	1444	Interview	Sexual assault 13.5 percent
Winfield and associates[17]	1157	Interview	Sexual assault 5.9 percent lifetime
Wyatt[18]	248	Interview	Completed rape 25 percent for Blacks and 20 percent for Whites

TABLE 8.2

▬▬▬▬

5 percent of the sample were unsure whether they had been raped.

▬▬▬▬▬▬▬▬▬▬▬

39 percent had experienced more than one rape in their lifetime.

▬▬▬▬▬▬▬▬▬▬▬▬▬▬▬

56 percent of the women surveyed indicated they had been raped one time.

attempted or actual rapes reported to the police in 1990 numbered 102,560. The National Crime Survey reported attempted or actual rapes for 1990 numbered 130,000. Although the National Women's survey did not include attempted rapes, the figure is still in excess of five times the previously accepted figure or number of rapes that occurred each year in the United States.

These figures indicate that rape in America is more common than previously thought, and rape is only one form of sexual violence that is perpetrated against women. Sexual violence can happen to any woman, at any time and in any place. No one is completely secure from this type of assault. The following sections will examine different aspects of this form of sexual violence.

Stranger Rape

There are still myths regarding the crime of rape. Some of these myths hold that women really want to be raped, that they like rough sex, and when they go bra-less they are asking for sex. These myths apply to stranger, marital, or acquaintance rape situations.

Definitions

Carnal knowledge of a female was one of the first terms used to connote sexual violence. It was defined as *penile–vaginal penetration.*[20] *Black's Law Dictionary* defines *carnal knowledge* as "coitus; copulation; the act of a man having sexual bodily connections with a woman; sexual intercourse."[21]

Traditional penal codes reflected this bias and misunderstanding of the crime of rape. Criminal codes are enacted by each state and the federal government setting forth various definitions of crime. This has resulted in a patchwork of different definitions applied to basically the same act. In an effort to establish uniformity within the area of criminal law, a distinguished group of scholars and attorneys worked together for several years in drafting a Model Penal Code (MPC). The purpose of this code was to set forth the most reasoned thinking on various crimes and encourage states to adopt these definitions of the various crimes so uniformity would be established throughout the United States. The Model Penal Code defines rape as:

A male who has sexual intercourse with a female, not his wife, is guilty of rape if:

(a) *he compels her to submit by force or by threat of imminent death, serious bodily injury, extreme pain or kidnapping to be inflicted upon anyone, or*

(b) *he has substantially impaired her power to appraise or control her conduct by administrating or employing without her knowledge drugs, intoxicants or other means for the purpose of preventing resistance, or*

(c) *the female is unconscious, or*

(d) *the female is less than 10 years old. Rape is a felony of the second degree unless (i) in the course thereof the actor inflicts serious bodily injury upon anyone, or (ii) the victim was not a voluntary social companion of the actor upon the occasion of the crime and had not previously permitted him sexual liberties, in which case the offense is a felony of the first degree.*[22]

The drafters of the Model Penal Code were not purposefully discriminating against women. However, it is clear that the MPC perpetuated the bias of the times. A reading of the Model Code reveals several flaws: the statute is gender biased, does not punish acquaintance rape as seriously as stranger rape, and does not provide for marital rape. The Model Penal Code only prohibits men from raping women. It makes no provision for female rape of a man. Secondly, although it "allows" that an acquaintance might rape his companion, this form of rape is not as serious as stranger rape, therefore it will not be punished as harshly. Finally, it would not be a crime for a husband to rape his wife under the code. Some states adopted the provisions of the code and others have modernized their criminal statutes relating to the crime of rape. Many statutes now define the crime of *rape* as "an unlawful act of sexual intercourse with another person against that person's will by force, fear, or trick."[23]

These statutes are gender neutral: Either a man or a woman may commit the crime. Secondly, the very definition allows for the charging and prosecution of marital rape. Finally, a person may be prosecuted for acquaintance rape under this statute. The only area that is not covered by these statutes is insertion of an object into the vagina during the assault.

Some authorities define rape as the penetration by a penis or other object into the mouth, vagina, or anal openings by force or fear.[24] There is a small but growing movement among the states to adopt this more modern definition of rape. Part of the rationale for the expanded definition is that rape is not a sexual crime, rather it is a violent assault on the victim and any type of forced penetration should be punished. This definition attempts to punish all forms of sexual assault. Additionally, it attempts to provide uniformity in an area where each state has adopted differing statutes regarding sexual violence. Other authorities suggest doing away with the term *rape* and using instead *sexual assault* or *sexual battery* and prohibiting oral, vaginal, or anal penetration by force or fear.[25] Someday we may move toward a more comprehensive definition of this type of sexual violence, but at present the great majority of statutes define rape in a manner similar to that discussed here. This definition in turn triggers reporting requirements by professionals in certain instances. Therefore the definition set forth here will be used for purposes of clarity and conformity with existing statutes. This should not give the impression that forcible anal intercourse or oral copulation is not a crime in most states. Under most statutes, these are considered separate offenses which are distinct from the crime of rape.

Legal Aspects

Rape carries with it certain physical, mental, and legal consequences. Many times during a rape the offender will perform or attempt to perform a variety of acts including vaginal, oral, and anal sex. As mentioned, each of these acts is considered a separate and distinct crime.

The crime of rape requires penetration of the penis into the vagina. The offense is complete on the slightest entry into the victim; therefore, it is possible for a woman to be raped and still retain her hymen. There is no requirement that the offender ejaculate for the crime to be complete.

As indicated, rape may be committed by force, fear, or trick. Forcible rape involves the offender using brute force to overpower the victim. He may use his fists, clubs, or other objects to strike the victim prior to raping her. The second situation occurs when the offender threatens the victim and she submits out of fear for her safety. This type of rape may not leave any physical scars, torn clothing, or other signs of physical violence. The third type of rape occurs when the offender tricks the victim. This is a broad category that includes sex with incompetents as well as the use of drugs and alcohol to render the victim incapable of consenting.

Victims are not the only ones asking rapists to wear condoms. The *New York Times* conducted an informal survey of rape crisis centers and concluded that more rapists are wearing condoms.[26] Rapists are not wearing condoms out of concern for the victim, they are wearing them to avoid receiving AIDS from the victim and to hinder prosecution. Condoms make the job of the prosecutor harder because there is no access to semen from which DNA samples might be obtained. The use of condoms by rapists reinforces the theory that the crime is a planned act of violence rather than an impulsive act.

FOCUS: Did She Consent When She Asked Him to Wear a Condom?

One common defense in rape cases is that the victim consented. This is especially true in fear or trick rapes, when the victim suffers no outward physical injuries.

In Texas, a recent rape trial caught the attention of the nation. The victim was single and lived alone. One evening after she returned from a friend's party she looked up and saw the defendant with a knife in his hand who had entered through a sliding glass door.

He approached her and demanded sex. The victim, fearing for her life, consented and asked the offender to wear a condom, which she supplied. The defendant was later arrested and tried for the crime of rape. He claimed the act was consensual in nature and pointed to the victim supplying him with a condom as proof of his assertion. The jury did not buy his story and he was convicted of rape.

Once the crime is complete and if the victim reports the offense to the authorities, the criminal justice system begins its slow and methodological prosecution of the offender. The rape victim will have to testify in open court about the incident. As late as the early 1960s, rape victims were treated as the criminals in sexual assault cases and defense attorneys were allowed to ask questions regarding their previous sexual experiences. There were a variety of theories that allowed for admission of this type of "evidence." Two of the more common theories involved the victim's reputation: (1) Because she had intercourse with other persons, she was therefore likely to have consented during this act. (2) Because of the proof that she was a person of loose morals, she was therefore willing to have sex with anyone, including this defendant. These antiquated and biased rules are no longer accepted in our judicial system. All fifty states and the federal government have adopted *rape shield laws,* which are statutes that prohibit the defendant or his attorney from questioning the rape victim regarding her previous sexual history or introducing any other evidence concerning her past sexual practices.[27]

Victim Selection

As with so many other aspects of sexual assault, we are not certain why certain rapists select certain victims. This is one of the many subjects in this area that needs further research. One study attempted to answer this question by interviewing convicted sexual predators. Stevens used other convicted felons to conduct a survey of sixty-one sexual offenders incarcerated in a maximum security prison.[28] Stevens trained thirteen incarcerated violent offenders enrolled in his class at a maximum security prison as student interviewers. They conducted interviews with convicted sexual predators, which resulted in sixty-one valid interviews.

The average respondent was thirty-two years old and had served seven years in prison at the time of the interview. The average rapist had attended eighth grade and was employed in a menial type of job before his arrest. The subjects averaged 3.4 prior adult arrests. Fifty-six percent of the sample was Black, 42 percent White, and 2 percent Hispanic.

The author cautions against accepting the word of criminals. However, the data show some interesting results: The most common characteristic for selecting victims was that the victims were perceived as "easy prey," meaning that the victims were thought to be vulnerable. In other words, either these predators selected victims who they thought could or would not resist an attack or an opportunity presented itself which allowed them to attack the victim.

Some of the predators viewed young women as easy prey. One predator talked about attacking sixty or seventy victims by scouting financial districts and looking for middle-class working women. Still other predators found that female shoppers were easy prey. They identified them by their demeanor. One predator stated, "If she's not watching what's happening all around her, then [she] doesn't know how to handle herself, how to use the things around her to hurt me, or get me caught." Finally, other predators wait for situations to develop in which the victim puts herself in a vulnerable position. For example, one predator attacked a woman in the parking lot by threatening to harm her young child unless she cooperated.

Stranger rape is a violent physical assault on women; however, it is not the most common form of sexual assault. Recent studies have indicated that more women are raped by persons they know than by strangers. The next section will examine this form of sexual violence—acquaintance rape.

Acquaintance Rape

Introduction

Intimate sexual violence includes marital and acquaintance rape. These forms of assault are not isolated incidents that occur to only a few women. *Rape in America* reported that only 22 percent of all women raped were sexually assaulted by someone they had never seen before or did not know![29] Nine percent of all victims were raped by their husbands or ex-husbands, 10 percent by boyfriends or ex-boyfriends, and 21 percent by other nonrelatives such as friends or neighbors. The remaining percentages were composed of fathers or stepfathers, other relatives, and a "not sure" category of 3 percent. This report indicates that approximately 683,000 women were raped in a one-year period. Using the figures provided in this report, that means in one year 61,470 women were raped by their husband or ex-husband, 68,300 women were raped by their boyfriend or ex-boyfriend, and 143,430 women were raped by other known acquaintances.

The Focus box illustrates forms of sexual violence faced by women on a daily basis. Some men and defense attorneys would argue that situations 1 and 3 were clearly not rape and that a man should not be responsible for getting inside the mind of his date. Depending on what further facts are added, situation 1 may

---

FOCUS: When Is It Rape?

1. A couple attending college decides to break up. They have been intimate for three years, engaging in oral, anal, and vaginal sexual activities. One week after they separate, the man arrives at the woman's apartment intoxicated and states they are going to have sex. The woman insists the relationship is over; however, the male gets angry, punches the wall, and demands sex. The woman knows he will not hit her and is therefore not frightened for her own safety, but gives in and they engage in sexual relations.

2. On a third date, the man double-shots his date's drinks. She is not an experienced drinker and passes out while they are engaged in heavy petting. The man proceeds to have intercourse with her.

3. A couple has been dating for three weeks. They both have had several drinks and are intoxicated. They engage in heavy petting and the woman responds physically, but says "Please darling, no." The man continues his sexual advances and the woman continues to respond physically, but also continues to say no. They finally engage in intercourse.

Are any of these examples acquaintance rape? Why? Who is responsible in these situations? Are both parties at fault?

have involved the use of force and therefore qualify as a sexual assault and rape. Situation 2 is clearly a rape by trick situation in which the victim was unable to give consent. Situation 3 may be classified as rape, because many authorities argue that when a woman says no, the advances by the man must stop. Others will argue that it may be rape depending on the victim's state of mind.

Sexual violence in dating relationships is not a new topic to social scientists and other professionals. As early as 1957, Kanin studied college students' sexual aggression. He found that over half of all college women (50 to 60 percent) reported being offended by sexual aggression whereas only 20 to 30 percent of college men admitted to such aggressive behavior.[30] This indicates a serious lack of empathy on the part of male college students as to what is appropriate behavior. Whereas a majority of the women found the acts aggressive, only 20 to 30 percent of the men found them to meet their definition of sexual aggression. Other researchers have confirmed these percentages and come to the conclusion that the double standard still exists in America.[31] This attitude in turn leads to situations in which date rape can and does occur.

Although sexual aggression in dating relationships has been studied for over thirty years, Americans still have problems in accepting the concept of rape by a person known to the victim. There are still individuals who want to believe that rape is committed in some dark alley by a sadistic monster and only "nice girls" who resist and whose resistance was overcome by physical force can be raped.

In assessing sexual violence during dating or courtship, Lloyd explained that sexual violence in a dating relationship does not necessarily lead to the breakup of the relationship.[32] Many victims reported that the relationship continued for some time after the violence. Lloyd also explained that violence in a dating situation occurs in a context of control by the aggressor.

Stranger rape at one time was thought to be the most common form of sexual violence. However, we now understand that intimate violence is more frequent than suspected. One survey reported that on a Midwestern campus 100 percent of all rapists knew their victims.[33]

Definition

Similar to marital rape, date or acquaintance rape situations are covered by the general definition of rape as set forth in the previous section. However, for purposes of explaining this special type of sexual violence, *acquaintance rape* is defined as the unlawful sexual intercourse accomplished by force or fear with a person known to the victim who is not related by blood or marriage.

The following actual cases* illustrate the continuing problems facing victims of acquaintance rape:

- A young woman reports to the police that she was kidnapped and raped by a former boyfriend. He had beaten her in the past, leading to his arrest on at

*Source: *The Response to Rape: Detours on the Road to Equal Justice*, (Majority Staff of the Senate Judiciary Committee), May 1993, pp. 18-19.

least one occasion. The prosecutor resists bringing rape charges due to the victim's prior relationship with her assailant, and offers the man a plea to reduced charges—a misdemeanor assault for which the attacker receives a six-month sentence and eighteen months probation. Less than a year later, the attacker brutally rapes and almost kills another woman.

- A group of young men meet a woman in a bar at night; they surreptitiously slip a tablet of LSD in her drink before leaving the bar with her. At the home of one of the young men, they slip her four more doses of LSD. The woman is then repeatedly raped with objects as a group cheers and takes pictures, which are later destroyed. One assailant stops the attack when someone suggests raping the woman with a statue of Christ. Three of the attackers are given immunity for providing statements helpful to the prosecution; one defendant pleads to evidence tampering and delivery of illegal drugs; he serves three months of an eight-month sentence in jail, with eight years probation. Not one of the defendants is convicted of sexual assault.

- A woman ends her engagement with a man. Several weeks later, he goes to her house and they get into an argument in his car. She tells the police that he dragged her into the back seat of the car and raped her. After the attack, she goes to the hospital and files a police report. The prosecutor in the case accepts the defendant's plea to "unlawful restraint"—a fourth degree felony with a two-year sentence—saying, "It's not like she didn't have sex with him before." The attacker serves six months and one day in jail.

Acquaintance rape will continue to be a serious problem in America as long as we socialize men to view women as inferior members of society who really want to be chased, conquered, and dominated. We must learn to view women as equals in interpersonal, social, and professional relationships.

Marital Rape

A recent article in the *Journal of the American Medical Association* discusses the various forms of family violence with a subsequent recommendation that the American Medical Association undertake a campaign to sensitize its members to marital rape.[34] The recommendation includes training and dissemination of protocols on identifying and treating victims of marital rape. As discussed, the medical community is slowly becoming aware of the need to respond to intimate sexual violence. Although there is more awareness now of marital and acquaintance rape primarily because of the media, many people, including professionals, have difficulty with the concept that a man can be accused and convicted of raping his wife or that a date who "consented" the evening before can raise the specter of rape the next day. Although the perception is slowly changing, there still remain those who believe sex is a matter of right in marriage or other intimate relationships.

Yllo cited several disturbing trends in marital rape.[35] She reported that data from recent studies indicated that approximately 10 to 14 percent of wives were forced by their husbands to have sex against their will. She further illustrated that because of the sexual nature of marriage, marital rape has not been regarded as a serious form of assault. Finally, Yllo stated that many rape crisis shelters and battered women's shelters often feel that marital rape is the responsibility of some other organization.

Historical Perspective

For centuries our society has believed that a man is entitled to sex with his wife. A man could not be charged or convicted of raping his wife in eighteenth century England. Wives were considered chattel and clearly subordinate to the husband.[36] Fathers had a property right or interest in their daughter's virginity and husbands in their wives' fidelity. The rape of an unmarried woman destroyed her value as a suitable bride and sexual mate. The rape of a married woman was an infringement on the property rights of her spouse and a disgrace to her husband.

The marital exemption for rape can be traced to Sir Matthew Hale, a seventeenth-century English jurist. Hale was the chief justice of King's Bench from 1671 to 1675. A book based on his writing was published after his death in 1736.[37] Geis in his review of early English common law indicated that Sir Matthew Hale's statement helped establish a precedent for spousal immunity from rape when he held: "But the husband cannot be guilty of rape committed by himself upon his lawful wife, for by their mutual matrimonial consent and contract the wife hath given up herself in this kind unto the husband which she cannot retract."[38]

Blackstone, the great English legal scholar, helped to perpetuate this reasoning. He stated that the legal existence of a woman is suspended during marriage, or at the very least incorporated into that of her husband. Blackstone's argument served to continue the legal fiction of unity of the person on marriage. Therefore, a wife was deemed to have irrevocably consented to sex when and where her husband wished.[39] This philosophy continued in England and elsewhere almost to modern times. R. E. Martin pointed out that Winston Churchill's mother could not refuse her husband's sexual advances even though he was suffering from incurable syphilis.[40]

The feminist movement in the 1970s sought to change the laws to allow for charges to be brought against a husband who raped his wife. It was not an easy victory. State- and Congressional-elected officials made such comments as: "But if you can't rape your wife, who can you rape?" and "[T]he Bible doesn't give the state permission anywhere in the Book for the state to be in your bedroom. . . ."[41] Unbelievable as it may seem now, there was a great deal of resistance to passage of any laws that would delete spousal immunity from the books and thus allow a wife to charge her husband with rape. Through the efforts of several dedicated groups and individuals, laws began to be amended to define marital rape as a specific crime.

As mentioned, many rape statutes now allow for the prosecution of a husband who rapes his wife. Therefore there is no separate legal definition of marital rape. However, for purposes of explaining and distinguishing this form of sexual violence from stranger rape, *marital rape* is defined as the unlawful sexual intercourse with a spouse or ex-spouse against her will by means of force or fear.

Finkelhor and Yllo conducted extensive research in the area of marital rape and classified marital rapes into three categories: force-only rapes, battering rapes, and obsessive rapes. A force-only rape occurs when the husband attempts to gain control over the type and frequency of sexual activity within the marriage. Finkelhor and Yllo compare this type of rape with Groth and Birnbaum's power rape. A battering rape involves the husband attempting to humiliate and degrade his spouse. These types of marital rapes are very similar to Groth and Birnbaum's anger rapes. The last type of marital rape is the obsessive rape. These rapes involve sexual sadism, fetishes, and forcible anal intercourse. This type of rape is similar to Groth and Birnbaum's sadistic rape.[42]

Factors Contributing to Marital Rape

Just as there are a number of theories as to why spousal abuse and stranger rape occur, so are there a variety of theories dealing with factors that encourage or promote marital rape. Previous chapters have discussed factors that increase the risk of family violence, including child physical and sexual abuse, spousal abuse, and marital rape. The following discussion focuses on factors and forces within our society that specifically encourage or contribute to marital rape. These factors include our historical perspective toward the family, spousal immunity, economics, and our culture's preoccupation with violence.

Historical Perspective toward the Family.   For generations the family has been viewed as the last stronghold of absolute privacy. What happened in the wedding bed was believed to be no one else's business. This concept of family privacy has caused delays and problems in researching issues such as marital rape. Additionally, women were raised with the belief that they had to "submit" to their husbands' sexual advances. Only recently have we begun to study the dynamics within the family bedroom, and women now understand that they do not owe sex on demand to their spouse.

Spousal Immunity.   As mentioned, early common law established the proposition that a husband could not be accused of raping his wife. Rape of a stranger was considered a violent and unspeakable act; however, rape of a wife was unknown. The wife was considered to be part of the husband and therefore he was immune from charges of rape brought by his spouse. Only recently have spouses been able to bring charges of rape against their husbands.

Economics.   Similar to other causes of family violence, economics and dependency play a role in promoting marital rape. In a marriage, both spouses are aware of the wife's economic dependency. Some men argue that they provide the paycheck so the wife must take care of the home. This "taking care of the home" includes, in the man's mind, sex on demand—any kind of sex.

Preoccupation with Violence.   Violence and its effect on family violence have already been discussed in detail earlier in this text. Because some films, books, and television devalue women, it is easier for men to utilize violence as an acceptable form of sexual expression.

Although none of these factors may be the single or sole cause for marital rape, they contribute along with other factors to a general climate of violence in America that promotes sexual violence against women.

Sexual Harassment

The title of this section has been purposely chosen. Sexual harassment is the overall umbrella under which specific forms of sexual violence take place. Although it is true that men have been targets of sexual harassment, most victims are women. Because sexual harassment is a form of violence against women, it is included in this chapter to allow for comparison between sexual violence within the family and sexual violence in the workplace. Only by understanding the full spectrum of sexual violence can we begin to respond appropriately to it.

We have faced discrimination in America since its founding. Lincoln began the process of doing away with discrimination when he freed the slaves, and for decades our courts have held that one citizen should not discriminate against another simply because of skin color. However, that battle still goes on in coffee shops that refuse to serve people of color, banks that decline to make home loans to persons living in certain locations, and many service-related businesses such as automobile dealers who simply ignore persons of different races. Discrimination against women simply because of their sex is one bias that is also reaching our collective consciousness. One offensive form of this discrimination is sexual harassment. Employment-based sexual harassment is dehumanizing and it changes the focus of employment from the woman's work performance to her sex. Additionally, it degrades women by reinforcing their traditionally inferior role in the workplace. The following sections will provide a brief overview of sexual harassment.

Introduction

Sexual harassment is a widespread phenomenon. One of the first work-related surveys of 9000 women found that nine of ten women reported instances of sexual harassment.[43] Probably the most comprehensive survey of sexual harassment ever done was conducted by the United States Merit System Protection Board in 1980. The board surveyed 23,000 federal employees and stated that 42 percent of all women reported being the subject of some form of sexual harassment.[44]

Demands for sexual favors in exchange for continuing employment have long been a common abuse of personal power in the workplace. The clandestine squeeze on the factory floor, the stolen kiss in the copy room, or the lewd suggestion regarding sex have been commonplace in American businesses for years. Until recently, the victim of such sexual violence has two choices: agree or lose her job. Additionally, she was led to believe that the activities that she found offensive were in reality common practice in the workplace. There was no legal recourse for victims of sexual harassment until the 1980s.

In 1964, we began the long process of outlawing all forms of discrimination. Congress passed Title VII of the Civil Rights Act of 1964 which prohibited employment discrimination based on race, color, religion, sex, pregnancy, or national origin.[45] Title VII provides that:

> *It shall be an unlawful employment practice for an employer—*
>
> 1. *to fail or refuse to hire or to discharge any individual, to otherwise to discriminate against any individual with respect to his compensation, terms, conditions, or privileges of employment, because of such individual's race, color, religion, sex, or national origin; or*
> 2. *to limit, segregate, or classify his employees or applicants for employment in any way which would deprive or tend to deprive any individual of employment opportunities or otherwise adversely affect his status an employee, because of such individual's race, color, religion, sex, or national origin.[46]*

Even though the language of the statute was clear, women continued to be exposed to discrimination because they were pregnant at the time or might become pregnant in the future. This continuing discrimination caused Congress to pass the Pregnancy Discrimination Act of 1978 which prohibited discrimination based on pregnancy, childbirth, or other related medical conditions.[47]

Many scholars believe the Civil Rights Act of 1964 was the basis for the current prohibition against sexual harassment. However, Congress never directly addressed that issue when it passed the act. In fact, sex was added as a prohibited classification in a last-minute attempt by opponents to block passage of the legislation.[48] Rather, courts and administrative agencies have used the Civil Rights Act as the foundation on which to base their rulings regarding sexual harassment.[49]

Definitions

There are a number of definitions of sexual harassment. From a traditional perspective, sexual harassment is a demand that a subordinate, usually a woman, grant sexual favors to retain a job benefit.[50] A more encompassing definition defines *sexual harassment* as the imposition of any unwanted condition on any person's employment because of that person's sex. Under this definition, harassment includes jokes, direct taunting, disruption of work, vandalism or destruction of property, and physical attacks.[51] Sexual harassment occurs in a wide variety of forms, including rape, pressure for sexual favors, sexual touching, suggestive looks or gestures, sexual joking or teasing, and the display of unwanted sexual material.

Sexual harassment may occur in either of two forms: quid pro quo harassment or hostile environment harassment. These are not mutually exclusive situations. Many times they will overlap and both forms may be present in the workplace.

Quid pro quo harassment occurs when an agent or supervisor of the employer uses his position to induce a female employee to grant him sexual favors. The exchange of continued employment or job benefits for sex suggests the name quid pro quo. The essence of a quid pro quo harassment is that the victim must choose between suffering economic disadvantage or enduring sexual advances.[52]

Hostile environment harassment occurs when unwelcome conduct of a sexual nature creates a hostile working environment. The conduct usually involves a series of incidents rather than a single episode of harassment. The essence of a hostile working environment form of harassment is that an individual is forced to work in an environment that, although it does not cause direct economic detriment, results in psychological or emotional harm or humiliation.

Barnes v. Costle established the principle that sex-based assignments or sexual advances in which the employer enforces the demand by threat of discharge or other adverse economic consequences violate Title VII of the Civil Rights Act.[53] In *Barnes,* the plaintiff alleged that she was hired as an administrative assistant to the director of the agency's equal employment opportunity division at the Environmental Protection Agency. Shortly after commencing employment, the director solicited her to join him after hours at social functions and stated that if she cooperated with him in a sexual affair her employment status would be enhanced. She refused these advances and her position was abolished. The appellate court held that such actions were a clear violation of Title VII of the Civil Rights Act.

In 1980, the Equal Employment Opportunity Commission (EEOC) adopted regulations in the form of guidelines that prohibited discrimination based on sex. These guidelines specifically state that an individual's response to unwelcome conduct of a sexual nature may not be made on the basis of any adverse employment decision.[54] Although the EEOC guidelines are not binding, they have been held to constitute a body of experience and informed judgments to which courts and litigants may properly resort for guidance.[55]

It wasn't until 1986 that a case concerning sexual harassment based on a hostile working environment was decided. In *Meritor Savings Bank v. Vinson,* the United States Supreme Court held that a working environment that is hostile to women may violate Title VII of the Civil Rights Act even without any question of economic detriment. In *Meritor,* the victim was hired by the bank as a teller and eventually advanced to the position of assistant branch manager. She alleged that a supervisor subjected her to sexual harassment for over four years. This harassment included sexual intercourse, fondling her in front of other employees, exposing himself to her, and even following her into the ladies' restroom. The Supreme Court upheld the victim's claim of sexual harassment based on the theory that the actions of the aggressor established a hostile working environment.

In 1993, the Supreme Court again addressed the issue of sexual harassment when it decided *Harris v. Forklift Systems, Inc.*[56] The Court extended its ruling in *Meritor* to include conduct that does not actually cause psychological injury. In *Harris,* the Court held that Title VII is violated when a workplace is permeated with unwelcome discriminatory intimidation, ridicule, and insult that are so severe or pervasive as to alter the conditions of the victim's employment. In essence, the court held that sexual harassment can occur if the environment can reasonably be perceived as hostile or abusive. The Supreme Court acknowledged that there is no clear line that determines whether a working environment is hostile, but noted that some factors can be examined as part of the circumstances of any case. These factors include frequency of the discriminatory conduct, severity of that conduct, whether it is physically threatening or humiliating or a mere offensive utterance, and whether it unreasonably interferes with an employee's work performance.

Tangri, Burt, and Johnson established three models or types of sexual harassment: the natural/biological model, the organizational model, and the sociocultural model.[57] Using data from the initial Merit Systems Protection Board 1980 survey, they partially tested these models.

The *natural/biological model* assumes that sexual behavior in the workplace is an extension of human sexuality. It is assumed that men and women possess strong sex drive, but the man whose sex drive is stronger takes the role of the aggressor. From this perspective, sexual harassment is not discriminatory in nature; it is simply the result of natural biological mating urges. This model presupposes that all sexual advances are mutual in nature and part of a courtship or mating behavior. We now understand that all advances are not in fact part of a courtship, and therefore this model fails to explain sexual harassment.

The *organizational model* is a result of the workplace environment which provides opportunities for sexual aggression. From this perspective, sexual harassment becomes an issue of power, not sex. This power is derived from the formal roles in an organizational context. For this model to be valid, only those women in positions of low hierarchical power would be targets of sexual harassment. Women have been harassed in a variety of positions, some of which were considered high on the organizational scheme. Therefore this model does not adequately explain sexual harassment.

The *sociocultural model* views sexual harassment as reflecting the more dominant position of men in our culture in which they are the source of economic and political power. This model suggests that sexual harassment is the result of a patriarchal power system in which men rule society. From this perspective, sexual harassment is based on the personal power of gender, in which men are dominant. Power is an important factor in sexual harassment. The male aggressor may control advancement, benefits, and even continued employment.

Sexual harassment doesn't exist only in the workplace. It has been called one of the best kept secrets on college campuses, and some feminists are concerned that certain professors have used their position of power to obtain sexual favors from students. Dziech and Weiner list the following actions which they consider as inappropriate behavior by professors:

- *Staring, leering, ogling.* These behaviors may be surreptitious or obvious. Professors, who by the very nature of their occupation must look at and/or observe students, should not cross over the boundaries of reason.

- *Frequently commenting on personal appearance of the student.* In an academic setting, professors should refrain from discussing apparel and physical characteristics of students.

- *Touching out of context.* Touching of students should be minimal and only to the extent necessary to carry out certain types of instruction.

- *Excessively flattering and praising the student.* This behavior, with others listed here, is especially seductive to students with low self-esteem or high expectations. By convincing the student that she is exceptional, the professor gains psychological access to her.

- *Injecting a "male versus female" tone into discussions with the student.* This type of disparaging remark about women and their abilities is a clear signal of a bias or negative perception on the part of the professor.
- *Persistently emphasizing sexuality in all contexts.* Pervasive emphasis on sex inside or outside the classroom is inappropriate.[58]

This discussion should not be construed to label every professor as a potential sexual harasser. However, even in academia, the controversy about professor–student relationships continues to be debated. In April 1993, the University of Virginia Faculty Senate was considering a policy that would prohibit faculty members from dating students. Representatives of the American Civil Liberties Union (ACLU) questioned the appropriateness of the actions, stating that the university might be infringing on privacy and associational rights of teachers. The ACLU instead recommended that the university beef up its sexual harassment codes. The University Faculty Senate proceeded to approve the no-dating policy. Many universities have sexual harassment codes and some are beginning to adopt a no-dating policy between students and faculty members. The relationship between students and faculty members is one of power. When a professor uses his position to extract sexual favors from a student, this becomes a serious quid pro quo form of sexual harassment.

Simply having agencies and courts establish procedures and processes to handle sexual harassment cases does not eliminate this behavior. The perception of women must be changed and they should be viewed as equals instead of sex objects. Only when women are approached as partners and equals will sexual harassment stop.

Summary

Sexual violence is a complex and far-ranging topic. The study of sexual violence has been and will continue to be hindered by a lack of agreement among the different professions on terminology and research methodology. All professionals agree that sexual violence continues to be a serious problem in the United States. Recent studies have indicated that women are more at risk from someone they know than from the stranger lurking in the darkness. Also, the consequences of any type of sexual violence are severe and in many instances long-lasting. We really should begin to think about a "war on rape" in addition to the "war on drugs."

We are slowly advancing in our perception of rape victims. No longer can only "nice" girls be raped. We have accepted that rape is a violent physical assault that has very little if anything to do with sexual gratification. Our legislatures have passed rape shield laws that now provide some protection to the victims of rape. These laws bar questions to the victim which require her to explain her previous sexual experiences to the judge and jury. As long as men rape women, lawyers will raise consent as a defense. However, as we become more educated as a nation, that rationalization will stop bearing creditability.

Sexual harassment continues to be a form of sexual violence in the United States and will continue as long as men view women as sexual trophies or playthings instead of equals. Only by continuing our education of society can we hope to put an end to this form of sexual violence.

Key Terms

Sexual violence is any intentional act or omission that results in physical, emotional, or financial injury to a woman.

Rape is an unlawful act of sexual intercourse with another person against that person's will by force, fear, or trick.

Rape shield laws are statutes that prohibit the defendant or his attorney from questioning the rape victim regarding her previous sexual history or introducing any other evidence concerning her past sexual practices.

Acquaintance rape is the unlawful sexual intercourse accomplished by force or fear with a person known to the victim who is not related by blood or marriage.

Marital rape is the unlawful sexual intercourse with a spouse or ex-spouse against her will by means of force or fear.

Sexual harassment is the imposition of any unwanted condition on any person's employment because of that person's sex.

Discussion Questions

1. Why is it so hard to define sexual violence?

2. In your opinion, what is the most acceptable theory on the cause of sexual violence? Justify your answer.

3. Should the definition of rape include more than sexual intercourse? Why? Why not?

4. Is victim selection an important issue in studying sexual violence? Isn't this a form of blaming the victim?

5. Should we call rape between nonstrangers "acquaintance rape"? Does that terminology degrade the crime into something less than what it is?

6. Should there be a requirement for independent evidence to support a charge of marital rape? Why? Why not?

Suggested Readings

P. Phillips, *Marx and Engels on Law and Laws*, (Barnes and Noble, Totowa, N.J.) 1980.

K. Millett, *Sexual Politics*,(Abacus, London) 1972.

S. Brownmiller, *Against Our Will: Men, Women and Rape*, (Penguin Books, New York) 1975.

L. Kelly, *Surviving Sexual Violence*, (University of Minnesota Press, Minneapolis) 1988.

D. E. H. Russell, *Sexual Exploitation*, (Sage, Beverly Hills, Calif.) 1884.

D. Russell, *The Politics of Rape,* (Stein and Day, New York) 1975.

D. Symons, *The Evolution of Human Sexuality,* (Oxford University Press, Oxford) 1979.

C. McCaghy, *Deviant Behavior: Crime, Conflict, and Interest Groups,* (Macmillian, New York) 1976.

A. N. Groth & J. Birnbaum, *Men Who Rape,* (Plenum Press, New York) 1979.

H. Wallace & C. Roberson, *Principles of Criminal Law,* (Longman, White Plains, New York) 1995.

R. E. Martin, *The Life of Lady Randolph Churchill,* (New York American Library, New York) 1969.

D. Finkelhor & K. Yllo, *License to Rape,* (Holt, Rinehart & Winston, New York) 1985.

B. Lindemann & D. D. Kadue, *Sexual Harassment in Employment Law,* (Bureau of National Affairs, Washington, D.C.) 1992.

A. M. Jaggar & P. S. Rothenberg, eds. *Feminist Frameworks,* 3rd ed., (McGraw-Hill, New York) 1993.

Endnotes

1. D. Russell, *The Politics of Rape,* (Stein and Day, New York) 1975.

2. D. Mosher & R. Anderson,"Macho Personality, Sexual Aggression and Reactions to Guided Imagery of Realistic Rape," 20 *Journal of Research in Personality,* 77–94 (1987).

3. D. Symons, *The Evolution of Human Sexuality,* (Oxford University Press, Oxford) 1979.

4. C. McCaghy, *Deviant Behavior, Crime, Conflict and Interest Groups,* (MacMillian, New York) 1976.

5. J. Rabkin, "Epidemiology of Forcible Rape," 49/4 *American Journal of Orthopsychiatry,* 634–647 (1979).

6. A. N. Groth, A. W. Burgess, & L. L. Holmstrom, "Rape: Power, Anger, and Sexuality," 134:11 *American Journal of Psychiatry,* 1239 (November 1977).

7. A. N. Groth & J. Birnbaum, *Men Who Rape,* (Plenum Press, New York) 1979.

8. For an excellent in-depth discussion of these issues see, M.P. Koss, "Detecting the Scope of Rape," 8/2 *Journal of Interpersonal Violence,* 198–222 (June 1993).

9. M. P. Koss, "Detecting the Scope of Rape," 8/2 *Journal of Interpersonal Violence,* 200–203 (June 1993).

10. M. R. Burt, Attitudes Supportive of Rape in American Culture (Final Report, Grant #ROIMH29023), National Institute of Mental Health, (National Center for the Prevention and Control of Rape, Washington, D.C.) 1979.

11. S. M. Essock-Vitlae & M. T. McGuire, "Women's Lives Viewed from an Evolutionary Perspective," I. Sexual Histories, Reproductive Success, and Demographic Characteristics of a Random Sample of American Women, 6 *Ethnology and Sociobiology,* 137–154 (1985).

12. D. G. Kilpatrick, C. L. Best, L. J. Veronen, A. E. Amick, L. A. Villeponteaux & G. A. Ruff," Mental Health Correlates of Criminal Victimization: A Random Community Survey," 53 *Journal of Consulting and Clinical Psychology,* 866–873 (1985).

13. S. Riger & M. T. Gordon, "The Fear of Rape; A Study in Social Control," 37 *Journal of Social Issues,* 71–92 (1981).

14. D. G. Kilpatrick, C. N. Edmunds, & A. K. Seymour, *Rape In America: A Report to the Nation,* (National Victims Center, Arlington, Va.) 1992.

15. D. E. H. Russell, *Sexual Exploitation,* (Sage, Beverly Hills, Calif.) 1884.

16. S. B. Sorenson, J. A. Stein, J. M. Siegel, J. M. Golding, & M. A. Burnam, "Prevalence of Adult Sexual Assault: The Los Angeles Epidemiologic Catchment Area Study," 126 *American Journal of Epidemiology,* 1154–1164 (1987).

17. I. Winfield, L. K. George, M. Swartz, & D. G. Blazer, "Sexual Assault and Psychiatric Disorders Among a Community Sample of Women," 147 *American Journal of Psychiatry,* 335–341 (1990).

18. G. E. Wyatt, "The Sociocultural Context of African American and White American Women's Rape," 48 *Journal of Social Issues,* 77–92 (1992).

19. Personal communication with Christine N. Edmunds, co-author and project director, National Victims Center, Washington, D.C.

20. L. B. Bienen, "Rape III—National Developments in Rape Reform Legislation," 6 *Women's Rights Law Reporter*, 171–213 (1981).

21. H. C. Black, *Black's Law Dictionary*, (West Publishing Co., St. Paul, Minn.) p. 213 (1990).

22. Model Penal Code Section 213.1 (American Law Institute, Chicago) 1985.

23. H. Wallace & C. Roberson, *Principles of Criminal Law*, (Longman, White Plains, New York) 1994.

24. D. G. Kilpatrick, C. L. Best, B. E. Saunders, & L. J. Veronen, "Rape in Marriage and in Dating Relationships: How Bad Is It for Mental Health?" 528 *Annals of the New York Academy of Sciences*, 335–344 (1988).

25. M. P. Koss, "Detecting the Scope of Rape," 8/2 *Journal of Interpersonal Violence*, 198 (June 1993).

26. Craig Wolff, "Rapists Increasingly Using Condoms," *The Fresno Bee*, A-7 (August 22, 1994).

27. See *Michigan v. Lucas*, 111 S. Ct. 1743 (1991) where the United States Supreme Court upheld the constitutionality of these statutes. See also, *Vermont Statute*, Title 13, Chapter 72, Section 3255 (3)(A)(B) for an example of a rape shield law.

28. Dennis J. Stevens, "Predatory Rapist and Victim Selection Techniques," 3¼ *The Social Science Journal*, 421 (1994).

29. D. G. Kilpatrick, C. N. Edmunds, & A. K. Seymour, *Rape in America: A Report to the Nation*, (National Victim Center, Arlington, Va.) 1992.

30. E. Kanin, "Male Aggression in Dating–Courtship Relationships" 63 *American Journal of Sociology*, 197–204 (1957).

31. Mary P. Koss & Sarah L. Cook, "Date and Acquaintance Rape Are Significant Problems for Women," Richard J. Gelles and Donileen R. Loseke, (eds.) *Current Controversies on Family Violence*, (Sage, Newbury Park, Calif.) 1993.

32. Sally A. Lloyd, "Physical and Sexual Violence during Dating/Courtship," in Richard J. Gelles, (ed.), *Vision 2010: Families & Violence, Abuse, & Neglect*, (National Council on Family Relations, Minneapolis) 1995.

33. T. Meyer, "Date Rape: A Serious Campus Problem That Few Talk About," *Chronicle of Higher Education*, A 15 (5 December 1990).

34. Council of Scientific Affairs, "Violence Against Women," *Journal of the American Medical Association*, 3/84 (267/23) (June 17, 1992).

35. Kersti Yllo,"Marital Rape," in Richard J. Gelles, (ed.), *Vision 2010: Families & Violence, Abuse, & Neglect*, (National Council on Family Relations, Minneapolis) 1995.

36. See Comment, "Abolishing the Marital Exemption to Rape: A Statutory Proposal, *U. Ill. L. Rev.* 201 (1983).

37. M. Hale, *The History of the Pleas of the Crown* (1736). The first American edition of the book, *Pleas of the Crown*, was published in 1874. See Comment, "Sexual Assault: The Case for Removing the Spousal Exemption from Texas Law," 38 *Baylor Law Review*, 1941 (1986).

38. G. Geis, "Rape and Marriage: Historical and Cross-Cultural Considerations," Paper presented at the annual meeting of the American Sociological Association, New York (1980). See also M. Hale, *The History of the Pleas of the Crown*, (1736) p. 629.

39. L. D. Waggoner, "New Mexico Joins the Twentieth Century: The Repeal of the Marital Rape Exemption," 22 *N. M. L. Rev.*, 551 (1992).

40. R. E. Martin, *The Life of Lady Randolph Churchill*, (New York American Library, New York) 1969.

41. J. Schulman, "The Marital Rape Exemption in the Criminal Law," 13/6 *Clearinghouse Review* (1980).

42. D. Finkelhor & K. Yllo, *License to Rape*, (Holt, Rinehart & Winston, New York) 1985.

43. Safran, "What Men Do to Women on the Job: A Shocking Look at Sexual Harassment," *Redbook*, 149 (Nov. 1976). Redbook received over 9000 responses to their questionnaire regarding sexual harassment.

44. "Sexual Harassment in the Federal Workplace—Is It a Problem?" (Merit System Protection Board 1981); see also W. Pollack,

"Sexual Harassment: Women's Experience vs. Legal Definitions," 13 *Harv. Women's L.J. 35* (Spring 1990) for a discussion of this and other surveys.

45. *42 U.S.C. 2000e to 2000e-17 (1964).*
46. *42 U.S.C. 2000e-2(a) (1982).*
47. *42 U.S.C. 2000e(k) (1982).*
48. *Wilson v. Southwest Airlines Co.,* 517 F. Supp. 292 at 297 fn. 12 (N.D. Tex. 1981).
49. *Meritor Saving's Bank v. Vinson,* 106 S.Ct. 2399, 2404 (1986).
50. B. Lindemann & D. D. Kadue, *Sexual Harassment in Employment Law,* (Bureau of National Affairs, Washington, D.C.) 1992.
51. See note, "The Dehumanizing Puzzle of Sexual Harassment: A Survey of the Law Concerning Harassment of Women in the Workplace," 24 *Washburn L.J.,* 574 (1985).
52. See *Barnes v. Costle,* 561 F.2d 983 (D.C. Cir. 1977).
53. 561 F.2d 983 (D.C. Cir. 1977).
54. 29 C.F.R. ss 1604.11(a).
55. *Meritor Saving's Bank v. Vinson,* 106 S.Ct. 2399, (1986).
56. 114 S.Ct. 367 (1993).
57. S. Tangri, M. Burt, & L. Johnson, "Sexual Harassment at Work: Three Explanatory Models," 38 *Journal of Social Issues,* 33–54 (1982).
58. B. W. Dziech & L. Weiner, "The Lecherous Professor," in A. M. Jaggar and P. S. Rothenberg, (eds.), *Feminist Frameworks,* 3rd ed., (McGraw-Hill, New York) 1993, pp. 323–327.

9

SPOUSES AS VICTIMS

Chapter Outline

Introduction to Spousal Abuse
Definition
Extent of the Problem
Dynamics of Battering

Theories on Spousal Abuse
Social Stress
Power
Dependency
Alcohol
Pregnancy
Marriage

The Criminal Justice Response to Spousal Abuse
Introduction
Factors Affecting Police Response
Arrest of Abusers
The Minneapolis Experiment
Other Replications

Summary

Key Terms

Discussion Questions

Suggested Readings

Learning Objectives

After reading this chapter, you should be able to:

- Explain why victims stay in abusive relationships
- Distinguish between the cycle theory of violence and the battered woman syndrome
- Define and give examples of the Stockholm syndrome
- Understand the various theories of spousal abuse
- Explain the advantages and disadvantages of mandatory arrest policies for those who assault their spouses

Introduction to Spousal Abuse

There is probably no more misunderstood form of violence than spousal abuse. Gelles has published a series of *Domestic Violence Factoids,* which are statements or sound bites used by various individuals or agencies when discussing family violence.[1] Gelles explained that many of these statements have taken on a life of their own and are presumed to be true or accurate. In many instances, this "truth" is based on misinterpretation or faulty analysis of research. The following are some of these factoids and Gelles's response:

Domestic violence is the leading cause of injury to women between the ages of fifteen and forty-four in the United States—more than car accidents, muggings, and rapes combined.

> *Gelles explained that as good a sound bite as this statement is, it is simply not true. The actual research that this statement is based on was a small survey of only one emergency room and the authors of the study stated that domestic violence* may *be a more common cause of emergency room visits than car accidents, muggings, and rapes.*

The March of Dimes reports that battering during pregnancy is the leading cause of birth defects and infant mortality.

> *Gelles responded that the March of Dimes knows of no such study.*

Nationally, 50 percent of all homeless women and children are on the streets because of violence in the home.

> *Gelles stated that this factoid can be attributed to Senator Biden, but there is no actual published scientific research supporting this figure.*

There are nearly three times as many animal shelters in the United States as there are shelters for battered women and their children.

> *Gelles indicated that although this is another great sound bite, there is no verified count of either type of shelter.*

As this discussion indicates, there is still a great deal of misinformation and controversy surrounding spousal abuse. These factoids should not be interpreted to mean that spousal abuse is not a serious and deadly problem. It is. However, to understand this form of violence, we must base our knowledge on facts or theories that are accepted within the various professions that deal with spousal abuse, not on sound bites.

Definition

There is no clear, single definition of spousal abuse. Different authorities include different acts within their definition and some authorities have established levels of spousal abuse. They categorize spousal abuse into two forms of violence. The lessor forms include yelling and throwing things and the more severe include striking and hitting.

As the practicum below indicates, there are shades of grey in any situation, and reasonable people may disagree as to what constitutes spousal abuse. For purposes of this chapter, *spousal abuse* is defined as any intentional act or series of acts that cause injury to the spouse. These acts may be physical, emotional, or sexual. Spouse is gender neutral and therefore the abuse may occur to a man or woman. The term includes those who are married, cohabitating, or involved in a serious relationship. It also encompasses individuals who are separated and living apart from their former spouses. Although there is some disagreement regarding the exact definition of spousal abuse, all scholars and authorities agree it exists. The next section will examine the extent of this form of family violence.

PRACTICUM: **Spousal Abuse**

Which of the following in your opinion would be considered spousal abuse:

- A man is upset at his girlfriend, who is late for a date. He calls her lazy and irresponsible.

- During a date, the man takes his date's arm and steers her to an exit, commenting that she is stupid for not seeing that this is the fastest way to leave the theater.

- A couple living together while attending college get into a yelling match, with each of them calling the other names.

- The same couple's argument escalates and the woman throws a textbook at her male friend. It misses and strikes the television.

- During a heated argument, the man grabs the woman's arms and shakes her.

- A husband yells at his wife and calls her an obscenity after she overdraws the bank account, causing him to bounce a check.

- The husband does not allow his wife access to any funds after she bounced three checks and almost caused him to lose his job at the bank.

- The wife is tired and wants to sleep, but the husband forces her to engage in sex.

- The wife does not enjoy anal sex, stating that it hurts her, but the husband forces her to engage in it once a month.

Extent of the Problem

Depending on whose study is reviewed, the extent of spousal abuse varies. In their landmark study of 8145 families, Straus and Gelles estimated that just over 16 percent, or one in six American couples, experienced an incident of physical assault during 1985. Projecting that number to the 54 million couples in America in that year leads to a startling figure of approximately 8.7 million couples who were involved in spousal abuse.[2] Other scholars point out that 20 percent of all women who go to emergency rooms for treatment have been battered.[3] These authorities cite figures that pertain to physical violence. As the definition here indicates, spousal abuse also includes psychological and sexual abuse. When a woman is emotionally abused, she may not go to an emergency room or even report the acts because she may believe she deserved the treatment and therefore it is not abuse. "After all, he didn't hit me" is a common refrain in some spousal abuse cases.

Although it is true that the definition of spousal abuse is gender neutral and in fact men can be battered by women, most of the victims of spousal abuse are women. In 1977, Steinmetz presented a paper entitled "The Battered Husband Syndrome." This presentation was the basis for an article dealing with husbands who are battered.[4] Steinmetz's research, which was widely publicized in the media, claimed that men were abused at a far greater rate than previously believed. Steinmetz went even further and claimed that wives abused their husbands more often and more severely than vice versa. This claim was attacked by feminists, professionals, and scholars. In 1988, Steinmetz and Lucca published a follow-up article discussing husband battering in more detail.[5] In this article, they continued to assert that husbands are battered and concluded that all forms of violence must be prevented by placing greater emphasis on changing the attitudes and values of a society that glorify violence.

One result of Steinmetz's position is the acknowledgment that both parties in an abusive relationship need to be evaluated. Some studies indicate that there are higher levels of female aggression by women toward their spouses than previously thought.[6] However, the type and severity of aggression is different than that experienced by women. As Campbell explained, most authorities agree that the detrimental effects of abuse affect women disproportionately.[7] Furthermore, Campbell stated that gender inequity is a significant risk factor in battering.

Although it may be true that some men are abused by women in an intimate relationship, the majority of all abuse is inflicted by men. Therefore the remainder of this chapter will examine the abused from the perspective of women as the victims.

One surprising result of some of these studies is the indication that spousal abuse may have declined in recent years. There are several explanations for this apparent decline. One is the existence of shelters for women who are abused. This escape valve allows them an option to escape an abusive relationship. Another is the widespread publicity that has occurred in recent years about spousal abuse. A third possible explanation is more effective punishment and better treatment for the assaultive partner.[8] Although the incidence of spousal abuse may be declining, many scholars believe its severity is increasing. Even with a decline in the number of reported cases in recent years, this form of family violence is still prevalent and requires any professional to be familiar with the nature and dynamics of spousal abuse.

Dynamics of Battering

One often-asked question is, "Why does the victim stay in an abusive relationship?" The reasons that women stay with abusive partners are complex and multifaceted. A number of theories attempt to explain the dynamics involved in battering. This section will briefly discuss some of the more well-known concepts in this area.

Lenore E. Walker is one of the leading authorities in the area of spousal abuse. She coined the term "cycle theory of violence" as a result of her research in the area of battered women.[9] This concept does not attempt to explain the cause of spousal abuse, rather it examines the dynamics of this form of family violence.

The *cycle theory of violence* sets forth the dynamics of battering in spousal abuse. Walker's theory has three distinct phases: the tension-building phase; the explosion or acute battering phase; and the calm, loving respite phase. These phases can vary in length and intensity depending on the relationship.

Tension-Building Phase.   As the tension-building phase implies, tension increases within the relationship, at which time the husband may engage in minor battering of his spouse. The wife attempts to calm him by agreeing to his demands, becoming more nurturing, or simply attempting to stay out of his way during this phase. The victim may rationalize that perhaps she is really at fault and deserves the abuse, accepting the batterer's faulty logic as her own. Women who have been in a battering relationship for an extended time know only too well that the minor battering will increase in time. A woman may try to withdraw more from the abuser in an attempt to avoid more conflict, but the tension in the relationship will continue to increase until the batterer explodes in a fit of rage.

Explosion or Acute Battering Phase.   During the explosion or acute battering phase, the abuser loses control and engages in major incidents of assaultive behavior. The intense, violent aggression is what distinguishes this phase from the minor or occasional battering that takes place in the first phase. When the first serious attack is over, both parties may feel shock, disbelief, and denial. For example, the woman may attempt to minimize her injuries.

Calm, Loving Respite Phase.   The calm, loving respite phase is characterized by contrite loving acts on the part of the abuser. The batterer may understand that he has gone too far during the previous phase and will beg forgiveness and promise never to let it happen again. The woman will want to accept the abuser's promises that he can change and that his loving behavior is an inducement for her to stay in the relationship.

Walker's theory is generally accepted both in academia and in the legal system. Her explanation for the dynamics of battering has been cited in numerous court decisions that deal with battered spouses.

Walker also presented the concept of the "Battered Woman Syndrome."[10] Some authorities prefer the term battered "woman's experiences" because they believe that the former (1) implies that there is one syndrome that all battered women develop; (2) has pathological connotations that suggest that battered women suffer from some sort of sickness; (3) does not make clear that, according to expert testimony, domestic violence refers to more than women's psychological reactions to violence; (4) focuses attention on the battered woman rather than on the batterer's coercive behavior; and (5) creates an image of battered women as suffering victims rather than active survivors.[11] However, because most court cases and the majority of experts still refer to this experience as the battered woman syndrome, that term will be used in this text. According to Walker, the ***battered woman syndrome*** theorizes that victims of spousal abuse gradually become immobilized by fear and believe they have no other options. As a result, these women stay in the abusive relationships, coping the best they can. The battered woman syndrome involves one who has been, on at least two occasions, the victim of physical, sexual, or serious psychological abuse by a man with whom she has an intimate relationship. It is a pattern of psychological symptoms that develop after someone has lived in a battering relationship. This is a gradual process of conditioning in which the victim feels both helpless and hopeless and, according to Walker, is one of the main reasons why spouses stay in these situations longer than people would expect. The abuse tends to follow the three-stage cyclical pattern of tension building, acute explosion, and loving contrition. The following responses are typical of women suffering from the battered woman syndrome: (1) traumatic effects of victimization induced by violence; (2) learned helplessness deficits; and (3) self-destructive coping responses to the violence.[12]

Very similar in dynamics to the battered woman syndrome is a condition referred to as the ***Stockholm Syndrome,*** which is a phenomenon that occurs when persons who are held as hostages, captives, or prisoners of war begin to identify with the captors. These victims are isolated, mistreated, and in fear for their lives. They become helpless, confined to the area in which they are ordered to stay, and dependent on their captors to supply everything they need to survive. They begin to develop positive feelings for their captors.[13] The syndrome was named after an incident in Stockholm, Sweden, where four bank employees were held hostage in the bank's vault for 131 hours by two perpetrators. When the victims were finally freed, they expressed gratitude toward the offenders for sparing their lives.

NiCarthy indicated that the dynamics of spousal abuse are very similar to techniques used to control or brainwash prisoners of war. NiCarthy wrote, "As stated in a report published by Amnesty International, these techniques induce 'dependency, dread and debility.' To the extent that a person is victimized by these techniques, she or he tends to become immobilized by the belief that she or he is trapped, cannot escape."[14] This heightening of fear, helplessness, dependency, and dread are all intertwined in the definition and dynamics of spousal abuse.

Dutton and Painter developed the ***traumatic bonding theory*** to explain why battered women stay in abusive relationships.[15] This theory holds that when a woman finally leaves an abusive partner, her immediate fears begin to diminish and her hidden attachment to her abuser begins to manifest itself. Emotionally drained and vulnerable, she becomes susceptible to her partner's loving contrite pressure to return. As her fears lessen and the needs previously provided by her partner increase, she may decide to give him another chance.[16]

Dutton's theory is based on the concepts of power distribution and emotional bonding that focus on the dynamics of the abusive relationship rather than on any personality defect or socioeconomic status of the victim. Dutton states that these two features—the existence of a power imbalance and the intermittent nature of the abuse—can explain why abused women stay with their abusers or even return to the relationship. Dutton theorized that when power imbalances exist in a relationship, the person of low power feels more negative in her self-appraisal, more incapable of fending for herself, and thus in need of the person with more power. This cycle of dependency and lowered self-esteem repeats itself over and over and eventually creates a strong affective bond to the high-power person.[17]

The second factor in traumatic bonding is the intermittent nature of the abuse. This occurs when the abusive partner periodically abuses the submissive partner by threats or physical acts. The time between these incidents is normally characterized by normal, socially acceptable behavior. Thus, the victim is subjected to negative arousal and the relief or release associated with its removal. This situation of alternating negative and pleasant conditions is known within learning theory as "partial or intermittent reinforcement." Dutton states that this situation is highly effective in producing persistent patterns of behavior associated with strong emotional attachment to the abuser that is hard to change or modify.[18]

These four theories or concepts are only a few of the many reasons advanced for why battered women stay in abusive relationships. At this time, controversy continues regarding why victims stay in these relationships. Victim service providers must understand these concepts so that they can educate not only the public but also members of the criminal justice profession.

Theories on Spousal Abuse

If we knew the causes of spousal abuse, we could correct them. To date, no one has yet come forward with a definitive answer to this problem. However, numerous scholars in different professions have studied this form of family violence and have developed a variety of reasons or causes for this type of abuse. Although several theories and studies exist in the area of spousal abuse, space dictates that only a few of the more well-known theories can be discussed.

Social Stress

The family system in America is a system of contradictions. Americans retreat from the city streets to their homes and install bars on their windows to keep out the violence. Yet the family structure is one of the most violent settings a person is likely to encounter.

For purposes of this discussion, a family is a group of persons who cohabitate. Marriage is not a requirement. Within this living arrangement, forces converge to cause stress. This increased level of stress in turn leads to a high rate of violence within the family. Many times this violence is directed at the spouse in the form of physical assaults. It should be pointed out that stress does not cause violence; it is one of the many responses available to persons who suffer from stress.

Family life has a different set of behaviors than other social settings. How the members within a family setting dress, talk, and act in their home is different from when they attend social functions. Additionally, violence in the form of physical punishment is accepted by many as a characteristic of the family. Parents can and do slap infants' hands to teach them to not touch the hot coffee pot. Thus, this form of physical violence may be used on loved ones for their own benefit. When stress occurs, there is already a preconditioned response or behavior that has been used, and therefore it is easier to use when one is under pressure.

Power

Power is the ability to impose one's will on another and make life decisions. Couples who share power or are equals in the decision-making process have the lowest level of both conflict and violence.[19] When a conflict arises, these families display the greatest resistance to the use of violence.

One characteristic of family violence is the use and abuse of power. Additionally, battered women report a feeling of powerlessness as a result of the spousal abuse they have suffered. If the husband desires power and control in the relationship, this represents one factor that may indicate a potential for violence.

Dependency

Some authorities argue that our society has fostered women's dependency. Women's financial and social success in many instances has been dependent on the man they marry. Although this is beginning to change, the "glass ceiling" still remains for the most part an impregnable barrier. A few examples illustrate this point: There are only two female United States Supreme Court justices, only six women are United States senators, and only a small percentage of women are chief executive officers of major corporations.[20] Statistically, after a divorce a man's standard of living increases, while a woman's declines.[21]

The meaning of marital dependency is subject to debate, but the most common meaning includes economic dependency. The wife has little or no earning power and is therefore dependent on her husband for the necessities of life. A variation on this theme of economic dependency results from the presence of children. Although a woman may be able to leave an abusive relationship and make ends meet, the addition of children multiplies the difficulties inherent in any separation. A third factor in dependence is society's expectation of women as caregivers and the further hidden message that a woman is not whole until she is married.[22]

Thus, *marital dependency* is a multifaceted concept that involves economic, emotional, and societal forces that result in a woman being dependent on her spouse for support. This dependency on a man and marriage for economic, emotional, and other support increases a woman's tolerance for physical abuse.

Straus and Gelles and their associates conducted an in-depth study of dependency and violence and reported that women whose dependency on marriage is high tend to suffer more physical violence than women whose dependency is low. Dependent wives have fewer alternatives to marriage and fewer resources within the marriage with which to cope or modify their husbands' behavior.[23] This dependency is a pair of "golden handcuffs" that bind the spouse to the abusive partner.

Alcohol

There is a common perception that men who drink alcohol beat their spouses. Therefore, so the reasoning goes, alcohol causes violence. Movies, books, and to some extent our own personal experiences support the concept that alcohol causes problems in relationships. The relationship between alcohol and abuse has been studied extensively, and several theories regarding alcohol and its relationship to violence exist. A few of the more common theories are listed here.

Disinhibition Theory. The disinhibition theory is based on the principle that alcohol releases inhibitions and alters judgment. Medical evidence regarding the effects of alcohol on the central nervous system supports this theory. However, recent research into the disinhibition theory reveals that alcohol interacts with individuals based on varying individual expectancies, which is only one aspect of the alcohol–violence equation.[24]

Social Learning and Deviance Disavowal Theory. Coleman and Straus argued that individuals learn violence by observing others who drink and become violent. This violent behavior is excused, pardoned, or justified because the individual was drunk and therefore not accountable for his or her actions.[25] Other scholars have suggested that individuals use alcohol to increase their sense of power and as an excuse for the exercise of unlawful force against others.[26]

Integrated Theoretical Models. Pernanem's research into alcohol and violence indicates numerous factors that interact in alcohol and violence. These factors may include the inherent conflict present in marriages.[27] A second factor is our society's expectation that drinking is an acceptable and expected form of male behavior.

These theories and studies have attempted to determine if alcohol causes spousal abuse. At this stage, there is no definitive answer, but a link between the two is apparent. However, there are persons who drink and do not abuse their spouses so it would appear that alcohol by itself cannot be defined as the cause of spousal abuse.

Pregnancy

Pregnancy and spousal abuse is a controversial subject, and studies indicate that there is a relationship between the two.[28] Despite this linkage, the question still remains of whether pregnancy contributes to domestic violence or whether it is simply another factor to be considered. Most studies are based on small samples and have internal validity problems; however, the Straus and Gelles survey of violence, using the National Family Violence Survey, determined that the rates of violence were higher for households in which the female partner was pregnant.[29] Subsequently, the authors concluded that previously reported associations between pregnancy and violence were not valid and that age is a more critical factor in determining violence than pregnancy. Young women have higher pregnancy rates and they experience violence more often than older women. Women under the age of twenty-five appeared to be at the highest level of risk.

Marriage

"The marriage license as a hitting license" was adopted in the early 1970s by Straus and Gelles when they discovered that married couples suffered assault at a much greater rate than strangers.[30] They reasoned that the common law tradition that allowed a husband to discipline his wife was alive and well in this modern age. However, more recent studies indicate that the highest rate of assault is among cohabiting couples. Additionally, violence is most severe in homes of cohabiting couples.[31]

Age may also be a factor, because dating and cohabiting couples tend to be younger than married couples. However, other research indicated that age and marital status have no relationship to violence. Therefore, significant relationships, whether they involve dating, cohabitation, or marriage, place women at risk. As indicated, cohabiting couples may be at a higher risk than married couples. In a more recent evaluation of the National Family Violence Survey, Straus and Gelles set forth the following factors as having more impact on the degree of risk a woman faces in a cohabiting relationship.

Isolation. Couples who are living together may be more isolated than married couples. Part of this isolation may be because of the stigma society attaches to cohabitation over marriage. This isolation allows for spousal abuse because of the lack of a supporting network of friends or family available for the abused spouse.

Autonomy and Control. Some persons prefer cohabitation over marriage with the thought that they can retain their own independence. However, any living arrangement brings with it duties, obligations, tensions, and the resulting disagreements. Some authorities point out that when the issue of control arises, violence occurs.[32] As the relationship becomes more serious, the issue of control becomes more important and violence is more likely to occur.

Investment in the Relationship. Cohabiting couples may share some characteristics that trigger violence while lacking others shared by married couples who stop the conflict from escalating into physical violence.[33]

As with other theories of spousal abuse, more study and research needs to occur before we can understand whether women who enter into any significant relationship are at risk of spousal abuse. This section has discussed various theories of spousal abuse, and it is clear that as of now we have not discovered a cure for this type of abuse. The cause of this type of violence may never be determined; therefore, is necessary for professionals in the field to understand the criminal justice response to spousal abuse.

The Criminal Justice Response to Spousal Abuse

Introduction

There are excellent texts and research material that discuss police and domestic violence.[34] This material provides an in-depth scholarly examination of the causes, effects, and police responses in this area. The purpose of this section is to acquaint readers with an overview of policing of spousal assault cases. This will allow them to have an understanding of some of the existing controversies in this highly debated area of domestic violence.

The term *spousal assault* is used to distinguish this form of family violence from spousal abuse. From a legal perspective, the term *spousal assault* is inaccurate. As will be discussed later in this chapter, in a majority of states an assault does not involve any physical injury to the victim. However, to be consistent with other professionals and writers in the field of family violence, **spousal assault** is used and defined as the act of intentionally inflicting physical injury on the spouse or other person who is cohabitating with the abuser. It is distinct and yet a part of spousal abuse in that all the dynamics that cause spousal abuse may be present in spousal assault. However, this form of assault may occur without the existence of the other forms of abuse, such as emotional or psychological injury, that typically accompany spousal abuse.

FOCUS: A Case of Indifference

Thurman v. City of Torrington, 595 F. Supp. 1521 (Conn. 1984).[35]

Starting in October 1982 and continuing until June 1983, Tracey Thurman repeatedly contacted the Torrington, Connecticut, police department begging for protection from her estranged husband, Buck. Tracey signed several sworn complaints against Buck; however, the police department considered the incidents a family matter and did not respond to them in the same manner as they did to "stranger assaults."

On the day of the final beating, Buck stabbed Tracey repeatedly. A police officer arrived and asked Buck for the knife but did not arrest or restrain him in any manner. Buck gave the officer the knife and then proceeded to stomp on Tracey's head in front of the officer. He then went inside the house and returned with their son and cursed and kicked Tracey in the head. This series of blows left her partially paralyzed. Other officers arrived, and

they did not arrest Buck until he tried to assault Tracey as she lay on the ambulance stretcher.

Tracey filed suit in federal court against the City of Torrington, its police department, and all twenty-four officers that she had contacted over the years about Buck's assaultive acts. She alleged that the police department and its officers had been negligent in responding to her and, further, that they had violated her constitutional rights to equal protection under the law by treating her differently than they would persons who were assaulted by strangers.

The jury awarded Tracey $2.3 million in damages. Although the city's insurance company paid the judgment, it indicated that it might not pay any future awards of any police department that refused or failed to educate their officers about domestic violence.[36]

Similar to many other areas of domestic violence, police response to spousal assault is still being researched and studied. As with so much of domestic violence and other criminal acts, we simply do not have the answers to the problem. Scholars such as Cynthia Bowman would even argue that we do not yet even understand what questions to ask.[37]

If spousal assault were like any other crime, the police response would be fairly simple: investigate, arrest, charge, and cooperate with the district attorney in the prosecution of the perpetrator. Unfortunately, spousal assault involves certain factors that make it unique. These factors will be explored in detail in this chapter. These forces all interact to cause law enforcement agencies to respond differently to spousal assault than they do to robberies, rapes, and other crimes of violence.

As the Thurman case described in the Focus box illustrates, spousal assault can have serious consequences for both the victim and any professionals who are involved with either the abuser or the victim. However, we are slowly beginning to acknowledge that spousal assault is one of the crimes society has ignored. *Thurman* and similar cases will be discussed in more detail in Chapter 15. Part of the reason for society's reaction to this form of domestic violence is the perceived difficulty in responding to physical assaults between adult family members. Another factor is our inability to classify those who assault their spouses into any identifiable category. Finally, as with other forms of family violence, we cannot with any certainty predict who will be the aggressor or victim in the area of spousal assault.

Factors Affecting Police Response

Law enforcement's acknowledgment and response to spousal assault have been slow in coming. Even today there are police officers who would rather not get involved in a "family matter." This should not be surprising in that the battering of women has existed for thousands of years. As indicated in Chapter 8, women were considered chattel and it was perfectly proper to "discipline" spouses as long as there was no permanent injury inflicted upon the wife.[38] There is clear evidence that numerous early laws accorded men rights and power over women.[39] The privacy that families enjoyed behind the closed doors of the home continued into modern times.

The *Journal of Marriage and the Family* did not even discuss spousal assault until 1971.[40] Slowly, however, scientific data emerged that indicated criminal violence occurred behind those closed doors. By the mid-1970s, numerous other studies began to elevate spousal abuse to the status of a national social problem.

Feminist groups, scholars, and others raised a hue and cry regarding this form of criminal conduct. Between 1975 and 1980, forty-four states passed some sort of legislation on domestic violence. Despite the existence of laws regarding spousal abuse, studies have indicated that police have been reluctant to enforce violations of this type of criminal conduct.[41]

No one single factor has resulted in this hesitation or reluctance to enforce the laws in the area of spousal assault. Scholars have examined this phenomenon in detail and have noted a series of influences that have affected police agencies' enforcement of spousal assault. These factors include call screening, beliefs regarding financial hardship on the family in the event of an arrest, the family argument theory, the classification of spousal assault as a misdemeanor, the victim's preference not to arrest, and perceived danger to the police in domestic violence situations.

Numerous police departments have engaged in **call screening,** which is downgrading by the law enforcement agency of the priority assigned to domestic violence calls for service. This call screening results in a slower response time by the police officer than for other calls of the same or similar seriousness. This dynamic allows the abuser to beat the victim and leave the scene of the crime before the arrival of the officers. In addition, the failure of police to respond in a timely manner may increase the power of the abuser over the victim and lead the victim to believe that she is truly alone and helpless.

Police officers were and are reluctant to arrest the abuser in the mistaken belief that an arrest would pose a financial hardship on the family. An **arrest** is the taking of a person into custody in the manner prescribed by law. In addition, many law enforcement officers believe arrest is a futile act in view of the lack of prosecution and lenient sentences imposed (if at all) by the courts.

Many officers would arrest only if, in their opinion, the injury to the victim was severe. This is clearly not the law; however, it illustrates the thinking and reluctance of police to intervene in a "family argument."[42]

Until recently another factor affecting the decision to arrest was the statutory limits on arrests for certain types of crimes. Traditionally, criminal violations are divided into two major classifications: felonies and misdemeanors. In the United States, this distinction is spelled out by statute or state constitution.[43] A **felony** is considered the most serious type of crime and is usually punished by imprisonment in state prison. Many statutes provide that all other crimes are misdemeanors. A **misdemeanor** is considered less serious and is punished by incarceration in local jails not to exceed one year. Normally, police may arrest persons who have committed felonies based on reasonable grounds or probable cause. **Probable cause** is that set of facts that would lead a reasonable person to believe a crime has been committed by the suspect. This felony arrest may occur even if the officers did not personally witness the offense. Misdemeanor arrests, on the other hand, require the officers to witness the crime. If they did not see the offense committed, they could request the victim to make a citizen's arrest and then on behalf of the citizen they would take the perpetrator into custody.

This distinction in the nature and classification of crimes had a direct impact on the ability of police officers to make arrests for domestic violence assaults. Many domestic violence disputes involve a battery. Most statutes define a **battery** as the unlawful application of force to the person of another.[44] Battery is the unlawful touching of another, whereas assault does not require any physical touching of the other person.[45] Absent serious injury, many state laws define battery as a misdemeanor. Thus until recently, officers could not make an arrest for spousal assault unless they witnessed the act or the victim was willing to make a citizen's arrest.

The victim's preference not to file charges also affected the police officer's decision not to arrest the offender. Several studies have indicated that many times victims of spousal assault did not want the police to make an arrest.[46] This resulted in the officers admonishing the offender and leaving the scene of the crime.

Many police officers perceive family disputes as potentially dangerous situations in which both parties, the abuser and the victim, may turn on the officer. Although there are conflicting studies as to whether family disputes are in fact more dangerous to police officers, the fact that many officers believe this to be the case can result in a delay in responding to these types of calls for service.[47] This perception may cause officers to delay in responding to spousal assault calls until they have a backup unit.

In the last several years, many states have passed mandatory arrest statutes that require the officer to arrest the suspect. These laws allow police to make arrests for misdemeanors not committed in their presence. The passage of these laws and their effectiveness is a subject of debate within the field of criminal justice. The following section will discuss the factors that resulted in the passage of these statutes.

Arrest of Abusers

In recent years, victims of family violence have turned to the courts in an attempt to require law enforcement departments to provide effective intervention and protection against spousal assault. Increasingly, courts have begun to listen and rule in their favor both on constitutional and tort grounds. However, lawsuits and personal liability did not result in the amendment of various state statutes mandating arrest of abusers. This development started in 1984 with a federally funded experiment in Minneapolis.

The Minneapolis Experiment

In the area of policing and domestic violence, there is probably no more controversial study than the Minneapolis Experiment dealing with the effect of arrest on those who batter their spouses. The dean of policing and domestic violence, Lawrence Sherman, was the architect of the 1984 Minneapolis Domestic Violence Experiment. This study was the first controlled evaluation of the effect of arrest on individuals who commit assaultive types of crimes against their spouses.[48]

The Police Foundation and the Minneapolis Police Department joined forces to conduct a controlled experiment to test the effectiveness of arrest on prevention or deterrence of domestic violence. Funded in part by the National Institute of Justice, the experiment utilized a lottery system of three possible actions by police when dealing with domestic violence.

Police officers responding to a domestic disturbance were required to utilize one of the following options:

1. arrest with at least one night incarceration
2. send the offender away from the scene of the disturbance or arrest him if he refused to leave
3. give the couple some form of advice, including mediation

The officers were not allowed to select which of these options would be used, rather they carried a pad of forms that listed the available options. When they encountered a situation that met the experiment's criteria, they were required to utilize the option listed on the top form.

The experiment involved only misdemeanor batteries in which both the victim and the suspect were present when the officers arrived at the scene of the disturbance. Cases involving serious threats or danger to the victim were excluded as were situations in which the victim demanded the officers arrest the suspect.

After the officers finished their assignment, they turned in a brief report to the researchers for follow-up. The research staff utilized two measures to determine the amount of repeated violence by the offenders: official police reports and victim interviews. Official police reports were monitored to determine if the suspect committed another similar offense within a specified time period. In addition, the research staff contacted the listed victims and conducted a detailed interview with subsequent interviews for a period of twenty-four weeks after the initial offense.

The experiment produced a sample of 314 cases that met all the criteria. The results indicated that the arrest option produced the lowest percentage of repeated violence of all the alternatives. Official police reports revealed that 10 percent of the arrested suspects committed a subsequent offense, 24 percent of those suspects who were sent from the home repeated acts of violence against their spouse, and 19 percent of the suspects who were advised by the officers committed another offense. Interviews with victims produced even more dramatic percentages: 19 percent of the arrest suspects, 33 percent of those suspects sent from the home, and 37 percent of those advised by the officers committed another offense.

Based on the results of the study, Sherman and his colleagues made three recommendations. The first and probably the least controversial was to change existing laws to allow the police to make warrantless arrests for misdemeanor spousal assaults not committed in their presence. The second recommendation was read to suggest that mandatory arrest was the preferred option in most cases of domestic violence. The final recommendation suggested that additional experiments be conducted in other cities to validate the results of the Minneapolis study.

The Minneapolis Experiment acted as a change agent within the criminal justice system. Armed with its results, advocates of mandatory arrest and other sanctions were able to find support in various state legislatures for long overdue reform of criminal statutes dealing with domestic violence. Eleven states adopted legislation that authorized warrantless arrest in misdemeanor domestic violence cases, and another sixteen states enacted mandatory arrest laws in family violence situations.[49]

Prior to the experiment, only 10 percent of police departments serving cities over 100,000 in population encouraged their officers to make arrests in domestic violence situations. Within five years of the announcement of the results of the experiment, 84 percent of all major police departments in the United States had adopted a policy that stated arrest was the preferred option in domestic violence situations.[50]

The Minneapolis Experiment was hailed as a breakthrough study of domestic violence and criticized by a number of prominent scholars as inadequate and flawed.[51] In retrospect, it may not matter whether the results of the study were accurate; its greatest contribution may be that it generated an incredible amount of debate within academia and the law enforcement profession regarding how we should respond to domestic violence.

Other Replications

One direct result of the Minneapolis Experiment was the funding of additional replications by the National Institute of Justice. Five additional studies were undertaken in the following locations: Metro-Dade (Miami), Colorado Springs, Milwaukee, Omaha, and Charlotte. What was consistent about these additional studies was the finding of inconsistency in the deterrent effect of arrest.

The Metro-Dade Experiment established two major categories with two sub-groups under each of these categories. The two major subdivisions were those suspects who were arrested and those who were not arrested. Each of these groups were further divided into subgroups that did or did not receive follow-up counseling by specially trained police officers.[52] The Metro-Dade Experiment clearly supports the theory that arrest is a deterrent to future domestic violence.

The Colorado Springs Experiment employed four options in its replication: (1) arrest and issuance of a restraining order; (2) counseling for the offender and issuance of a restraining order; (3) issuance of a restraining order; and (4) restoring order at the scene of the crime without arrest or use of a restraining order. The Colorado Springs Experiment supports the hypothesis that arrest in some situations does in fact act as a deterrent to future violence.[53]

The Milwaukee Experiment was carried out in a city that in May 1986 had adopted a citywide policy of mandatory arrest for domestic violence cases.[54] However, the study did not involve arrests of all offenders, rather it utilized three options: full arrest, short arrest, or warning. The full arrest involved taking the suspect into custody pursuant to existing policy and allowing him bail in the amount of $250. The short arrest required officers to arrest the suspect but allowed him to be released on his own recognizance preferably within two hours after arrest. The warning option utilized a standard warning of arrest if the officers had to return to the location at any time during the same day.

The results were obtained by a review of police records and follow-up interviews with the victims. The researchers found that there was a clear initial deterrent effect in both the full arrest and short arrest situations as compared with the warning only option. However, this deterrence did not last and there appeared to be no long-term difference between the arrest options and warning option.

The original Minneapolis Experiment and these three replications may lead one to conclude that arrest does in fact deter either short-term or long-term spousal assault. Unfortunately, the Omaha and Charlotte replications came to the opposite conclusion. These studies were conducted in the same manner as the other replications and indicated that arrest does not deter future violence.

The Omaha Experiment randomly assigned eligible police calls regarding domestic violence into three categories when both the suspect and the victim were present.[55] These classifications were arrest, separation, or mediation. In those cases in which the suspect had already left the scene of the crime when the police arrived, the police randomly assigned him to a warrant or no warrant group.

The police relied on five conditions when making their determination of whether to include the suspect within the experiment: (1) the existence of probable cause to arrest for misdemeanor assault; (2) a clearly identifiable victim and suspect; (3) both the victim and suspect were adults; (4) the victim and the suspect must have cohabitated some time during the year preceding the assault; and (5) neither party had an outstanding arrest warrant. Although the Omaha Experiment excluded felony domestic violence cases, a majority of the calls for service involved physical injuries to the victim.

The results of the experiment were measured in two ways: review of police reports and victim interviews. Contrary to the Minneapolis Experiment, the Omaha study concluded that arrest of a suspect at the scene of the domestic assault did not have any greater deterrent effect than the other two options.[56] However, the issuance of a warrant for an offender who was absent from the scene of the crime at the time the officers arrived did appear to extend significantly the time frame in which the victim was free from further violence in comparison with those situations in which the police simply informed the victim that she had the right to obtain a warrant for the suspect.

The Charlotte Experiment tested three distinct alternatives to domestic violence.[57] Police responses included advising the couple, issuing a citation to the offender, or arresting the offender. Excluded from the study were situations in which the victim insisted on the arrest of the suspect, the suspect threatened or assaulted the officer, or the officer believed the victim was in imminent danger. Similar to the other replications, the Charlotte Experiment evaluated the effect of these alternatives using only two methods: police reports and victim interviews. The results indicated no significant difference in the deterrent effect of advising, citing, or arresting the offender.

These replications indicate that no clear answer exists as to whether arrest deters those who commit spousal assault. Scholars have found different interpretations in the data collected by these studies. Some authorities suggest that arrest may have a harmful effect on the victim, since there is statistical support for the position that arrest may lead to future violence rather than deter spousal assault. Others have hypothesized that arrest will deter certain types of suspects such as those who are employed or have something to lose as a result of the arrest. What is clear at this juncture is the need for more study in this area of domestic violence. If simply arresting the offender does not prevent spousal assault, we must look to other alternatives to determine if there are other mechanisms that may stop this form of family violence.

As a result of these studies and other factors, many police departments have adopted policies that encourage or mandate the arrest of a spouse abuser. To ensure the effectiveness of these policies, some police departments have created special domestic violence units, trained personnel on the dynamics of spousal abuse, and created sophisticated tracking and monitoring communication systems.[58]

For arrest to be an effective domestic violence intervention policy, there must be a coordinated and integrated response to the problem on the part of the criminal justice system. If police, prosecutors, judges, and probation and parole agencies all respond appropriately and the victims feel that the system is committed to protecting them and their children, we will have taken a major step forward in responding to this type of violence.[59]

Summary

Although spousal abuse has been intensely researched in the past years, it is still one of the most commonly misunderstood issues within family violence. Our society has placed women in inferior and subordinate positions throughout history, and even today some segments of our society continue to treat them as property rather than partners. These beliefs contribute to the interpersonal dynamics that result in violence against women. The nature and extent of spousal abuse is staggering. Current figures indicate women today are being brutalized at alarming numbers.

One common question asked by both professionals and laypersons is, "Why does the victim stay in such a relationship?" It is clear today that there are a number of dynamics that occur in a battering relationship. These dynamics many times bind victims to their abusers more tightly than if they were handcuffed to them.

There are numerous theories to explain why men batter women. In fact, there are so many theories that entire textbooks are devoted to explaining them. Yet no one theory is accepted by all scholars, practitioners, or professionals in the field as the theory that explains spousal abuse. Even though no one theory prevails, professionals should be aware of the more common and well-known studies of spousal abuse. They include studies of social stress, power, dependency, alcohol, pregnancy, and marriage.

The criminal justice system is still searching for ways to respond to spousal abuse. As a result of a number of factors, there are mandatory arrest policies in effect in a number of jurisdictions. This may stop the immediate battering but will not solve the problem. We must continue to search for ways to prevent this type of abuse. Only by stopping it before it occurs can we grow as a nation and society.

Key Terms

Spousal abuse is any intentional act or series of acts that cause injury to the spouse. These acts may be physical, emotional, or sexual. Spouse is gender neutral and therefore the abuse may occur to a man or a woman. The term includes those who are married, cohabitating, or involved in a serious relationship. It also encompasses individuals who are separated and living apart from their former spouse.

Cycle theory of violence sets forth the dynamics of battering in spousal abuse.

Battered woman syndrome theorizes that victims of spousal abuse gradually become immobilized by fear and believe they have no other options. As a result, these women stay in the abusive relationships coping the best they can. The battered woman syndrome involves one who has been, on at least two occasions, the victim of physical, sexual, or serious psychological abuse by a man with whom she has an intimate relationship. It is a pattern of psychological symptoms that develop after somebody has lived in a battering relationship.

Stockholm syndrome is a phenomenon that occurs when persons who are held as hostages, captives, or prisoners of war begin to identify with the captors.

Traumatic bonding theory explains why battered woman stay in abusive relationships. This theory holds that when a women finally leaves an abusive partner, her immediate fears begin to diminish and her hidden attachment to her abuser begins to manifest itself. Emotionally drained and vulnerable, she becomes susceptible to her partner's loving contrite pressure to return. As her fears lessen and the needs previously provided by her partner increase, she may decide to give him another chance.

Power is the ability to impose one's will on another and make life decisions.

Marital dependency is a multifaceted concept that involves economic, emotional, and societal forces that result in a woman being dependent on her spouse for support.

Spousal assault is used and defined as the act of intentionally inflicting physical injury on the spouse or other person who is cohabitating with the abuser.

Call screening. This is downgrading by the law enforcement agency of the priority assigned to domestic violence calls for service.

Arrest is the taking of a person into custody in the manner presented by law.

Felony is considered the most serious type of crime and is usually punished by imprisonment in state prison.

Misdemeanor is considered less serious and is punished by incarceration in local jails not to exceed one year.

Probable cause is that set of facts that would lead a reasonable person to believe a crime has been committed by the suspect.

Battery is the unlawful application of force to the person of another.

Discussion Questions

1. Can you narrow the definition of spousal abuse? What would you exclude and why?

2. Do we really know the extent of spouse abuse? Why is it important how many spouses are abused?

3. Which of the theories regarding the dynamics of battering do you believe is the major reason spouses stay with their abuser? Justify your answer.

4. Isn't Dutton's theory of traumatic bonding just another form of the battered woman syndrome? Why? Why not?

5. Which of the theories regarding spouse abuse do you believe is the major reason one spouse abuses the other?

6. What can we do to improve the criminal justice system's treatment of abused spouses?

Suggested Readings

M. A. Straus & R. J. Gelles, *Physical Violence in American Families*, (Transaction Publishers, New Brunswick, N.J.) 1990.

V. B. Hasselt, R. L. Morrison, A. S. Bellack, & W. Frazier, (eds.), *Handbook of Family Violence*, (Plenum, New York) 1988.

R. J. Gelles, (ed.) *Vision 2010,* (National Council on Family Relations, Minneapolis) 1995.

R. T. Ammerman & M. Hersen, (eds.) , *Case Studies in Family Violence,* (Plenum, New York) 1991.

L. E. Walker, *The Battered Woman,* (Harper & Row, New York) 1979.

L. E. Walker, *The Battered Woman Syndrome,* (Springer, New York) 1984.

D. J. Sonkin, (ed.), *Domestic Violence on Trial,* (Springer, New York) 1982.

M. D. Pagelow, *Family Violence,* (Praeger, New York) 1984.

D. G. Dutton, *The Domestic Assault of Women,* (UBC Press, Vancouver, B.C.) 1995.

E. S. Buzawa & C. G. Buzawa, (eds.), *Domestic Violence: The Changing Criminal Justice Response,* (Auburn House, Westport, Conn.) 1992.

A. M. Jaggar & P. S. Rothenberg, (eds.), *Feminist Frameworks,* 3rd ed. (McGraw Hill, New York) 1993.

L. W. Sherman, *Policing Domestic Violence,* (The Free Press, New York) 1992.

F. G. Bolton & S. R. Bolton, *Working with Violent Families,* (Sage, Newbury Park, Calif.) 1987.

W. R. LaFave & A. W. Scott, Jr., *Criminal Law,* 2nd ed. (West Publishing Co., St. Paul, Minn.) 1986.

R. M. Perkins & R. N. Boyce, *Criminal Law,* 3rd ed. (Foundation Press, Inc., New York) 1982.

M. Steinman, (ed.), *Women Battering: Policy Responses,* (Anderson Publishing Co., Cincinnati) 1991.

Endnotes

1. R. J. Gelles, *Domestic Violence Factoids,* http://www.umn.edu/mincava/factoid.htm (file created October 16, 1995).

2. M. A. Straus & R. J. Gelles, *Physical Violence in American Families,* (Transaction Publishers, New Brunswick, N.J.) 1990, pp. 96–98.

3. E. Stark & A. Flitcraft, "Violence Among Intimates: An Epidemiological Review," in V. B. Hasselt, R. L. Morrison, A. S. Bellack, & W. Frazier, (eds.), *Handbook of Family Violence,* (Plenum, New York) 1988, pp. 292–317.

4. Suzanne Steinmetz, "The Battered Husband Syndrome," 2 (3/4) *Victimology,* 499–509 (1978).

5. S. K. Steinmetz & J. S. Lucca, "Husband Battering," *Handbook of Family Violence,* V. B. Van Hasselt, R. L. Morrison, A. S. Bellack, & M. Hersen, (eds.), (Plenum, New York) 1988.

6. K. D. O'Leary, J. Barling, I. Arias, A. Rosenbaum, J. Malone, & A. Tyree, "Prevalence and Stability of Physical Aggression between Spouses: A Longitudinal Analysis," 57 *Journal of Consulting and Clinical Psychology,* 263–268 (1989).

7. Jacquelyn Campbell, "Violence Toward Women: Homicide and Battering," in Richard J. Gelles, (ed.), *Vision 2010,* (National Council on Family Relations, Minneapolis) 1995.

8. E. W. Gondolf & E. R. Fisher, "Wife Battering," *Case Studies in Family Violence,* R. T. Ammerman & M. Hersen, (eds.), (Plenum, New York) 1991, pp. 273–274.

9. L. E. Walker, *The Battered Women,* (Harper & Row, New York) 1979.

10. L. E. Walker, *The Battered Woman Syndrome,* (Springer, New York) 1984.

11. See *People v. Humphrey,* 96 *Daily Journal D.A.R.* 10609 at 10612 where the California Supreme Court addressed this issue.

12. M. A. Douglas, "The Battered Women Syndrome," in D. J. Sonkin, (ed.), *Domestic Violence on Trial,* (Springer, New York) 1982.

13. M. D. Pagelow, *Family Violence,* (Praeger, New York) 1984, p. 308.

14. G. NiCarthy, *Getting Free: A Handbook for Women in Abusive Relationships,* (Seal Press, New York) 1986, pp. 117–118.

15. D. G. Dutton & S. L. Painter, "Traumatic Bonding: The Development of Emotional Attachments in Battered Women and Other Relationships of Intermittent Abuse," 6 *Victimology,* 139 (1981).

16. D. G. Dutton, *The Domestic Assault of Women,* (UBC Press, Vancouver, B.C.) 1995.

17. Id. at p. 190.

18. Id. at p. 191.

19. Demie Kurz, "Battering and the Criminal Justice System: A Feminist View," in Eve S. Buzawa & Carl G. Buzawa, (eds.), *Domestic Violence: The Changing Criminal Justice Response,* (Auburn House, Westport, Conn.) 1992.

20. For an excellent discussion of these issues, see K. Spiller, "The Feminist Majority Report: Corporate Women and the Mommy Track," in A. M. Jaggar & P. S. Rothenberg, (eds.), *Feminest Frameworks,* 3rd ed. (McGraw Hill, New York) 1993, pp. 316–318.

21. See K. Newman, "Middle-Class Women in Trouble," in A. M. Jaggar & P. S. Rothenberg, (eds.), *Feminist Frameworks,* 3rd ed. (McGraw Hill, New York) 1993, pp. 319–323.

22. M. Roy, "A Current Study of 150 Cases," in M. Roy, (ed.), *A Psychological Study of Domestic Violence,* (Van Nostrand Reinhold, New York) 1977.

23. D. S. Kalmuss & M. A. in Straus, "Wife's Marital Dependency and Wife Abuse," in M. A. Straus & R. J. Gelles, *Physical Violence in American Families,* (Transaction Publishers, New Brunswick, N.J.) 1990, pp. 379–380.

24. K. J. Sher, "Subjective Effects of Alcohol: The Influence of Setting and Individual Differences in Alcohol Expectancies," 46 *Journal of Studies on Alcohol,* 137–146 (1985).

25. D. H. Coleman & M. A. Straus, "Alcohol Abuse and Family Violence," *Alcohol, Drug Abuse and Aggression,* E. Gottheil, K. A. Druley, T. E. Skoloda, & H. M. Waxman, (eds.), (Charles C. Thomas, Springfield, Ill.) 1983, pp. 104–124.

26. D. C. McClelland, W. N. Davis, R. Kalin, & E. Wanner, *The Drinking Man,* (Free Press, New York) 1972.

27. K. Pernanem, "Theoretical Aspects of the Relationship between Alcohol Use and Crime," *Drinking and Crime: Perspectives on the Relationships Between Alcohol Consumption and Criminal Behavior,* J. J. Collins, Jr., (ed.), (Guilford Press, New York) 1981.

28. A. Helton, "Battering during Pregnancy," 86 *American Journal of Nursing,* 910–913 (1986).

29. R. J. Gelles, "Violence and Pregnancy: Are Pregnant Women at Greater Risk of Abuse?" in M. A. Straus & R. J. Gelles, *Physical Violence in American Families,* (Transaction Publishers, New Brunswick, N.J.) 1990, p. 282.

30. M. A. Straus & R. J. Gelles, "How Violent Are American Families? Estimates From the National Family Violence Survey and Other Studies," in G. T. Hotaling, D. Finkelhor, John T. Kirkpatrick, & M. A. Straus, (eds.), *New Directions in Family Violence Research,* (Sage, Beverly Hills, Calif.) 1988.

31. J. E. Sets & M. A. Straus, "The Marriage License: A Comparison of Assaults in Dating, Cohabitating, and Married Couples," in M. A. Straus & R. J. Gelles, (eds.), *Physical Violence in American Families,* (Transaction Publishers, New Brunswick, N.J.) 1990, pp. 227–244. Published earlier in 4 *Journal of Family Violence,* 161–180 (1989).

32. J. E. Stets & M. A. Pirog-Good, "Violence in Dating Relationships," 50 *Social Psychology Quarterly,* 237–246 (1987).

33. See J. E. Sets & M. A. Straus, "The Marriage License: A Comparison of Assaults in Dating, Cohabitating, and Married Couples," in M. A. Straus & R. J. Gelles, *Physical Violence in American Families,* (Transaction Publishers, New Brunswick, N.J.) 1990, pp. 227–244.

34. See for example, Lawrence W. Sherman, *Policing Domestic Violence,* (The Free Press, New York) 1992; Frank G. Bolton & Susan R. Bolton, *Working with Violent Families,* (Sage, Newbury Park, Calif.) 1987; and Eve S. Buzawa & Carl G. Buzawa, (eds.), *Domestic Violence, The Changing Criminal Justice Response,* (Auburn House, Westport, Conn.) 1992.

35. The judgment was later reduced to $1.9 million.

36. M. Buddy & K. Taylor, "Please, Somebody Help Me," *20/20 News,* January 23, 1986.

37. See Cynthia Grant Bowman, "The Arrest Experiments: A Feminist Critique," 83/1 *Journal of Criminal Law and Criminology,* 201–208 (1992) in which Bowman argues that current research in the area of spousal assault is flawed because it is usually conducted from the abuser's perspective, ignores feminist thinking, and does not consider various social factors.

38. Lisa A. Frisch, "Research That Succeeds, Policies That Fail," 83/1 *Journal of Criminal Law and Criminology,* 209 (1992).

39. For an excellent discussion of these laws see, Arnold Binder & James Meeker, "The Development of Social Attitudes Toward Spousal

Abuse," in Eve S. Buzawa & Carl G. Buzawa, (eds.), *Domestic Violence, The Changing Criminal Justice Response*, (Auburn House, Westport, Conn.) 1992.

40. John E. O'Brien, "Women Abuse: Facts Replacing Myths," 33 *Journal of Marriage and the Family*, 362–398 (1971).

41. Edna Erez, "Intimacy, Violence and the Police," 39 *Human Relations* 265–281 (1986).

42. Eve S. Buzawa & Carl G. Buzawa, *Domestic Violence, The Criminal Justice Response*, (Sage, Newbury Park, Calif.) 1990, p. 44.

43. Wayne R. LaFave & Austin W. Scott, Jr., *Criminal Law*, 2nd ed. (West Publishing Co., St. Paul, Minn.) 1986, p. 30.

44. Rollin M. Perkins & Ronald N. Boyce, *Criminal Law*, 3rd ed., (Foundation Press, Inc., New York) 1982, p. 152.

45. Wayne R. LaFave & Austin W. Scott, Jr., *Criminal Law*, 2nd ed. (West Publishing Co., St. Paul, Minn.) 1986, p. 684.

46. See Donald Black, *The Manners and Customs of Police*, (Academic Press, New York) 1980, p. 189.

47. For an excellent discussion of this area see, Sherman, *Policing Domestic Violence*, pp. 30–31.

48. Lawrence W. Sherman & Richard A. Berk, "The Specific Deterrent Effects of Arrest for Domestic Assault," 49 *American Sociological Review*, 261 (1984).

49. Jacob R. Clark, "The Minneapolis Study: Policy Gets Made Despite Cautions," *Law Enforcement News*, 9 (March 31, 1993).

50. J. David Hirschel & Ira Hutchinson, "Police-Preferred Arrest Policies," in Michael Steinman, (ed.), *Women Battering: Policy Responses*, (Anderson Publishing Co., Cincinnati) 1991, p. 59.

51. See Delbert S. Elliot, "Criminal Justice Procedures in Family Violence Crimes," in Lloyd Ohlin & Michael Tonry (eds.), *Family Violence*, (University of Chicago Press, Chicago) 1989, p. 458 which cites the study as a landmark study on the effectiveness of alternative police responses to family violence and compares that position with Richard Lempert, "Humility is a Virtue," 23 *Law & Society Review*, 146 (1989) which argues that the experiment lacked a scientific basis.

52. Antony Pate, Edwin E. Hamilton, & Annan Sampson, *"Metro-Dade Spouse Abuse Replication Project, Draft Final Report*, (National Institute of Justice, Washington, D.C.) 1991.

53. Richard A. Berk, Alec Campbell, Ruth Klap, & Bruce Western, "A Bayesian Analysis of the Colorado Springs Spouse Abuse Experiment," 83/1 *Journal of Criminal Law and Criminology*, 170 (1992).

54. Lawrence W. Sherman, Janell D. Schmidt, Dennis P. Rogan, Douglas A. Smith, Patrick R. Gartin, Ellen G. Cohn, Dean J. Collins, & Anthony R. Bacich, "The Variable Effects of Arrest on Criminal Careers: The Milwaukee Domestic Violence Experiment," 83/1 *Journal of Criminal Law and Criminology*, 137 (1992).

55. Franklyn W. Dunford, David Huizinga, & Delbert S. Elliot, "The Omaha Domestic Violence Police Experiment," Final Report to the National Institute of Justice, (National Institute of Justice, Washington, D.C.) 1989.

56. Id. at p. 34.

57. J. David Hirchel, Ira W. Hutchinson III, Charles W. Dean, Joseph J. Kelly, & Carolyn E. Pesackis, "Charlotte Spouse Assault Replication Project." Final Report to the National Institute of Justice, (National Institute of Justice, Washington, D.C.) 1991.

58. *Grants to Encourage Arrest Policies*, (Office of Justice Programs, Washington, D.C.) 1996.

59. B. J. Hart, "Coordinated Community Approaches to Domestic Violence," presented at the Strategic Planning Workshop on Violence Against Women, sponsored by the National Institute of Justice in Washington, D.C., March 31, 1995.

10

CHILD VICTIMS

Chapter Outline

Types of Child Abuse
  Physical Child Abuse
  Child Neglect
  Sexual Child Abuse

Extent of the Problem
  Physical Child Abuse
  Child Neglect
  Child Sexual Abuse

Cycle of Violence
  Definitions
  Cycle of Violence and Family Violence
  Cycle of Violence and Aggression

Other Theories Regarding Child Abuse
  Theories of Physical Child Abuse
  Theories of Child Neglect
  Theories of Child Sexual Abuse

Special Types of Child Abuse
  Sibling Abuse
  Munchausen Syndrome by Proxy
  Ritual Abuse

Summary

Key Terms

Discussion Questions

Suggested Readings

Learning Objectives

After reading this chapter, you should be able to:

- Distinguish between the different types of physical child abuse
- Recognize when poor parenting becomes child neglect
- Understand the dynamics involved in child sexual abuse
- Distinguish between the different theories regarding child abuse
- Explain some excuses used by parents to justify the acts of aggression between siblings
- Understand the controversies surrounding the topic of ritualistic child abuse

Types of Child Abuse

Physical Child Abuse

Is a parent unfit or considered abusive if, while bathing his one-year-old daughter, she slips from his grasp and hits her head against the faucet causing a cut over her eye that requires two stitches? Is this child abuse? Although some might blame the father for not being alert to that possibility, others would not classify him as a child abuser. Accidents happen. They are a part of growing up and, painful as they may be to the parent and the child, they are part of a normal, healthy relationship. Thus, not all injuries sustained by children can be classified as child abuse. If not all injuries are child abuse and parents have a right to inflict corporal punishment on children as a form of discipline, how do we draw the line and define physical injuries to children?

Numerous authorities have defined child abuse. Part of the problem in this area has been the continued struggle to agree on what the term *child abuse* means. Van Hasselt, Pagelow, Gelles, and other scholars in the field have excellent discussions and definitions of this condition.[1] For purposes of this text and ease of understanding, we have accepted the following definition: *Physical child abuse* may be defined as any act which results in a nonaccidental physical injury by a person who has care, custody, or control of a child.

There are two key aspects to this definition—the act is intentional or willful and the act resulted in a physical injury. An accidental injury does not qualify as child abuse. In the previous example, an accidental slip in a bathtub would not qualify as child abuse even if the child received an injury that required several stitches. Child abuse as discussed in this chapter is manifested by physical injury that can be proved or documented. Simply yelling at the child is not child abuse within the meaning of this definition. Nor is spanking the child on the hand, the face, or the buttocks if those acts do not result in a physical injury that can be documented. Although it is true that any form of spanking causes injury in the form of pain and some trauma to the child, unless the force is sufficient to leave marks, most medical and legal authorities will not classify these acts as child abuse. This lack of a clear definition is part of the problem of physical child abuse. The next section will address the issue of child neglect, an area that is even more emotional and hard to define.

PRACTICUM: When Is It Child Abuse?

Situation 1: A three-year-old boy is running around the supermarket, knocking down cans of food and does not stop when his grandmother asks him to. The grandmother takes the child by the arm and the child starts yelling, "You're hurting me!" Assume there is no physical injury to the child. Is it child abuse? What if the child is just acting out?

Situation 2: The father leaves the four-year-old child in the fenced-in backyard with the family pet, a collie. The child hits the dog, who bites her arm. Assume there is no history of aggression on the part of the dog. Is it child abuse?

Situation 3: A mother is babysitting the next door neighbor's five-year-old girl. She has a six-year-old boy. She decides to give them a bath together. The boy keeps touching the girl's genital area. Is it child abuse?

Situation 4: An older brother decides to tease his younger sister. When their parents are gone, he holds her down and tickles her until she cries. Is it child abuse?

Child Neglect

In the past twenty years, numerous texts, articles, and studies have dealt with the subject of neglect. The literature runs the gamut from examining assessment techniques of neglect[2] to listing the different forms of this abuse.[3] Except for rare instances, child neglect does not receive the public attention that child sexual and physical abuse generates. Part of the reason for this lack of emphasis may lie in the definition and nature of child neglect.

Child neglect is the negligent treatment or maltreatment of a child by a parent or caretaker under circumstances indicating harm or threatened harm to the child's health or welfare. Although this appears at first glance to be a simple and straightforward statement, it covers a wide range of activities or omissions that impact on the physical and emotional well-being of a child. At what point does mere inattention or lack of knowledge translate itself into child neglect? This definition would require an act or omission that results in harm or threatens to cause harm to the child's health or welfare. This act or omission may be physical or psychological. A strict interpretation of this definition would require that parents or caretakers guard their children like prisoners. However, this is unrealistic because children are mobile. They get into drawers, cabinets, and every corner in the house and yard. Therefore, as Figure 10.1 illustrates, we are dealing with a continuum that stretches from momentary inattention to gross inaction.

Somewhere on the line in Figure 10.1 acceptable parenting ends and child neglect begins. Although no specific place on this line establishes child neglect, it

Momentary inattention ———————————— Gross action or inaction

FIGURE 10.1   Child Neglect Continuum

is a common form of child abuse. The next section addresses another aspect of child abuse—sexual abuse of children.

Sexual Child Abuse

Child sexual abuse is sexual exploitation or sexual activities with children under circumstances which indicate that the child's health or welfare is harmed or threatened.[4] This definition includes inappropriate sexual activities between children and adults. The inappropriate behavior may be between family members or between a stranger and the victim. *Intrafamilial sexual abuse* includes incest and refers to any type of exploitative sexual contact occurring between relatives. *Extrafamilial sexual abuse* refers to exploitative sexual contact with perpetrators who may be known to the child (neighbors, babysitters, live-in partners) or unknown to the child.[5]

One major problem with this definition is the requirement that the child be harmed. From a legal perspective, harm to the victim is not an element of the crime of child sexual abuse. If certain physical acts occur, the crime is complete. In criminal proceedings, it is not necessary to prove that the perpetrator intended to harm or actually harmed the child. However, this definition is useful in exploring the consequences of child sexual abuse, and retaining the requirement of an injury to the child will allow for such a discussion.

The following acts are examples of child sexual abuse: exposing one's sexual organs to the child, voyeurism, touching the sex organs of the child, mutual or self-masturbation with the child, oral sex, intercourse, and anal sex. In addition, allowing the child to view or participate in pornographic or obscene movies is considered child abuse.

Child sexual abuse may be distinguished from rape in that the perpetrator may use a variety of different "techniques" to achieve the objective of sexual gratification. Rape normally involves sexual acts as the result of force or fear. Child abuse offenders may also use force or fear; however, they also employ other pressures or influences to accomplish their goal. These actions include manipulation of the child (psychologically isolating the child from other loved ones), coercion (using adult authority or power on the child), force (restraining the child), threats or fear (informing the child if they tell, no one will love them).[6]

Extent of the Problem

Physical Child Abuse

The physical battering of children is not a new phenomenon. Children have suffered trauma at the hands of their parents and caretakers since the beginning of recorded history. In Egypt, upon the birth of Moses, the pharaoh ordered the death of all male children. King Herod also ordered infanticide on a large scale when Jesus was born.

Early history records the practice of burying infants alive in foundations of buildings and bridges.[7] Excavations of Canaanite dwellings have uncovered jars of infant bones in the foundation of buildings.[8] Although officially outlawed, this practice continued in seventeenth-century Europe and children were found buried in the foundations of London Bridge.

Plato (428–348 B.C.) and Aristotle (348–322 B.C.) both urged the killing of infants born with birth defects. Children with birth defects, female infants, and the children of poor families were killed as a matter of course several hundred years before the birth of Christ. In Rome, the law of the Twelve Tables prohibited raising a child with a defect or deformity. In Sparta, infants were examined by a local council of elders, who had the power to throw those children considered unfit into a canyon.[9]

Infanticide was not the only form of abuse practiced by early civilizations. During the Middle Ages, families would often mutilate or sever limbs from children so as to make them more effective beggars. The histories of the European school system are filled with records detailing beatings and abuse by teachers inflicted on their young charges.

The industrial revolution was characterized by repeated maltreatment of children. Young children were forced to work long hours under inhumane conditions in factories or other heavy industries. Many were beaten, shackled, or starved to force them to work harder at their tasks.

In 1874, an eight-year-old child named Mary Ellen Wilson was discovered by a social worker to have been beaten and starved by her adoptive parents. The worker referred the case to the New York Police Department, which refused to take any action because there were no laws on the books that addressed the abuse of children by their parents or caretakers. In an effort to save the child, the city filed charges against the caretakers utilizing a statute that prevented cruelty to animals. The adoptive mother was sentenced to one year in jail, and the resulting publicity surrounding Mary Ellen's plight led to the formation of the Society for the Prevention of Cruelty to Children in 1875.

From this beginning, we have expanded our concern and care for abused children. Every state has laws preventing the physical abuse of children. The phenomenon of child abuse has generated many studies. One commonly cited study was conducted by the American Association for Protecting Children. The information contained in this annual report indicated that in 1982 almost 1 million children were abused and neglected.[10] Other studies report figures ranging from 200,000 to 4 million. Some researchers even take the position that there is no method of obtaining reliable data in this field.[11] Even the federal government has failed to establish standards for reporting child abuse. The FBI's Uniform Crime Reports (UCR) is the accepted method of reporting crimes on a nationwide basis. The UCR publishes crime statistics reported by 16,000 law enforcement agencies. However, it provides no specific information on crimes against children. With the exception of murder, the UCR does not list the victim's age. The National Center on Child Abuse and Neglect (NCCAN), a division within the U.S. Department of Health and Human Services, has commissioned studies to provide a national estimate of the incidence of child maltreatment.

Many authorities believe that the number of reported cases of child abuse is only the tip of the iceberg. This is particularly true for those children between the ages of twelve and nineteen. This age group is far less likely than younger victims to report crimes, especially when the offender is not a stranger.[12] Part of the problem with determining the magnitude of physical child abuse may have something to do with the definition itself.

By defining the characteristics or hallmarks of physical child abuse differently, the research data can also differ significantly. Researchers select their sample populations based on criteria that differ from scholar to scholar and study to study. Some social scientists view physical child abuse in the context of determining whether the child is "at risk," whereas those working in the criminal justice field emphasize physical evidence. This multifaceted approach to understanding physical child abuse presents both problems and opportunities for growth. As mentioned earlier, the problem is reaching consensus on the definition of physical child abuse and how we respond to it. The opportunities for growth are based on the premise that professionals can and should learn from each other. The social worker may learn of the difficulties in proving certain types of abuse while at the same time teaching the prosecuting attorney to accept the seriousness of a situation that might not otherwise be apparent from a legal perspective.

Child Neglect

Some scholars have stated that child neglect is the most common form of maltreatment. According to Green, the reported cases of neglect in New York outnumbered those of physical abuse by 11 to 1 in 1987.[13] Other studies indicated that physical abuse is more prevalent than neglect. No matter who is right, child neglect is an important topic all professionals should understand. Neglect is less obvious than physical or sexual abuse and it may continue for years without any outsider even being aware that the child they see daily is a victim. Neglect has many faces, forms, and appearances. There are serious cases in which a child's life is threatened and more mundane acts when the child is simply neglected on a daily basis.

Child Sexual Abuse

The American people have a widespread interest in child sexual abuse; however, the true magnitude of this problem is difficult to establish. There is a general agreement among both scholars and professionals in the field that the incidence of child sexual abuse reporting is understated.[14] Estimates on the number of child sexual abuses vary from source to source. Finkelhor's 1979 study of 796 college students indicated that 19 percent of the women and 9 percent of the men had been subjected to sexual abuse as children.[15] A later study by Finkelhor of 521 Boston parents indicated that 15 percent of the women and 6 percent of the men had been sexually abused by the age of sixteen.[16] Russell's survey of 930 San Francisco women found that 28 percent had been victims of child sexual abuse before the age of fourteen.[17] In 1985, the *Los Angeles Times* conducted a random survey of 2627 adults across the United States. The survey revealed that 27 percent of the women and 16 percent of the survey participants had been molested as children. The total percentage (combining men and women) for those who suffered child

TABLE 10.1   Classification of Offenders

Stranger as the offender	approximately 8–10 percent
Family member as the offender	approximately 47 percent
Acquaintance as the offender	approximately 40 percent

sexual abuse was 22 percent.[18] In 1991, researchers came to the conclusion that as many as 10 to 15 percent of all boys and 20 to 25 percent of all girls had experienced at least one instance of sexual abuse prior to the age of eighteen.[19]

Rape in America, which was published by the National Victims Center, indicates sexual violence occurs at a much higher rate than previously expected.[20] This study was discussed in more detail in Chapter 8 dealing with women and sexual violence, but it illustrates that sexual violence is still a major problem in America. Based on this study, the National Victims Center estimates at least 12.1 million women in the United States have been subjected to sexual violence as children or adults.

Utilizing some of these statistics, we can project the possible prevalence of child sexual abuse in the United States today.[21] The most conservative estimate indicates 10 percent of all women and 2 percent of all men have been molested. Our census indicates a population of 60 million minors within the United States. Using these figures we can project that there are 210,000 incidents of child sexual abuse that occur every year. Comparing this number with the 44,700 cases reported to professionals clearly indicates a lack of reporting of this type of abuse.[22]

Although the figures may vary from study to study regarding the types and incidents of child sexual abuse, there is some agreement among researchers that the classification of offenders shown in Table 10.1 is a valid estimate:[23]

The true extent of child victimization is unknown; however, simply discussing this subject raises our awareness and makes it more likely that we will acknowledge its existence. Professionals must not only be aware that it occurs, they should also have a basic understanding of some of the more common theories dealing with causation of child abuse. The next section will examine one popular theory in this area, the cycle of violence.

Cycle of Violence

Some scholars would argue that the most effective method of stopping child abuse is to break the cycle of violence. The cycle of violence theory is discussed as a distinct and separate aspect of child abuse. Simply separating it from the other theories should not imply that this is the definitive answer to why people commit aggressive acts, rather it is singled out for examination because professionals and laypersons constantly refer to it as a scientifically accepted fact. As with other causes or theories of family violence, there is no way to prove or disprove the cycle of violence theory. However, because of the widespread acceptance of this theory, it is necessary to explore fully both the premises on which it is founded and the criticisms directed to it.

The cycle of violence concept has generated continuing controversy among researchers for several decades. Scholars have attempted to determine whether violent tendencies can be inherited from the family of origin as a result of observing it or being a victim. Other scholars have attempted to explain criminal behavior by reference to this cycle.[24]

Definitions

The most commonly used term to describe the process involved in this concept is the "cycle of violence"; however, this theory is also known as the "intergenerational transmission of violence theory." Because many authors, researchers, and commentators use the former, that is the term that will be used in this text. The *cycle of violence theory* asserts that violent behavior is learned within the family and bequeathed from one generation to the next. This theory holds that children who are victims of child abuse or who witness violent aggression by one spouse against the other will grow up and react to their children or spouses in the same manner. The childhood survivor of a violent family develops a predisposition toward violence in his or her own family. Thus, so this theory holds, we have a never-ending chain of violence that is passed from one generation to the next. There have been numerous studies on the cycle of violence, and the results of these studies will be discussed later in this section.

Cycle of Violence and Family Violence

The sources for most studies of the cycle of violence theory are case studies, clinical interviews, self-reporting, and agency records. One widely cited study in support of the cycle of violence theory is Steele and Pollock's research which appeared in Helfer and Kempe's *The Battered Child Syndrome* in 1968.[25] Their study involved sixty parents who were referred to them as a result of their children being treated for child abuse. Steele and Pollock gathered data by testing and interviewing the parents. The parents stated that as children they had experienced intense, pervasive, continuous demands from their own parents. Lost within the conclusions of the study was the fact that some parents were physically abused and others were not. The researchers had cautioned against drawing too many inferences from their research; however, their study is constantly cited as evidence supporting the cycle of violence theory.

Straus conducted an extensive study by interviewing 1146 families with children.[26] The results of the study indicated an 18 percent rate of generational transmission of violence. The results of this study may have been low because the researchers limited the definition of abuse to physical acts that occurred during adolescence. As discussed in Chapter 2, child abuse is more likely to occur at a younger age with a gradual tapering off in incidents as the child reaches the teenage years.

During this same time period, Hunter and Kilstrom interviewed 282 parents of newborn infants.[27] These researchers followed the parents and determined that the intergenerational transmission of violence was 18 percent. However, 82 percent of the parents who were abused as children did not abuse their offspring. Those parents appeared to be able to break the cycle of violence because of social support, healthy children, and a more supportive relationship with one of their own parents. Hunter and Kilstrom's study is suspect because it examined only infants who had been admitted to an intensive care nursery. In addition, there was no extended follow-up of the families or their children.

In 1984, England and Jacobvitz concluded a major study of 160 single-parent mothers.[28] Each mother had at least one child under the age of five. The sample was divided into three groups: severe physical child abuse, including being struck by objects or burned; borderline child abuse, including weekly spankings; and, finally, those children who were being raised by another caretaker. The researchers found a 70 percent intergenerational transmission of violence for those mothers who had suffered severe abuse as a child.

In 1990, Cappell and Heiner analyzed 888 childrearing families and measured the incidence of aggression in the respondent's families.[29] The presence or absence of aggression was classified into family member relationships: husband to wife aggression, wife to husband aggression, and respondent to child aggression. These researchers found that women who witnessed or experienced violence as children were more likely to discipline their own children aggressively. Perhaps more important, these scholars suggested that children who are raised in a violent family learn or inherit vulnerability. Cappell and Heiner theorize that this intergenerational transmission of vulnerability causes men and women to provoke violence, accept violence as normal, and select aggressive partners. These scholars rightfully explain that this research is limited because the same group was composed only of intact couples.

Cycle of Violence and Aggression

Dodge and his associates examined the effect of the cycle of violence on development of aggressive tendencies in children.[30] They studied a representative sample of 309 four-year-olds in kindergarten. This research was multi-site in nature, with children being selected from Nashville and Knoxville, Tennessee, as well as Bloomington, Indiana. The researchers interviewed the mothers, evaluated the children, and received responses regarding the children's behavior from school personnel, peer ratings, and direct observation.

They found that children who had been physically abused were more aggressive toward other children than those who had not been harmed.[31] The teacher-rated aggression index for abused children was 93 percent higher than for nonabused children. The researchers also found that abused children were less able to process information and solve interpersonal problems. Although the authors accurately point out several caveats to their study, it does demonstrate the harm inflicted on children by abuse.

This harm may translate into future acts of aggression that take the form of crime against society. One comprehensive study in this area of child abuse and delinquency was undertaken by Widom in 1989.[32] She followed 1575 cases from childhood through young adulthood. The study compared arrest records of two groups:

- One group was composed of 908 children with documented histories of abuse or neglect.
- The control group was composed of 667 children with no reported incidents of child abuse.

These groups were tracked through official records over the next fifteen to twenty years. The children were eleven years old or younger at the time of the abuse; therefore, an inherent weakness in the Straus research was avoided. The study classified abuse into three distinct areas: physical, sexual, and neglect cases. Court and probation records were the source of data for the initial acts of abuse, and subsequent arrest data were obtained from federal, state, and local law enforcement agencies.

The study found that children who had been abused were more likely to commit crimes as juveniles and adults than the control group. Further, these children were arrested more often for violent crime (11 percent) than the nonabused children (8 percent). Those children who were physically abused were more likely to be arrested for a violent crime. Interestingly, this study pointed out that the next biggest arrest rate for violent crimes was for those children who had been neglected.

As this discussion illustrates, the cycle of violence theory continues to dominate the literature. This and other theories of family violence will continue to be researched in an attempt to find the cause of family violence, predict its occurrence, and search for a cure.

Other Theories Regarding Child Abuse

Theories of Physical Child Abuse

Rather than attempt to describe all acceptable theories of the causes of child abuse, this section will set forth one model that encompasses several different theories. Cynthia Crosson Tower established a series of categories that grouped several theories into three distinct models: (1) the psychopathological model; (2) the interactional model; and (3) the environmental–sociological–cultural model.[33]

The *psychopathological model* stresses the characteristics of the abuser as the primary cause of abuse. The abuser's personality predisposes the abuser to injure the child. This model includes three separate approaches to child abuse: (1) the psychodynamic model; (2) the mental illness model; and (3) the character-trait model.

The psychodymanic model is based on the work of C. Henry Kempe and Ray Helfer. This model theorized that a lack of bonding between the parent and child is an important factor in child abuse. This theory assumes that the abuser was part of a cycle of parental inadequacy. These individuals are unable to bond with children and when a crisis occurs, they respond with abusive acts. This model also assumes the abuser will engage in role reversal. In other words, the parents expect the child to nurture them instead of vice versa.

The mental illness model sets forth the proposition that the parent's mental illness is the primary cause of child abuse. This is an easy theory for laypersons to accept because its easy to believe that anyone who would repeatedly beat or torture a child must be crazy. Justice and Justice suggested this model as a viable category.[34] Although some scholars have found abusive parents to be mentally disturbed, many others argue that abusive parents do not fit any existing psychiatric classification. For example, Kempe found that fewer than 5 percent were psychotic.

The character-trait model focuses on specific traits of abusers without regard to how they acquired these traits. Scholars such as Merrill and Delsordo have categorized abusive parents by specific traits that cause child abuse.[35] Merrill's study included such traits as hostility, rigidity, passivity, dependence, and competitiveness. Delsordo's categorization of abusive parent's traits included mental illness, frustration and irresponsibility, and severe disciplinarian and misplaced abuse.

The *interactional model* views child abuse as a result of a dysfunctional system. This category of abuse focuses on the following factors in child abuse: (1) the role of the child, (2) chance events, and (3) the family structure.

The role of the child and the perceptions of the parent toward that child are viewed as a cause of child abuse by some scholars. Martin suggests that abuse not only requires a certain type of adult, but also that certain acts of the child trigger the abuse. If the parent has certain expectations that the child does not meet, abuse may occur.[36]

"Chance events" is the somewhat inaccurate name given to events which prevent the parent from bonding with the child. This lack of attachment is viewed as a predisposition toward child abuse. Lynch suggests that difficulties in pregnancy, labor, or delivery can have a bearing on the attachment of the mother to the child.[37]

The family structure model theorizes that child abuse is a result of a dysfunctional family. The adult members of the family blame the child for their own shortcomings, and this leads to abuse.

The *environmental–sociological–cultural model* views child abuse as a result of stresses in society that are the primary causes of abuse. This category of abuse includes the following causes of child abuse: (1) the environmental stress model; (2) the social learning model; (3) the social psychological model; and (4) the psychosocial systems model.

The environmental stress model accepts the proposition that factors such as lack of education, poverty, unemployment, or occupational stress result in child abuse. As these outside forces build, the parent or caretaker is unable to cope and reacts by hitting or injuring the child.

The social learning model emphasizes the inadequacy of the parenting skills of abusive parents. These parents never learned appropriate responses to child-rearing and therefore their lack of skill leads to frustration. This frustration in turn causes abusive behavior.

The social psychological model assumes stress results from a number of social and psychological factors including marital disputes, unemployment, or too many or unwanted children. These factors induce stress that causes the individual to react to the child in an abusive manner.

The psychosocial systems model stresses that abuse results from interactions within the family. The family as a system is out of balance and incapable of caring for the child. The child becomes the target for family members' frustration, and abuse is the result.

As this discussion indicates, several theories attempt to explain who the abusers are and why they abuse children. Although no authority can point to one single cause of child abuse, it is clear that it continues to occur. The causes of child physical abuse are multifaceted; therefore, it is necessary to review who are the victims or recipients of this violence to attempt to understand this phenomenon more fully.

Theories of Child Neglect

Are poor children neglected and rich kids well cared for? Unfortunately, a substantial number of people in society equate poverty with neglect, but simply being poor does not make a neglectful parent. There are children who live at the edge of poverty or below the poverty level and are loved and nurtured. On the other hand, there are children who live in $1 million homes but are neglected or psychologically abused on a daily basis. The causes of neglect are varied and wide ranging.

Polansky and his colleagues in their classic text, *Damaged Parents: An Anatomy of Child Neglect*, established three major causes of neglect: (1) economic causes, (2) ecological causes, and (3) personalistic causes.[38] The *economic theory* suggests that neglect is caused by stress as a result of living in poverty. The *ecological theory* views the family behavior and neglect as a result of social causes. The *personalistic theory* attributes child neglect to individual personality characteristics of the caretakers.

Numerous studies have indicated that poverty is an important factor in the parents' ability to care for their children, and the question must be asked, "Does poverty cause neglect, or is poverty the result of the parents' inability to function?"[39]

Some scholars have indicated that families who neglect their children live in an environment that is unfriendly and characterized by low morale and hopelessness.[40] As indicated, the issue is whether environment causes neglect or whether the environment is a characteristic of the parents' inability to function.

The more reasoned approach seems to be that of the personalistic theory. In this approach, neglect is viewed as being caused by complex maladaptive interactions and/or lack of essential caretaking behaviors that are influenced by the level of parental skill, knowledge deficits, and other stress factors.[41] The following is a list of some important characteristics of parents or caretakers who neglect their children:[42]

Inability to plan: These parents lack the ability to establish goals, objectives, and direction. These parents may have low frustration levels and little ability to delay gratification.

Lack of knowledge: Parents have little or no knowledge about children's needs, housekeeping skills, cooking, etc.

Lack of judgment: Parents may leave a young child alone and unsupervised.

Lack of motivation: Parents lack energy, have little desire to learn, and have no other standard of comparison. These parents are apathetic or ineffective in that they are withdrawn and feel that nothing is worth doing.

There are other models that profile personalities of neglectful parents or caretakers, and no one study or theory has gained universal acceptance. The next section will examine an even more controversial subject—the reason why perpetrators molest young children.

Theories of Child Sexual Abuse

Numerous studies indicate that child abusers do not fit any stereotype. The common lay perception that all abusers are ugly old men who prey on children is simply not true, but researchers have attempted to find a common thread or factor that connects all child abusers. They have examined the degree of violence, the age of the victim, the age and education of the offender, preoffense social and occupational adjustment, alcohol abuse, physiological responses of offenders, and aggression. Conti reviewed the literature in this area and described the following factors that were considered important when evaluating characteristics of abusers:[43]

1. Measurement of sexual arousal is essential to discriminate between various categories of sexual offenders.
2. The role of sexual fantasies with children is important due to its connection to deviant sexuality. Fantasies about children coupled with masturbation during these fantasies serve as a form of rehearsal for contact with the victims.
3. The types of rationalizations used by adult offenders who have sexual relations with children commonly take the form of statements or thoughts to the effect: "A child who doesn't resist really wants to have sex," or "Having sex with a child is the best way to teach her about sex," or "You become closer to the child when you share sex with him," and so on.

In addition to the various forms of psychopathology present in child abuse, Finkelhor established four factors involved in sexual abuse.[44] He called this theory the *four preconditions model of sexual abuse*, which establishes preconditions that create a personal and social context for expressing sexually abusive behaviors. These preconditions include: (1) motivation to abuse sexually; (2) overcoming internal inhibitors; (3) factors predisposing to overcome external inhibitors; and (4) factors predisposing to overcome the child's resistance.

Precondition I: Motivation to Abuse Sexually.   The motivation to abuse a child sexually includes emotional congruence, sexual arousal, and blockage. Emotional congruence involves satisfying an emotional need by relating to the child in a sexual manner. Sexual arousal occurs when the child becomes the source of sexual gratification. Blockage occurs when other alternative forms of sexual satisfaction are not present, not available, or less satisfying. The motivation to abuse a child is based on individual as well as sociological grounds. Individual explanations include the need for power and control, unconscious reenactment of a previous childhood trauma, and biological abnormality. Sociological reasons include the male-oriented society that demands male dominance, child pornography, and erotic portrayal of children in the media.

Precondition II: Overcoming Internal Inhibitors.   The perpetrator must overcome internal controls that would prevent him from sexually abusing the victim.

Some of these controls are overcome by use of alcohol or drugs, existing psychosis, inability of the offender to identify with the needs of the victim, weak criminal sanctions against offenders, and child pornography.

Precondition III: Factors Predisposing to Overcome External Inhibitors.   These conditions are outside the control of the perpetrator. These factors include social situations such as the type and amount of supervision a child receives, lack of a parental figure who is close to or protective of the victim, and unusual sleeping or living arrangements. Additionally, the lack of social support for mothers, barriers to equality, and erosion of the family's social networks contribute to the ability of the offender to overcome external inhibitors.

Precondition IV: Factors Predisposing to Overcome the Child's Resistance. These factors concern the victim's ability to resist the sexual advances. The child may be emotionally insecure, deprived, or lacking in sexual experience or knowledge. The victim may feel powerless, or a situation of trust exists between the offender and the victim.

There is no distinct or clear answer as to why adults sexually abuse children. The offender may commit these acts for a variety of reasons. Both psychological forces and social structure enter into this complex mesh of forces to allow individuals to engage in sexual activities with young victims.

We traditionally think of the abuser as a man and the victim as a girl. However, studies indicate that boys may be the victim of sexual abuse at a higher rate than previously thought. One study in San Jose, California, indicates a rise in the reported incidents of sexual abuse of boys.[45] Between 1970 and 1975, only 5 percent of the reported victims of sex abuse were boys. However, this figure rose to over 22 percent by 1986.[46]

Boys who are victims of abuse may not report the acts or incidents for several reasons. First, boys may not want to be viewed as victims or sissies or be perceived as weak. Second, boys normally do not have to account for their movements and are given greater degrees of freedom and less protection through supervision and therefore parents may not notice unusual behavior that may indicate sexual abuse. And third, our stereotypes lead us to look for abuse with girls, not with boys.[47]

The high-risk years for child sexual abuse range from between four and nine years old.[48] At the former age, children are naive and sexually curious, and by the time they reach the age of nine, their loyalty, desire to please, and trust of adults are traits manipulated by offenders to accomplish their goal of molestation. Generally, sexual abuse is terminated by the time the child reaches fourteen. This termination occurs because the victim may threaten the offender with disclosure or engage in activities, such as running away, that would lead authorities to suspect abuse.[49]

Contrary to popular belief, the actual physical attractiveness of the female child has little if anything to do with whether the child is a victim of molestation. Additionally, the seductiveness of the female child is now discounted as a contributing factor in sexual abuse situations. Although we may be able to dispel certain stereotypes about female victims, there needs to be more research on the issue of male victims. Two scholars have isolated at least one factor that may identify why certain male children are molested. Finkelhor and Porter suggested that the less assertive boys are more likely to be victims of sexual abuse.[50]

Children are at a higher risk of sexual abuse if they are socially isolated, left alone, and unsupervised. If the mother is absent from the home for long periods, either because of work or other commitments, the child is more likely to be abused. Some authorities theorize that the presence of a stepfather in the home adds to the risk of sexual abuse.[51] These factors establish situations in which the child becomes vulnerable to the perpetrator.

We are still researching and learning about the characteristics of those who abuse and why certain children are chosen for abuse over others. Misconceptions and stereotypes have contributed to the confusion in this very important area. We do not have all the answers on why and who is involved in child sexual abuse, but we are making progress.

There are normally two situations or factual patterns that occur in child sexual abuse: one is a sudden, violent assault by a stranger and involves the use of force or fear, and the other involves sexual activities by a perpetrator known by the child. The former is the classic rape of the victim which is discussed in detail in Chapter 7. This section discusses those situations in which the offender knows or is related to the victim. As with most relationships, child sexual abuse requires interaction between the perpetrator and the victim. There is often a progression of acts that lead to the sexual encounter. Tower established five stages or phases of child sexual abuse: the engagement phase, sexual interaction, the secrecy phase, the disclosure phase, and the suppression phase.[52]

The engagement phase involves the perpetrator gaining access to the victim. This access may occur as a result of a living arrangement, a trip, babysitting, or any other situation in which the offender has an opportunity to discuss sex with the child without supervision of any other adult. The adult may offer rationalizations or attempt to convince the victim that sex is proper. Comments such as "This is how daddies teach their daughters about sex" and "You will make me and your mommy happy by doing this" are examples of verbal communications that occur during this stage. The perpetrator may engage in what appears to be "accidents" to see how the child responds. Acts such as walking in while the child is bathing or allowing the child to see the adult nude or view the offender's genitals are examples of these types of actions. If the child reacts negatively to these tentative approaches, some offenders will back off and try another approach.

The sexual interaction phase involves actual sexual contact. This may range from viewing the child nude or having the child observe the adult without clothes, fondling the child and vice versa, oral sex, or sexual penetration. Groth established two categories of sexual contacts: pressured sex and forced sex.[53]

Pressured sex involves the perpetrator attempting to convince the child to engage in sexual activity. This is accomplished by bribing or rewarding the child with attention, praise, or material goods. If the child refuses the advances, the perpetrator will not resort to force to achieve sexual contact. Forced sex involves the threat of harm or use of force to complete the act. The perpetrator may use his position of authority as an adult to obtain compliance from the child. Other offenders will carry out the act in the traditional sexual assault form of rape.

The secrecy phase involves the perpetrator convincing the child to remain silent about the acts. This allows the offender to continue with sexual relations over an extended period of time. The adult may threaten, blackmail, or bribe the child to remain silent. The most common tactic is intimidation.[54] Statements such as "If they found out, your daddy would have to leave you and your mommy" are common forms of threats that may occur during this stage of sexual exploitation.

The disclosure phase may occur relatively soon after the act or at a later time when the victim is an adult. The disclosure may occur accidentally when the participants are observed in the act of sex or when the child visits a physician and is diagnosed as the victim of sexual abuse. Intentional disclosure involves the child informing someone of the actions of the perpetrator. Many victims of sexual abuse do not disclose its existence until they are adults and out of the reach, authority, or power of the offender. Occasionally, adult women will disclose the activity because they are afraid the perpetrator may be molesting a younger brother or sister.

The suppression phase occurs after disclosure or discovery of the abuse and involves caretakers attempting to force the child to recant the accusations of abuse. If the molester is a father figure or sole support for family, pressure may be brought on the child to keep quiet. Some families will promise the child that it will not happen again. Other techniques involve telling the child that a loved one will go to prison if the child continues to tell others of the molestation. The purpose of these activities is to get the child to recant so that no action will be taken by the authorities.

This discussion has focused on the progression of sexual abuse. In these situations, the offender is usually known to the victim. These activities may occur with a relative or a caretaker who is associated with the family. Child sexual abuse is a serious form of victimization that has longlasting consequences for the victim. However, there are other forms of child abuse that also have long-term consequences for their victims. The next section will address some of these special types of child abuse.

Special Types of Child Abuse

Sibling Abuse

Sibling abuse is probably the most common form of family violence in the United States. Gelles and Cornell stated this fact in another manner when they wrote that the most commonly victimized family members are siblings.[55] If sibling abuse is in fact the most common form of family violence, why is there such a reluctance on the part of society and professionals to discuss it? There are very few texts devoted exclusively to this topic. Most academic articles dealing with child abuse may include as an afterthought a discussion of sibling abuse. Two areas of sibling abuse that are being examined in some detail are incest and the abuse of a sibling by parents.

There are a variety of reasons for this lack of discussion regarding sibling abuse. We consider sibling aggression to be a normal part of growing up.

As the Focus box indicates, we have all heard excuses for sibling aggression. They are common refrains in families with more than one child. As a society we tend to minimize sibling aggression. Yet early studies in New York and Philadelphia

---

FOCUS: Sibling Abuse and Excuses

How many of the following excuses have you heard used to justify one sibling's acts toward another?

Don't worry about it, its just normal sibling rivalry.

They were just playing doctor.

Kids will be kids.

He really didn't mean to hurt his sister; he loves her.

It's only normal childhood curiosity.

Kids are always calling each other names.

I told him not to hit her again.

They will grow out of it.

---

indicated that 3 percent of all homicides committed in those cities were committed by siblings against siblings![56] In another classic study of sibling abuse, Steinmetz found that parents did not consider their children's physical aggression toward siblings as abuse. They would even talk with friends, neighbors, and relatives about the aggression—viewing it as an inevitable part of siblings growing up.[57]

No one has accurate figures on the nature, type, or extent of sibling abuse. However, most authorities agree that it is the most common form of family violence. The popular media first addressed this issue in 1979 with a report in *U.S. News & World Report* that stated 138,000 children aged three to seventeen had used a weapon on a sibling within the last year.[58] In a 1980 study, Straus, Gelles, and Steinmetz reported that 82 percent of parents of children surveyed considered sibling violence to be the most common form of intrafamily violence.[59] In another early study, Steinmetz (1981) found that a clear majority of children used physical violence to resolve conflict with their siblings.[60]

In 1988, Pagelow presented the findings of her study of 1025 college students at three university campuses in southern California at the annual meeting of the Pacific Sociological Association. Pagelow's survey revealed that almost half of the siblings living at home at the age of twelve were either aggressors or victims of violent acts of kicking and punching. Ten percent said their siblings beat them, and 4 percent stated that their siblings had threatened them with a gun or knife or used a gun or knife against them.

In 1992, Carson and Daane presented the results of their study of 3357 students in an Indiana school district at the annual meeting of the American Sociological Association. Seventy-four percent of the students approved of hitting their sibling if they were reacting to being hit first. Forty-three percent approved of striking their sibling if that sibling broke the stereo. Thirty-eight percent believed it was appropriate to hit their sibling if that sibling made fun of the aggressor in front of friends. Almost one-quarter of all students surveyed approved of hitting their sibling if there was an argument and the other sibling did not listen to reason.

These and other studies indicate that sibling abuse is a common form of family violence. Its existence can no longer be denied; however, we are still studying its nature, causation, and extent. As with many other forms of family violence, there is no one single definition of sibling abuse.

The question then must be, do we really need a separate definition of sibling abuse, or would other definitions within this text cover most if not all of the situations that arise in which children commit acts of violence toward their siblings? Earlier in this chapter, *physical* child abuse was defined as any act that results in a nonaccidental physical injury by a person who has care, custody, or control of a child. Many acts of sibling abuse occur when the older or more powerful sibling has care or control over the victim. However, there are acts of sibling abuse that occur within the home when parents are present but unaware of the acts of the abusing sibling. Therefore, the definition of physical child abuse does not cover all situations that might arise in sibling abuse. Although it is possible to draft a broad definition of child abuse that would cover acts of sibling abuse, by defining it as a separate and distinct form of child abuse, its importance in any study of family violence is highlighted.

Sibling abuse is any form of physical, mental, or sexual abuse inflicted by one child in a family unit upon another. This definition covers the various types of abuse that will be discussed later. Additionally, it does not require that the children be related by birth. There are situations in which children from different marriages end up in the same household. Finally, the definition uses the term *child*. This term requires further explanation. There are reported incidents of one sibling abusing the other after they have reached the age of eighteen. However, it appears that the vast majority of abuse occurs when the victim and/or the abuser are under the age of adulthood. Therefore *child* is defined as a person under the age of legal majority. This age is typically stated to be eighteen. It should be clear that this definition does not include abuse of different children within the same family by an adult member of the household.

Munchausen Syndrome by Proxy

One type of child abuse has recently become a topic of discussion.[61] ***Munchausen Syndrome by proxy*** is defined as a psychiatric disorder whereby individuals intentionally produce physical symptoms of illness in their children. It is still being researched but has surfaced as a diagnosis in a number of cases.[62]

The term "Munchausen syndrome" was coined by Richard Asher in 1951 to describe patients who fabricated histories of illness. These individuals described complex medical histories and often displayed symptoms of the alleged disease. These fabrications invariably led to complex medical interventions and hospitalizations. Asher named this disorder after Baron von Munchausen. Hieronymous Karl Fredrich von Munchausen was an eighteenth-century German baron and mercenary officer in the Russian cavalry. The baron was famous for dramatizing his "amazing" adventures. Some might describe him as a world-class teller of tall tales.

There is some debate as to who first used the term "Munchausen syndrome by proxy." Money used it in 1976 to describe four children who were so severely abused that they were dwarfed.[63] However, in 1977 Meadow also used the term to describe the more commonly accepted definition of this form of abuse. Meadow examined two children who were being poisoned by a parent. The parent knew what was happening but encouraged the medical professionals to search for a diagnosis. This diagnostic process was painful and dangerous to the children.[64]

The warning signs of the disorder include: repeated hospitalizations and medical evaluations without definitive diagnosis; inappropriate symptoms and/or medical signs that are inconsistent; signs and symptoms that disappear when away from the parent; a parent who welcomes medical tests of the child, even if they are painful; increased parental uneasiness as the child recovers; and a parent who is less concerned with the child's health and more concerned about spending time with hospital staff.[65]

Today, professionals in the field have come to the conclusion that Munchausen syndrome by proxy is of continuing concern. Some authorities predict that 10 percent of these child victims will die at the hands of their parents.[66] Professionals in the field must recognize this form of child victimization and respond accordingly.

Ritual Abuse

On a daily basis, we are beginning to hear tales of horror and disgust involving children being victimized in so-called satanic cults. Adults who were victims are coming forward and shedding light on this new form of family violence. Just as we were slow in accepting the fact that fathers were molesting their young daughters, so are we as a society hesitant to believe that many of the described practices of ritualistic abuse occur. Child abuse, neglect, and sexual molestation are difficult to accept, but satanic ritualistic abuse not only causes harm to our children, it also strikes a cord in our collective consciousness as to the evil that is perpetrated by our species. It is for these reasons that we must examine this controversial and highly emotional issue.

Professionals are only now beginning to treat survivors of ritualistic abuse. However, controversy rages as to the validity of many of the claims made by these survivors and the extent of their abuse. Other scholarly works in the field are silent or only briefly touch on this new issue.[67] Even though this is a relatively new form of family violence and we are still researching its causes and consequences, it is included in this text for purposes of familiarizing students with the general nature and types of ritualistic abuse.

During the early twentieth century one of the most important figures in the development of magic and mysticism appeared. His name was Aleister Crowley and he published the book *Magick in Theory and Practice.*[68] Crowley's book was a "how to" for neophytes who wanted to experiment with magic. It told them what to do, what to say, and how to feel. For those who were unable to achieve the desired psychological state, Crowley recommended the use of various drugs including hashish, mescaline, or cocaine.

The 1960s and 1970s were decades of rebellion in the United States. The Age of Aquarius was upon us. The concept of mind-expanding drugs gained widespread acceptance. During this period of change, it was popular to question authority and beliefs. The advent of birth control, the first stirrings of the women's movement, and the breakdown of traditional roles all combined to force change in America. Magic, free love, and drugs were accepted tenets in our life.

During this period, Anton LaVey established the Church of Satan and drafted *The Satanic Bible*. Although he was denounced as a fraud by some, LaVey had a far greater impact than most people were willing to admit. He took the position that individuals could make a conscious choice to live in a world without God and then he thrust this idea upon the general public.[69] A passage from *The Satanic Bible* illustrates the logic and allure of LaVey's teaching:

> *Satanists are encouraged to indulge in the seven deadly sins as they need hurt no one; they were only invented by the Christian Church to [e]nsure guilt on the part of its followers. Their Christian Church knows that it is impossible for anyone to avoid committing these sins, as they are things which we, human beings, most naturally do.*[70]

It should be stressed that the Church of Satan does not condone ritualistic child abuse. It is listed in the telephone pages and has its headquarters or grotto in San Francisco.

In 1980, the reading public was shocked by a book that brought the specter of satanism and ritualistic abuse directly into their homes. *Michelle Remembers*, a book written by psychiatrist Lawrence Pazder and Michelle Smith, recounts a tale of satanism and ritual abuse that occurred to Michelle as a child at the hands of a satanic cult in Victoria, Canada.[71] The book describes how Michelle recovered her memories during therapy. One memory included a claim that she was a designated bride of Satan and was to be presented to him at a ceremony that occurs only every twenty-eight years during the Year of the Beast. One of the most controversial portions of *Michelle Remembers* details how she resisted Satan's attempts to claim her with the help of the Virgin Mary.

In the late 1980s, tales began to surface of massive sexual abuse at daycare centers. Americans were angered and repulsed by allegations of ritualistic child abuse allegedly perpetrated on scores of preschool children by Peggy McMartin Buckey and her son, Raymond Buckey, at the Virginia McMartin Preschool in Manhattan Beach, California. Several children testified that they had been subjected to satanic rituals, including animal sacrifices and sexual abuse inside churches. After one of the longest and most expensive trials in the United States, all the defendants were acquitted. Although the defendants were found not guilty, the trial raised our consciousness regarding this new form of child abuse.

The nature and extent of allegations of sexual abuse of children in daycare settings in recent years is a controversial subject among clinicians. Cases of sexual abuse in daycare often involve numerous factors that differ from what clinicians are typically confronted with in cases of intrafamilial sexual abuse. These factors include the young age of the child victims, the involvement of multiple victims and multiple perpetrators, women as perpetrators, use of extreme threats, and in some cases ritualistic activities.[72]

Ritualistic child abuse in daycare centers is a particularly disturbing type of reported daycare center abuse. Children who have been ritualistically abused describe participation in group ceremonies, use of chants and songs, adults dressed in costumes and masks, threats with supernatural powers often involving

Satan or demons, the sacrifice of animals, the ingestion of blood, feces, and urine, and murders.[73]

The definition of ritualistic child abuse is still evolving. One of the most cited definitions was established by the Los Angeles County Commission for Women in 1989. This commission set forth the following definition of *ritual abuse:*

> *A brutal form of abuse of children consisting of physical, sexual, and psychological abuse, and involving the use of rituals. Ritual does not necessarily mean satanic. However, most survivors state that they were ritually abused as part of satanic worship for the purpose of indoctrinating them into satanic beliefs and practices. Ritual abuse rarely consists of a single episode. It usually involves repeated abuse over an extended period of time.*[74]

As the definition states, ritualistic child abuse does not have to involve religion. However, most of the survivors claim the ritualistic abuse was definitely tied to satanic worship. All rituals are not evil. The word *ritual* is defined simply as the established form for a ceremony, a system of rites, any formal and customarily repeated act or series of acts.[75] It is only when ritual is combined with abuse that we as a society can intervene. We have established that ritualistic child abuse involves long-term repeated abuse of the most severe form. These abuses may be inflicted and believed justified because of certain religious tenets held by the cult or organization.

It would be easy to explain satanism as the creation of a deranged mind. Doing so would permit us to dismiss it as something so out of the ordinary that it doesn't bear thinking about, except in a curious nonanalytical way. But this approach does not allow for a complete understanding of this form of family violence. Although historians still dispute the historic nature and extent of satanism and many present-day scholars continue to discount stories of ritualistic child abuse, the fact remains that more people are coming forward and claiming to be victims of this type of abuse. It is therefore imperative that professionals in the field have a general understanding of ritualistic abuse.

Summary

At this stage in the development of our society, we cannot prevent all forms of child abuse so we must be alert to its existence and understand some of the more common theories on how and why it occurs. We have won half the battle if we are aware that child abuse occurs in all segments of our society. On the other hand, we must be willing to accept reasonable explanations of injuries. Children are active human beings—as such they will trip, fall, and run into objects. Our goal is to be able to distinguish between a normal injury and a nonaccidental one. This ability may save a child's life.

In many instances, there is no clear line between simply poor parenting and neglect. Each situation must be evaluated on its own merits, and professionals must look at the totality of the circumstances in determining whether the child is a victim of neglect. The causes of neglect are varied and do not simply rest on the assumption that poverty is the cause. The rich and famous can, and do, subject their children to acts that are clearly child neglect.

Child sexual abuse is one of the most emotional areas of family violence. It is a crime that occurs in secret and may last only moments or for years. Even the definition of child sexual abuse is shrouded in controversy. Although we cannot explain why it occurs, some scholars have established certain theories or characteristics regarding child sexual abuse.

Unlike other forms of child abuse, sexual molestation may not leave scars that are visible to other persons. Sexual abuse in children takes many forms. Scholars have established certain steps or a progression in the nonviolent sexual abuse of children. These include a gradual increase in sexual activity culminating in intercourse.

The consequences of child sexual abuse are traumatic and long lasting and various scholars have attempted to study the ramification of this type of child maltreatment. Although disagreement exists among these authorities, all agree that it is a serious problem that must be studied and hopefully a solution found to ease the pain of the survivors of sexual abuse.

The victimization of children is an emotional and complex topic. Not only are children kidnapped, raped, and killed by strangers, sometimes they face a worse fate in their own homes. Understanding the types, extent, and theories surrounding child abuse will benefit any professional who works in the criminal justice field.

Key Terms

Physical child abuse may be defined as any act which results in a nonaccidental physical injury by a person who has care, custody, or control of a child.

Child neglect is the negligent treatment or maltreatment of a child by a parent or caretaker under circumstances indicating harm or threatened harm to the child's health or welfare.

Child sexual abuse is sexual exploitation or sexual activities with children under circumstances which indicate that the child's health or welfare is harmed or threatened.

Intrafamilial sexual abuse includes incest and refers to any type of exploitative sexual contact occurring between relatives.

Extrafamilial sexual abuse refers to exploitative sexual contact with perpetrators who may be known to the child (neighbors, babysitters, live-in partners) or unknown to the child.

Cycle of violence theory asserts that violent behavior is learned within the family and bequeathed from one generation to the next.

Psychopathological model stresses the characteristics of the abuser as the primary cause of abuse. The abuser's personality predisposes the abuser to injure the child.

Interactional model views child abuse as a result of a dysfunctional system.

Environmental–sociological–cultural model views child abuse as a result of stresses in society that are the primary causes of abuse.

Economic theory suggests that neglect is caused by stress as a result of living in poverty.

Ecological theory views the family behavior and neglect as a result of social causes.

Personalistic theory attributes child neglect to individual personality characteristics of the caretakers.

Four preconditions model of sexual abuse establishes preconditions that create a personal and social context for expressing sexually abusive behaviors.

Sibling abuse is any form of physical, mental, or sexual abuse inflicted by one child in a family unit upon another.

Child is defined as a person under the age of legal majority. This age is typically stated to be eighteen.

Munchausen syndrome by proxy is a psychiatric disorder whereby individuals intentionally produce physical symptoms of illness in their children.

Ritual abuse is a brutal form of abuse of children consisting of physical, sexual, and psychological abuse, and involving the use of rituals. Ritual does not necessarily mean satanic. However, most survivors state that they were ritually abused as part of satanic worship for the purpose of indoctrinating them into satanic beliefs and practices. Ritual abuse rarely consists of a single episode. It usually involves repeated abuse over an extended period of time.

Discussion Questions

1. If a child is injured and the physician is uncertain of whether the injury is physical child abuse, should the physician alert the police? Why? Why not? Would it make any difference if the physician knew the parents and had been to their home for a social event?

2. What is the most serious form of physical child abuse? Why?

3. If a child has been seriously injured by his mother, should that child ever be returned to the mother's care? Why?

4. Should convicted child abusers be required to inform all social partners of their crimes? What if the criminal is dating someone who has small children and she asks him to watch her children while she goes to work for the day?

5. Based on your reading, what is the most single important cause of neglect? Why?

6. Based on your reading of this chapter, can you provide a more comprehensive definition of child sexual abuse? What about a more specific definition?

7. If you were a professional working in an environment that includes young children and you observed a child exhibiting symptoms that led you to suspect child sexual abuse, what would you do?

8. Should we punish or treat child molesters? Because some would argue that you can never cure a pedophile, does this mean we should lock the offender up forever?

Suggested Readings

Vincent B. Van Hasselt, et al., (eds.), *Handbook of Family Violence*, (Plenum Press, New York) 1988.

R. T. Ammerman & M. Hersen, *Assessment of Family Violence*, (John Wiley & Sons, New York) 1992.

R. Helfer & C. H. Kempe, (eds.), *The Battered Child*, 2nd ed. (University of Chicago Press, Chicago) 1974.

G. Gerber, C. Ross, & E. Zigler, (eds.), *Child Abuse: An Agenda for Action*, (Oxford University Press, New York) 1980.

R. Ammerman & M. Hersen, (eds.), *Case Studies in Family Violence*, (Plenum Press, New York) 1991.

D. Cicchetti & V. Carlson, (eds.), *Child Maltreatment*, (Cambridge University Press, Cambridge, Mass.) 1989.

D. Finkelhor, *Child Sexual Abuse: New Theories and Research* (Free Press, New York) 1984.

D. G. Kilpatrick, C. N. Edmonds, & A. K. Seymour, *Rape in America: A Report to the Nation*, (National Victims Center, Arlington, Va.) 1992.

Cynthia Crosson Tower, *Understanding Child Abuse and Neglect*, 2nd ed. (Allyn & Bacon, Boston) 1993.

N. Polansky, M. Chambers, E. Buttenwieser, & D. Williams, *Damaged Parents: An Anatomy of Child Neglect*, (University of Chicago Press, Chicago) 1981.

M. A. Straus, R. J. Gelles, & S. K. Steinmetz, *Behind Closed Doors: Violence in the American Family*, (Doubleday, New York) 1980.

D. K. Sakheim & S. E. Devine, *Out of Darkness*, (Lexington Books, New York) 1992.

Endnotes

1. See for example, Vincent B. Van Hasselt, et. al., (eds.), *Handbook of Family Violence*, (Plenum Press, New York) 1988.

2. R. T. Ammerman & M. Hersen, *Assessment of Family Violence*, (John Wiley & Sons, New York) 1992.

3. J. Meyers, *Evidence in Child Abuse and Neglect*, 2nd ed. (John Wiley & Sons, New York) 1992.

4. This is a shortened version of the definition contained in the Child Abuse Prevention and Treatment Act of 1974 which is one of the most widely adopted statutes defining child sexual abuse.

5. D. A. Wolfe, V. V. Wolfe, & C. L. Best, "Child Victims of Sexual Assault," in V. B. Van Hasselt, R. L. Morrison, A. S. Bellack, & M. Hersen, (eds.), *Handbook of Family Violence*, (Plenum Press, New York) 1988.

6. J. R. Conte, "Victims of Child Sexual Abuse," in R. T. Ammerman & M. Hersen, (eds.), *Treatment of Family Violence*, (John Wiley & Sons, New York) 1990, pp. 64–65.

7. S. Radbill, "A History of Child Abuse and Infanticide," in R. Helfer & C. H. Kempe, (eds.), *The Battered Child*, 2nd ed. (University of Chicago Press, Chicago) 1974.

8. C. F. Potter, "Infanticides," in M. Leach, (ed.), *Dictionary of Folklore, Mythology and Legend*, vol. 1, (Funk & Wagnalls, New York) 1949.

9. N. C. Sorel, *Ever Since Eve: Personal Reflections on Childbirth*, (Oxford University Press, New York) 1984.

10. American Association for Protecting Children, Inc. *Highlights of Official Child Neglect and Abuse Reporting*, (American Humane Association) 1983.

11. R. Uviler, "Save Them from Their Saviors: The Constitutional Rights in the Family," in G. Gerber, C. Ross, & E. Zigler, (eds.), *Child Abuse: An Agenda for Action*, (Oxford University Press, New York) 1980, pp. 147–155.

12. U.S. Department of Justice, Bureau of Justice Statistics, *Criminal Victimization in the United States, 1987*, (Government Printing Office, Washington, D.C.) 1989, Table 4.

13. Arthur H. Green, "Child Neglect," in R. Ammerman & M. Hersen, (eds.), *Case Studies in Family Violence*, (Plenum Press, New York) 1991, p. 135.

14. C. R. Hartman & A. W. Burgess, "Sexual Abuse in Children: Causes and Consequences," in D. Cicchetti & V. Carlson, (eds.), *Child Maltreatment*, (Cambridge University Press, Cambridge, Mass.) 1989, p. 98.

15. D. Finkelhor, *Sexually Victimized Children*, (Free Press, New York) 1979.

16. D. Finkelhor, *Child Sexual Abuse: Theories and Research*, (Free Press, New York) 1984.

17. D. Russell, *Rape in Marriage*, (Macmillan, New York) 1982.

18. L. Timnick, "22% in Survey Were Child Abuse Victims," *Los Angeles Times*, 1 (25 August 1985).

19. Friedrich, Grambsch, Broughton, Kuiper, & Beilke, "Normative Sexual Behavior in Children," 88 *Pediatrics*, 456 (1991).

20. D. G. Kilpatrick, C. N. Edmonds, & A. K. Seymour, *Rape in America: A Report to the Nation*, (National Victims Center, Arlington, Va.) 1992.

21. D. Finkelhor, *Child Sexual Abuse*, supra.
22. The figure of 44,700 comes from the National Incidence Survey of 1981. See *National Study of the Incidence and Severity of Child Abuse and Neglect: Technical Report Number 1*, K. Bergdorf & J. Edmonds, (eds.), (Washington, D.C., DHHS Publication No. (OHDS) 81-30326) 1981.
23. C. R. Hartman & A. W. Burgess, "Sexual Abuse of Children," p. 98–99.
24. L. J. Siegal, *Criminology*, 3rd ed. (West Publishing Co., St Paul, Minn.) 1989, p. 188.
25. B. Steele & V. Pollock, "A Psychiatric Study of Parents Who Abuse Infants and Small Children," in R. Helfer & C. H. Kempe, (eds.), *The Battered Child Syndrome*, (University of Chicago Press, Chicago) 1968. It is interesting to note that later editions of this classic book on child abuse do not contain the article. For example, see the 4th edition published in 1987.
26. M. A. Straus, "Family Patterns in a Nationally Representative Sample," 3 *International Journal of Child Abuse and Neglect*, 23 (1979).
27. R. Hunter & N. Kilstrom, "Breaking the Cycle in Abusive Families," 136 *American Journal of Psychiatry*, 1320 (1979).
28. B. England & D. Jacobvitz, "Intergenerational Continuity of Parental Abuse: Causes and Consequences." Paper presented at the Conference on Biosocial Perspectives in Abuse and Neglect, York, Maine (1984).
29. C. Cappell & R. B. Heiner, "The Intergenerational Transmission of Family Aggression," 5(2) *Journal of Family Violence*, 135 (1990).
30. K. A. Dodge, J. E. Bates, & G. S. Pettit, "Mechanisms in the Cycle of Violence," 250 *Science*, 1678 (December 1990).
31. Id. at p. 1681.
32. C. S. Widom, "The Cycle of Violence," *Research in Brief, National Institute of Justice* (US Department of Justice, Washington, D.C.) October 1992.
33. Cynthia Crosson Tower, *Understanding Child Abuse and Neglect*, 2nd ed. (Allyn and Bacon, Boston) 1993.
34. B. Justice & R. Justice, *The Abusing Family*, (Human Services Press, New York) 1976, p. 37.
35. See J. D. Delsordo, "Protective Casework for Abused Children," 10 *Children*, (1963) 213–218.
36. H. P. Martin, (ed.), *The Abused Child*, (Ballinger, Cambridge, Mass.) 1976.
37. M. Lynch, "Risk Factors in the Child: A Study of Abused Children and Their Siblings," in H. P. Martin, (ed.), *The Abused Child*, (Ballinger, Cambridge, Mass.) 1976, pp. 43–56.
38. N. Polansky, M. Chambers, E. Buttenwieser, & D. Williams, *Damaged Parents: An Anatomy of Child Neglect*, (University of Chicago Press, Chicago) 1981, p. 21.
39. See L. Young, *Wednesday's Children*, (McGraw-Hill New York) 1964; and S. N. Katz, *When Parents Fail*, (Beacon Press, Boston) 1971.
40. I. Wolock & B. Horowitz, "Child Maltreatment and Maternal Deprivation Among AFDC Families," 53 *Social Service Review*, 175–184 (1979).
41. D. J. Hansen & V. M. MacMilian, "Behavioral Assessment of Child Abuse and Neglectful Families: Recent Development and Current Issues," 14 *Behavior Modification*, 225–278 (1990).
42. H. B. Cantwell, "Child Neglect," in C. H. Kempe and R. E. Helfer, (eds.), *The Battered Child*, (University of Chicago Press, Chicago) 1980, pp. 183–197.
43. See J. Conti, "The Effects of Sexual Abuse on Children: A Critique and Suggestions for Future Research," 10 *Victimology: An International Journal*, 110–130 (1985); and J. Conti, I. Berliner, & J. Schurman, "The Impact of Sexual Abuse on Children: Final Report," Available from the authors at the University of Chicago, 969 E. 60th Street, Chicago, Ill., 60637.
44. D. Finkelhor, *Child Sexual Abuse: New Theories and Research*, (Free Press, New York) 1984.
45. E. Porter, *Treating the Young Male Victims of Sexual Assault*, (Safer Society Press, Syracuse, N.Y.) 1986.
46. Id.
47. A. N. Groth, *Men Who Rape*, (Plenum Press, New York) 1979.
48. D. J. Gelinas, "The Persisting Negative Effects of Incest," 46 *Psychiatry*, 312–322 (1983).

49. C. A. Courtios, "Studying and Counseling Women with Past Incest Experience," 5, *Victimology: An International Journal*, 322–334 (1980).

50. D. Finkelhor, *Child Sexual Abuse* See note #51 (1984) and E. Porter, *Treating the Young Male Victim of Sexual Assault*. See note #45 (1986).

51. D. Finkelhor, *Child Sexual Abuse*, (Free Press, New York) 1984.

52. C. C. Tower, *Understanding Child Abuse and Neglect*, 2nd ed. (Allyn and Bacon, Boston) 1993.

53. A. N. Groth, *Men Who Rape*, (Plenum Press, New York) 1979.

54. E. D. Farber, J. Showers, C. F. Johnson, J. A. Joseph, & L. Oshins, "The Sexual Abuse of Children: A Comparison of Male and Female Victims," 13 *Journal of Clinical Child Psychology*, 294–297 (1984).

55. Richard J. Gelles & Claire Pedrick Cornell, *Intimate Violence in Families*, 2nd ed. (Sage, Newbury, Calif.) 1990, p. 85.

56. See M. Bard, "The Study and Modification of Intrafamily Violence," in J. L. Singer, (ed.), *The Control of Aggression and Violence*, (Academic Press, New York) 1971 for study of homicides in Philadelphia; and M. Wolfgang, *Patterns in Criminal Homicide*, (John Wiley, New York) 1958 for the study of homicides in New York.

57. S. K. Steinmetz, *The Cycle of Violence: Assertive, Aggressive, and Abusive Family Interaction*, (Prager, New York) 1971.

58. "Battered families: A growing nightmare," *U.S. News & World Report*, 60–61 (15 January 1979).

59. M. A. Straus, R. J. Gelles, & S. K. Steinmetz, *Behind Closed Doors: Violence in the American Family*, (Doubleday, New York) 1980.

60. S. K. Steinmetz, "A Cross-Cultural Comparison of Sibling Violence," 2 (3/4) *International Journal of Family Psychiatry*, 337–351 (1981).

61. See for example, David D. P. Jones, "The Syndrome of Munchausen by Proxy," 18 *Child Abuse and Neglect*, 769 (1994).

62. E. J. Kudsk & J. A. Nolan, "Munchausen Syndrome by Proxy: The Case for Adult Victims," paper presented at the annual meeting of Academy of Criminal Justice Sciences, Boston, (March 1995).

63. J. Money, "Munchausen's Syndrome by Proxy: Update," *Journal of Pediatric Psychology*, 583 (November 1986) discussing an earlier article that appeared in the *Bulletin of the American Academy of Psychiatry and the Law* in 1976.

64. R. Meadow, "Munchausen Syndrome by Proxy: The Hinterland of Child Abuse," *The Lancet*, 351 (1977).

65. S. J. Boros & L. C. Brubaker, "Munchausen Syndrome by Proxy," *FBI Law Enforcement Bulletin*, 16 (June 1992).

66. Id. at p. 20.

67. See D. Cicchetti & Vicki Carlson, (eds.), *Child Maltreatment*, (Cambridge University Press, Cambridge, Mass.) 1989; C. C. Tower, *Understanding Child Abuse and Neglect*, 2nd ed. (Allyn and Bacon, Boston 1993); R. T. Ammerman & M. Hersen, *Assessment of Family Violence*, (Wiley & Sons, New York) 1992 which do not discuss ritual abuse; and compare C. C. Kent, "Ritual Abuse," *Case Studies in Family Violence*, R. T. Ammerman & M. Hersen, (eds.), (Plenum Press, New York) 1991; and D. K. Sakheim & S. E. Devine, *Out of Darkness*, (Lexington Books, New York) 1992 which covers the entire realm of ritualistic abuse.

68. A. Crowley, *Magick in Theory and Practice*, (Dover, New York) 1924. Reprinted in 1976.

69. C. Raschke, *Painted Black: Satanic Crime in America*, p. 123.

70. A LaVey, *The Satanic Bible*, (Avon Books, New York) 1969, p. 77.

71. M. Smith & L. Pazder, *Michelle Remembers*, (Congdon & Lattes, New York) 1980.

72. For an excellent discussion of this area, see S. J. Kelly, R. Brant, & J. Waterman, "Sexual Abuse of Children in Day Care Centers," 17 *Child Abuse & Neglect*, 71–89 (1993).

73. Id.

74. *Ritual Abuse: Definitions, Glossary, The Use of Mind Control*. (Ritual Abuse Task Force. Los Angeles County Commission For Women) September 15, 1989).

75. *Webster's Ninth New Collegiate Dictionary* (Merriam-Webster Inc., Springfield, Mass.) 1987, p. 1018.

11

ELDER VICTIMS

Chapter Outline

Elder Abuse
    Extent of the Problem
    Definition

Theories of Elder Abuse
    Cycle of Violence
    Psychopathology
    Social Exchange Theory
    Family Stress Theory
    Neutralization Theory

Elder Victimization
    Sexual Assault
    Other Violent Crimes
    Fraud
    Burglary

Summary

Key Terms

Discussion Questions

Suggested Readings

Learning Objectives

After reading this chapter, you should be able to:

- Discuss the nature and extent of elder abuse in the United States
- Define issues that affect the validity of examining the problem of elder abuse
- Explain the different causation theories of elder abuse
- Describe the various types of criminal victimizations and their impact on elders

Elder Abuse

Although we became aware of certain forms of family violence in the 1960s and 1970s, it wasn't until the 1980s that the plight of elder victims entered our national consciousness as a problem that must be dealt with. One of the first studies dealing with elder abuse was published in 1979. Block and Sinnott entitled their work "The Battered Elder Syndrome: An Exploratory Study." They contacted twenty-four agencies in Maryland and surveyed 427 professionals and 443 elders. They found twenty-six cases of elder abuse. Unfortunately, the study went no further, but it was the first step in the long process of recognizing that elders can be victims of family violence.[1] By 1988, the research examining elder abuse consisted of over 200 research papers.[2] Today, that number continues to expand rapidly. Although several problems exist in the study of elder abuse, defining the term itself and determining its extent are two of the most controversial and difficult to resolve.

Extent of the Problem

How pervasive is elder abuse? Domestic elder abuse, like other forms of family violence, occurs behind closed doors in the privacy of the home. One significant study of elder abuse published in 1988 by Pillemer and Finkelhor involved 2020 Boston elders who were sixty-five and older and living on their own or with their families. This research found a rate of 32 abused elders per 1000. The results of this survey would translate into over 1 million abused elders in the United States in 1988.[3]

Estimates on the nature, type, and prevalence of elder abuse continue to vary widely. In 1989, one congressional committee estimated that 1.5 million cases of elder abuse occur each year.[4] More shocking is the fact that this figure has steadily increased by 0.5 million each year since 1980.[5] Callahan claims that between 4 and 10 percent of all elders suffer abuse.[6] Other researchers believe the figure is higher, contending that only one in six incidents of elder abuse is ever reported to the authorities.[7]

Controversy continues regarding who is abused and who is the abuser—is it the children who abuse the parents, or the elder's wife, or the husband? This confusion is further illustrated by the fact that some authorities believe that victims are primarily women over the age of seventy-five,[8] whereas others believe that the wife is the one who perpetrates the abuse.[9] Other scholars argue that adult children inflict abuse on their parents. The Boston survey indicated elders were abused more by their spouses than by their children. This result is somewhat skewed once it is understood that elders live with spouses more than adult children and therefore the chance is greater of being abused by a spouse than by an adult child. Although both men and women may be victims of elder abuse, the abuse inflicted by husbands is more severe than that inflicted by wives. More research is necessary to determine the extent and nature of elder abuse, but the central issue is that abuse is likely to be inflicted by the people with whom the elder is living.

There is a continuing failure to report and act on this form of abuse and Decalmer lists two major factors that may contribute to this failure:

1. There is a failure to understand the size, severity, and nature of the problem because of the conflicting definitions of elder abuse.
2. The number of controlled studies and the case reporting methods that are used in most of the research in this area have produced difficulties in estimating the true extent of the various acts of abuse and neglect.[10]

In addition, methodology and sampling procedures differ from study to study. Some research focuses on the elderly population, other studies examine agency records, and still other investigations poll professionals. As a result, there are no definitive figures that are accepted by all scholars and researchers.

Definition

The term *elder abuse* was first used during congressional hearings in the late 1970s. The House Select Committee on Aging, chaired by Representative Claude Pepper (The Pepper Commission) examined the mistreatment of the elderly and introduced the term *elder abuse* to the nation.[11] However, coining a term does not always clearly define the parameters for the scholars and professionals trying to do the research.

Some scholars, when examining elder abuse, have included persons under the age of sixty in their research, whereas others simply include everyone who is over the age of sixty regardless of the circumstances.[12] Well-respected authorities defined elder abuse as occurring only between those who share a residence with the victim, and in other studies out-of-home caretakers were included.[13] The debate, confusion, and inability to agree on any acceptable conceptual framework from which to study elder abuse continue to cause problems in this area.

In an effort to clarify this confusion, some authorities attempted to develop a list of definitions involving abuse of the elderly by establishing typologies. Unfortunately, these typologies lacked uniformity and resulted in more confusion. Hudson and Johnson pointed out that some typologies differed considerably in defining neglect, whereas others classified withholding of personal care as physical abuse and/or psychological abuse.[14] As a result of this continuing confusion, other researchers began to attempt to frame the definition of elder abuse from a conceptional perspective. For example, some scholars placed the issue of elder abuse within the broad category of inadequate care.[15] However, the same problems that were faced in trying to establish an acceptable typology were present in the effort to conceptualize the whole issue.[16]

Several prominent scholars including Wolf, Pillemer, and Godkin subsequently distilled these various definitions down to a multifaceted definition that classified elder abuse into five areas:

1. *Physical abuse* includes the infliction of physical pain or injury, physical coercion, sexual molestation, or physical restraint.
2. *Psychological abuse* includes the infliction of mental anguish.
3. *Material abuse* includes the illegal or improper exploitation and/or use of funds or resources.
4. *Active neglect* includes the refusal or failure to undertake a caretaking obligation.
5. *Passive neglect* includes the refusal or failure to fulfill a caretaking obligation.[17]

This discussion clearly illustrates the difficulty in attempting to define the term *elder abuse* and helps to explain the continuing scholarly debate and controversy. Based on this confusion and conflict, a simple, clear definition of elder abuse may not be possible. However, for purposes of consistency with other definitions contained in this text, **elder abuse** is defined as conduct that results in the physical, psychological, or material harm, or neglect or injury to an elder. This definition applies both to domestic and institutional abuse. **Material** in the context of elder abuse refers to the exploitation or use of resources. An **elder** is a person sixty-five years or older. The initial age determination of sixty-five years is based on common acceptance of that age by most authorities, scholars, and professionals.[18] This age group may be further subdivided into those between sixty-five and seventy-five who are called the young-old and those above seventy-five who are referred to as the old-old.[19]

Elder abuse can occur in a domestic or institutional setting. Pillemer and Moore explained that despite two decades of state and federal regulation of nursing homes, abuse of the elderly still occurs on a regular basis.[20] The focus of this section will be on the domestic abuse aspect of this form of violence, as more research has been done in this area. However, abuse of the elderly in nursing homes and long-term care institutions is a fact of modern life and should not be forgotten or overlooked when considering the overall plight of the elderly in our society.

Theories of Elder Abuse

Authorities may disagree as to the exact cause of elder abuse, but they generally agree that it is similar to other forms of family violence and that it crosses all social and economic lines. Most researchers agree that elder abuse is not an isolated event, rather it is a repetitive pattern of acts by the abuser toward the victim.

Cycle of Violence

The cycle of violence or intergenerational transmission of violence theory has already been discussed in detail in Chapter 10. Galbraith argues that it has proven ineffective in predicting elder abuse.[21] Wolf and Pillemer also point out that those who abuse elders do not necessarily grow up in families characterized by violence.[22]

Psychopathology

The *psychopathology theory* is based on the premise that abusers suffer from mental disorders that cause them to be violent. Wolf found a high prevalence of mental illness among elder abusers.[23] This approach seems to have greater validity in explaining elder abuse than in explaining either child or spousal abuse. Researchers have found psychopathology present in cases of physical and verbal abuse of elders.[24] Other scholars indicate that a number of abusers have had previous hospitalizations for serious psychiatric disorders, such as schizophrenia and other psychoses.[25]

Social Exchange Theory

One *social exchange theory* assumes that dependency in relationships contributes to elder abuse; that is, that increased dependency of the victim on the abuser results in acts of violence. Other research studies support this theory.[26] The abuser's financial dependency on the victim also has been found to be a factor in a number of studies of elder abuse.[27]

The loss of mutual resources between the elder and the caretaker also contributes to the deterioration of the relationship. This results in the caretaker perceiving the relationship as unfair, with a subsequent increase in hostility toward the elder.[28]

A second social exchange theory assumes that the dependency of the abuser on the elder victim causes abuse. This concept focuses on adult children becoming dependent on the elder for material rewards, such as housing and finances. Because these children perceive themselves as weaker and less powerful than the elder, abusing the elder is a way to equalize the balance of power and gain control over the relationship.[29]

Family Stress Theory

The family stress theory is one of the most widely accepted theories of elder abuse.[30] The *family stress theory* is based on the premise that providing care for an elder induces stress within the family. This stress may take many forms, including economic hardship, loss of sleep, intrusions into normal family privacy routines, and other activities which may cause the caregiver to feel resentment toward the elder. Adult children may have to give up economic security to provide care for an aged parent or other close relative. In addition, the physical toll of caring for an ill elderly person can sometimes overwhelm the adult child, which results in a loss of control and subsequent abuse.[31] However, even this theory is subject to controversy. Phillips suggests that stress levels may not be as important a factor in causing elder abuse as previously believed.[32]

Neutralization Theory

The *neutralization theory* was originally developed by Sykes and Matza to explain juvenile delinquency in our society.[33] This theory views the delinquent as being affected by the norms and values of a larger social system rather than a counterculture. This concept holds that delinquents show guilt and shame for their antisocial behavior.[34] To commit criminal or antisocial acts, persons develop techniques of neutralization. These techniques are rationalizations or justifications for their behavior. Matza established five techniques that allow individuals to justify their acts:

1. *Denial of responsibility.* The person may claim that something else, such as alcohol, made him commit the criminal act.
2. *Denial of injury.* Juveniles may believe that even though they violated the law, no one was really hurt. For example, theft of an automobile is okay because the owner's insurance company will replace it with a new model anyway.
3. *Denial of victim.* Delinquents may claim that the victim had it coming and therefore their acts were justified under the circumstances.
4. *Condemnation of the condemners.* Juveniles may shift the blame to others, calling them corrupt or incompetent.
5. *Appeal to higher loyalty.* Some offenders will claim they violated the law to satisfy a higher authority or goal.

Tomita has applied the neutralization theory to elder abuse and suggests that, although it cannot be used to establish a direct cause, it may viewed as reasons employed by abusers to justify their acts.[35] She examines each technique of neutralization and explains how it is utilized by the perpetrators to justify their abuse of elders.

1. *Denial of responsibility.* In these situations, the abuser claims the mistreatment was caused by forces beyond his control, such as poverty, bad parents, etc.
2. *Denial of injury.* The abuser will rationalize that the injury was not really that serious because the victim did not have to go to the emergency room. In material abuse situations, the abuser will justify her actions by stating that the parent can afford to give away property or assets.
3. *Denial of the victim.* Abusers may state that the victim doesn't need help, that she is only attempting to gain attention. For example, the abuser may refuse to dress the victim, claiming the victim wants attention, when in reality, the victim cannot dress herself.
4. *Condemnation of the condemners.* In these situations, the abuser condemns protective services or other agencies for interfering with the family.
5. *Appeal to higher loyalty.* The abuser may believe he must act a certain way to satisfy his spouse.

As this discussion illustrates, several theories attempt to explain why people abuse the elderly. Just as with other causes of family violence, no single theory is universally accepted by all scholars. Continued research is needed in this area to determine if a cause can be established.

FOCUS: Triads

Community Involvement in Fighting Elder Victimization

A new concept that emphasizes community cooperation in combating elder victimization is succeeding in a number of areas throughout the nation. This innovative concept is the triad program.

Triads are formed when the local police and sheriff's department agree to work cooperatively with senior citizens to prevent the victimization of the elderly in the community. The three groups share ideas and resources to provide programs and training for vulnerable and often fearful elderly citizens.

A triad program usually begins when a police chief, a sheriff, or a leader in the senior citizen community contacts the other two essential participants to discuss a combined effort. Although each entity may already have programs in place to reduce the victimization rate among the elderly, the three-way involvement of triads adds strength, resources, and greater credibility.

Most traids include representatives from agencies that serve older persons, such as the Agency on Aging, senior centers, and Adult Protective Services. Law enforcement leaders then invite seniors and those working with them to serve on an advisory coun-

cil, often called Seniors and Lawmen Together (SALT).

Some triads establish programs to prevent elder abuse through education and to address the plight of seniors in personal care homes. For example, in Columbus, Georgia, the plight of some seniors in such facilities came to the attention of a very active SALT council. Learning that older residents were suffering from abuse and neglect, the SALT council devised a strategy to investigate specific situations.

To begin, the council enlisted the assistance of the sheriff's office and the police and health departments. Through these agencies, a search warrant of the homes was obtained, proper lodging and care was arranged for those seniors living in unhealthy and unsafe conditions, and a plan for more careful monitoring of such homes was initiated.

The essence of the triad program is cooperation. This program allows the service providers—law enforcement—to work together with the consumers—senior citizens. Through positive programs that affect safety and quality of life, mutual respect and appreciation evolves between the law enforcement community and citizens.

Source: Adapted from Betsy Cantrell, "Triad, Reducing Criminal Victimization of the Elderly," *FBI Law Enforcement Bulletin,* 19–23 (February 1994).

Elder Victimization[36]

Even with programs such as triads, the incidence of elder victimization continues to escalate in our society. This section will examine a few of the more common crimes committed against elders. Not only are elders preyed upon by family members because of their frail condition, they are also prime targets for certain kinds of criminals who seek easy targets.

Sexual Assault

For many elderly women who were raised during a time when sexual matters were never discussed publicly, becoming a victim of a sexual assault can be a traumatic experience that the elder is not able to process. Some elders are still surrounded with embarrassment about sexual activity and have never discussed it even with their children. To these elders, the thought of having to discuss sexual acts in public is unthinkable. Many older victims believe it is the worst form of lost dignity. They may experience shame in discussing the case or participating in a medical examination with law enforcement officers present. They may have been required to perform sexual acts that they have never participated in before, which only adds to the humiliation.

Elderly rape victims often sustain injuries different from those experienced by younger victims. Vaginal linings are not as elastic as those of younger women because of hormonal changes. This may cause increased sexual trauma including infections, bruising, and tears that never fully heal. More alarmingly, many elders have brittle bones, such as the pelvis and hips, that can be more easily broken or crushed by the weight of the rapist.

Intervention with the elderly is critical and may afford the victims some choices they may not have otherwise had. For example, victim assistance professionals can offer to work with the victim on a relocation plan if that is her desire and she has the financial ability to move from the place of the attack. If the elder agrees, the victim service provider can work with family members to help educate them about the special needs of the victim as a result of the crime. If there is no family, close contact should be maintained with the victim to help increase her feelings of self-worth.

Other Violent Crimes

Elder victims are the least likely to be physically injured during the commission of a violent crime. However, if they are injured, these injuries tend to be more serious because of their frailty and aging bodies. Bones become more brittle with advanced age and break more easily than those of a twenty year old. One study points out that when elders are physically injured during a violent crime, they are twice as likely as any other age group to be seriously injured and require hospitalization.[37] However, the elderly as a whole are significantly less likely than younger age groups to become victims of most types of crime, including violent crime.[38] This may be because they are not as mobile and therefore do not go out in public as much as their younger counterparts and therefore are not as easily approached or victimized.

Most homicide victims over the age of sixty-five were killed during the commission of another felony and were more likely to be killed by a stranger. The elderly are also less likely to protect themselves during the incident and may suffer injuries that younger victims would avoid. A purse snatcher may cause a younger victim to stumble and regain her stability, whereas the same incident may cause an elderly victim to fall and break her hip.

Fraud

The elderly are targeted for crimes involving finances more than any other victim population. Although elderly victims may not sustain any physical injury as a result of this type of crime, the psychological impact can be devastating. The loss of one's entire life savings can create severe and debilitating depression. Many victims blame themselves for the loss and because of this can suffer additional health problems relating to depression such as loss of appetite, decreased interest level, increased withdrawal, and diminished sleep. Some victims feel ashamed that they didn't recognize the "con" and become reluctant to report the crime because they think family members will blame them for mismanagement of their funds and seek to terminate their financial independence.

A majority of the elderly live on fixed incomes and the impact of a financial crime can be devastating to them. They may lose their life savings and even their homes. This may result in the loss of their independence, which many elderly people value more than money itself.

Victim service providers can provide the elderly and their families with information on the victim's right to file civil actions against the perpetrator. The elderly may need help in rearranging their finances as a result of the loss. The courts should be asked to allow for an expiated payment schedule on any restitution plan. The elderly victim may need the funds now, not three or five years from now.

Burglary

For many of the elderly, the home becomes the center of their world as they gradually lose friends and their own mobility. They retire from jobs, family members begin to die, and outside activities decrease due to increasing physical or mental limitations. This imposed isolation explains, in part, why a majority of the elderly are victimized near or in their homes.

The loss of certain possessions, especially those that have sentimental value, can have a great impact on an older person. The loss of other material items such as televisions can further restrict an elder's outside contact with the world. Many victims may want to relocate after a burglary but may not have the financial ability to do so. Once their home has been invaded, they may never feel safe again.

Victim service providers should work with other organizations in the community to assist elderly victims. The local law enforcement agency may provide advice and assistance in evaluating the elder's home to determine if other points of entry should be made more secure. Neighborhood Watch participants should be alerted to the fact that their neighbor was victimized and to increase their vigilance of any suspicious activity which might involve the perpetrator returning to an "easy target." Additionally, every Agency on Aging operates an information and referral line that can refer the elderly to a variety of services.

Summary

Elder abuse has become still another form of violence in our society. Authorities cannot agree on a definition, and as a result the outcome of different studies vary widely regarding the nature, cause, and extent of this type of violence. Elder abuse, like other forms of family violence, is not an isolated event, rather it is a pattern of behavior that increases both in intensity and frequency over time. The rich, poor, college educated, and uneducated suffer from elder abuse. The dynamics and etiology of this type of abuse are still being theorized, with some theories holding more promise than others. Continued research is of paramount importance if we are to understand and intervene in this type of behavior.

It is a grim fate that awaits our maturing population: that after years of productivity and work, we could face the prospect of being beaten and shamed by other members of our society. As a society, we owe it to ourselves and those who will come after us to actively pursue detection and prevention of this form of violence.

Key Terms

Elder abuse is defined as conduct that results in the physical, psychological, or material harm, or neglect or injury to an elder.

Material in the context of elder abuse refers to the exploitation or use of resources.

Elder is a person sixty-five years or older.

Psychopathology of elder abuse is based on the premise that abusers suffer from mental disorders that cause them to be violent.

Social exchange theory of elder abuse assumes that dependency in relationships contributes to elder abuse.

Family stress theory regarding elder abuse is based on the premise that providing care for an elder induces stress within the family.

Neutralization theory was originally developed by Sykes and Matza to explain juvenile delinquency in our society. This theory views the delinquent as being affected by the norms and values of a larger social system rather than a counterculture.

Discussion Questions

1. Is elder abuse more or less serious than child abuse? Why?

2. Do you agree with the definition of elder abuse contained in the text? Draft another definition that you believe is more appropriate and justify your answer.

3. Which of the theories discussing elder abuse do you favor? Why?

4. What is the most serious type of crime that an elder can experience? Why?

5. What is more important in your mind for an elderly victim—independence or security from further victimization? Why?

Suggested Readings

B. Schlesinger & R. Schlesinger, (eds.), *Abuse of the Elderly: Issues and Annotated Bibliography*, (University of Toronto Press, Toronto) 1988.

Peter Decalmer & Frank Glendenning, (eds.), *The Mistreatment of Elder People*, (Sage, London, England) 1993.

V. B. Van Hasselt, et al. (eds.), *Handbook of Family Violence*, (Plenum Press, New York) 1988.

R. S. Wolf & K. A. Pillemer, *Helping Elderly Victims: The Reality of Elder Abuse*, (Columbia University Press, New York) 1989.

R. Filenson & S. R. Ingman, (eds.), *Elder Abuse: Practice and Policy*, (Human Sciences Press, New York) 1989.

R. T. Ammerman and M. Hersen, (eds.), *Assessment of Family Violence, A Clinical and Legal Sourcebook*, (John Wiley & Sons Inc, New York) 1992.

M. R. Block & J. D. Sinnott, (eds.), *The Battered Elder Syndrome: An Exploratory Study*, (University of Maryland Center on Aging, College Park, Md.) 1979.

Endnotes

1. M. R. Block & J. D. Sinnott. "The Battered Elder Syndrome: An Exploratory Study," (Center on Aging, University of Maryland) 1979.
2. B. Schlesinger & R. Schlesinger, (eds.), *Abuse of the Elderly: Issues and Annotated Bibliography*, (University of Toronto Press, Toronto) 1988.
3. K. A. Pillemer & D. Finkelhor, "The Prevalence of Elder Abuse: A Random Sample Survey," 28(1) *The Gerontologist*, 51 (1988).
4. U.S. House of Representative, Select Committee on Aging, "Elder Abuse: Curbing a National Epidemic," (Hearings) (Washington, D.C. GPO) December 10, 1990.
5. Id.
6. J. J. Callahan, "Elder Abuse: Some Questions for Policymakers," 28 *The Gerontologist*, 453–458 (1988).
7. J. I. Kosberg, "Preventing Elder Abuse: Identification of High Risk Factors Prior to Placement Decision," 28 *The Gerontologist*, 43–50 (1988).
8. U.S. House of Representative, Select Committee on Aging, "Elder Abuse: A Decade of Shame and Inaction" (Hearings) (Washington, D.C. GPO) May 1, 1990.
9. K. A. Pillemer & D. Finkelhor, "The Prevalence of Elder Abuse: A Random Sample Survey," 28(1) *The Gerontologist*, 51 (1988).
10. Peter Decalmer & Frank Glendenning, (eds.), *The Mistreatment of Elder People*, (Sage, London, England) 1993, p. 35.
11. "Elder Abuse," 1 (17) Infolink, (National Victims Center, Washington, D.C.) 1992.
12. Karl Pillemer & J. J. Suitor, "Elder Abuse," V. B. Van Hasselt, et al. (eds.), *Handbook of Family Violence*, (Plenum Press, New York) 1988.
13. Compare M. R. Block & J. D. Sinnott. "The Battered Elder Syndrome: An Exploratory Study," (Center on Aging, University of Maryland) 1979 with S. Steinmetz & D. J. Amsden, "Dependent Elders, Family Stress and Abuse," T. H. Brubaker, (ed.), *Family Relationships in Later Life* (Sage, Beverly Hills, Calif.) 1983.
14. M. F. Hudson & T. F. Johnson, "Elder Abuse and Neglect: A Review of the Literature," in C. Eisdorfer, et al., (eds.), 6 *Annual Review of Gerontology and Geriatrics* (Springer, New York) 1986.
15. T. A. O'Malley, H. C. O'Malley, D. E. Everitt, & D. Sarson, "Categories of Family-Mediated Abuse and Neglect of Elderly Persons," 32(5) *Journal of the American Geriatrics Society*, 362–369 (1984).
16. Id.
17. See R. S. Wolf & K. A. Pillemer, *Helping Elderly Victims: The Reality of Elder Abuse* (Columbia University Press, New York) 1989; and M. A. Godkin, R. S. Wolf, & K. A. Pillemer, "A Case-Comparison Analysis of Elder Abuse and Neglect," 28(3) *International Journal of Aging and Human Development*, 207–225 (1989).
18. R. Bachman, "Elderly Victim," *Special Report, Bureau of Justice Statistics*, (U.S. Department of Justice, Washington, D.C.) 1992.
19. M. D. Pagelow, *Family Violence*, (Praeger, New York) 1984, p. 359.
20. K. A. Pillemer & D. W. Moore, "Abuse of Patients in Nursing Homes: Findings from a Survey of Staff," 29(3) *The Gerontologist*, 314 (1989).
21. M. W. Galbraith, "A Critical Examination of the Definitional, Methodological and Theoretical Problems of Elder Abuse," in R. Filenson, & S. R. Ingman, (eds.), *Elder Abuse: Practice and Policy*, (Human Sciences Press, New York) 1989, pp. 35–42.

22. R. S. Wolf & K. A. Pillemer, *Helping Elderly Victims: The Reality of Elder Abuse,* (Columbia University Press, New York) 1989.

23. R. S. Wolf, C. Strugnell, & M. Godkin, *Preliminary Findings from Three Model Projects on Elder Abuse,* (University of Massachusetts Medical Center, (Worcester, Mass.) 1982.

24. T. Hickey & R. L. Douglas, "Mistreatment of the Elderly in the Domestic Setting: An Exploratory Study," 71 *American Journal of Public Health,* 500–517 (1981).

25. R. S. Beckman & R. D. Adelman, "Elder Abuse and Neglect," in R. T. Ammerman & M. Hersen, (eds.), *Assessment of Family Violence, A Clinical and Legal Soucebook,* (John Wiley & Sons Inc, New York) 1992, p. 238.

26. J. L. Davison, "Elder Abuse," in M. R. Block & J. D. Sinnott, (eds.), *The Battered Elder Syndrome: An Exploratory Study,* (University of Maryland Center on Aging, College Park, Md.) 1979, pp. 49–55.

27. R. S. Wolf, M. Godkin, & K. A. Pillemer, *Elder Abuse and Neglect: Report from the Model Projects,* (University of Massachusetts Medical Center, University Center on Aging, Worchester, Mass.) 1984.

28. S. K. Steinmetz, *Duty Bound: Elder Abuse and Family Care,* (Sage Publications, Newbury Park, Calif.) 1988.

29. G. J. Anetzberger, *The Etiology of Elder Abuse by Adult Offspring,* (Charles C. Thomas, Springfield Park, Ill.) 1987.

30. S. K. Steinmetz, *Duty Bound: Elder Abuse and Family Care,* (Sage Publications, Newbury Park, Calif.) 1988.

31. R. J. Gelles, "An Exchange/Social Control Theory," in D. Finkelhor, G. Hotaling, R. J. Gelles, & M. A. Straus, (eds.), *The Dark Side of Families: Current Family Violence Research,* (Sage, Beverly Hills, Calif.) 1983.

32. L. Phillips, "Theoretical Explanations of Elder Abuse: Competing Hypotheses and Unresolved Issues," in K. Pillemer & R. Wolf, (eds.), *Elder Abuse: Conflict in the Family,* (Auburn House Publishing Co., Dover, Mass.) 1986.

33. G. M. Sykes & D. Matza, "Techniques of Neutralization: A Theory of Delinquency," 22 *American Sociological Review,* 664–670 (1978).

34. J. F. Short, Jr. & Fred Strodtbeck, *Group Process and Gang Delinquency,* (University of Chicago Press, Chicago) 1965.

35. S. K. Tomita, "The Denial of Elder Mistreatment by Victims and Abusers: The Application of Neutralization Theory," 5(3) *Violence and Victims,* 171 (1990).

36. This section has been adapted from Ellen Alexander, "Elderly Victims of Crime," *National Victim Assistance Academy Text,* (Office for Victims of Crime, Washington, D.C.) 1996, which was funded by a federal grant.

37. *Elder Victimization,* (Bureau of Justice Statistics, Washington, D.C.) 1987.

38. *Highlights from 20 Years of Surveying Crime Victims, 1973–1992,* (Bureau of Justice Statistics, Washington, D.C.) October 1993.

12

HATE CRIMES

Chapter Outline

Cultural Awareness
> *Introduction*
> *Cultural Awareness Training*

Hate Crimes
> *Introduction*
> *Legal Aspects of Hate Crimes*
> *Identifying Bias Crimes*
> *Typology of Offenders*

Cultural Awareness Case Study

Summary

Key Terms

Discussion Questions

Suggested Readings

Learning Objectives

After reading this chapter, you should be able to:

- Explain why it is important to understand different cultures
- List the elements of an effective cultural diversity program
- List the indicators of bias crimes
- Explain the different types of bias crime offenders

FOCUS: Hate Crimes in America

- In New York, a white teenage boy was arrested for chasing two Hispanic girls with a baseball bat while yelling racial slurs.
- In Kansas, a developmentally disabled woman is raped by a caretaker.
- In Woodland Hills, California, posters depicting swastikas and KKK symbols are discovered at California State University, Hayward. These posters urge homosexuals to "go back to your closets."

- A number of African-American places of worship are burned.
- There is a reported rise in the militia movement in America.
- White supremacist groups have become more visible and active in the last ten years.
- In 1994, the Southern Poverty Law Center listed more than 270 hate groups as being active in the United States.

To understand hate crimes fully, victim service providers must be sensitive to cultural issues. Each victim of a crime needs to be treated as an individual. However, some victims face more difficult tasks than others, necessitating a more comprehensive approach from the service provider. This difficulty may arise because of the nature of the crime; that is, a murder victim's family will suffer more trauma than the victim of a car theft. Other victims face difficult times because they are from special populations that are different from the established cultures in our country. This difference may be based on skin color, sex, religious beliefs, sexual orientation, or a number of other factors that make people culturally different. This text cannot possibly address all the issues facing the victims who are members of special groups. Its purpose is to examine selected special victim populations and suggest specific methods professionals should use when responding to crimes committed against them.

Cultural Awareness

The United States has traditionally been a melting pot of different peoples who have come to its shores and taken their unique place in our society. We pride ourselves on our diversity and multiculturalism. However, the other side of this coin reflects a darker side to our relationship with these groups. Clashes between ethnic and racial minority groups and other more established cultures in the United States have escalated over the last ten to twenty years. Additionally, new refugees, recent immigrants, and other minority groups are prime targets for certain types of perpetrators. These victims face an almost overwhelming task when attempting to pursue redress in the criminal or civil justice system. Victim service providers need to be aware of these issues when dealing with these victims.

Introduction

Simply saying to those who work in the criminal justice system that a victim comes from a different culture and is different from the rest of us does not automatically guarantee sympathetic treatment and/or an understanding response to that victim's special needs. Stereotyping must be guarded against, and relying on third-hand information when responding to the needs of minority victims should be avoided. Different cultures may not be as homogeneous as they appear on the surface, and care should be taken to not attribute characteristics to special populations based on conversations or interactions with one member of the group. The person being interviewed may be advocating personal beliefs, which may not represent the feelings of other members of that particular culture. It is essential that professionals working in the criminal justice profession be both culturally sensitive and careful to validate their information if possible.

Cultural awareness can be defined as the understanding an individual has regarding different cultures. The term *culture* includes different races, religions, genders, ages, physical disabilities, and gay or lesbian issues. Therefore, cultural awareness encompasses a wide range of issues, any of which may confront those working within this field. The next section will provide some guidelines for professionals to use when evaluating cultural awareness programs or setting up such training programs.

PRACTICUM: Cultures and Misunderstanding[1]

The Officer's Perspective

A Nigerian cab driver runs a red light. An officer pulls him over in the next block, stopping the patrol car at least three car lengths behind the cab. Before the officer can exit his patrol car, the cabbie gets out of his vehicle and approaches the officer. Talking rapidly in a high-pitched voice and making wild gestures, the cab driver appears to be out of control.

The officer steps from his vehicle and yells for the cab driver to stop, but the cabbie continues to advance until he is about two feet from him. The cab driver does not make eye contact and appears to be talking to the ground. Finally, the officer arrests the cabbie for disorderly conduct and resisting arrest.

The Cab Driver's Perspective

Although most Americans know to remain in their cars, the Nigerian exited his cab to show his respect by not troubling the officer to leave his own vehicle. The Nigerian ignores the command to stop advancing on the officer because

in his eyes he is not even close to the officer. The social distance for conversation in Nigeria is much closer for conversations than in the United States. For Nigerians, it may be less than fifteen inches, whereas two feet represents a comfortable conversation zone for Americans.

Anglo-Americans expect eye contact during conversation; the lack of it usually signifies deception, rudeness, defiance, or a means to end a conversation.

In Nigeria, however, people often show respect and humility by averting their eyes. The Nigerian believes he is sending a message of respect by averting his eyes and talking to the ground.

1. Is either party at fault in this encounter?
2. Is the officer responsible for understanding other cultures? Is the cabbie responsible for conforming to the standards of the country in which he is working?
3. List ways to avoid such situations.

Cultural Awareness Training

The Practicum indicates how important cultural awareness or sensitivity training is within the criminal justice system. This is an emerging area to which victim service providers can contribute greatly, and in which they should take the lead. They should become knowledgeable regarding different cultures within their community and be prepared to conduct training sessions regarding the customs and traditions of those cultures and their responses to crime and the criminal justice system.

They have an opportunity to provide a valuable service to future victims by ensuring that those in the criminal justice system respond appropriately to members of different cultures. Occasionally, law enforcement agencies will contact victim service providers and ask that they provide cultural awareness or sensitivity training to members of their organization. Unfortunately, this request for training occurs after an incident involving a minority victim has resulted in adverse publicity being directed toward the department. The victim service provider should use this request as an opportunity to "train the trainers" regarding what is an appropriate cultural awareness training program.

No single technique or program will work for all agencies. Professionals may find themselves adapting programs or training techniques to fit specific situations. There are a number of different techniques that may be used to train professionals in the area of cultural awareness.

St. George lists a variety of factors that trainers should consider when conducting cultural awareness training.[2] These factors include multidimensional learning from several perspectives, learning that is relevant and structured to meet specific needs, that is behavior-based, so that students express their feelings by actions, that is empathetic to the feelings and concerns of community minority members, that is practical in nature, and that allows for controversy and provides follow-up support.

Shusta and his associates recommended a multifaceted cultural awareness training program.[3] They suggested that the trainer should use a variety of training aids and techniques to accomplish the objective of teaching cultural awareness. These techniques include the following strategies:

Lectures.   Lectures should be interspersed between other activities and include local demographics. This information may be obtained from city and county departments, housing authorities, state and federal census data, and community-based organizations. Lectures should introduce students to cultural-specific information about the various subcultures within a community.

Role-playing.   Role-playing should include communication skills. Role-playing is intended to create a realistic environment in which the participants may interact and be trained to respond in an appropriate manner.

Simulations.   The purpose of simulations is to allow the participants to identify their own feelings and thereby achieve a better understanding of others. A number of commercial simulation packages specifically designed for cultural awareness programs are on the market.

Work Groups or Presentations.   The work group or presentation aspect of a cultural awareness program allows the participants to discuss various issues. Small groups are a useful technique that allow participants to express their feelings more freely than if they were in a large group.

Critical Incidents or Case Studies.   In critical incidents or case studies, participants are asked to bring in news stories of actual conflict expressing hate or bias based on ethnicity, gender, or sexual orientation. An experienced facilitator interjects comments and asks questions of the students regarding their reactions to the incidents. Students discuss how they would have responded to the situation and how they can avoid similar situations in the future.

Local Culture Video Profiles and Cross-Cultural Films.   Local agencies or universities might cooperate in producing a video that examines local cultural groups. Students might be assigned to write the script, direct, or even act in the video. In this day of inexpensive camcorders, videos are relatively easy to make and show. Students learn by researching local information for the production.

Experiential Assignments.   Students are assigned to spend time in a minority community or work environment. They return to class and explain their reactions and feelings based on their experience.

Interactive Computer Video.   Probably the most innovative tool available to trainers is the interactive computer video. Students use computers and computer disks (CDs) to move through interactive sessions dealing with cultural issues. Students cannot progress from one stage until they have successfully completed all tasks at prior steps.

As indicated, many scholars advocate cultural awareness training as a continual process. An example of one successful cultural awareness project is the federally funded Head Start program. This program teaches parenting skills to families, provides medical and social services to children, and prepares them for school. Congress has established a series of performance standards for Head Start programs.[4] Some of these performance standards are excellent examples of continuing cultural awareness training. Although these standards obviously apply to a preschool classroom setting, they are easy to modify to make them relevant to a variety of situations. Samples of Head Start performance standards are listed here:

45 Code of Federal Regulations 1304.2-2 Education Services and Objectives and Performance Standards
(c) The education services component of the plan shall provide for a program which is individualized to meet the special needs of children from various populations by:
(1) Having a curriculum which is relevant and reflective of the needs of the population served.

This standard can be accomplished by including in each classroom materials and activities that reflect the cultural background of the children. Examples of materials include books, records, posters, maps, dolls, and clothing. Activities may include celebrating cultural events and holidays, serving food related to other cultures, and enjoying stories, music, and games representative of children's background.

> *(2) Having staff and program resources reflective of the racial and ethnic population of the children in the program.*

This standard may be accomplished by having an adult present who speaks the primary language of the children and who is knowledgeable about their heritage. This adult may be a teacher or aide, other member of the center staff, a parent or family member, or a volunteer.

> *(3) Include parents in the curriculum development and having them serve as resource persons.*

Parents can be valuable resources in planning which activities reflect the children's heritage. Teachers may request suggestions from parents on ways to integrate cultural activities into the program. For example, parents may wish to plan holiday celebrations, prepare foods unique to various cultures, recommend books, records, or other materials for the classroom, act as classroom volunteers, or suggest games, songs, and art projects that reflect cultural customs.

As this discussion indicates, there is no easy answer to the problem of dealing with minority populations. Feelings, perceptions, and past experiences all enter into our reactions to those that are different from us. Unfortunately, there are those members of our society that do more than simply feel uncomfortable around members of other cultures or other minority groups. As indicated in the Focus box at the beginning of this chapter, there are groups that engage in acts of violence that are directed at special populations. The next section will discuss hate crimes and their impact on our society.

Hate Crimes

Introduction

Hate violence has a long history in the United States. However, some sources are suggesting that it has increased in the recent past.[5] Accurately measuring the number of hate crimes that are committed is extremely difficult because the Hate Crime Statistics Act of 1990, although it requires reporting, is still a relatively new procedure. Additionally, two other factors contribute to the lack of meaningful statistics in this area: The lack of training by law enforcement causes many officers to fail to

**TABLE 12.1   Bias Crimes by Motivation and Type as Reported
to the FBI for 1992**[6]

Bias Motivation	Crimes against Persons	Crimes against Property	Total Bias Offenses	% against Persons	% against Property
Race	4015	1053	5068	79	21
Ethnicity/National Origin	680	166	846	80	20
Religion	492	751	1243	40	60
Sexual Orientation	774	175	949	81	19
Total	5961	2145	8106	73	27

recognize incidents of racial violence, and there is natural reluctance on the part of many victims of hate crimes to report such incidents to law enforcement agencies.[7]

Acts of racial violence reflect a racial prejudice or interpersonal hostility that is based on the view that different cultures do not merit treatment as equals or that they deserve blame for various problems within society. Many minority cultures are viewed in a certain manner.[8] These stereotypes are race-based generalizations about a person's behavior or character that are typically not substantiated in scientific data. This stereotyping may act as a trigger to violence in different cultures. Stereotyping does not cause violence; however, physical violence is easier to perform on a dehumanized victim. Attackers may believe that the minority is "invading their turf." This may occur when a minority family moves into a traditional neighborhood and has not had any previous experience with that particular culture. Attackers may also claim that minority cultures are taking jobs that rightfully belong to "real" Americans. These and other rationalizations deny minority cultures status as accepted citizens.

Persons of color and certain religious groups have traditionally been the target of hate crimes. These groups have been victimized both on a national and international scale. They continue to be victimized today. For example, in New York in 1988, 30 percent of all bias incidents were committed against African-Americans and another 30 percent were perpetrated against Jews. In Los Angeles in that same year, the majority of racial incidents were against African-Americans, and more than 90 percent of religiously motivated incidents were against Jews.[9] The arson of African-American churches is but another example of the continuing victimization of persons of color.[10]

Disabled persons are also victims of hate or bias crimes. As the number of disabled persons in our nation has increased, so too has the number of hate crimes and abuse against them. Some perpetrators seek out disabled victims because their disability makes them "easy prey" for this type of offender. An example is a developmentally disabled woman with the intellectual ability of a seven-year-old child who may be sexually assaulted by a caretaker. A ***disabled person*** is one who has a physical or mental impairment that substantially limits one or more of the major life activities of that individual, or that person has a record of such impairment, or that person is regarded as having such an impairment. Major life activities include walking, seeing, hearing, speaking, breathing, learning, and working.

Antigay and antilesbian violence became a national issue with the murders of San Francisco Mayor George Moscone and City Supervisor Harvey Milk. Their deaths became symbols of both the strength of the homosexual community and the hostility that is directed at them. Attacks against gays infected with HIV/AIDS have increased in the last several years.[11]

Women also have been the subject of hate and bias crimes. They continue to be targets of violence because of their gender. Many states include gender as a classification within their hate crime statutes. Crimes against women, including sexual assault and spousal abuse, will be discussed in Chapter 8. The next section examines the conflict between the First Amendment of the U.S. Constitution, which protects freedom of expression, and prosecuting hate or bias crimes.

Legal Aspects of Hate Crimes

Prosecuting a perpetrator for violation of a hate crime raises several emotional and constitutional issues. The First Amendment prohibits the federal government and the states from enacting any law that unduly regulates a person's freedom of expression.[12] However, from the founding of our nation, the Supreme Court has held that such freedom of expression is not unlimited. There are situations in which conduct or other activities, although expressing beliefs or thoughts, are outside the scope of First Amendment protection.

Hate crimes deal with both the expression of beliefs and action. The expression of beliefs reflects hatred or loathing toward a certain group, and the action is criminal in nature. Thus, crafting a criminal statute that regulates hate crimes is no easy task. In 1992, the Supreme Court struck down a local hate crime ordinance in St. Paul, Minnesota, which criminalized the use of hate symbols, such as the burning of a cross, on the grounds that it violated an individual's right to freedom of expression.[13]

On June 11, 1993, in *Wisconsin v. Mitchell,* the U.S. Supreme Court unanimously upheld the constitutionality of Wisconsin's hate crime statute, which increased penalties for crimes motivated by hate or bias.[14] Todd Mitchell was a nineteen-year-old Black who was outraged over a scene in the film *Mississippi Burning* that depicted a young black child being attacked by a white racist. Upon seeing a fourteen-year-old white boy, Mitchell asked his companions if they wanted to "get that white boy." They attacked the white boy, leaving the victim comatose for four days with possible brain damage. Mitchell was convicted for aggravated battery, and the sentence was doubled from two to four years after it was proved he had intentionally selected his victim based on race. Mitchell challenged the constitutionality of the hate crime enhancement statute, claiming that it violated the First Amendment guarantee of freedom of expression.

The U.S. Supreme Court upheld the statute, stating bias or hate crimes were valid for three main reasons:

1. While the government cannot punish an individual's abstract beliefs, it can punish a vast array of depraved motives for crime, including selecting a crime

victim based on race, religion, color, disability, sexual orientation, national origin, or ancestry;

2. Hate crimes do not punish thoughts, rather they address the greater individual and societal harms caused by bias-related offenses in that they are more likely to provoke retaliatory crimes, inflict distinct emotional harms on their victims, and incite community unrest; and

3. Hate crime penalty enhancement laws do not punish people because they express their views.

As indicated, laws prohibiting certain conduct will be considered constitutionally valid. Nonthreatening bigoted expression is still protected as long as it does not evolve into bias-motivated action. When such beliefs are the basis for hate or bias crimes, professionals in the field should be able to identify them. The next sections discuss factors that may indicate that the offense was a hate crime.

Identifying Bias Crimes

To identify hate or bias crimes, we must first define these offenses. In this text, hate crime and bias crime are used interchangeably. Finn and McNeil define hate crimes as "words or actions designed to intimidate an individual because of his or her race, religion, national origin or sexual [preference]."[15] In the Hate Crimes Statistics Act of 1990, *bias crimes* are those offenses that are motivated by hatred against a victim based on race, religion, sexual orientation, ethnicity, or national origin.[16] Many states have also adopted hate crime statutes that prohibit the same or a similar type of conduct. As indicated, hate or bias crimes are not new; what is new is that we are beginning to recognize these crimes and respond to them.

Recognizing bias crimes involves an evaluation of a number of factors. There is no generally accepted foolproof list of indicators that indicate the offense is motivated by bias or hate of a particular group. However, the Office for Victims of Crime has identified seven general categories that should be examined when evaluating criminal acts.[17] These factors include cultural differences, written or oral comments, use of symbols, representation of organized hate groups, prior hate crimes, victim–witness perceptions, and lack of other motive. Depending on the situation, one of these factors standing by itself may strongly indicate that the offense may be classified as a bias or hate crime. Conversely, several of these indicators may not present conclusive evidence that the crime was motivated by hate or bias. Each case should be evaluated on its own merits.

Racial, Ethic, Gender, and Cultural Differences

Is the victim of a different culture than the offender? Investigators may not be able to establish this fact from the victim. They may have to look for other indicators that point to any cultural differences between the victim and the offender. These other factors include the cultural diversity of a number of locations, including the place of attack, the victim's home, or the workplace. Inquiry should be made as to whether the victim was engaged in activities that represent or promote a group, such as a gay rights march. Did the incident occur on a date that has a special significance to certain cultures, such as Martin Luther King's birthday? Even if the victim is not a member of any recognized cultural or ethnic minority, that person may have supported such a group and the attack may be in reprisal for that activity. Finally, questions must be asked as to whether there is a history of violence between the victim's culture and any other group.

Written or Oral Comments or Gestures
Inquiry should be made as to whether the attackers made any comments or gestures before, during, or immediately after the attack. These comments may refer to the victim's race, sexual orientation, or gender. Likewise, the attackers may make certain gestures indicating their own affiliation with another group.

Drawings, Markings, Symbols, and Graffiti
Care should be taken to look for any drawings or symbols that may indicate membership in a group. These may be on the victim's house, place of work, house of worship, or where the attack occurred.

Representations of Organized Hate Groups
Sometimes hate groups will call members of the media and take credit for a bombing, burning, or other act of violence. They may also leave their trademark at the scene of the crime. For example, a burning cross may be found outside the victim's home.

Previous Existence of Bias or Hate Crime Incidents
Did the incident occur in a location where previous hate crime have occurred? If there have been a series of crimes involving victims of the same culture, or the incidents occurred in the same location that is frequented by members of a specific culture, those facts may indicate that the crimes are motivated by hate or bias. Interview the victims to determine if they have received previous harassing mail or phone calls based on their affiliation or membership in a group.

Victim–Witness Perception
Victims should be questioned to determine if they perceive the crime as motivated by bias. This may not always be accurate, but the victims' input in this area is always critical.

Lack of Other Motives
If there is no other motive for the incident and the victim is a member of minority culture, the fact that it may be motivated by bias or hatred of that group should always be considered.

As indicated, the presence or absence of these factors does not establish the existence of a hate-related crime. In fact, there are several caveats that must be exercised when evaluating these crimes. These caveats might appropriately be called false-positive factors. These factors include the following:

Requirement for a Case-by-Case Assessment.   Each crime must be evaluated on its own merits. The existence or nonexistence of bias or hate as the motivation for the offense must be evaluated in light of all facts and circumstances surrounding the crime.

Misleading Facts.   Care must be taken not to rush to judgment in what appears to be a hate crime. There may be other facts that negate this first impression. For example, the victim may tell the officers that the perpetrator used a racial epithet during the assault. Further investigation may reveal that the victim and the offender were both of the same race or culture.

Feigned Facts and Hoaxes.   Some offenders may leave hate symbols in an effort to give the false impression that the offense was motivated by bias or hatred when in fact is was simply an ordinary crime. Other perpetrators may leave symbols or signs of certain groups as a hoax or to mislead investigators.

On occasion, determining whether the offense is really a hate crime may be difficult. Even if police officers cannot prove that the offense was a hate crime, the victim may believe that hate or bias was in fact the motivation. The effect of such crime on victims is unique and in many cases more devastating than other crimes because of the psychological impact on the victim.[18]

The victim must live with the realization that the crime was not a random act of violence; rather, the victim was targeted or selected for victimization based on beliefs, race, culture, religion, or sexual preference. Bias crimes are "message crimes" that send a message of terror to the victim because the victim is different from the majority of other Americans. Some victims of bias crimes may not have any community support systems within their communities. They may have recently arrived in the United States and may not have developed a support base within the general community or their specific culture. Other victims may fear discovery of their status and therefore decline to report suspected hate crimes. This aspect of this type of victimization is especially true for closeted gays and lesbians, undocumented aliens, and those who suffer from other disabilities such as HIV/AIDS infection.

Bias crimes also impact the victim's immediate community and culture. Such crimes increase tension with the minority community and raise the specter of retaliation by members of that community. As a result of these factors, bias or hate crimes pose special problems for victim service providers.

Typology of Offenders

Understanding more about those who commit hate crimes allows victim service providers to help the victim understand some of the dynamics involved in this type of crime. Although research is still being developed in this area, Levin and McDevitt have established three categories of offenders: thrill-seeking offenders, reactive offenders, and mission offenders.[19]

The thrill-seeking offenders are generally groups of teenagers that are not otherwise associated with any other formal hate group. They engage in these acts for a variety of reasons, including an attempt to gain a psychological or social thrill or rush, a desire to be accepted by others, or to be able to brag about the act at a later time. Almost any member of a minority group may be a target of these groups. They generally operate outside of their own area or neighborhood and actively look for targets and opportunity. Because these attacks are random and usually fail to follow any pattern, it is often difficult to identify the perpetrators of these types of hate crimes.

The reactive offenders have a sense of entitlement concerning their rights or lifestyle that does not extend to the victim. They usually do not belong to any organized hate group but may associate with one to mitigate a perceived threat to their way of life. When a victim acts in such a manner as to cause these offenders to feel that their lifestyle is threatened, they may react with violence. They will commit hate crimes to send a message to the victim and/or the victim's community that will cause the victim to stop whatever action is threatening the perpetrator's rights or lifestyle. These crimes normally occur within the offender's own community, school, or place of work. Examples of these types of hate crimes include burning crosses at a minority's new home in a predominately white neighborhood, beating a minority who takes a job in a traditionally white occupation, and other acts of violence directed at maintaining the status quo.

The mission-oriented offenders may suffer from a mental illness, including psychosis. They may experience hallucinations, withdrawal, and impaired ability to reason. These offenders may believe they have received instructions from a higher deity to rid the world of this "evil." They typically have a sense of urgency about their objectives and believe that they must act before it is too late. The victim is usually a member of a group that is targeted for elimination. These perpetrators will look for victims in the victim's own neighborhood. An example of this type of offender was Marc Lepine, who killed fourteen women at the University of Montreal, stating that he hated all feminists.

Sapp and his associates developed a typology of hate offenders based on their ideology.[20] They believed that ideology is used by hate groups to serve as a symbolic set of ideas that provides the group with a perceived social legitimacy. Ideology is a way of thinking used by a group to express its beliefs and social values. Sapp classified hate groups into three basic categories: Christian conservatism based on the identity movement, white racial supremacy, and patriotism and survival.

Christian conservatism based on the identity movement uses passages in scripture identifying certain groups as superior to others and the notion that a nation, rather than being a geographic, political, or economic entity, is a culture grouped according to bloodlines and shared history. Racial identity thus becomes the basis for national identity.

These groups may adopt a postmillennial view that holds that the second coming of Christ cannot happen until Christians purge the Earth of sin and establish the Holy Land.[21] As Gale points out, this is potentially a blueprint for genocide in that it allows these groups to cleanse the Holy Land of "sinners." Therefore, mass murder of inferiors and those who oppose the groups and their churches is mandated.[22]

White racial supremacy groups also include racial purity proponents. Racial purity is concerned with the purity of the Aryan race or God's children. Refugees, illegal aliens, legal immigrants, Jews, Blacks, Hispanics, Asians, and non-Christians are all considered a threat to white racial purity theorists. The Ku Klux

---

FOCUS: What Is Racism?

Over sixty years ago, Ruth Benedict penned a definition of racism that is still valid today. "Racism is the dogma that one ethnic group is condemned by nature to congenital inferiority and another group is destined to congenital superiority. It is the dogma that the hope of civilization depends upon eliminating some races and keeping others pure. It is the dogma that one race has carried progress with it throughout human history and can alone ensure future progress. . . . [R]acism is essentially a pretentious way of saying that 'I belong . . . . For such a conviction, in the most gratifying formula that has ever been discovered, for neither my own unworthiness nor the accusations of others can ever dislodge me from my position. . . .' It avoids all embarrassing claims by 'inferior' groups about their own achievements and ethical standards."[24]

Klan is an example of a white supremacy group. Its founding fathers stated that its purpose was the maintenance of the supremacy of the white race in the republic because that race is superior to all other races.[23]

Patriotism and survival groups have recently come to the attention of the general public because of the incidents in Idaho and Montana involving various members of militia groups. These groups offer an attractive ideology to some conservative groups in America. They point out the economic troubles, including unemployment, and blame these problems on refugees and other nonwhite groups. They argue that special interests control the government and decry the moral bankruptcy of our leaders.

These groups blame lax courts for encouraging criminals. They target the media because they believe the media glorify criminals and are responsible for the total breakdown of morals in America. Some of these groups use quotes from the Constitution as a basis for their beliefs and argue that they are no longer subject to the laws of the United States.

Bias and hate crimes do not simply happen, they are motivated by a variety of feelings, beliefs, and emotions. The result is intimidation of the individual as well as the community. Victim service providers must understand these crimes and their impact to assist these victims properly.

Cultural Awareness Case Study

You live in a medium-sized community with a wide range of cultures and subcultures. These groups include people from South America and the Far East. Within the last several months, there have been reports of the use of excessive force on the part of law enforcement officers when they encountered these minorities. The minority groups have responded by picketing city hall and threatening recall campaigns against the local elected officials.

You are the local victim–witness coordinator and have spoken at a variety of meetings regarding cultural awareness and its impact and importance to victims.

The chief of police has asked you to assist his department in the establishment of a cultural awareness program. You understand that for such a program to be successful it must be continuing and multifaceted. Reread the Head Start performance standards listed in this chapter. Revise them so that they could apply to a local law enforcement agency instead of a school setting. For example, instead of a parent providing suggestions, you may want to substitute a leader of a minority group.

Summary

Cultural awareness is more than a series of "politically correct" sayings and posters that hang in an office. Victim service providers are in unique positions to serve both the victims and the criminal justice agencies within the system. They can act as advocates for the victims and as cultural awareness trainers to law enforcement agencies.

Hate or bias crimes continue to happen in this country. Victim service providers must be aware of the dynamics involved in these crimes from both the offenders perspective and the victim's position. The commission of a hate crime not only affects the individual victim, it impacts the victim's entire community. A message of terror is sent to these victims, their families, and their communities. Service providers must be able to offer advice, guidance, and support to these special victims.

Key Terms

Cultural awareness is the understanding that an individual has regarding different cultures.

Disabled person is one who has a physical or mental impairment that substantially limits one or more of the major life activities of that individual or that person has a record of such impairment or that person is regarded as having such an impairment.

Bias crimes are those offenses that are motivated by hatred and directed against a victim based on race, religion, sexual orientation, ethnicity, or national origin.

Discussion Questions

1. List the various cultures that exist in your city. Explain how they are different from the mainstream population of your area. What do you know of the history and culture of these populations?

2. What is the most important aspect of a cultural awareness program?

3. Save your local newspaper for one week and list all the incidents involving hate crimes. How do these crimes compare with the material listed in the book? Discuss each crime using the criteria set forth in the book.

4. Are there any other groups that you can identify that might be subject to hate crimes?

5. Should membership in organizations that espouse hate doctrine be a crime? Why? Why not?

Suggested Readings

Robert M. Shusta, Deena R. Levine, Philip R. Harris, & Herbert Z. Wong, *Multicultural Law Enforcement*, (Prentice-Hall, Englewood Cliffs, N.J.) 1995.

Marlene A. Young, *Victim Assistance Frontiers and Fundamentals*, (Kendall/Hunt Publishing, Dubuque, Iowa) 1993.

Robert J. Kelly, (ed.), *Bias Crimes: American Law Enforcement and Legal Responses*, (Office of the International Criminal Justice Administration, Reading, Berkshire, United Kingdom) 1993.

National Bias Crimes Training for Law Enforcement and Victim Assistance Professionals, Office for Victims of Crime, (U.S. Department of Justice, Washington, D.C.) January 1995.

Endnotes

1. Adapted from Gary Weaver, "Law Enforcement in a Culturally Diverse Society," *FBI Law Enforcement Bulletin*, 1 (September 1992).
2. Joyce St. George, "Sensitivity Training Needs Rethinking," 7/347 *Law Enforcement News*, 8–12 (Nov. 30, 1991).
3. Robert M. Shusta, Deena R. Levine, Philip R. Harris, & Herbert Z. Wong, *Multicultural Law Enforcement*, (Prentice-Hall, Englewood Cliffs, N.J.) 1995.
4. 45 Code of Federal Regulations 1304 et. seq. (1992).
5. "1990 Audit of Anti-Semitic Incidents," Anti-Defamation League of B'nai B'rith, New York (1991).
6. *Characteristics of Hate Crime in 1992*, U.S. Department of Justice, (Federal Bureau of Investigation, GPO, Washington, D.C.) 1993.
7. For example it was not until January 1995 that the Office for Victims of Crime published a *National Bias Crimes Training Manual for Law Enforcement and Victim Assistance Professionals* (U.S. Department of Justice, Washington, D.C.) 1995.
8. Harry H. L. Kitano, "Asian-Americans: The Chinese, Japanese, Koreans, Philipinos and Southeast Asians," 454 *Annals American Academy of Political & Social Science*, 125 (1981).
9. R. J. Kelly, (ed.), *Bias Crimes: American Law Enforcement and Legal Responses*, (Office of the International Criminal Justice Administration, Reading, Berkshire, United Kingdom) 1993.
10. But see Fred Bayles, "Church Arsons not all Linked to Racism," Associated Press, *Fresno Bee*, A-1 (July 5, 1996) where the reporter points out that after reviewing six years of federal, state and local data, the Associated Press found arsons increasing, but with only random links to racism. Of the seventy-three African-American church arsons since 1995, fewer than twenty cases had clear links to racism. On the whole, the Associated Press reported that church arsons increased across the nation.
11. Kevin Berrill, "Gay and Lesbian Crime Victims: What We All Can Do," 10/12 *NOVA Newsletter*, 3 (Washington, D.C.).
12. See Edwin J. Delattre & Daniel L. Schofield, "Combating Bigotry in Law Enforcement," *FBI Law Enforcement Bulletin*, 27 (June 1966).
13. *R.A.V. v. City of St. Paul*, 112 S. Ct. 2538 (1992).
14. 113 S. Ct. 2194 (1993).
15. Peter Finn & Taylor McNeil, *The Response of the Criminal Justice System to Bias Crimes: An Exploratory Review*, (Abt Associates, Inc., Washington, D.C.) 1987.
16. Public Law 101–275 (1990).
17. *National Bias Crimes Training for Law Enforcement and Victim Assistance Professionals*, Office for Victims of Crime, (U.S. Department of Justice, Washington, D.C.) January 1995.
18. Marlene A. Young, *Victim Assistance Frontiers and Fundamentals*, (Kendall/Hunt Publishing, Dubuque, Iowa) 1993.

19. Jack Levin & Jack McDevitt, *The Rising Tide of Bigotry and Bloodshed*, (Plenum, New York) 1993.

20. Allen D. Sapp, Richard N. Holden, & Michael E. Wiggins, "Value and Belief Systems of Right-Wing Extremists," in Robert J. Kelly, (ed.), *Bias Crimes: American Law Enforcement and Legal Responses*, (Office of the International Criminal Justice Administration, Reading, Berkshire, United Kingdom) 1993.

21. Normal Geiser, *Moody Monthly*, 129–131 (October 1985).

22. William Gale, *Racial and National Identity*, (pamphlet) (Ministry of Christ Church, Glendale, Calif.) undated.

23. William P. Randel, *The Ku Klux Klan: A Century of Infamy*, (Chilton Books, New York) 1965, pp. 15–16.

24. Ruth Benedict, "Race: Science and Politics," in Jacques Baryan, (ed.), *Race: A Study in Modern Superstition*, (MacMillian, New York) 1937, pp. 153–154.

13

SPECIAL VICTIM POPULATIONS

Chapter Outline

HIV/AIDS Victims
   Medical and Psychological Aspects of HIV/AIDS
   Victim Service Issues
   Specific Victim Populations

Disabled Victims
   Introduction
   Legal Issues
   Types of Victimization
   Emerging Issues

Gay and Lesbian Victims
   History
   Definitions
   Gay and Lesbians as Victims of Crime
   Intimate Violence
   Extent of the Problem
   Legal Aspects of Gay and Lesbian Abuse

Summary

Key Terms

Discussion Questions

Suggested Readings

Learning Objectives

After reading this chapter, you should be able to:

- Understand the HIV/AIDS disease
- Explain how the HIV/AIDS disease impacts victims of crime
- Distinguish between the various victim populations that are impacted by the HIV/AIDS disease
- Discuss the victimization of disabled persons
- Understand the dynamics involved in gay and lesbian abuse

HIV/AIDS Victims[1]

HIV/AIDS is the black plague of the nineties. It causes normally rational professionals to become emotional at the thought that they may have been exposed to AIDS. We are still learning the consequences of this disease; however, two facts remain constant—persons with AIDS die because of the infection, and at present there is no known cure. It is therefore critical that professionals in this area understand how to respond to victims that have been exposed to this disease.

Medical and Psychological Aspects of HIV/AIDS

AIDS is the acronym for the medial term *acquired immune deficiency syndrome*. The "acquired" portion of the term means that the condition is not a birth defect, but was acquired from another person after birth. The "immune deficiency" portion of the term means that the immune system is repeatedly attacked by infections and diseases until it becomes so weak that it cannot perform its job. The "syndrome" portion of the term means that a series of signs or symptoms occur together and characterize this particular abnormality. The term AIDS should normally only be used when the person has become seriously ill and has fulfilled the Center for Disease Control's criteria for a formal diagnosis as AIDS. Otherwise, the more correct description is HIV+, or HIV positive, for persons who have the HIV disease or infection.[2]

HIV stands for *human immunodeficiency virus*, which overcomes and destroys the body's natural immune system. As the immune system deteriorates, the person's body is unable to protect itself from infections and diseases. The person dies from a disease or infection. The person does not die from AIDS or HIV, rather death results from one or more of the infections that overcome the person's weakened immune system.

There are two primary types of human immunodeficiency virus, or HIV: HIV-1 is the most common and deadly and HIV-2 acts in the same way as HIV-1, but reproduces more slowly. Almost all infected persons in the United States suffer from HIV-1. Once a person is infected with HIV, there is no known cure. The progression of the disease can be slowed with medication, but it cannot be stopped. Most cases result in death; however, there are some persons known as "nonprogressive long-term survivors," who have the virus, but it does not destroy their immune system and they do not become sick and die from the disease. Researchers continue to study these individuals in an attempt to learn why the virus affects them differently than the majority of the infected population.[3]

HIV disease is a disease that has various phases, running the spectrum from wellness to illness.[4] Normally, the virus replicates itself in the lymph glands and then begins to dump copious amounts of itself into the bloodstream, thus setting the stage for progression of the disease. There are five phases in the HIV infection:

Phase 1.   Asymptomatic incubation period, which lasts from four to six weeks. Phase 1 is often called the window period because the infected person has HIV present and replicating in the blood but generally has no detectable symptoms. This is a dangerous period because infected persons have no idea that they are contagious. At some point during this phase, the first antibody is produced and the infected person converts from HIV negative to HIV positive. This conversion is called the *seroconversion.*

Phase 2.   Acute primary infection, which lasts from one to two weeks. During phase 2, the person will experience some symptoms of early infection, but may not recognize the cause of the symptoms. For example, the person may attribute aches, pains, and swollen glands to the flu. The infected person has sufficient antibodies in his or her system to detect the HIV virus during this phase.

Phase 3.   Asymptomatic phase, which lasts three to fifteen years. This phase is characterized by seemingly good health while HIV continues to replicate in the blood and certain tissues and begins slowly to erode the body's immune system. The length of this phase will vary from person to person depending on a number of factors, including the person's overall general health, the person's self-care, and the medical treatment received.

Phase 4.   Symptomatic phase with persistent generalized lymphadenopathy, which lasts one to three years. Serious symptoms signal the beginning of phase 4. Infections that a normal healthy person would fight off will make an HIV+ person ill. The symptoms for this phase include fever, night sweats, diarrhea, enlargement of the lymph glands, weight loss, oral lesions, fatigue, rashes, and cognitive slowing.

Phase 5.   AIDS case, which lasts from one to three years. This condition meets the Center for Disease Control's criteria for the definition of AIDS. As the person approaches death (end-stage AIDS), it is common to have multiple symptoms. The person dies as a result of infections and disease.[5]

HIV is not transmitted by animals or insects or by using swimming pools or hot tubs. It cannot be transmitted after contact with an infected person's clothes, or use of the same toilet seat, eating utensils, drinking glasses, or telephone. There has never been a case in which HIV was transmitted due to kissing or CPR. For HIV to be passed from one person to another, there must be an infected party, an uninfected party, and a route of entry to get particles of the virus from the donor to the recipient. HIV has been found in blood, semen, saliva, serum, urine, tears, breast milk, vaginal secretions, lung fluid, and cerebrospinal fluid. However, the fact that the virus is in those fluids does not mean it is transmissible via those fluids. The three most common routes of HIV transmission are: sexual transmission, blood-to-blood transmission, and mother-to-child transmission.

Most cases of HIV transmission occur as a result of sexual activities. Anal intercourse carries the highest risk of transmission because the fragile tissues of the anus and rectum may tear as a result of the friction of intercourse. Vaginal intercourse is also a high-risk practice with an infected person. Oral sex with a man or woman, although lower in risk than anal or vaginal intercourse, may also transmit the virus. Because of the violent nature of most sex crimes, there is a great concern that victims may be exposed to HIV.

Blood-to-blood transmission can also occur in a variety of ways. Using infected needles can transmit the disease. This method of transmission is common among drug users and is of concern to health workers who receive needle sticks during their work with patients. The virus may be transmitted when contaminated blood or body fluids come into contact with open wounds. This is an area of concern in domestic violence cases when one party may get infected blood into an open wound of another person.

Mother-to-child transmission occurs when the virus is transmitted to the fetus of a pregnant woman. This is the most common form of pediatric transmission. A newborn may also become infected as a result of breast-feeding from an HIV positive mother.

AIDS and HIV present social, psychological, and medical problems. AIDS has changed our view of public health and has affected how we judge others. People with HIV disease respond like all others in a crisis situation. Learning that one has HIV is a severe stressor because of the inevitable result—death. Service providers must understand that there is no right or wrong way to respond to this life-threatening disease.

When individuals learn they are infected with HIV, they may react with a wide range of emotions similar to those experienced by victims of crime. That trauma of victimization has been discussed in detail in Chapter 5. Once they have passed through these emotions, they must face the physical, social, and psychological aspects of living and dying with this disease. As death becomes more imminent, AIDS victims begin to plan for their death. This process becomes difficult and sometimes impossible because they may be coping with HIV-related dementia.

The major characteristic of dementia as a result of HIV is the presence of a dementia that is judged to be the direct pathophysiological consequence of the HIV disease. The major features of this type of dementia are forgetfulness, slowness, poor concentration, and difficulties with problem solving. The infected person may exhibit apathy and social withdrawal and occasionally experience delirium, delusions, or hallucinations.[6]

Victim service providers must remember that AIDS is a medical disease that has additional social and psychological aspects. Because some victims of crime may become infected by the virus, professionals must be knowledgeable regarding the disease and be prepared to address sensitive issues. The next section will examine some of these issues.

Victim Service Issues

Since society acknowledged the existence and impact of the HIV disease, victim service providers have attempted to deal with the impact of this disease on the victims they serve. Most service providers focused solely on victims of rape. However, with the passage of time and expansion of knowledge regarding the disease, victim service providers now must understand how the HIV disease affects victims of child sexual abuse and other violent crimes. Service providers must also be ready to deal with persons who are infected with the disease and who are victimized. Additionally, they must respond to family members, friends, and colleagues of these victims who bring their own concerns, biases, and feelings to their interactions with victim service providers.

HIV/AIDS disease is a medical condition and therefore it is considered confidential information. Victim service providers must always remember that they cannot disseminate the medical status of a victim suffering from this disease without their express permission. Victim providers must be capable of explaining the consequences to victims of disclosing or not disclosing their condition to others.

Creating a safe and open environment in which a victim, family member, friend, or colleague will feel secure enough in raising the HIV/AIDS issue is a critical first step in responding to these victim's special needs. By creating this safe environment, victims will receive a message that they are with someone who has some knowledge of the disease and is open to discussing it. Victims must be reassured that the professional is not sitting in judgment on them or their lifestyle.

The displaying of AIDS awareness posters in the office may assist in establishing this open environment. These posters can be obtained from local AIDS service organizations, county health departments, and the Center for Disease Control. Information regarding the disease should be made available in brochures. Many victims have found lists of local AIDS service organizations to be very helpful.[7]

Raising the issue of HIV/AIDS with a victim who may be at risk is one of the most difficult tasks undertaken by a victim service provider. This topic may be made easier by the open and safe office environment. Victims may not want to discuss this topic for a variety of reasons: They may not realize they are at risk; they may understand that they are at risk but be fearful of discussing the risk with anyone; or they may already know they are infected and decide not to disclose that fact.

Victim assistance professionals should take the time to review the victim's risk of infection and motivation for being tested. They should explain the testing process, including the various test results. They may need to consider a collaborative response to a victim's inquiry by using a local AIDS service provider. Victim service providers should never deliver the victim's HIV/AIDS test results. This would possibly introduce an uncomfortable aspect to an already existing relationship, as the victim professional may become a constant reminder of the moment the positive results were delivered to the victim.[8]

One controversial issue in the criminal justice field today involves involuntary testing of offenders. In recent years, several states have passed laws that give victims of sexual assault access to information about the HIV status of their offender.[9] These laws apply to those arrested, convicted, or who have pled guilty to crimes involving sexual penetration or other exposure to an offender's bodily fluids. At the federal level, sexual assault victims can request an order requiring the HIV testing of the defendant if the court finds there is probable cause to believe that the defendant committed the offense, that the victim has received appropriate counseling, and that the information is necessary for the health of the victim.

If the offender is positive, it does not mean that the victim will have contracted the virus, but simply learning of the offender's status may cause the victim unnecessary emotional upheaval. The victim must also be tested to be absolutely sure that the virus was or was not transmitted. Other professionals fear that imposing mandatory testing on offenders will lead to mandatory testing of other groups or professions. This continues to be a hotly debated topic.[10] The Practicum below lists distinct classes of persons in our society. Discuss the advantages and disadvantages of mandatory testing of these persons.

If we adopt mandatory testing of offenders and other groups for the HIV/AIDS disease, isn't it also reasonable to test those groups for additional diseases, such as all other sexually transmitted diseases?

Professionals in this field normally work with persons who have already experienced the trauma of victimization. Most victim assistance providers do not encounter a person who has a life-threatening illness such as the HIV/AIDS virus. When they work with these victims, it is with the knowledge that the victim will surely die as a result of this disease. It is therefore critical that everyone in the criminal justice system understand the effect on victims of the HIV/AIDS disease.

Specific Victim Populations

Victim service providers must not only understand the HIV/AIDS disease, but they must also be able to relate to specific victim populations that might be exposed to the disease. This section will focus on those victims for which HIV/AIDS is a concern. The victim populations include victims of rape, child victims, family violence victims, and HIV+ persons who are victimized.

PRACTICUM: Who Should Undergo Mandatory Testing for HIV/AIDS Disease?

Sexual predators	Professional athletes
Physicians, dentists, nurses	Law enforcement personnel
Members of the military	All persons above the age of fifteen

Victims of Rape

Contrary to news reports and discussions carried on in a variety of settings, there has been no *documented* case of HIV being transmitted during the rape of an adult in the United States. This is not to say that such a transmission has not occurred, only that at present, the Center for Disease Control, which officially tracks AIDS cases, does not classify cases by consensual or nonconsensual sex. Additionally, given the nature of the disease, it is difficult to link exposure to the virus to a rape. However, the concern about the disease and exposure to it is a very real concern for victims of rape and their consensual sexual partners.[11]

Even as enlightened as we like to think our society is about crime and victimization, victims of rape are still reluctant to report such assaults. Although many victims have experienced difficulty disclosing their rape to their significant partners, the additional factor of possible exposure to HIV may make disclosure even more difficult. The grieving process that normally occurs after a rape may now be extended and deepened because of the added fear regarding HIV.[12] These issues will continue to confront victim service providers as they work with victims of rape until we find a cure for the HIV/AIDS disease.[13]

Child Victims

The Center for Disease Control reports that there were 6209 pediatric cases of AIDS in the United States as of the end of 1994. Children who are sexually assaulted are considered to be at higher risk than adult victims of sexual assault. This increased risk is based on two factors: (1) Child victims may be repeatedly assaulted over a long period of time by the same perpetrator; and (2) Children are at a greater risk of injury during penetration and as a result there is a higher likelihood of transmission of the virus during the sexual act.

Victim service providers must assist parents in making informed decisions regarding how much information to give to a young child who has been sexually assaulted by an HIV+ perpetrator. The victim service provider should work closely with the AIDS service provider regarding counseling and other support techniques for both the child and the parents.[14]

Family Violence Victims

Family violence occurs every day from the mansions of Brentwood to the slums of New York. This type of violence crosses all ethnic, social, and sexual boundaries and its victims include Blacks, Hispanics, Asians, and homosexuals. Some family violence victims are forced to participate in drug usage with the abuser and his friends. Additionally, the abuser may be using drugs or engaging in sexual acts with multiple partners that exposes him to the disease. He can then pass the virus along to his partner during "consensual" sexual relations. The victim's request for use of a condom or other device may be met with violence by the abuser.

Shelters for battered women have traditionally been places of sanctuary for these victims. The spread of HIV/AIDS disease has added another complication to the heavy burden carried by these shelters. Victim service providers must ensure that staff working in the shelters understand the medical and legal aspects of the disease so as not to traumatize further those residents who are HIV+.

HIV+ Persons Who Are Victimized

Persons who are HIV+ are no different from the rest of society as it relates to becoming a victim of a violent crime. What is different is that some persons have been victimized merely because of their real or perceived HIV status. Other HIV+ victims must decide if they are going to disclose their status to authorities when reporting crimes of violence.

HIV-related violence covers a wide spectrum of acts from simple verbal abuse, to harassment, to job discrimination and actual physical attacks. The person's appearance may suggest that he or she is at risk of carrying HIV. Certain groups, such as homosexuals, drug users, and those wearing AIDS support ribbons and other symbols, have suffered HIV-related violence.

A person who is living with HIV must expend a great deal of energy on day-to-day survival, including taking medications, attending medical appointments and treatment sessions, and going to support groups. Suffering criminal victimization with its attendant responsibilities of reporting the crime, interviewing with law enforcement officers, attending court, and facing the perpetrator can add a tremendous amount of stress to the victim's life. This increased stress can dramatically impact the victim's health. For this and other reasons, HIV+ victims may decide not to pursue reporting victimization. Still others may report, but as the burdens of appearing in court increase, they may opt to drop the charges. Victim service providers must be aware of the dynamics of this form of victimization and respond accordingly by supporting the victim.

Disabled Victims

Introduction

Disabled victims have the same rights as any other victim; however, they remain one of the largest categories of victims to be neglected by our criminal justice system.[15] This is because they are not afforded the same type of access, legitimacy, or respect as other victims. For example, as the Practicum on page 230 illustrates, some material in the criminal justice system is in several different languages, but very few agencies may have information in Braille. This section will provide victim service providers with an overview of some of the problems faced by disabled persons.

Crimes against persons with developmental and other severe disabilities is a problem similar to other forms of violence.[16] Some research indicates that the level of violence against children and adults with developmental and other severe disabilities is as much as five times higher than against the general public, that such crimes are reported at a much lower rate, and that there are indications of lower rates of prosecution and conviction.[17]

One of the first issues confronting victim service providers is how to respond to victims of crimes who also have a disability.[18] Each type of disability may require a different response on the part of the victim service provider. For example, a victim with a hearing impairment will have different needs than a victim with a sight impairment. However, there are certain rules that apply to all crime victims who are disabled.

PRACTICUM: Disability and Crime

It was late in the evening when John was returning home from the local convenience store with a carton of milk and some other groceries. It was cold and rainy, and John was hurrying as fast as he could to reach his apartment, when two persons grabbed him from behind and pulled him into an alley.

They took his wallet, trashed his bag of groceries, and proceeded to kick him in the ribs, legs, and head. Several other people walked by the attack but did nothing to render assistance. The perpetrators fled only when they heard a police siren. John gave a report to the police and was informed by the investigating officer of his right to contact the local victim–witness office. Several days later, John went downtown to that office. He had to ride ten stories in a crowded elevator and was late for the scheduled appointment. Once inside the office, he was asked to have a seat and waited approximately thirty minutes before he finally was interviewed regarding his victimization. After the interview with a victim service provider, John wanted to take some of the information home so he could study his rights as a victim more closely. Unfortunately the office did not have any pamphlets in his language—John was blind.

1. What are the issues faced by a victim service provider in this situation?
2. What problems did John encounter? How would you attempt to solve those problems? Assume you do not have any additional funds in your agency.

- Look directly at the victim when speaking. Deliberately averting your eyes is impolite and can be uncomfortable.
- Feel free to ask a disabled victim how you should act or communicate most effectively if you have any doubts about correctness in the situation.
- Address and speak directly to the disabled person, even if the person is accompanied or assisted by a third-party nondisabled person.
- Feel free to offer physical assistance to a disabled person, such as offering your arm if the need arises, but do not assume the person will need it or accept it.
- Ask a disabled victim about any personal needs that will require special services or arrangements, and then attempt to make arrangements to meet those needs.
- Do not stare or avoid looking at a visible disability or deformity or express sympathy to the disabled victim.
- Do not tell the disabled victim you admire his or her courage or determination for living with the disability. The disabled person doesn't want to be thought of as a hero.
- Do not avoid humorous situations that occur as a result of a disability. Take your cue from the victim.[19]

These suggestions should be used as guidelines when working with disabled persons. Victim service professionals must understand that the disabled person, like all other victims, is an individual and must be approached and interacted with as a separate and distinct individual. For years, people with disabilities tolerated discrimination and hardship as a result of society's reaction to their disability. Congress finally addressed this issue when it enacted the Civil Rights Act of 1964 and the Americans with Disabilities Act of 1990.

Legal Issues

There are approximately 43 million Americans with one or more disabilities. These disabilities may be mental, physical, or both. They may be congenital (occurring at birth) or adventitious (occurring after birth). As indicated earlier in this chapter, a *disabled person* is one who has a physical or mental impairment that substantially limits one or more of the major life activities of that individual, or that person has a record of such impairment, or that person is regarded as having such an impairment. This definition is founded on the language contained in the Americans with Disabilities Act (ADA) of 1990. This is one of the most comprehensive pieces of civil rights legislation passed by Congress since the Civil Rights Act of 1964. The ADA was enacted by Congress to protect the employment and accessibility rights of persons suffering from disabilities. Any agency receiving any type of governmental funding (federal, state, or local) must comply with the provisions contained in the ADA.

Some authorities state that persons with developmental and other severe disabilities represent approximately 10 percent of the population of our country (1.8 percent developmental disabilities, 5 percent adult onset brain impairment, 2.8 percent severe major mental disorders). As many as 30 percent to 40 percent of all families may have loved ones or close friends with developmental or other severe disabilities. These numbers may increase as our population ages. Fifteen percent of Americans over the age of fifty-five have cognitive disabilities, and 25 percent of those over the age of seventy-five suffer from this form of disability.[20]

Disabilities covered by the law include physical and mental impairments. Physical disabilities include physiological disorders or conditions, disfigurement, or loss of use of any body system. Specific examples include cerebral palsy, epilepsy, multiple sclerosis, AIDS/HIV infections, cancer, heart disease, and diabetes. Mental impairments include any mental or psychological disorder, such as mental retardation, organic brain syndrome, emotional or mental illness, and specific learning disorders.

Victim service providers must anticipate serving disabled victims. They must work with local governmental agencies and be prepared to provide a wide variety of services to those disabled persons in need of their help. They should become familiar with the ADA and be spokespeople for disabled victims within the criminal justice system.

Types of Victimization

Disabled persons can be victimized in the same way as other persons; however, their response to crime is different from other victims. Crimes against disabled persons are underreported for a number of reasons: There may be communication and mobility barriers; the disabled person may be unable to report the crime because of a mental or developmental reason, or the person may be dependant on others to do so; and finally, some reporting agencies fail to record the fact that the victim was disabled.[21]

One researcher reported that 60 percent of all persons who have mental disabilities become victims of crime sometime during their life, and 60 percent of all hearing-impaired women will be victims of sexual assault.[22] Another source indicates that many disabled people do not receive any form of sex education, and some of them are socialized to obey others without question. Consequently, they do not complain or report acts of sexual maltreatment.[23] Disabled individuals in institutions are twice as likely as those in the community to be abused.[24]

Although the data are extremely limited, there is reason to believe that substantial numbers of disabled persons are victims of domestic abuse. These studies also indicate that hearing-impaired women have a high probability of becoming victims of domestic violence.[25] For years, professionals have acknowledged that there is a higher risk of child abuse if the child is suffering from a disability.[26]

Emerging Issues

The realization that disabled victims present unique challenges to those in the criminal justice system is just being acknowledged at local, state, and federal jurisdictions. California has assembled a task force to study these issues, and this group has formulated a series of recommendations regarding the treatment of disabled crime victims.[27] These recommendations still need further study and revision, but they represent an important first step in this newly emerging area of victimization of the disabled. The following is a brief summary of these recommendations:

The Legal Process

Each service provider should have a criminal justice coordinator. Knowledgeable service professionals and disability advocates should be available to assist the police, prosecutors, and courts. Each developmental disabilities regional center and other primary care or case management service agencies should have a twenty-four-hour phone number to respond to requests for information on an emergency basis. Criminal justice organizations should have specialized staff for cases involving persons with disabilities. This will allow for the gathering of information and building of expertise by those in the system. It will also provide a single point of contact for service organizations. There should be sentence enhancements when disabled persons are victims. This protects those who cannot protect themselves. Regular and relatively comprehensive training on disabled victims should occur for police, prosecutors, judges, defense attorneys, probation officers, victim–witness officers, and others in the criminal justice system.

Reporting laws should be amended to require mandatory reporting of possible crimes against disabled victims. Persons that deal with the disabled on a regular basis should receive training in recognizing criminal acts against these victims and how to report them. Multidisciplinary teams including disabled victims should be formed in all local jurisdictions. These teams should meet on a regular basis to address various problems encountered by disabled victims. These teams should review sudden, unexpected deaths or major traumatic injuries to the disabled when the death or injury occurs in an institution, residential or other service facility.

Victim Support

Each community should develop multidisciplinary teams to provide victim support cooperatively. Each team should include, as a minimum, victim service providers, sexual assault advocates, and service providers who work with the disabled. All case management agencies should have a designated staff person to serve as an advocate for disabled victims. There should be a coordinated public relations campaign to encourage disabled victims to report all crimes committed against them.

Risk Reduction and Prevention

Curriculums and required training for residential programs, vocational training, day programs, recreational programs, and special education should be modified to include personal safety training skills for disabled persons. This training should include self-defense skills, individual rights, assertiveness training, social skills, and training about the criminal justice system. All education and service plans for disabled clients should include a personal safety plan as a component. Crime prevention should involve the client, service providers, family, and friends. Special training should be conducted for family members on how to overcome isolation, facilitate attachments, support family relationships, and increase and improve communication skills of the client and family members. Safer living environments are necessary to prevent victimization of the disabled. The more connected and integrated these persons are with their community, the lower the risk of victimization. Steps should be taken to break down the traditional barriers that exist between the disabled and the community. Adult protective service agencies should have adequate resources to investigate reported abuse of the disabled.

Institutional Abuse. There is a critical need to improve standards for screening and hiring of staff in institutions that serve the disabled. Staff training in institutions needs to be improved and updated. Use of the "buddy system" for mentoring new and problem employees should be implemented. Advocacy systems that are independent of any institutional provider should be created and supported. Ombudsperson programs need to be expanded to address these concerns. Administrators and professional staff must be actively present in all institutions to monitor and supervise staff and the clients. Management staff must be held accountable for abuse that occurs in their institutions and yet must also be encouraged to report such abuse. They must look beyond individual cases and accept the moral and professional responsibility to care for these individuals.

Gay and Lesbian Victims

This section is included because gay and lesbian victimization is often overlooked. One unique aspect of their victimization deals with intimate violence between gay and lesbian couples. Some people respond negatively to the discussion of this type of aggression. To accept that reaction is to deny reality and fail to anticipate issues that affect many professionals who work in the area of victim services. The fact of the matter is that gays and lesbians are victims of crime and they do live, work, and love with same-sex partners.

History

The history of the gay and lesbian struggle for equal treatment does not necessarily belong in a text on victimology. However, society's reactions to same-sex living arrangements need to be explored for professionals to understand some of the dynamics involved in a gay or lesbian relationship. Understanding these relationships will allow professionals to react properly when faced with a situation that involves gay or lesbian victimization.

Historically, homosexual behavior can be traced back to ancient Greece, where homosexuality was viewed as natural in many segments of Greek society. Plato's *Symposium* extolled the virtues of homosexual behavior and indicated that homosexual lovers would make the best soldiers.[28] One scholar indicates that homosexuality was not considered socially deviant behavior until the time of Thomas Aquinas and St. Augustine, both of whom argued that it was unnatural because it did not lead to conception.[29] In 1980, the DSM-III-R reclassified homosexual behavior as an alternative sexual lifestyle rather than deviant behavior. This view is not accepted by all members of our society. Even in the medical community there remains a core of professionals whose opinion is that homosexuality is unnatural sexual behavior.

Definitions

Homosexual, gay, or lesbian—these terms evoke strong emotional responses from certain segments of our society. However, to discuss gay and lesbian victimization accurately, one needs to put that response aside and start with a clear understanding of what these terms mean.

- *Homosexuality* is defined as the manifestation of sexual desire toward a member of one's own sex.
- *Gay* is defined as a male homosexual or a socially integrated group oriented toward and concerned with the welfare of homosexuals.
- *Lesbian* is defined as a female homosexual.[30] Lesbianism is believed to have been named from the Isle of Lesbos, where the practice of lesbianism was reputed to have been general in ancient days.

Even these terms are subject to debate and interpretation, especially among members of the gay and lesbian community itself. If the gay and lesbian community cannot agree on certain definitions, it becomes very difficult to research victimization within those communities.

Gays and Lesbians as Victims of Crime

Antigay and antilesbian violence is a pervasive problem throughout the United States.[31] Research, surveys, studies, and community-based analyses of gay and lesbian victimization have all indicated that gay men and lesbian women are victimized at a higher rate than the general population.[32]

Additionally, the discovery and spread of AIDS with its high mortality rate has affected the homosexual community disproportionately and has generated additional fear, hatred, and discrimination against members of the gay and lesbian community. Although victimization existed before the discovery of AIDS, evidence suggests that the spread of this virus within the homosexual community has increased the prejudice that already existed.

Since 1984, the National Gay and Lesbian Task Force Policy Institute has produced an annual report on gay and lesbian violence.[33] This report uses data collected from programs in nine cities—Boston, Chicago, Columbus, Detroit, Minneapolis/St. Paul, New York, Portland, Los Angeles, and San Francisco.

Over one-third of all hate crimes committed against gay or lesbian victims involved two or more perpetrators. Data indicate that gay and lesbian offenses involve a higher number of perpetrators per incident than other hate crimes. The FBI lists the average perpetrator–victim ratio for all forms of hate crimes as 1 to 1.19.[34] Gay and lesbian victims are often surprised and outnumbered by their assailants, and therefore fighting back may not be a viable option.

Forty-three percent of the incidents involved physical assaults. The level of injury suffered by the victims was high, with only 37 percent escaping without any injury, 28 percent suffering minor injuries, 16 percent requiring outpatient medical treatment, 17 percent requiring admission to the hospital, and 3 percent of the attacks resulting in the death of the victim. These figures dispel the myths that the majority of hate crimes against gay or lesbian victims involve simple intimidation or verbal threats.

In the past thirty years, there has been a considerable body of knowledge and research accumulated on sexual coercion in heterosexual relationships. Marital rape is discussed in depth in this text in Chapter 8. However, there is very little research into the area of gay men as victims of nonconsensual, or forced, sex. Waterman and her associates conducted one of the first studies of sexual coercion in gay male and lesbian relationships.[35] The results of their research indicate that forced sex is a considerable problem for gay men.

Hickson and his associates reviewed incidents of nonconsensual sexual activity among 930 gay men living in England and Wales.[36] Hickson points out that the vast majority of research dealing with sexual assault on men has focused on prison populations. The presumed sexual orientation of men who rape other men has been subject to some debate. Hickson correctly states that men rape other men for the same reasons they rape women, and that male rape is rarely, if ever, a homosexual problem. Of the 930 men interviewed, 257, or 27 percent, stated that they had been subjected to nonconsensual sex at some point in their lives. After deleting 10 of the men who were assaulted by women, and 28 respondents who declined to discuss the event or could not remember the details, the remaining 219 subjects' sexual history was examined.

Hickson's research indicated a broad range of different types of sexual assaults on gay men. These assaults included older men touching younger boys, sexual assault of the victim by a heterosexual man after the victim had identified himself as gay, and a large number of assaults that occurred between gay men.

Just as female victims of male battering are reluctant or incapable of reporting or leaving the abusing spouse, so are same-sex victims. However, gay and lesbian victims face additional problems when it comes to disclosure or detachment from the abuser. Many of these problems are unique to the lesbian or gay community and have contributed to a lack of academic research in this area of victimology.

Intimate Violence

As indicated earlier, gays and lesbians live together as same-sex partners. These living arrangements sometimes result in one of the partners becoming a victim of intimate violence. As more gays and lesbians acknowledge this form of abuse, it will be incumbent upon professionals to understand the dynamics that are involved and to offer support and treatment to the victims.

Gay and lesbian couples face the same kind of violence that occurs in a heterosexual relationship. Some authorities refer to gays and lesbians who live together as a family as a *nontraditional family.* By some estimates, there are several million nontraditional families in the United States.[37] Many of these families include children from previous marriages, adoptions, or artificial insemination of a lesbian partner. These are family units in every aspect except for the issuance by the state of a marriage license. Polikoff states that these nontraditional families are defined by their sharing of emotions and their financial interdependence in the relationship.[38]

Gay and lesbian couples have struggled for years to be accepted in society and accorded the same rights as heterosexual couples. The U.S. Census Bureau annual survey in 1990 revealed 4.47 million households of unmarried adults with 1.6 million of this number composed of members of the same sex.[39] One complex issue facing these couples is gay or lesbian abuse.

In comparison to other forms of family violence, there is very little research in the area of lesbian and gay abuse. However, some scholars in academia have set forth definitions of gender-specific abuse. For example, Hart defines lesbian battering as "that pattern of violent and coercive behaviors whereby a lesbian seeks to control the thoughts, beliefs or conduct of her intimate partner or to punish the intimate for resisting the perpetrator's control over her."[40] Island and Letellier published one of the first studies on gay abuse and defined gay domestic violence as "any unwanted physical force, psychological abuse, material or property damage inflicted on one man by another."[41] Both definitions involve dynamics similar to heterosexual spousal abuse. Some authorities might argue that gay and lesbian abuse should have its own definition because of the nature of the relationship; however, if one accepts that position, then heterosexual couples who live together but are not married should have their own definition of abuse. To approach this topic in such a manner would be to splinter all relationships into separate groups and lose sight of the overall dynamics that are involved in an abusive relationship. The definition of family violence used in this text does not require that the parties be married or even be of different sexes. *Family Violence* is defined as any act or omission by persons who are cohabitating that results in serious injury to other members of the family. Because this term covers gay and lesbian abuse, it will be used to promote the fact that this type of aggression is in fact a form of family violence.

To acknowledge that lesbian and gay couples face many of the same problems as heterosexual couples is to accord a legitimacy to their status. There is a segment of the population that refuses to accept same-sex relationships as a legitimate expression of society's values. This viewpoint is only one reason why there is so little research in this area of family violence. However, there are other reasons for the failure to explore this type of aggression. Many of these reasons are unique to the lesbian and gay community and will be discussed later in this section.

Extent of the Problem

The true extent of lesbian and gay family violence has never been accurately determined. Some researchers argue that battering within same-sex relationships is the same as it is for heterosexual couples, approximately 25 to 35 percent.[42] Other authorities have stated that domestic violence is the third most severe health problem facing gay men.[43]

The lesbian and gay communities themselves have contributed in some instances to the lack of hard scientific evidence concerning this form of family violence. Lesbian communities may be reluctant, for ideological reasons, to admit that one woman can batter another. To do so is contrary to the idea of a peaceful woman-centered world. However, there is more discussion within the lesbian community regarding battering than in the gay community. Gays may be reluctant to discuss gay abuse because very simply, as one scholar put it, "the gay community would rather not know."[44]

When Yale University conducted a study dealing with battered women and the effectiveness of restraining orders, they discovered that gay and lesbian abuse was so extensive they needed to include this segment of the population in the study.[45] There is a great deal of conflict among authorities as to whether gay men or lesbians are the more violent of the two. Some researchers claim that lesbians seem to be more aggressive than gay men or heterosexual women.[46] Other authors state that there is some evidence to support the theory that violence may occur more frequently between gay men than lesbians.[47] However, all parties to this debate agree that these conclusions are tentative at best, and more empirical research needs to be conducted in this area. Although there has been no definitive study on the different types of abuse suffered by gay couples, there is support for the proposition that they suffer the same type of abuse as lesbian couples.

There is still a great deal of misinformation regarding AIDS, its effect, and how it may be acquired. Gay or lesbian victims who are HIV positive may feel that they do not have any support system available to them other than the abusing partner. Also, if the abuser has AIDS or is HIV positive, the victim may feel a great deal of remorse at the thought of reporting the partner to law enforcement agencies or otherwise abandoning him or her.[48]

The abuser may also prevent the victim from disclosing the abuse or leaving the relationship by threatening to "out" the victim. *Outing* is disclosure of the victim's sexual preference. The abuser may threaten to tell the victim's friends, family, or others unless the victim agrees to conceal the abuse. Even if the victim is open about sexual preference, the batterer may exploit fears of sexist and heterosexual stereotypes to convince the victim that reporting the incident is useless.

Lesbian and gay victims face additional pressure from their peers within the gay community. Some authorities point out that the gay community's failure to acknowledge family violence within its ranks is based on a fear that acknowledgment of such behavior will lead to increased derision from the heterosexual community, by adding credence to the homophobic attitude that gay men and lesbians are deviates.[49]

Another problem facing lesbian and gay victims is the critical shortage of support services and/or organizations that offer support for same-sex victims of family violence. Specialized counseling services for gay and lesbian victims of family violence are available in only a few cities: New York, San Francisco, Seattle, and Minneapolis.[50] No city has established an emergency shelter specifically for gay men or lesbian victims of family violence.[51] Although some lesbian victims may be able to use battered women's services and/or shelters, this option is not available to gay men.

Legal Aspects of Gay and Lesbian Abuse

Gay and lesbian victims face additional hurdles when they attempt to prevent further abuse by their partners. These obstacles include outdated, and in many cases homophobic, attitudes by law enforcement officers, attorneys, and even members of the judiciary system. Simply reporting the incident may cause the victims to suffer more humiliation and pain from a system that is ill equipped to deal with this form of family violence.

Law enforcement officers and members of the judicial system have historically been reluctant to acknowledge gay and lesbian abuse. In many instances, this leaves the victims without assistance from the legal system. Therefore, abused gays and lesbians are generally less likely to report incidents of domestic violence to the police.

There are reported cases in which members of the judiciary system have made comments reflecting their negative feelings toward gay and lesbian couples. In *Constant A. v. Paul C.A.* the court awarded custody of the children to the father stating, ". . . once the father established the mother's lesbian relationship and his own legitimate and stable heterosexual relationship, a presumption arose favoring the preferability of the traditional relationship."[52]

Although many professionals in the criminal justice system are aware of the dynamics involved in male battering of women, they may be unwilling to accept the fact that these same kinds of dynamics are operating in same-sex battery. This lack of knowledge on the part of police and the judicial system works to the advantage of the abuser this way: It is not uncommon for the abuser to claim that he or she is in fact the victim. Because many gay and lesbian couples may be the same size physically, the stereotypical view that the larger person is always the aggressor in a relationship may prevent professionals from seeing the facts as legitimate. Even assuming professionals within the criminal justice system are willing to act on allegations of same-sex battering, the laws in sixteen states do not cover same-sex, nonrelated cohabitants.

Some states make certain sex acts criminal even when they occur between consenting adults. In *Bowers v. Hardwick,* the U.S. Supreme Court upheld the right of states to impose criminal sanctions on acts that occur in the privacy of one's bedroom.[53] Although sodomy statutes among consenting adults are criminal in only six states, misinformation and fear may allow the perpetrator to threaten the victim with disclosure of certain sex acts that might be considered criminal. As stated in *Baker v Wade,*

> *"the existence of these criminal laws, even if they are not enforced . . . does result in stigma, emotional stress and other adverse effects. The anxieties caused to homosexuals—fear of arrest, loss of jobs, discovery, etc.—can cause severe mental health problems."*[54]

This discussion may lead one to believe that there is no hope for gay and lesbian victims. This is not the case. Therapists are beginning to discuss gay and lesbian relationships more often.[55] Those in academia continue researching issues of gay and lesbian victimization.[56] An example of a local program that provides support for victims of gay and lesbian abuse is the New York City Gay and Lesbian AntiViolence Project. It provides a number of services for gay and lesbian victims including:

- Telephone counseling and crisis intervention
- Short-term in-person counseling
- Assistance in obtaining orders of protection
- Police advocacy and precinct accompaniment
- Crime victims' compensation filing and advocacy
- Court advocacy, monitoring, and accompaniment
- Information and referrals
- Community education and outreach
- Volunteer training
- Hospital accompaniment
- Advocacy with other service agencies

These activities are similar to those offered to heterosexual victims by a number of social service agencies. As more gays and lesbians accept the fact that it is all right to come out of another closet and admit that they have been victims, the sooner we will accept this form of aggression as a part of the totality of the circumstances that must be addressed when studying victimology.

Summary

This chapter is a general overview of a serious issue within the criminal justice system. Special population victimization continues and in some instances is on the increase. Because the United States is becoming more diverse with the passage of each year, victim service providers need to become very aware and sensitive to the needs of these special victims. More important, they need to act as the spokespeople for these victims to individuals and agencies within the criminal justice system.

HIV/AIDS is a terrible disease with deadly consequences for any infected person. Victims of crimes may suffer a second trauma if there is the possibility that they were exposed to the virus during the commission of the crime. Victim service providers must be sensitive to these victims' special needs.

Disabled victims and gay or lesbian victims are only two of the many special populations that exist in the United States. However, their victimization carries special problems and issues that must be addressed by those within the criminal justice system. Because of their status, these victims may not report crimes. Additionally, they may be victimized a second time during the criminal justice process. Victim professionals must be aware of these potential problems when dealing with these special populations.

Key Terms

Disabled person is one who has a physical or mental impairment that substantially limits one or more of the major life activities of that individual or that person has a record of such impairment or that person is regarded as having such an impairment.

Homosexuality is defined as the manifestation of sexual desire toward a member of one's own sex.

Gay is defined as a male homosexual or a socially integrated group oriented toward and concerned with the welfare of homosexuals.

Lesbian is defined as a female homosexual.

Nontraditional family occurs when gays or lesbians live together as a family.

Family Violence is defined as any act or omission by persons who are cohabitating that results in serious injury to other members of the family.

Outing is disclosure of the victim's sexual preference.

Discussion Questions

1. Should victims who are HIV+ be treated any differently than other victims? Why?

2. Should a person suffering from the HIV/AIDS disease be required to disclose that fact to family members? to sexual partners? to workplace associates? to friends?

3. Should there be stiffer criminal penalties for perpetrators who commit crimes when HIV+? What if they were unaware of their infection?

4. Explain how you would work with a sight-impaired victim, a hearing-impaired victim, and a victim confined to a wheelchair. What problems or issues do you see that they will face in the criminal justice system?

5. Assume that a gay man has approached you and told you he had been raped by men who called him a "faggot." However, he doesn't want to report the crime to the police because his parents do not know he is gay. What advice can you offer him? What are the issues raised by this situation?

Suggested Readings

Jack Levin & Jack McDevitt, *The Rising Tide of Bigotry and Bloodshed*, (Plenum, New York) 1993.

William P. Randel, *The Ku Klux Klan: A Century of Infamy*, (Chilton Books, New York) 1965.

J. Boswell, *Christianity, Social Tolerance, and Homosexuality*, (Univ of Chicago Press, Chicago) 1980.

Kerry Lobel, (ed.), *Naming the Violence: Speaking Out about Lesbian Battering*, (The Seal Press, Seattle, Wa.) 1986.

Endnotes

1. This section has been adapted from *HIV/AIDS and Victim Services: A Critical Concern of the 90s,* sponsored by a grant from the Office for Victims of Crime, (National Victims Center, Arlington, VA) February 1996, Chapters II, III, and IV [hereinafter cited as *HIV/AIDS and Victim Services*]

2. *HIV/AIDS and Victim Services* pp. II-1–II-2.

3. *HIV/AIDS and Victim Services* pp. II-3–II-4.

4. *HIV/AIDS and Victim Services* p. II-5.

5. *HIV/AIDS and Victim Services* pp. II-5–II-8.

6. *HIV/AIDS and Victim Services* pp. II-30–II-32.

7. *HIV/AIDS and Victim Services* p. III-3.

8. *HIV/AIDS and Victim Services* p. III-5.

9. See for example, Florida Code Section 960.003 (1) (1994).

10. *HIV/AIDS and Victim Services* p. III-18.

11. *HIV/AIDS and Victim Services* pp. IV-1–IV-2.

12. *HIV/AIDS and Victim Services* p. IV-7.

13. *HIV/AIDS and Victim Services* pp. IV-21–IV-30.

14. *HIV/AIDS and Victim Services* pp. IV-31–IV-33.

15. Much of the material in this section has been adapted from *Focus on the Future: A Systems Approach to Prosecution and Victim Assistance*, sponsored by a grant from Office for Victims of Crimes, (U.S. Department of Justice, Washington, D.C.) (National Victims Center, Arlington, Va.) 1992.

16. Kathi Wolfe, "Bashing the Disabled: the New Hate Crime," 9/11 *The Progressive*, 24 (Nov. 1995).

17. This paragraph was adapted from the *Draft Report, Criminal Justice Task Force for Persons with Developmental Disabilities, Victim of Crime Section* (Office of Criminal Justice Planning, Sacramento, Calif.) October 1, 1996, p. 1 (hereinafter referred to as *Task Force for Persons with Developmental Disabilities*)

18. L. Merkin & M. J. Smith, "A Community-Based Model Providing Services for the Deaf and Deaf–Blind Victims of Sexual Assault and Domestic Violence," 13(2) *Sexuality and Disability*, 97–106 (1995).

19. "Eight Do's and Don'ts in Working with Disabled Victims of Crime," *Focus on the Future: A Systems Approach to Prosecution and Victim Assistance*, (National Victims Center, sponsored by a grant from the Office for Victims of Crimes, U.S. Department of Justice, Washington, D.C.) 1992, p. C-13.

20. Adapted from *Task Force for Persons with Developmental Disabilities*), p. 1.
21. Cheryl G. Tyiska, "Responding to Disabled Victims of Crime," 8/12 *NOVA Network Information Bulletin,* (NOVA, Washington, D.C.) 1990. p. 10.
22. George Marshall Worthington, "Sexual Exploitation and Abuse of People with Disabilities," 7/2 *Response to Violence in the Family and Sexual Assault,* 43 (1984).
23. *Sexual Exploitation of Handicapped Students: Teachers Training Manual,* (Seattle Rape Relief Disabilities Project, Seattle, Wash.) 1981.
24. Cathy McPherson, "Bringing Redress to Abused Disabled Persons," 8/12 *NOVA Network Information Bulletin,* 14 (NOVA, Washington, D.C., 1990).
25. Louise Melling, "Wife Abuse in the Deaf Community," 7/1 *Response to Violence in the Family and Sexual Assault,* 12 (1984).
26. Denise Aiello & Lee Capkin, "Services for Disabled Victims: Elements and Standards," 7/5 *Response to Violence in the Family and Sexual Assault,* 14, (1984).
27. Adapted from *Task Force for Persons with Developmental Disabilities,* p. 11–22.
28. W. Masters, V. Johnson, & R. Kolodny, *Masters and Johnson on Sex and Human Loving,* (Little Brown & Co., Boston) 1968.
29. J. Boswell, *Christianity, Social Tolerance, and Homosexuality,* Ill.: (Univ. of Chicago Press, Chicago) 1980.
30. *Webster's New Collegiate Dictionary,* (G & C Merriam Co., Springfield, Mass.) (1981).
31. Valerie Jenness, "Social Movement Growth, Domain Expansion, and Framing Process: The Gay/Lesbian Movement and Violence Against Gays and Lesbians as a Social Problem," 42/1 *Social Problems,* (February 1995).
32. Gregory M. Herek, "Hate Crimes Against Lesbian and Gay Men," 44/6 *American Psychologist,* (June 1989).
33. *AntiGay/Lesbian Violence in 1994: National Trends, Analysis and Incident Summaries,* (New York City Gay and Lesbian AntiViolence Project, New York) 1994.
34. *Characteristics of Hate Crime in 1992,* (U.S. Department of Justice, Federal Bureau of Investigation, GPO, Washington, D.C., 1993) p. 9
35. Carolyn K. Waterman, Lori J. Dawson, & Michael J. Bologna, "Sexual Coercion in Gay Male and Lesbian Relationships: Predictors and Implications for Support Services," 26/1 *The Journal of Sex Research,* 118 (February, 1989).
36. Ford C. I. Hickson, Peter M. Davies, Andrew J. Hunt, Peter Weatherburn, Thomas J. McManus, & Anthony P. M. Coxon, "Gay Men as Victims of Nonconsensual Sex," 23/3 *Archives of Sexual Behavior,* 281 (1994).
37. Nan D. Hunter & Nancy D. Polikoff, "Custody Rights of Lesbian Mothers: Legal Theory and Litigation Strategy," 25 *Buffalo Law Rev.,* 691 (1976).
38. Nancy Polikoff, "This Child Does Have Two Mothers: Redefining Parenthood to Meet the Needs of Children in Lesbian-Mother and Other Nontraditional Families," 78 *Georgia Law Rev.,* 459 (1990).
39. Arlene F. Saluter, "Marital Status and Living Arrangements: March 1990," *U.S. Bureau of the Census, Series P-20,* no. 450 (May 1991), p. 73.
40. Barbara Hart, "Lesbian Battering: An Examination," Kerry Lobel, (ed.), *Naming The Violence: Speaking Out About Lesbian Battering,* (The Seal Press, Seattle, Wash.) 1986, p. 173.
41. David Island & Patrick Letellier, *Men Who Beat the Men Who Love Them,* (Harrington Park Press, New York) 1991. p. 27.
42. Claire M. Renzetti, *Violent Betrayal, Partner Abuse in Lesbian Relationships* (Sage Publications, Newbury Park, Calif.) 1992, pp. 17–18.
43. Island & Letellier, *Men Who Beat the Men Who Love Them,* p. 14.
44. David Island & Patrick Letellier, *Men Who Beat the Men Who Love Them,"* at 10, 36.
45. Gary Brown et al., "Starting a TRO Project: Student Representation of Battered Women," 96 *Yale Law Rev.* 1985 (1987).
46. Mac D. Hunter, "Homosexuals as a New Class of Domestic Violence Subjects Under the New Jersey Prevention of Domestic Violence Act of 1991," 31 *University of Louisville Journal of Family Law,* p. 557 (1992/93).

47. Denise Bricker, "Fatal Defense: An Analysis of Battered Women's Syndrome, Expert Testimony for Gay Men and Lesbians Who Kill Abusive Partners," 58 *Brooklyn Law Rev.*, 1379 (Winter 1993).

48. "Violence Against People with HIV/AIDS," Pamphlet prepared by the New York City Gay & Lesbian AntiViolence Project, (New York 1991).

49. Mindy Benowitz, "How Homophobia Affects Lesbians' Response to Violence in Lesbian Relationships," in *Naming the Violence,* p. 200.

50. Phyllis Winfield, "Rare Program Aids Battered Lesbians, Gays: Violence Mirrors Heterosexual Incidents," *Seattle Times,* September 24, 1990, at E3.

51. Judy Mann, "A Grant in Trouble," C3 *Washington Post,* (July 5, 1995).

52. 496 A.2d 1 at 7 (1985).

53. 478 U.S. 186, (1986).

54. 553 F.Supp. 1121 (N.D. Tex. 1982), appeal dismissed, 743 F.2d 236 (5th Cir. 1984), Cert. denied 478 U.S. 1022 (1986).

55. See for example a special section entitled, "Gay and Lesbians Are Out of the Closet," in *The Family Therapy Networker,* (January/February 1991).

56. Gwat-Yong Lie and Sabrina Gentlewarrier, "Intimate Violence in Lesbian Relationships: Discussion of Survey Findings and Practice Implications," 15 (1/2) *Journal of Social Service Research,* 41 (1991).

14

NEGLIGENCE AND INTENTIONAL TORTS

Chapter Outline

Introduction

Negligence
Introduction
Elements of Negligence

Wrongful Death
The Parties
Elements of Damage

Assault and Battery
Defined
Fear versus Contact

False Imprisonment
Defined
The Confinement Requirement

Mental Distress
Intent Requirement
Conduct Requirement

Joint Tortfeasors
The Parties
Civil Conspiracy
Apportionment

Defenses to Intentional Torts
Self-Defense
Defense of Others

Defense of Property
Consent
Necessity
Authority of Law

Summary

Key Terms

Discussion Questions

Suggested Readings

Learning Objectives

After reading this chapter, you should be able to:

- Compare and contrast negligence and intentional torts
- Explain the difference between torts and criminal acts
- Distinguish between the torts of assault and of battery
- Explain why the tort of mental distress is important to victims
- Understand the various defenses to negligence and intentional torts

Introduction

This chapter deals with negligence and the intentional torts of wrongful death, assault, battery, false imprisonment, and intentional infliction of mental distress. The great majority of all victim-related issues occur in the area of tort law and therefore it is important to understand the basic rules that apply to an action based on tort.

A tort may be based on negligence or on intentional acts. *Negligence* is a complex legal concept that under certain circumstances holds persons liable for acting, or failing to act, in a certain manner. Many persons, including victims of crime, have been injured because of the negligence of another party.

Many other issues relating to victims arise because of an intentional act of another. Intentional torts include wrongful death, assault, battery, false imprisonment, and intentional infliction of mental distress. Each of these torts requires the perpetrator to act with a certain state of mind or intent. The intent required for these types of injuries requires that the tortfeasor intend to cause some physical or mental effect on another person. There is no requirement that the tortfeasor intend to harm the victim. The intent to harm is irrelevant as long as the tortfeasor intended the act.[1] The law also calls a tortfeasor's actions intentional even if he didn't desire a certain type of occurrence but knew with substantial certainty that it would occur as a result of his actions.

In the majority of intentional torts, a certain doctrine applies. The doctrine of *transferred intent* holds that so long as the tortfeasor had the necessary intent to act in a certain manner toward one person, he will be held liable for torts committed against any other person who happens to be injured. Many states incorporate this doctrine into their criminal codes that establish criminal liability.[2]

The significance of proving intent relates to the award of damages. If the jury finds that the tortfeasor acted intentionally, the jury may award nominal damages even if no injury occurred to the plaintiff. *Nominal damages* are token damages, for example, $1.00. Although this may seem insignificant, many jurisdictions also allow the prevailing party to recover attorneys' fees. In this case, the award of token damages may allow the victim to recover attorneys' fees and the costs of the suit. An intentional tort victim may also recover punitive damages if the jury finds that the defendant's acts were outrageous or malicious. As discussed later in this chapter, punitive damages are to punish the tortfeasor.

Each of these torts has a "companion" criminal act. Although there are differences between the criminal and civil acts, they are similar in many ways. Table 14.1 compares some of the more common criminal acts with their companion civil tort.

One significant difference between a criminal case and a civil case is the amount of evidence necessary to prove the case. Normally the criminal process will have been completed prior to the civil trial. If the defendant is found guilty in the criminal action, this fact may be presented in the subsequent civil action to prove culpability. Even if the perpetrator is found not guilty in the criminal case, the victim still has the right to pursue a civil cause of action because of the difference in the burden of proof between the two types of proceedings. In criminal cases, the government must prove the case beyond a reasonable doubt, whereas in civil cases the plaintiff need only present a preponderance of the evidence. Table 14.2 illustrates the difference between the two levels of proof.

The difference in the burden of proof is important because unlike criminal proceedings, there is no double jeopardy bar to filing a civil action after an acquittal in the criminal case. In criminal cases, the double jeopardy clause of the Fifth Amendment prevents the state from refiling the criminal charges if the defendant is acquit-

TABLE 14.1   A Comparison of Torts and Crimes

Intentional Torts	Crimes
Wrongful Death	Murder Involuntary manslaughter Voluntary manslaughter Negligent manslaughter
Assault	Assault or Stalking
Battery	Battery or any sexual crime such as rape, sodomy, or oral copulation
False Imprisonment	False Imprisonment
Mental Distress	Stalking

TABLE 14.2

Possible Amount of Proof

0 - 100%

Beyond a Reasonable Doubt

0 - 90–95%

Preponderance of the Evidence

0 - - - - - - - - - - - - - - - 51%

ted.[3] This prohibition, however, does not apply to the filing of civil cases. Therefore, even if the defendant is acquitted in a criminal action, a civil intentional tort action may be filed. This is exactly what happened in the O. J. Simpson saga. After Mr. Simpson was acquitted of the double murder of his ex-wife, Nicole Brown Simpson, and her friend, Ronald Goldman, both families of the victims filed civil actions against O. J. Simpson. Both families prevailed in the civil action when the jury found Mr. Simpson liable for the wrongful death of Nicole and Ronald.

Victims file civil actions against their perpetrators for a variety of reasons. They may believe that they did not receive appropriate satisfaction as a result of any criminal proceedings. The defendant may have been acquitted or convicted of a lessor charge than the victim believes is proper. Victims may also feel mistreated by the criminal justice system and have a desire to be in control of the proceedings instead of merely being a witness. Many victims may also want to receive more compensation for injuries than is available in the criminal justice system.

Negligence

Introduction

Often we hear others refer to the fact that someone was negligent. The lay or common meaning of the term *negligent* simply means someone was careless or slipshod in performing some act. The term *negligence* in tort law is a far more complex and confusing concept. The legal definition of **negligence** comprises several components including a duty, a breach of that duty, proximate cause, and actual injury. Under the concept of negligence the injured party must show that the tortfeasor had a legal duty that required him to conduct himself according to certain standards, so as to avoid harming others. The plaintiff must also prove that the defendant breached or failed to conform his conduct to that standard. Once these two elements have been established there must be proof that they were the proximate cause or causal link between the defendant's acts and the injury suffered by the plaintiff. Finally, there must be proof of actual damages as distinguished from intentional torts that allow for recovery of nominal damages even without proof of actual injury.

Elements of Negligence

The above-mentioned definition of negligence contains several distinct elements. Each of these must be proved before the injured party can recover damages. The problem with negligence is that there are many grey areas in each of these elements. For ease of understanding, only basic concepts will be discussed in this text.

The injured party must prove that the defendant owed a legal duty to avoid unreasonable risk to others. Courts utilize a balancing test to determine if the defendant's conduct exposed the victim to unreasonable harm. The test is simply whether a reasonable person would have recognized the risk of harm and sought to avoid it.[4]

In applying this test, courts will often examine the situation using an objective test. Juries will be asked to view the defendant's conduct from a reasonable person's point of view. If a reasonable person of ordinary prudence in the defendant's position would have avoided harming the victim, the defendant will be found negligent if the actions injured the plaintiff.

The defendant must fail to conform his conduct to the legal duty. This duty to others many times is determined by the relationship between the defendant and the victim. Some relationships impose a higher standard of care or duty on the defendant than others. These special or third-party relationships will be discussed in Chapter 15.

The victim must also show a close causal relationship between the defendant's acts and the injury. This is known as the *proximate* or *legal cause* of the injury. This is the one area of negligence that gives lawyers, judges, and juries the most problems. For example, suppose two drivers are intoxicated and run into each other. Who is at fault? Suppose one driver had two drinks and the other driver had ten drinks? The short answer is that the law will presume that each driver will be held to be a proximate or legal cause of the accident. Therefore if the defendant has "caused" the injury to the victim, the law may hold him liable. However, the issue is further complicated by another concept that deals with foreseeability of harm.

Foreseeability is viewing harm as a set of dominoes. When the defendant acts in certain ways, his actions cause other effects similar to pushing over one domino in a line. The public policy question is how far down that line of toppling dominoes will the courts look in holding the defendant accountable. The generally accepted rule is that if the injuries were a direct result of the defendant's action, the defendant will be held liable even if the injuries were not the kind one would normally expect as a result of the act.[5] This position is based on several rationales including the fact that many serious cases arise from single acts of negligence that are caused by large corporations, government, or utilities. These entities are able to bear the burden of compensating the victim who had no reason to guard against that particular loss.

Finally, the victim must suffer actual damage or injury. The extent of the victim's injury may not be easy to determine. This aspect of negligence may require the services of expert witnesses to explain how the victim was injured, the extent of those injuries, and how long they will last.

Victims may not be aware of the true extent of their injuries. Care should be taken when advising victims to settle with insurance companies immediately after the incident. There are some injuries that do not show up right away and most settlement agreements prevent the victim from asking for additional money for other injuries that are discovered after the settlement. Many states allow victims of negligence up to one year before they lose their right to sue. Victims should be advised to consult their own insurance company as well as an attorney and have a thorough medical examination before signing any settlement.

Wrongful Death

Wrongful death actions may be brought based on negligence, strict liability, or intentional acts by the defendant. They are discussed in this chapter because many wrongful death causes of action arise from criminal acts that are based on homicide statutes. When a perpetrator kills the victim, her family must cope with the loss. Additionally, the family may have been deprived of the economic support that the victim would have contributed over her lifetime.

The Parties

In common law, when a person died, his right to recover for any injuries was extinguished upon death. This rule also applied to his heirs so that they were precluded from recovering damages they suffered as a result of the loss of a loved one. Every state has modified this common law rule by adopting survival statutes and wrongful death statutes.

Survival statutes modify the common law rule by allowing the decedent's claim for personal injuries to be brought by his heirs. Many of these states also allow the filing and maintenance of a personal injury action against the defendant's estate if he dies before the filing of the civil case. Most states have special *wrongful death statutes* which allow a defined group of individuals to recover the loss it sustained as a result of the victim's death. The parties that may sue under these wrongful death statutes are the decedent's spouse, children, and parents. Because wrongful death actions are based on statutorily created rights, courts are reluctant to expand the scope of these remedies. Thus, live-in lovers who are not legally married may be denied recovery.[6]

Elements of Damage

Certain types of damages are unique to wrongful death cases and include loss of companionship, sexual intercourse, and moral guidance of the decedent. Some states also allow for grief or other mental suffering of the survivors as an element of damages.

When a child is murdered and a civil action is brought by her parents, it is sometimes hard to establish pecuniary loss on the part of the parents, because it is generally agreed that the cost of raising and educating a child is more than any earning she could be expected to contribute to her parents. However, many courts are now allowing damages for loss of companionship of the child.

A very emotional issue that sometimes arises in wrongful death cases involves the doctrine of unjust enrichment. This common law rule prohibits persons, in wrongful death cases it would be the perpetrator, from profiting from their own wrongdoing. The doctrine of unjust enrichment is implemented by court decisions that are founded upon "Salyer's Rules or Statutes." These are statutes that prohibit a murderer from profiting from his illegal acts. There are numerous court decisions that prevent intrafamilial killers from gaining an economic advantage because of their actions. For example, in one famous case, a husband murdered his wife and then filed to become the administrator of her estate. As the administrator, he would have been entitled to fees for his services to the estate. The court rejected his claim because he had been convicted of her murder.[7]

Assault and Battery

Assault and battery are common intentional torts. Many laypersons confuse assault with battery and vice versa. It is not uncommon for an assault and battery to occur during the commission of a crime. However, it must be understood that although they are discussed together for purposes of comparison, they are distinct and separate intentional torts. You may have an assault without a battery and you may also have a battery without an assault.

Defined

The tort of *assault* has been defined as the intentional causing of an apprehension or offensive contact.[8] The defendant has committed the tort of assault when he has caused the victim to believe that she will be subjected to harmful or offensive contact. The interest that is being protected is the victim's freedom from apprehension of wrongful contact. Assault can therefore occur even if no actual contact occurs between the defendant and the victim.

The tort of *battery* has been defined as the intentional infliction of harmful or offensive bodily contact.[9] The tort of battery includes touching or contact that causes injury to the victim as well as any bodily contact that is considered offensive. The standard used to determine if the contact is offensive is whether an ordinary person would have been offended by the contact.

Fear versus Contact

As the previous definitions indicate, the key distinction between an assault and battery is whether the victim experienced fear or was touched in a harmful or offensive manner by the defendant. Some states argue whether words alone may constitute an assault. The states requiring more than words mandate that the words be accompanied by some overt act that adds to the threatening character of the words. Other states and the *Restatement of Torts* indicate that there may be situations in which words by themselves without any overt act are sufficient to constitute the tort of assault.[10] This distinction between threats and overt acts was also a dilemma faced by law enforcement agencies who responded to threats made by perpetrators prior to the adopting of the stalking laws. Most criminal assault statutes required that the defendant have the present ability to inflict injury upon the victim. Stalking statutes allow law enforcement to take action based on a threat to harm the victim in the future.[11]

Because the tort of assault protects the peace of mind of the victim, she must be aware of the threat. The victim need only experience apprehension. Apprehension is not necessarily the same emotion as fear. In other words, the victim only need be concerned rather than scared. The threat must be directed at the victim and not a third person. If a family member is threatened, the victim may experience apprehension or even fear, but cannot recover based on the traditional tort of assault. As will be discussed later, the modern tort of infliction of mental distress would apply in these types of situations.

Unlike assault, the tort of battery may be committed even if the victim is unaware of the contact at the time it occurs. For example, the perpetrator may slip something in the victim's drink causing her to pass out. He then engages in sexual intercourse with her. The crime of rape and the tort of battery have both occurred even though at the time of the contact the victim was unconscious.

False Imprisonment

Defined

The tort of *false imprisonment* is defined as the intentional infliction of a confinement. The victim must show that the perpetrator intended to confine her. She must be confined within definite physical boundaries. Simply blocking the victim's path or preventing him from entering a particular place does not meet the requirement of this tort. However, if the victim initially consents to the confinement there is no tort. If the perpetrator is under a duty to release the victim and fails to do so, the tort has been committed. For example, a victim may meet the perpetrator at a bar and agree to a ride home with him. There is no false imprisonment during the ride to the victim's home. Once they arrive at the victim's home and the perpetrator refuses to allow the victim to leave the car unless the victim has sex with him, the tort of false imprisonment occurs. This is true even though the victim agreed to ride in the perpetrator's car.

The Confinement Requirement

The essence of the confinement requirement is that the victim is held within certain limits, not simply prevented from entering certain places. Thus preventing the victim from entering a store is not false imprisonment, whereas holding him in an office within that store would be such a tort. Confining the victim to a locked room clearly meets the definition of this tort. However, there are other instances of more subtle acts that will give rise to the tort of false imprisonment. If the perpetrator threatens the victim with force if he tries to escape from an unlocked building and the perpetrator has the apparent ability to carry out the threat, the tort of false imprisonment is complete. Unlike assault, the tort of false imprisonment may occur if the perpetrator threatens harm to family members if the victim does not remain in a particular room or tries to escape.[12] The threat or duress that confines the victim must be of imminent harm. Threats of future harm are not sufficient. The tort of false imprisonment usually does not occur in a vacuum. Perpetrators usually commit other torts such as assault and battery in connection with the false imprisonment. Victim service providers should always be aware that several intentional torts may arise from one crime. For example, the offense of kidnapping may give rise to the intentional torts of assault, battery, false imprisonment, and mental distress.

Mental Distress

The intentional tort of infliction of mental distress is a relatively new tort. An increasing number of jurisdictions are recognizing that victims suffer mental problems as a result of criminal or other intentional acts and these jurisdictions are allowing these victims to sue for damages alleging infliction of mental or emotional distress. The tort of *mental distress* has been defined as the intentional or reckless infliction, by extreme or outrageous conduct, of severe emotional or mental distress. This tort does not require any physical harm or injury to the victim.

Intent Requirement

Unlike the majority of other intentional torts, the doctrine of transferred intent does not generally apply to the infliction of emotional distress. The most common reason given for precluding the application of this doctrine is that it would open the floodgates of litigation by unrelated parties. Professor Prosser points out that if the doctrine of transferred intent were allowed in emotional distress cases, millions of Americans who witnessed President Reagan being shot on television would be able to sue John Hinckley for infliction of emotional distress.[13]

The courts have fashioned one important exception in this area that deals with family members who witness the defendant injure or harm another family member. However, this exception is quite narrow and requires that the defendant know of the plaintiff's presence so that the infliction of mental distress is a reasonable consequence of the defendant's actions toward the other family member. For example, in a California case, the plaintiff watched the defendant beat up her father, and as a result of observing the beating she suffered severe emotional distress. The court held that because there was no allegation or proof that the defendant knew of her presence, nor that he intended to cause her emotional distress, her claim was invalid and the case dismissed.[14] However, the *Restatement of Torts* would liberalize this position and allow for recovery by victims who witness injury to others even if they are not related so long as the victim suffers physical illness as a result of the incident.[15]

Conduct Requirement

For the victim to recover damages, she must show that the defendant's conduct was extreme and outrageous. The defendant is not liable for insults or hurt feelings. The Restatement of Torts points out that certain conduct does not meet the standard of outrageous. Nonqualifying conduct includes ". . . mere insults, indignities, threats, annoyances, petty oppressions, or other trivialities."[16] The test that is normally applied requires that the conduct be so outrageous in character and so extreme as to go beyond all possible bounds of decency and be regarded as atrocious and utterly intolerable in a civilized society.[17] Once the victim has shown that the defendant's conduct was extreme and outrageous, she must also prove that she suffered severe emotional distress. Most jurisdictions require as a minimum that the victim show that as a result of the defendant's conduct she sought and received medical treatment.

Joint Tortfeasors

The issue of liability and damages will be addressed in more detail later in this text; however, certain aspects of liability are unique to intentional tortfeasors and they will be briefly examined in this chapter. Some crimes by their very nature involve more than one perpetrator. Clearly, when several members of a gang rape a woman, they are all criminally and civilly liable for their intentional acts.

Certain situations occur in which persons assist the perpetrator in committing the crime, but are not physically present at the crime scene. Under both criminal and civil law these other parties may be held liable. Other situations involve two or more defendants who are liable for some or all of the harm inflicted upon the victim. However, this is a complex area with many technical rules regarding knowledge, participation, and capability. When the issue of accomplice or accessory liability arises, it may become very frustrating and confusing for both the victim and the service provider who is working with the victim.

The Parties

Understanding who the parties are and what their role is in the crime sets the stage for determining their liability. Perpetrators are guilty of crimes if they commit certain acts that meet all the elements of a particular offense. As discussed, they may also be civilly liable for certain intentional torts that correspond to their criminal acts. In addition, other persons may be guilty or civilly liable for the same acts if their conduct satisfies certain requirements, even though they did not engage in the conduct prohibited under the substantive offense.

Society has determined that certain acts which assist in the commission of a crime should be prohibited although they do not directly satisfy the requirements or elements of the offense. The common law concept that held other parties liable for the perpetrator's criminal act was known as *aiding and abetting*. Over the years we have modified this concept and codified it into two separate forms of liability: an accomplice or an accessory. An *accomplice* is one who solicits another to commit a crime, or aids or agrees to aid another in planning the crime, or having a legal duty to prevent the offense fails to do so.[18] An *accessory* is a person who with the necessary intent harbors or conceals the perpetrator, provides aid, destroys evidence, warns the other party, or supplies false information to the police.[19] These parties will be held criminally and civilly liable as if they directly participated in those offenses.

Several special problems arise with accomplice and/or accessory liability. What happens if a person originally encourages or assists in the commission of a crime and then upon further reflection withdraws his support prior to the completion of the offense. Most jurisdictions require that to escape criminal and civil liability the accomplice must do certain acts that render his prior assistance useless or provide a timely warning to the victim or attempt to prevent the crime.[20] Is a person an accessory to a crime if she observes a criminal act and fails to report it to the proper authorities? Simply observing a crime and failing to report it absent some sort of relationship or duty to report has been held to not make that person an accessory. There are many reasons why persons do not report crimes and although we may morally condemn them, the state of the law is that they are not civilly or criminally liable for failing to report these offenses.

Civil Conspiracy

There are several criminal acts that give rise to civil liability in which one of the perpetrators does not directly participate in the commission of the crime. The most common offense is conspiracy. *Conspiracy* is an agreement between two or more persons with the specific intent to commit a public offense, followed by an overt act committed for the purpose of accomplishing the objective of the agreement.[21] For example, two perpetrators may plan a robbery of a local store. The first offender may plan the crime and the second offender may be the one who enters the establishment and actually carries out the crime. Under both criminal and civil laws, each perpetrator is responsible for the crime and its consequences.

There are also special problems or issues in the area of responsibility or liability of coconspirators. Withdrawal from the conspiracy after the commission of the overt act is no defense to liability. The rationale for this position is that once the overt act is complete, the danger to society has occurred and it is immaterial whether the ultimate objective of the conspiracy is attained. The coconspirators are liable for all crimes committed by each member of the conspiracy, when it was a reasonably foreseeable result of the conspiracy and done in furtherance of it.[22]

Apportionment

Many situations involve two or more perpetrators who have committed a crime in which a victim was injured. In some cases, it is difficult to determine which individual perpetrator caused the injury to the victim. In these situations the law deems the injury to the victim as indivisible and each perpetrator is liable for the entire harm. This concept is known as *joint and several liability*. For example, if several perpetrators physically attacked the victim and the victim suffered a broken arm but could not tell which of the offenders broke his arm, all the perpetrators could be held liable for the injury. The effect of this rule is to allow victims to sue and collect from each defendant or all of them. The victim cannot collect more than the overall damages. (The victim cannot collect twice.) The modern trend is to place limits on the doctrine of joint and several liability and many states now limit the victim's recovery in these types of cases to the tortfeasor's equitable share of damages.

There are, however, certain situations or injuries that are not theoretically divisible into portions or shares of damage. If the victim dies as a result of concerted or independent acts by two perpetrators, each will be liable for all damages flowing from that death because death is not apportionable. This is true for any other single personal injury. Similarly, if the victim's property is burned or otherwise destroyed, court will not require that apportionment occur. They will treat this as an indivisible result with all tortfeasors being held liable for the entire amount of damage.

As indicated, joint and several liability applies only where the victim's harm is not capable of apportionment between or among the perpetrators. If there is a way to prove that a certain portion of the injury to the victim is the result of one perpetrator and the remaining portion is the result of the act of another perpetrator, then each defendant will be responsible only for the harm attributable to him.[23] Certain types of injuries and their resulting fiscal impact can be clearly divided into parts or definite amounts. The classic example is the victim who is shot in a drive-by shooting by two gang members each acting independently of each other. One gang member's bullet enters the victim's arm and the other gang member's bullet enters the victim's leg. In these situations, each gang member will be liable only for the injury he has caused. However, if the two gang members acted in concert, each will be liable for the injuries directly caused by the other. All parties are wrongdoers acting in concert and each participant is liable for harm to a third person arising from the tortious conduct of the other because he has induced and encouraged the tort.[24]

Once liability has been determined, victims must be careful regarding how they approach settlement with any of the joint tortfeasors. A victim who has a cause of action against several perpetrators may settle with one while pursuing a lawsuit against the remaining offenders. Until recently how the victim settled with individual defendants could have grave consequences on her ability to recover from the others.

In common law, if a victim gave a *release* (a formal document absolving the party of all liability normally given in exchange for payment of money) to one of the tortfeasors, this release was held to relieve all the other defendants of liability as well. This rule was based on the common law fiction that a plaintiff had only one indivisible cause of action against all joint tortfeasors and it could not be extinguished as to one defendant and remain viable as to the remaining parties. The majority of states have now abolished this common law rule; however, most of them hold that if the release is silent on the question of continuing liability of the remaining defendants, the nonsettling defendants are relieved of continuing liability. Thus, absent a "reservation of rights" or other saving language in the settlement document, a release of one tortfeasor ordinarily releases all other tortfeasors.

Defenses to Intentional Torts

Simply establishing that the perpetrator injured the victim does not end the inquiry. Just as there are defenses that persons accused of crimes may raise in criminal actions, so are there the same or similar defenses that may be asserted in civil actions. This is especially true if there was no criminal case filed or it was dismissed on a technicality and no conviction or plea entered. If that is the case, then many of the defenses that would have been raised in the criminal case will most likely be used by the perpetrator in the civil case in an attempt to escape liability.

Self-Defense

Just as criminal law recognizes the privilege of self-defense, so does civil law. The rules regarding the use of self-defense are substantially the same in both situations. In understanding self-defense it is important to distinguish between deadly and nondeadly force. A person is justified in using deadly force only to protect oneself or others from what the person reasonably believes is imminent, unlawful deadly force.

The concept of self-defense includes the components of proportionality and necessity. *Proportionality* mandates that the force used in self-defense not be out of proportion to the force necessary to protect the person from the threatened harm. Necessity requires that a person only use force to prevent imminent, unlawful deadly force. Therefore, a person is normally not authorized in using deadly force to combat threats of future harm.

This is the dilemma faced by many battered spouses. There have been numerous cases and articles dealing with situations in which the battered spouse kills her abusing partner.[25] The victim may have attacked and killed the abuser defending herself from his physical assault or in some cases he may threaten her with harm in the future such as when he awakes or returns home. In some cases, she has responded with force as the abuser enters the home or while he is sleeping or passed out. The abused spouse believes in her own mind that she will be killed or seriously injured. She has no doubt regarding the offender's ability to carry out any threats because she has experienced his violent behavior in the past.

When the spouse kills another under a subjective opinion that they face death or danger, several jurisdictions have called this an "imperfect" form of self-defense. The courts are divided in this area with some courts authorizing the use of deadly force and others claiming the use of force was improper with the result that the abused spouse faces criminal charges for homicide.[26] This imperfect self-defense is what the Menendez brothers used in their high-profile murder trial in which they were accused of murdering their mother and father. The brothers alleged that their father was going to kill them when they threatened to expose the fact that he had sexually molested them for years. The jury rejected this defense and found the brothers guilty of homicide.

The general rule is that the nonaggressor or original victim does not have a duty to retreat before using deadly force to defend oneself. However, the aggressor may not normally use deadly force in self-defense of his actions. Most states deny the defense to those who initiate the fight. However, if the aggressor starts the fight, then clearly tries to retreat, deadly force may be used if the retreat is unsuccessful.

Defense of Others

A person is authorized in using force to defend another from imminent attack. The defender is justified in using the same amount or type of force in defending others as in self-dense. Some early cases required the defender to be related to the one being attacked, but modern cases have done away with this requirement and a person can now use force to defend a stranger.

Defense of Property

There is a right to use force to defend both real and personal property. The property owner can only use as much force as is reasonable to protect the property. There is authority for the position that the owner must first make a verbal demand that the perpetrator stop before using force, unless it appears that the harm is imminent or that the request to stop is useless. Although a property owner may use reasonable force to defend property, a person may not use deadly force to protect the property. Nor can a person use any force to reclaim property not in possession. The law does not favor self-help. A person also may not use mechanical devices such as spring guns in defending the home from theft or trespass. Spring guns are triggered to go off when a perpetrator enters the premises. In a widely discussed case, the defendant owned an unoccupied boarded-up farmhouse that had been broken into and vandalized a number of times. The defendant placed a shotgun in a bedroom and rigged it so that when a person entered the bedroom, the gun would discharge. The plaintiff entered the house to steal some jars he thought were antiques. When he entered the bedroom, the gun discharged striking him in the leg. In the civil trial that followed, the plaintiff (intruder) was awarded damages for his injuries and the property owner's claim of defense of property was denied. On appeal, the court stated that a property owner may not use deadly force to defend his property against a trespasser, unless the latter is committing a felony of violence or endangering human life by his act. Further what a property owner may not do directly, he may not do indirectly by a spring gun or other mechanical device.[27]

Consent

If the victim gives consent, the defendant will not be liable for any injuries. The defense of consent is frequently used in sexual assault cases. The perpetrator will claim the victim consented to the sexual acts and if there are physical injuries, the offender will attempt to dismiss them stating that the victim enjoyed or asked for rough sex. A number of sexual assault cases involve situations in which consent is an issue. These areas include lack of capacity to consent, exceeding the scope of consent, and duress causing consent.

Lack of Capacity to Consent.   This situation occurs when for a variety of reasons the victim, as a matter of law, is unable to give consent. Young children are incapable of consenting to sexual acts. For example, a defendant would never raise the issue of consent when the victim of his sexual advances was five years old. Adults who are developmental disabled may also be incapable of consenting to sexual acts. Persons who are unconscious because of excessive drinking or the use of drugs cannot give consent. Thus the male college student who engages in sexual acts with his date who has passed out cannot raise the defense of consent.

Exceeding the Scope of Consent.   If the victim gives actual consent to certain acts, the offender will not be able to raise the defense of consent if he goes substantially beyond the scope of that consent. In these situations the perpetrator argues that the victim consented to having sex and the victim states that she may have consented to certain acts, such as kissing and petting, but not sexual intercourse. Because there may be no physical evidence to support the victim's position, it becomes an issue of credibility in which the victim gives one statement and the perpetrator claims the events occurred in a different manner.

Duress Causing Consent.   Recently in Texas, a woman was in her home alone at night and a stranger entered through a window. The intruder stated he was going to have sex with her. The women fearing that she might get AIDS asked that he wear a condom during the act. She placed the condom on his penis and they engaged in sexual intercourse. Immediately after the perpetrator fled the scene the women called the police and they arrested the offender. He claimed consent arguing that she had invited the acts by urging him to wear a condom. One Texas grand jury refused to indict the defendant for rape; however, a second grand jury did indict him.

Another situation involves the defendant threatening the victim with a weapon and causing her to comply with his demands for sex. In this situation, there may not be any physical evidence that supports the victim's claim of rape, but clearly such a fact pattern meets all the elements of the crime of rape and the torts of assault and battery.

Necessity

The defense of necessity is based on a balancing of the evil that faces a person. For example, a person trapped on a hill during a snowstorm may have a choice of breaking into a cabin or freezing to death. The person understands that he is committing a crime (of burglary or trespass) by breaking into the cabin, but he also realizes that to stay out in the unprotected environment will result in his death. Although the person may have committed a criminal offense in breaking into the cabin, the defense of necessity will allow him to escape punishment. A person cannot raise this defense if the threatened harm will occur sometime in the future. In other words, a person cannot simply enter a store and take food claiming that a snowstorm is coming and he needs food to exist.

Two types of emergencies justify a person in harming another's property: cases of public necessity and cases of private necessity. When the person injures another's property in order to prevent harm to a substantial number of persons or to himself, the defense is based on public necessity. When the person is protecting only his own interest or the interest of a few citizens, the defense is based on private necessity. Public necessity defenses normally arise when the interference or damage to the lands of another is necessary or appears to be necessary to prevent a disaster to the community or a substantial number of persons within the community.[28] Private necessity defenses arise when a person injures private property to protect his property or the person or property of a third party if there is no other way to prevent the harm.[29]

Authority of Law

Acts committed by persons under authority of law are generally considered a valid defense. For example, a law enforcement officer who executes a valid warrant and uses proper procedures in doing so has a defense against a lawsuit based on the tort of false imprisonment by the person arrested. When an officer makes an arrest based on an arrest warrant that is valid on its face and uses proper procedures in making the arrest, the officer will have a valid defense even if it is later shown that the arrest warrant was invalid. Arrests without a warrant are complex and confusing. An officer or private citizen may make an arrest for a felony or misdemeanor which is committed in her presence. An officer may also make a warrantless arrest for a felony not committed in her presence if she has reasonable cause to believe the defendant committed it. The officer is privileged even if it later turns out that no crime was committed or that she arrested the wrong person so long as her beliefs were reasonable at the time of the arrest. Private citizens will lose their immunity if no felony was committed; however, like the officer they will still retain the immunity even if they arrested the wrong person if their beliefs were reasonable.

Summary

A significant number of victims will decide to file a civil lawsuit against the perpetrator who injured them during the commission of a crime. Victims file these actions for a variety of reasons. As a result, victim service providers must be familiar with civil causes of actions that allow victims to recover for their injuries. Negligence is a complex legal doctrine that holds parties liable for injuries suffered as a result of a breach of duty owed to the victim.

Additionally, a number of other torts correspond to the more common criminal offenses. These civil actions include the intentional torts of wrongful death, assault, battery, false imprisonment, and mental distress. Additionally, victim advocates must be familiar with the basic rules regarding liability of joint tortfeasors, issues surrounding the common defenses to these torts, the various types of intent necessary to commit these torts, and the different levels of proof in a criminal and civil case.

The intentional tort of wrongful death is one of the most emotional torts victim service providers must handle. The primary victim of this crime is dead and the remaining victim must deal with grief regarding the loss of a loved one as well as the complexities of pursuing a civil lawsuit. Victim service providers must understand who can recover and be prepared to discuss issues regarding damages which may be available to the remaining family victims.

There are a number of defenses to intentional torts. Many of these civil defenses are the same ones that will be raised in any criminal action. In many homicides, for example, the defendant will claim to have been provoked by the deceased and was simply acting in self-defense. Understanding the various defenses to intentional torts is an important aspect of this area of victims' rights.

Key Terms

Transferred intent holds that so long as the tort-feasor had the necessary intent to act in a certain manner toward one person, that person will be held liable for torts committed against any other person who happens to be injured.

Nominal damages are token damages, for example, $1.00.

Negligence comprises several components including a duty, a breach of that duty, proximate cause, and actual injury.

Survival statutes modify the common law rule by allowing the decedent's claim for personal injuries to be brought by his heirs.

Wrongful death statutes allow a defined group of individuals to recover the loss it sustained as a result of the victim's death. The parties that may sue under these wrongful death statutes are the decedent's spouse, children, and parents.

Assault is the intentional causing of an apprehension or offensive contact.

Battery is the intentional infliction of harmful or offensive bodily contact.

False imprisonment is the intentional infliction of a confinement.

Mental distress is the intentional or reckless infliction, by extreme or outrageous conduct, of severe emotional or mental distress.

Conspiracy is an agreement between two or more persons with the specific intent to commit a public offense, followed by an overt act committed for the purpose of accomplishing the objective of the agreement.

Release is a formal document absolving the party of all liability normally given in exchange for payment of money.

Discussion Questions

1. Should we be able to obtain insurance that covers us in the event of a negligent act on our part? If we didn't have insurance, would we be more careful in our actions?

2. What is the most important element in the tort of negligence? Why is it more critical than the other elements?

3. Other than wrongful death, what is the most serious intentional tort? Justify your answer.

4. Should people be held liable for acts of others? Why? Why not?

5. Should we have a "no-fault" tort system and pay those that are injured instead of arguing over who is at fault and which defense may apply? Would such a system save us money?

6. Which is the most important defense to the intentional torts? Why?

Suggested Readings

Wade Prosser, & Schwartz, *Cases and Materials on Torts*, 5th ed. (West Publishing Co., St. Paul, Minn.) 1984 w/ 1988 Supp.

Endnotes

1. *Vosburg v. Putney*, 50 N.W. 403 (Wis. 1891).
2. See H. Wallace & C. Roberson, *Principles of Criminal Law*, (Longman, White Plains, N.Y.) 1996.
3. The double jeopardy clause applies to state and federal actions. *Benton v. Maryland*, 395 U.S. 784 (1969).
4. *U.S. v. Carroll Towing Co.*, 159 F2d 169 (2nd Cir. 1947).
5. See the classic case of *In Re Polemis*, 3 K.B. 560 (Eng. 1921) for a full discussion of this concept.
6. See *Steed v. Imperial Airlines*, 524 P.2d 801 (Cal. 1974) where the court held that a stepchild was not a heir under the wrongful death statute and therefore could not recover damages even though the child suffered loses of economic support and moral guidance.
7. *Brown v. Blue*, 724 S.W. 2d 400 (Tex. App. 1986).
8. See *Restatement Second of Torts*, Section 21, American Law Institute (1995).
9. See *Restatement Second of Torts*, Section 13, American Law Institute (1995).
10. See *Restatement Second of Torts*, Section 31, American Law Institute (1995).
11. H. Wallace, "A Prosecutors Guide to Stalking," *The Prosecutor*, 26 (January/February 1995).
12. See *Restatement Second of Torts*, Section 40A, American Law Institute (1995).
13. Wade Prosser & Schwartz, *Cases and Materials on Torts*, 5th ed. (West Publishing Co., St. Paul, Minn.) 1984 w/ 1988 Supp, p. 64.
14. *Taylor v. Vallelunga*, 339 P.2d 910 (Cal. App. 1959).
15. See *Restatement Second of Torts*, Section 40A, American Law Institute (1995).
16. See *Restatement Second of Torts*, Section 46, American Law Institute (1995).
17. See *Restatement Second of Torts*, Section 46 Comment d, American Law Institute (1995).
18. Model Penal Code Section 2.06.
19. Model Penal Code Section 242.3.
20. Model Penal Code Section 2.06(6)(c) and Commentaries, Part 1, Section 2.06, p. 326.
21. See CALJIC No. 6.10.
22. See *Pinkerton v. United States*, 328 U.S. 640 (1949).
23. See *Restatement Second of Torts*, Section 433A Comment d, American Law Institute (1995).
24. See *Bierezynski v. Rogers*, 239 A.2d 218 (Del. 1968) which set forth this principle when dealing with two defendants engaged in drag racing on a public highway where one of the defendants struck the victim. The court held both were liable for injuries.
25. See H. Wallace, "The Battered Women Syndrome: Self-defence and Duress as Mandatory Defences?" *The Police Journal*, 133 (April–June 1994). (Note title uses English spelling.)
26. H. Wallace, *Family Violence: Legal, Medical and Social Perspectives*, (Allyn & Bacon, Boston) 1996.
27. *Katko v. Briney*, 183 N.W. 2d 657 (Iowa 1971).
28. For a case dealing with public necessity by public officials, see *Surocco v. Geary*, 3 Cal. 69 (1853); and for a case dealing with public necessity by a private person see *Harrison v. Wisdom*, 54 Tenn. 99 (1872).
29. See *Ploof v. Putnam*, 71 A. 188 (Vt. 1908) for a discussion of the defense of private necessity.

15

THIRD-PARTY LIABILITY AND INSURANCE

Chapter Outline

Introduction

Duty to Protect
  Landlords
  Other Relationships

Classifications of Parties
  Business Visitors or Invitees
  Licensees
  Trespassers

Theories of Liability
  Limited Duty Rule
  Prior Similar Incidents Rule
  Totality of the Circumstances Rule

Unlawful Activity
  Accidental Loss
  Intentional Acts

Life Insurance
  Introduction
  Accidental or Intentional Death

Homeowners' Insurance
  Introduction
  Sexual Assaults

Automobile Insurance
  Types of Coverage
  Uninsured and Underinsured Insurance
  No-Fault Insurance

Liability Insurance

Workers' Compensation
  Arising Out of and In the Course of Employment
  Benefits
  Exclusive Remedy

Summary

Key Terms

Discussion Questions

Suggested Readings

Learning Objectives

After reading this chapter, you should be able to:

- Distinguish between the various types of duty to protect persons entering upon lands
- Compare and contrast the different theories of liability
- Understand the distinction between intentional acts and accidental loss and how this distinction affects insurance
- Describe how life insurance policies are structured
- Discuss how the existence of automobile insurance may benefit victims of crime
- Explain workers' compensation laws and how these laws impact victims

Introduction

Many times victim service professionals must explain the complexities of criminal and civil law to victims. A question that always arises in these situations involves the obligation or duty of third parties and their failure to act to prevent injury. This chapter will examine the rights, duties, and liabilities of third parties. It is important to understand these concepts because typically, most perpetrators or their families will not have insurance or any other method to compensate victims for their injuries. In these situations, victims should determine if there are third parties that may be liable for their injuries.

Most intentional torts or negligence involves misfeasance which requires an affirmative act that results in harm to the victim. However, certain situations occur in which nonfeasance or the failure to act may also cause liability to attach. Most nonfeasance cases involve persons who have some relationship with the victim and observe that the victim is in danger, but fail to render assistance although they could do so easily and safely.

Several years ago in Queens, New York, thirty-eight citizens either watched or heard twenty-eight-year-old Kitty Genovese being attacked by a knife-wielding assailant. She was stalked and then stabbed many times during a thirty-minute period. Although she screamed for help, none of these citizens came to her aid. Finally, a neighbor of the victim called the police and they responded in less than two minutes. Unfortunately, it was too late for Ms. Genovese, who died of multiple stab wounds.[1] None of the thirty-eight citizens who observed or heard the attack were indicted by the state or sued by the victim's family. As sad as this scenario is, it highlights the general rule that a person is not generally liable criminally or civilly on the grounds that they failed to act.

As appalling as these facts are, this is still the law in most jurisdictions. Courts, however, have established several important exceptions to this general rule that allow victims of crime to take actions against third parties. Some of these exceptions are based on a duty to protect persons who enter upon the land of another.

Duty to Protect

A number of theories exist that hold property owners liable to persons injured on their property. One approach is to determine if the property owner owed a duty to protect the person from criminal acts of third parties. This is a confusing and often contradictory area of tort law. Courts using this approach have focused on a variety of factors in determining whether a landowner has a duty to protect those who enter upon their property. One of the most common situations deals with landlords and their tenants.

Landlords

Traditionally, landlords had no duty to protect tenants from acts of third parties. However, the classic case of *Kline v. Massachusetts Avenue Apartment Corporation* established the concept that landlords owed a duty to their tenants.[2] Kline moved into the apartments when the management provided a certain level of security. This security decreased during her residency. As a result, assaults, robberies, and larcenies increased. The landlord had notice of these events and was even urged by Kline to take steps to secure the building. The victim was subsequently assaulted and robbed in a common hallway of the apartment.

Kline sued and the court held the landlord liable stating that (1) the hallways were in the exclusive control of the landlord who was the only one with the power to make the area safe, (2) the court found an implied contract to continue to provide the same level of safety as was present when the victim rented the apartment, and

(3) the landlord was similar to an innkeeper and was in the best position to protect the guest from harm. The *Kline* court adopted a standard of "reasonable care" to determine whether a landlord fulfilled the duty of protection and held that when criminal acts were probable and predictable, a duty arose for the landlord "to take steps to protect tenants from foreseeable criminal acts committed by third parties."[3]

In *O'Hara v. Western Seven Trees Corporation*, the court found the landlord negligent for failing to protect the victim from a rape that occurred inside her apartment.[4] Before moving in, there had been several other rapes in the complex. Although the owners were aware of these facts, they assured O'Hara that the premise was safe and patrolled at all times by professional guards. The court found that liability attaches for failure to exercise reasonable care under the circumstances. Using *Kline* as a basis for its reasoning, the court held that the landlord was under a duty to secure the common areas, and the fact that the rape occurred inside the victim's apartment was not material.

In *L.M.S. v. Angeles Corporation*, the Alabama Supreme Court held that an apartment complex had a duty to maintain the victim's apartment in a safe condition.[5] The tenant was raped by a man who entered her apartment through her living room window. The tenant alleged that the landlord had failed to maintain her window in a safe condition and that had led to the sexual assault. The court held that the landlord knew or should have known of the condition that could result in an attack on the victim.

However, not all courts have found landlords liable for criminal acts committed on their premises. In *Cramer v. Balcor Property Management*, the South Carolina Supreme Court held that there was no duty imposed on a landlord to provide protection to tenants against the criminal acts of third parties.[6] A woman was murdered in her apartment in 1990. An unknown third party had pried open a sliding glass patio door, entered her apartment, and killed her. Her estate brought an action against the apartment alleging negligence. The court held that the mere fact of the existence of a landlord–tenant relationship does not by itself establish a duty to protect the tenant from criminal acts of third parties.

Other Relationships

The duty to protect applies to parties other than landlords. In *Young v. Huntsville Hospital*, the court found the hospital negligent for failing to protect a patient from a sexual assault.[7] The victim entered the hospital suffering from kidney stones. A male intruder entered her hospital room at approximately 6:00 A.M. and raped her while she lay helpless under heavy pain medication. The victim sued and the appellate court held that a special relationship was established because of the victim's status as a patient.

In *Snell v. O'Halloran, Inc.*, the court found a saloon owner negligent for failing to protect a patron from an attack in the saloon's parking lot.[8] After an argument regarding the use of a pool table, another patron followed the victim out of the saloon and attacked him in the parking lot. Four hours later, he died because of the beating. The court held that the owner knew or should have known that an attack on a patron was about to take place and thus should have intervened.

In *Erichsen v. No-Frills Supermarkets of Omaha, Inc.*, the Nebraska Supreme Court imposed a duty on business owners to use reasonable care to keep their premises safe for patrons from the criminal acts of third parties.[9] The victim, Janis L. Erichsen, was shopping at a No-Frills Supermarket. When she returned to her car, she was attacked and robbed by Terry Bennett, who sprayed her with mace and stole her purse. Bennett ran to his car in which an accomplice waited. The victim recovered from the mace and ran to the car in an attempt to regain her purse. In the ensuing struggle she became entangled in the seatbelt of the car and was dragged for over a mile by the perpetrators. She suffered third-degree burns on her feet and legs and tore her knee caps off. She subsequently underwent numerous surgeries to remove rocks from her body and to reconstruct her knees. She filed a personal injury action against the store, alleging that No-Frills owed her a duty to protect her from criminal activity. The Nebraska Supreme Court agreed with Erichsen, holding that since ten crimes had occurred in the No-Frills parking lot or surrounding area within the last sixteen months, there was a sufficient history of criminal activity to make such activities reasonably foreseeable thereby imposing a duty on the owner of property.

All courts, however, do not take such a sweeping view of victims' rights. In *Ann M. v. Pacific Plaza Shopping Center*, the California Supreme Court held that evidence of prior similar incidents of violent crime on the landowner's premise is almost always a prerequisite for finding that a landowner has a duty to provide security guards.[10] In that case, Ann M. brought a civil action against Pacific Plaza Shopping Center after she was raped on the premises. She was an employee in a photo shop located in a secluded area of the shopping center and was able to present evidence that there had been assaults and robberies in the shopping center previously, and that other employees and tenants were concerned about their safety. She alleged that the shopping center was negligent in failing to provide adequate security to protect her from unreasonable harm. The court held that because the financial and social burden of hiring security guards is so significant, a high degree of foreseeability is required to find that a landlord has a duty to provide these security measures. The court found that Pacific Plaza did not have notice of any violent criminal sexual assaults occurring on its premises. The court found that the prior physical assaults and robberies that occurred on the defendant's property were not similar enough in nature to the violent rape that the plaintiff had suffered to impose a duty on Pacific Plaza to hire security guards.

As this discussion suggests, determining whether there is a duty to protect persons who enter upon another's property can be a confusing and complex task. In an attempt to clarify this area of law, courts have turned to other methods of viewing the parties' roles and responsibilities. One of the simplest and most common methods of analyzing the rights of the parties is based on the traditional common law classification as to the nature of their visit to the property.

Classifications of Parties

Courts may examine the nature of the parties' relationships in evaluating any duty owed by the owner of property to persons entering upon that property. This relationship may require the property owner to act in certain ways or to maintain the property in a safe condition. The three most common classifications of parties are business visitor or invitee, licensee, or trespasser.

Business Visitors or Invitees

Certain occupations or businesses have always had a duty to furnish assistance to their customers. These customers are classified as business visitors or invitees. Common carriers such as railroads, bus lines, and airlines are mandated to go to the assistance of their passengers. In *Lopez v. Southern California Regional Transit District,* the court held the public carrier liable for injuries to passengers traveling on its bus.[11] The passengers were injured because of an altercation that occurred on the bus. The driver was notified of the situation, but failed to take any action. In holding the district liable, the court stated that because of the special relationship between the common carrier and its passengers, the district had a duty to protect them from the assaults. The court further held that passengers have no control over who enters the bus and are dependent upon the driver to control the situation.

Innkeepers are in much the same situation and because of the special relationship that exists between the business and its guests, innkeepers are mandated to protect their guests from certain types of injuries. In a famous case, the actress Connie Francis was sexually assaulted in her room at a Howard Johnson Motel. She filed suit and recovered monetary damages from the motel chain for failing to provide adequate room security.

Courts have extended to business relationships the concept of a duty of care owed to guests. Most jurisdictions now accept the rule that any business must furnish a warning, and assistance, to its patrons. The modern view is that owners of property owe a duty not only to those invited onto the property, but also to members of the public who enter the property to conduct business. In other words, owners owe a duty to those they invite onto the property to conduct business, as well as to those that a reasonable person would foresee would enter upon the property for purposes for which the property is held open to the general public. It is not necessary that the person make a purchase on the premises to be classified as an invitee as long as that person had a general business relationship with the owner of the property.

Invitees are owed a reasonable duty of care by owners of businesses. Owners must inspect their premises for hidden dangers. This does not mean that the owners must find and remedy all hidden dangers, only that they exercise reasonable care in making the inspections. What constitutes reasonable care will vary with the nature of the business conducted on the property. Thus the owner of a private home who invites a door-to-door salesperson to enter has a lesser duty than the owner of a large department store who has hundreds of patrons each day.

Owners must use reasonable care to exercise control over third parties. Business owners must take reasonable security measures to protect customers from attacks or thefts. Private businesses are not the only classifications of property owners that owe invitees a duty of care. Courts have also recognized that in certain situations, public institutions such as universities also owe a duty to protect their students from injury. In *Peterson v. San Francisco Community College District*, the court held a community college liable for injuries suffered by a student as a result of a foreseeable criminal assault in the college's parking lot.[12]

Licensees

A licensee is another type of relationship that requires owners of property to exercise a certain duty of care. A *licensee* is a person who has the owner's consent to be on the property, but who is not conducting business on the property. Licensees are owed a duty of care, but it is lower than that of the business visitor or invitee. The main category of persons who are classified as licensees are social guests. These persons, even though they are invited by the owner, do not attain the status of "invitee" because that term is reserved in tort law for persons who are conducting business on the property.

In *Barmore v. Elmore*, the victim and the defendant were members of a fraternal organization.[13] The victim went to the defendant's home to discuss lodge business. While he was at the home, the defendant's mentally ill son attacked him with a knife. The victim sued claiming that the defendant owed him a duty to keep the premise reasonably safe. The court found that the victim was a mere licensee and not an invitee, because the discussion of the lodge benefitted the lodge and not the defendant. Because the victim was only a licensee, the defendant had no duty to maintain the premise in a safe condition, but merely a duty to warn him of known dangers. The evidence established that the defendant was unaware that his son posed a danger to others.

As *Barmore* points out, the main difference between the duty owed to a licensee and an invitee is that there is no duty to inspect for unknown dangers for a licensee. The justification for this distinction is that a social guest is only a licensee because guests understand that the owner does not take any special precautions for their safety. Although licensees do not rate the same duty of care as an invitee, owners of property that know of a dangerous condition on their property must warn the licensee of this danger. However, the owner of property is under no duty to inspect the premise for hidden dangers.

Trespassers

The general rule is that owners of property owe no duty to a trespasser to make their land safe, or to protect a trespasser in any other way. The rationale behind this position is that property owners should be able to use their property as they see fit, without worrying about the safety of those who have no right to be on it. There are exceptions to this general rule however, most notably the attractive nuisance doctrine. This theory holds that a landowner is liable to a child if that child enters upon the property to use or enjoy a condition that reasonable persons agree would entice or beckon children.

Some states are beginning to reject the complex and confusing classification scheme that determines the standard of duty owed a person entering upon land.

The California Supreme Court rejected the old classification and adopted an approach that asks whether in the management of the property, the owner has acted as a reasonable person in view of the possibility of injury to others.[14] Other states continue to used the invitee, licensee, and trespasser classification to determine liability.

Theories of Liability

Most courts accept the general principle that a property owner owes a duty to protect other persons if a crime or injury is foreseeable. Foreseeability is a complex legal theory that is beyond the scope of this chapter. However, simply defined, *foreseeability* states that a person is liable only for those consequences of his or her negligence which were reasonably foreseeable at the time he or she acted or, having a duty to do so, failed to act. Defining foreseeability is only the first step to understanding the duty owed by property owners to victims injured on their property. There are a number of legal theories or justifications for holding third parties liable for injuries of persons on their property without regard to their status as visitors, licensees, or trespassers. Unfortunately, the law is not uniform and different states have adopted different rationales.

Limited Duty Rule

One common rule is the *limited duty rule* which defines liability as arising only in those situations in which the criminal act was imminent.[15] Courts following this rationale usually require proof that the property owner knew of or had reason to know that a crime was going to occur and thus could have prevented it. The limited duty rule is based on the theory that protecting citizens from criminal activity is the responsibility of the government and not the duty of private businesses. Interestingly, this rule holds that a past history of criminal acts on the premises is not sufficient to give rise to a duty to protect customers. For example, in *Ortell v. Spencer Co.* the fact that there were over eighty assaults, thefts, robberies, or burglaries within a two-block area surrounding a convenience store, including eight incidents in the store itself, was not sufficient to create a duty to protect a customer who was robbed and sexually assaulted on the premises.[16] This rule has been criticized as making recovery for criminal acts almost impossible.[17]

Prior Similar Incidents Rule

The *prior similar incidents rule* holds that liability is determined by the number of prior criminal acts occurring on or near the premises.[18] The fact that similar criminal activity has occurred is considered a critical element under this rationale. Both the type of criminal activity and its timeliness and location are considered in establishing liability using the prior similar incidents rule. In *Atamina v. Supermarkets Gen. Corp.*, the court found the business liable, holding that there was a duty to protect a rape victim who was assaulted in the same supermarket's parking lot where there had been five previous assaults.[19] Under this approach, the fact that there was no prior crime on the premises is almost always a bar to the victim's suit. For example, in *Feder v. Banker's Trust Co.*, the bank was not liable for damages when bank customers were robbed after leaving the bank because the bank had experienced no previous crime.[20] This rule has been criticized as allowing businesses "one free crime" before imposing liability.[21]

Totality of the Circumstances Rule

The *totality of the circumstances rule* will consider prior crimes and a variety of other circumstances in determining liability. Thus, even though there have been no prior criminal acts completed on the premises, the fact that the business maintains poor lighting in its parking lot and is located in a high–crime rate neighborhood may establish liability under the totality of the circumstances rule.[22]

This rule has been criticized as establishing liability for businesses that have a crime-free environment on their premise simply because they are located in a general area of the city that may have a high crime rate. Poor areas of most inner cities have some level of criminal activity and under this rule, liability might attach because of location rather than other factors.

Third parties can be individuals or businesses. Persons other than the perpetrator may have contributed to the victim's injury. However, like the perpetrator, these parties may not have sufficient funds or resources to make the victim whole. Once it has been determined that a third party has insurance, the methods of recovery from those insurance policies must be evaluated. The remainder of this chapter examines the various sources of recovery from insurance policies.

Unlawful Activity

The unlawful activity area of insurance deals with unlawful contracts or activity. Most courts will hold that any insurance policy that violates public policy, a statute, or is an integral part of some prohibited activity is void and unenforceable. Additionally, many courts will not allow the insured to recover any premiums paid for the policy. The U.S. Supreme Court has held that any insurance policy that endangers the public interests or "injuriously affect[s] the public good, or which is subversive of sound morality, ought never to receive the sanctions of a court of justice or be made the foundation of its judgment."[23] However, in many situations there is "no clear bright line" that distinguishes between unlawful activity and cases involving lawful, unique, factual situations. These types of cases involve property as well as individuals.

Accidental Loss

Insurance coverage is provided for accidental loss and not for intentional acts. Thus, even when there is no limitation expressly spelled out in the insurance policy, courts have recognized various implied exceptions to insurance coverage, including certain types of losses and certain types of conduct. Most insurance policies include a requirement that the loss be *caused by accident*.[24] In addition to using "accidental" terminology, most policies set forth explicit limitations or restrictions on the type of loss that will be covered.

The principle that insurance policies will cover only accidental loss means that no proceeds will be paid if it is determined that the loss was intentionally caused by the insured. The fact that most intentional torts involve acts that also constitute violations of criminal codes supports the judicial position that "an insurer may not contract to indemnify an insured against the civil consequences of . . . willful criminal conduct."[25] For example in *Haser v. Maryland Casualty Company,* a passenger in a taxi was raped by the driver and another passenger. When the victim attempted to collect from the taxi cab's insurance company, the court disallowed payment of any funds from the insurer on the ground that such coverage would be contrary to public policy because the acts were intentional.[26]

Intentional Acts

Arson is a common crime that sometimes causes the victim to suffer a huge financial loss. If the owner of a building intentionally burns it down, the loss is not considered accidental and the owner would receive no property insurance payment. However, if a building is destroyed as a result of arson by a third party who has no connection to the owner, fire insurance will provide indemnification and pay the proceeds listed in the policy.

Courts have ordered payment when items were stolen by a husband after the spouse filed for divorce and obtained a restraining order barring the husband from the premise.[27] The courts view this situation as one in which the spouse did not intend to suffer the loss even though her husband committed an intentional act of theft. This is a classic example of how the perspective from which an act is viewed changes the rules regarding whether insurance proceeds are recoverable.

Although courts will usually bar recovery if the acts of the insured are classified as intentional, victims have found a variety of ways to seek compensation from insurance companies by pleading distinct or alternate theories of recovery in their complaints. Even if it is clear that the perpetrator acted intentionally, there may be others who also bear some or all of the responsibility for the perpetrator's acts. For example, a business may have hired a parking lot attendant who had a known history of assaultive behavior. If the attendant assaults the victim, there are several alleged theories that will allow the victim recovery from the business' insurance company.

Life Insurance

Introduction

Life insurance is a contract to make specific payments upon the death of the person whose life is insured. There are several parties involved in life insurance policies: (1) the insurer or company which issued the policy; (2) the owner of the policy, who has the power to name or change the beneficiary and the obligation to pay the premiums; (3) the person whose life is the subject of the policy, known as the insured (or *cestui que vie*); and (4) the beneficiary to whom the proceeds are paid. In many instances, most of these parties will be the same people. For example, the owner of the policy and the insured, in most situations, are the same.

Life insurance policies usually provide for benefits to be paid in the event of the insured's death, with two major exceptions: (1) when the death results from criminal activities by the insured, or (2) when the death is a result of suicide. Absent these situations, the policy will be paid without undue inquiry. Many life insurance policies provide additional funds in the event that death results from accidental means. These policies double the amount of the payment to the beneficiary and are known as "double indemnity" clauses.

Many life insurance policies expressly deny coverage when the insured is engaged in criminal activities. In *Powell v. New York Life Insurance Company*, the court ruled in favor of the insurance company.[28] The insured decedent, while beating his wife, was shot and killed by his son. The court upheld the policy language excluding payment of the accidental death benefit if the death resulted from the commission, by the insured, of an assault or other felony. Even in the absence of express language in the policy denying coverage, many courts will deny benefits under a life insurance or accidental insurance policy on an implied exception based on public policy grounds. The courts will rule that when a death was a reasonably foreseeable risk or consequence, insurance coverage should be denied. For instance, courts have upheld the denial of coverage when the insured died as a result of a self-administered injection of heroin.[29] The rationale for this position is that when death results from criminal activities, the death did not occur as a result of accidental means.

The courts and many state legislatures have addressed the issue of suicide by the insured. The great majority of insurance policies include clauses that limit the insurance company's liability in the event the insured commits suicide within a specified number of years (usually one or two) from the commencement of the coverage.[30] Following this specified period, most insurance policies are required to pay the death benefits.[31]

Accidental or Intentional Death

One critical issue in the area of accidental or intentional death is determining which perspective is used in analyzing whether a loss was accidental or intentional. Most jurisdictions hold that the determination of whether a loss was accidental is based on the point of view of the person whose economic interest is protected by the insurance policy.[32] Most of the time that person is the insured. For example, in property insurance cases, the person who sustains the financial loss as a result of damage to the property is normally the insured.

In life insurance cases, the economic interest that is being protected is the beneficiary's, not the person whose life is covered by the insurance. The beneficiaries are the ones who receive economic benefit as a result of the death of the insured. Therefore, if the insured dies as a result of a homicide committed by anyone other than a beneficiary, the death is not intentional from the beneficiary's perspective. This means that payment of the life insurance proceeds to the beneficiary is required. This area becomes more complex in cases involving the death of an insured who participated in a fight or altercation. Most courts will order payment of the proceeds if the insured did not start or provoke the fight.[33] Many courts view such an incident from the decedent's point of view. Even if he initiated the fight, some courts will examine whether death was a foreseeable result. If death was not foreseeable, benefits will be paid because the death will be presumed to be accidental.

Homeowners' Insurance

Introduction

Most homeowners' insurance policies include fire and casualty coverage. *Fire insurance* generally covers any loss by fire, other than that deliberately caused by the insured, to property specifically listed on the policy. *Casualty insurance* generally includes coverage for legal liability, burglary and theft, accidents and health, and/or property damage.

In some situations, perpetrators have committed crimes against victims who have subsequently sued the offender and the offender's insurance company. Many of these actions involve the perpetrator's homeowner's policy. A number of courts hold that intentional acts such as crimes are specifically excluded from coverage.

Sexual Assaults

One fast-growing and controversial area of homeowners' insurance litigation involves claims for sexual assault.[34] There is no "clear bright line" that establishes the insurer's liability in this area. The result is a series of often conflicting case decisions that only add to the stress suffered by victims.

When sexual abuse or exploitation is discovered, some victims or their families pursue civil remedies to recover for injuries suffered because of the crime. These civil actions involve suing the perpetrator and adding as a party in the lawsuit the perpetrator's insurance company. The rationale for such a tactic is that most individuals do not have sufficient personal funds to make the victim whole, whereas insurance companies have thousands of dollars for just such a purpose.

Most courts deny coverage to the insured perpetrator of sexual abuse when the offender is an adult and the victim is a minor. In many of these cases the courts rely on the *inferred intent rule* that states intent to injure is inferred as a matter of law from the act of abuse itself.

In *Goldsmith v. Physicians Insurance Company,* an adult homeowner was sued for sexually abusing three minor boys.[35] The homeowner's insurance policy specifically excluded coverage for bodily injury expected or intended by the insured. The court denied coverage acknowledging that its decision might mean innocent victims of sexual abuse would not be able to recover damages for all their injuries. However, the court found it more important to uphold the principle that perpetrators of intentional acts not be able to escape having to personally compensate their victims. In explaining its position regarding the rule of inferred intent the court stated:

> *The courts following the majority approach have concluded that sexual miscon-
> duct with a minor is objectively so substantially certain to result in harm to the
> minor, that the perpetrator cannot be allowed to escape society's determination
> that he or she is expected to know that. Hence, these courts infer the intent to
> harm as a matter of law.*[36]

This approach was followed in *Nationwide Mutual Insurance Co. v. Abernathy*, which involved a homeowner's policy that excluded coverage for bodily injury expected or intended by the insured.[37] In this case, the insured adult was sued for sexually abusing one of his minor-aged music students over a period of seven years. He pled guilty to criminal charges arising out of these acts and the parents of the child filed a civil action against him and his homeowner's insurance to recover for injuries arising out of the molest. The child's damages included mental, emotional, and psychological harm and the medical costs associated with treating these injuries. The North Carolina Court of Appeals denied coverage finding that as a matter of law, an adult who abuses a child intends, or at least expects, to harm the child.

In certain situations the inferred intent rule does not apply. Various jurisdictions are split in regard to whether the rule applies in situations involving abuse committed by a minor. In *Fire Insurance Exchange v. Diehi*, a minor-aged boy committed two sexual assaults on a minor-aged girl.[38] The perpetrator was between seven and nine years old and the victim was between four and six years old. The boy's parents had a homeowner's policy that excluded intentional acts committed by the insured or members of that family. In finding that the insurance company was required to pay for the victim's injuries, the court stated that there was no evidence that an average seven- to nine-year-old child could reasonably foresee that his sexual acts could harm another child. The court acknowledged the majority rule regarding inferred intent; however, it held that it would be untenable to apply that objective adult standard in cases of sexual abuse by a child.

The jurisdictions are also split on whether to apply the inferred intent rule when the sexual abuse involves abuse by an adult of another adult. In *Aetna Life & Casualty Co. v. Barthelemy*, an eighteen-year-old female college student alleged that a nineteen-year-old male college student had sex with her while they were both intoxicated.[39] She charged the perpetrator with battery, negligent or reckless conduct, and reckless infliction of emotional distress. It was stipulated by all parties that the man was covered by his parent's homeowner's policy. That policy had the standard exclusion for expected or intended acts or injuries by the insured. The Third Circuit held that for the exclusion to apply, the insured must specifically intend to cause harm, not merely intend to do the act. The court distinguished this situation from those involving adults who sexually molest children by pointing out that the victim was eighteen, she consented to the act, no criminal charges had been filed, and that both participants were intoxicated. The court concluded by finding that the perpetrator was covered by his parents' policy.

Homeowners' policies were originally established to protect the insured homeowner against accidental or unexpected losses such as fire or theft of property. However, as victims continue to search for methods of obtaining redress from perpetrators, homeowners' insurance presents a viable alternative that under some limited circumstances allows for recovery. This is not a turning aside of the original intent in establishing homeowners' insurance, rather it is an acknowledgment by courts and society that victims have a right to be made whole and they may look toward insurance policies as one alternative.

Automobile Insurance

Since the first automobile traveled a public thoroughfare, accidents and injuries have occurred. States have responded with legislation in an attempt to provide indemnification for those injured in these accidents. Automobile accidents are the primary source of tort claims for serious injury and death in the United States.[40] This has resulted in numerous statutes that regulate automobile insurance within the various states.

Types of Coverage

Most automobile insurance policies provide coverage for accidents that occur, without regard to whether those events were the fault of the insured or another party. The principle coverage in automobile insurance policies are of three types: (1) *collision coverage,* which applies to damage to the insured automobile resulting from a collision with another object such as a car, tree, lamppost, etc.; (2) *comprehensive coverage,* which applies to damage to an insured vehicle resulting from acts of nature such as earthquakes, fires, or other acts such as theft; and (3) *medical payments,* which provide for payment of medical expenses that arise out of injuries resulting from operation of the automobile.

One of the first questions to be answered when a person is involved in an automobile accident is, "Who is the insured person?" Victims may determine the identity of the principle insured by reading the names listed on the declarations page, which is the front page contained in most automobile insurance policies. The liability coverage in automobile insurance policies normally extends to the named insured and members of that family who reside in the same household. Traditionally, this means that family members who meet certain requirements such as age are covered when operating the insured automobile and when driving other vehicles. Additionally, most policies provide for insurance coverage of the identified vehicle so that nonfamilial members who operate that particular vehicle will also be covered. Therefore, victims should review both the relationship of the tortfeasor to the named insured and examine who owned the vehicle that the tortfeasor was driving. Depending on the facts, there may be the option of recovering from either or both of these sources.

Until recently some automobile policies excluded specific persons or classes of persons from recovering damages. Insurance companies developed coverage limitations that excluded family members from recovering from any other family member residing in the same household. These limitations were designed to prevent collusive or fake lawsuits filed by one family member against another. Insurance companies believed that fraudulent lawsuits would be significantly reduced if claims between family members were precluded.[41] At the time these exclusions were developed, society had accepted that family members should not be able to sue each other. There was widespread acceptance of public policies that endorsed intrafamilial immunity (family members were precluded from suing each other), interspousal immunity (except for divorce, spouses could not sue each other), and guest statutes (which prevented guests from suing the persons who invited them onto their property). These limitations no longer apply, but they serve as an historical reminder of how public attitudes can affect a victim's ability to recover for injuries.

Uninsured and Underinsured Insurance

Two other types of automobile insurance need to be briefly reviewed: uninsured and underinsured motorist insurance. Uninsured motorist insurance is included in most automobile insurance policies. It is first-party insurance, which means that insurance proceeds are paid by the insurance company to the person who is listed as the insured in the policy. It is also a "fault-based" type of coverage because it will pay benefits only when the insured is legally entitled to recover damages from an uninsured driver. In other words, the insured must not be at fault or cause the accident.[42]

Uninsured motorist policies list three distinct classes of insured: (1) the named insured and members of the insured's family who are residents of the same household, (2) persons who are injured by riding in the insured's vehicle, and (3) persons who sustain consequential damages as a result of the injuries suffered by the insured.

Underinsured motorist insurance is designed to address situations in which the victim suffers injuries whose cost to treat far exceed the normal coverage mandated by the various states' financial responsibility laws. These are laws that require the driver of a car to maintain a certain minimum level of insurance as a condition of being able to legally operate a motor vehicle. This type of insurance allows an insured to raise the amount of coverage in the policy to a level that the insured believes will protect him or her from financial loss in the event of an accident.

No-Fault Insurance

The final form of automobile insurance that needs to be examined is called no-fault insurance. No-fault insurance requires that persons injured in automobile accidents be indemnified for medical expenses, lost wages, and the cost of replacement services. This type of insurance is usually referred to as personal injury protection (PIP).

Starting in 1925 and continuing into the 1960s, states examined the possibility of establishing some form of mandatory no-fault insurance. In 1965 Professors

Keeton and O'Connell published a seminal text in the area of automobile insurance.[43] This text, *Basic Protection for the Traffic Victim*, conducted an in-depth study of the automobile insurance compensation system and concluded that neither the first-party insurance nor the state financial responsibility laws provided sufficient coverage and compensation for victims who were seriously injured in automobile accidents. Keeton and O'Connell then proposed an extensive no-fault insurance system for traffic victims. No-Fault insurance differs from traditional automobile insurance in three ways: (1) it replaces the "fault-based" system with one that eliminates fault in certain circumstances, (2) it substitutes first-party insurance for third-party insurance, and (3) it limits recovery to purely pecuniary losses.

Massachusetts was the first state in the nation to adopt such a no-fault automobile insurance system. Many states have followed Massachusetts' lead and have adopted no-fault systems. These statutes generally preclude victims from suing the perpetrator if their injuries are below a certain amount. However, all states allow victims to sue if they suffer serious physical injury. This allows victims to sue for pain and suffering as well as financial losses.[44]

Liability Insurance

Another common form of insurance is *comprehensive general liability insurance,* also known as third-party liability insurance, which is purchased by a business that desires liability protection from acts by third parties that may arise out of a broad range of risks. The most common form of this insurance in use today is the commercial general liability (CGL) policy. This type of policy provides coverage for bodily injury and property damage which the insured becomes legally obligated to pay as damages. CGL coverage extends to a wide spectrum of activities including customers' personal injury lawsuits. CGL normally requires that the injury result from "an accident, including continuous or repeated exposure to substantially the same general harmful conditions."

Victims of crimes may be successful in suing CGL insurance companies by alleging negligence on the part of the insured.[45] Coverage has been found to exist even though the employee was engaged in intentional crimes. Often the offender will have little if any resources, and victims may look to the insurance company based on a theory of negligence in hiring or supervising the perpetrator. In *Silverball Amusement, Inc. v. Utah Home Fire Insurance Company,* an employee with a prior history of violence molested a nine-year-old child and plead guilty to first-degree sexual assault.[46] The child filed a civil action against the company claiming it was negligent in hiring the perpetrator. The court held the insurer was obligated to provide coverage because the victim was alleging negligence against the company and the fact that the perpetrator's act was intentional could not be used as defense by the company. The court stated that the concept of negligent hiring does not mean that the employer intended its employees inflict harm on others. In *Society of the Roman Catholic Church of the Diocese of Lafayette v. Interstate Fire & Casualty Co.,* two priests molested thirty-one children between 1976 and 1983.[47] The parties agreed that the abuse had occurred and settled all the claims but were unable to agree among themselves on the allocation of loss. Therefore a dispute existed between the primary carrier, excess carriers, and the diocese, who was self-insured, as to who would pay which portion of the judgment. The court held that all the parties would contribute based on the percentage of coverage it had at the time of the molestation.

Not all lawsuits against CGL insurance carriers are successful. *Lopez v. New Mexico Public Schools Insurance Authority* involved a teacher who was accused of molesting a student.[48] The school board and school district were also named parties. The defendants were insured under a CGL policy that excluded sexual assaults by any employee of the insured. The court held that the insurer had no duty to defend or indemnify its insured for any tort claims arising out of the sexual assault. Court decisions on the issue of liability insurance continue to create confusion in this area. Victims and professionals who work in this area need to be aware of the evolving case law.

Workers' Compensation

One complex area of the law involves workers' compensation laws. These laws are a form of strict liability and are completely statutory in nature. Every state has adopted some form of workers' compensation law that compensates employees for on-the-job injuries without regard for fault. The no-fault or strict liability approach applies even if the employer has a perfect safety record and takes every possible precaution to make the workplace a safe environment.

Many states have separate workers' compensation boards or panels. The state mandates certain benefits be awarded in the event of a job-related injury. If either party disagrees with this statutory award, that party may ask for a hearing. Most statutes are worded in such a manner as to give a preference to compensating the worker for any injuries suffered during employment. If one party is unhappy with the award, that party may appeal the decision.

Arising Out of and In the Course of Employment

The typical statute applies to all injuries that arise out of and in the course of employment. There is an abundance of litigation in this area of workers' compensation. Normally, purely personal activities are not covered by the law. For example, if the employee left the workplace and went to a commercial mall to do some personal shopping, many statutes would disallow coverage if the employee were injured while in the mall.

Some statutes deny coverage if the worker is injured while intoxicated on the job. Similarly, other workers' compensation statutes do not provide coverage if the worker is engaged in illegal activities at the time of the injury. Finally, approximately one-third of the states deny coverage if it can be shown that the worker willfully disregarded safety regulations.

The jurisdictions are split on whether injuries suffered by employees traveling to or from their employment would be covered under the arising out of employment concept. *Wilson v. Workers' Compensation Appeals Board* involved a school teacher that was transporting homework that she had graded at home back to school when she was injured in a car accident.[49] The court held she was not covered by workers' compensation because she graded the papers at home for her own convenience and therefore it was considered purely personal in nature. Even in California, where *Wilson* was decided, several exceptions allow for coverage when traveling to and from employment. Other states allow for coverage in this area.

The modern trend in workers' compensation law is to treat attacks by third parties that injure employees as within the scope of the law. This is true even if employees' duties do not require them to deal with a specific attacker or the specific assault occurred after hours so long as the injury arose out of activities that are somehow related to the victims' employment. For example, one court awarded benefits to an employee who was attacked after normal working hours by a perpetrator when the employee tried to prevent him from stealing company equipment.[50]

Benefits

A worker recovers specific benefits that are listed in the statute. The employee is limited to recovery of direct expenses and loss of earning power and is almost never allowed to recover for pain and suffering associated with the injury. The awards are for loss of earning capacity and do not consider the severity of the injury.

Most states have a limit on the amount an employee can recover. This is normally referred to as the *average wage* of the typical worker. The statute then awards a portion of this amount for a specified time. In the event of total or permanent disability, most statutes award two-thirds of this amount for the remainder of the worker's life.

Exclusive Remedy

An understanding of workers' compensation law is important because many courts have held that it is the exclusive remedy available to an employee injured on the job. Thus, even if the employer were clearly negligent and allowed an unsafe work condition to exist with resulting injuries to an employee, the only remedy would be under the workers' compensation laws. Although workers' compensation laws are the exclusive remedy for employees, it does not prevent them from suing third parties who, under common law theories, are liable for the worker's injuries.

Fortunately, for victims of crimes that occur while they are on the job, the courts have limited workers' compensations laws to nonintentional acts by the employer. In other words, if victims can prove that the employer intentionally caused the injury, they can use the common law torts as a basis for recovery. This is the complete opposite of most insurance law in which allegations of intentional acts might bar recovery! This would allow for damages for pain and suffering as well as punitive damages if appropriate. The intentional nature of the act must be an actual intent to injure. Most courts will not allow recovery for failure to follow the law even if the employer knowingly failed to observe safety regulations that resulted in the employee's injury.[51]

Summary

When victims of crime attempt to obtain compensation from the perpetrators, they may find that these individuals have little or no assets. Many offenders may not have insurance. However, there is another alternative. More crime victims are suing the owners of the property where the criminal activity occurred. These law-suits may provide the victim of a crime with funds that will compensate them for their loss.

Liability for injuries that occur on another's property may involve a number of legal theories. One approach analyzes the relationship between the property owner and the victim. The status of the victim may determine the nature and duty of care owed by the property owner. Other courts have looked at different theo-ries of liability to determine the duty of care.

Victim service providers must be aware of these different aspects of tort law that may provide victims with the right to recover for their injuries. It is not uncommon to allege several different theories in the complaint. Once discovery has commenced, and all the facts are known, the victim can then select the best theory of recovery and proceed with the lawsuit with some certainty of success.

Many perpetrators of crimes do not have any assets that allow the victim of a crime to obtain payment for injury suffered as a result of the incident. In these sit-uations, victims have looked to other sources in an effort to make them whole financially. Insurance is one of the most common sources available to victims of crime.

There are a number of different types of insurance by which victims may be able to receive a monetary award to compensate them for their injuries. Insurance law is a complex area that is constantly changing because of the enactment of new laws, as well as the issuance of court decisions changing existing laws. One com-mon principle in the area of insurance is that it applies to accidental loss and usu-ally does not cover intentional acts or crimes committed by the insured.

Even with the intentional act exclusion, victims of crime may still be able to recover if they can show that other parties were responsible for the perpetrator's acts, or that although the perpetrator acted willfully the consequences were not intended. Additionally, in the area of workers' compensation law, intentional acts are covered if they result in injury to the victim while employed.

Victim service providers must be aware of the various types of insurance poli-cies and be able to explain them to victims of crime. Suing insurance companies is not a matter of finding a "deep pocket to gouge" so much as it is attempting to compensate victims of crime for serious financial losses imposed on them by crim-inals. Society has made a determination that under some circumstances, insurance companies are better suited to bear this loss than the victim.

Key Terms

Licensee is a person who has the owner's consent to be on the property, but who is not conducting business on the property.

Foreseeability holds that a person is liable only for those consequences of his or her negligence which were reasonably foreseeable at the time he or she acted or, having a duty to do so, failed to act.

Limited duty rule defines liability as arising only in those situations in which the criminal act was imminent.

Prior similar incidents rule holds that liability is determined by the number of prior criminal acts occurring on or near the premises.

Totality of the circumstances rule will consider prior crimes and a variety of other circumstances in determining liability.

Life insurance is a contract to make specific payments upon the death of the person whose life is insured.

Fire insurance generally covers any loss by fire, other than that deliberately caused by the insured, to property specifically listed on the policy.

Casualty insurance generally includes coverage for legal liability, burglary and theft, accidents and health, and/or property damage.

Inferred intent rule states that intent to injure is inferred as a matter of law from the act of abuse itself.

Collision coverage applies to damage to the insured automobile resulting from a collision with another object such as a car, tree, lamppost, etc.

Comprehensive coverage applies to damage to an insured vehicle resulting from acts of nature such as earthquakes, fires, or other acts such as theft.

Medical payments provide for payment of medical expenses that arise out of injuries resulting from operation of the automobile.

Comprehensive general liability insurance also known as *third-party liability insurance*, is purchased by a business that desires liability protection from acts by third parties that may arise out of a broad range of risks.

Discussion Questions

1. Should duty be determined by the nature of the landowner's occupation?

2. Should we treat invitees different than licensees?

3. Compare the various theories of liability and list each of their shortcomings. Which theory is best from the property owner's perspective? Which theory is best from the victim's perspective?

4. Should intentional acts be covered by insurance? If they were covered should the insured have to pay more for such coverage?

5. Should workers' compensation laws be no-fault? Why? Why not?

Suggested Readings

Keeton & Wydiss, *Insurance Law,* (West Publishing Co., St. Paul, Minn.) 1988.

Prosser & Keeton, *Hornbook on Torts,* 5th ed. (West Publishing Co., St. Paul, Minn.) 1984 with 1988 Supp.

Endnotes

1. For a more complete account of the attack, see *New York Times*, 27 March 1964.
2. 439 F.2d 477 (D.C. Cir. 1970).
3. Id. at 484, 485.
4. 75 Cal. App. 3d 798 (1977).
5. 621 So.2d 246 (Ala. 1993).
6. 441 S.E.2d 317 (1994).
7. 595 So.2d 1386 (Ala. 1992).
8. No. A-91-617, 1993 Neb.App. LEXIS 221 (Neb.Ct.App. April 20, 1993).
9. 518 N.W.2d 116 (1994).
10. 836 P.2d 207 (Cal. 1993).
11. 710 P.2d 907 (Cal. 1985).
12. 685 P. 2d 1193 (Cal. 1984).
13. 403 N.E.2d 1355 (Ill.App.Ct.1980).
14. *Rowland v. Christian*, 443 P.2d 561 (Cal. 1968).
15. See Sharp, "Paying for the Crimes of Others? Landlord Liability for Crimes on the Premises," 29 *S. Texas L. Rev.* 11 (1987) and *Henley v. Pizitz Reality Co.*, 456 So.2d 272 (Ala. 1984).
16. 477 So. 2d 299 (Ala. 1985).
17. *Nappier v. Kincade*, 666 S.W.2d 858 (Mo. Ct. App. 1984).
18. *Brown v. National Supermarkets, Inc.* 678 W.W.2d 307 (Mo.Ct. App. 1984).
19. 369 A.2d 38 (N.J. 1976).
20. 509 N.Y.S.2d 447 (N.Y. App. Term 1986).
21. See Comment, "Business Inviters' Duty to Protect Invitees from Criminal Acts," 134 *University of Penn. L. Rev.* 883 (1986).
22. *Issaacs v. Huntington Memorial Hosp.*, 695 P.2d 653 (Cal. 1985).
23. *Ritter v. Mutual Life Ins. Co.*, 169 U.S. 139 (1989).
24. See *Haser v. Maryland Casualty Company*, 78 N.D. 893, 53 N.W. 2d 508 (1952) discussed in detail in the text.
25. *Ambassador Insurance Company v. Montes*, 78 N.J. 477, 483, 388 A.2d 603, 606 (1978).
26. *Haser v. Maryland Casualty Company*, 78 N.D. 893, 53 N.W. 2d 508 (1952).
27. *Simon v. Security Insurance Company*, 390 Mich. 72, 210 N.W. 2d 322 (1973).
28. 120 So.2d 33 (Fla. App.2d Dist. 1960).
29. *Gordon v. Metropolitan Life Insurance Company*, 256 Md. 320, 260 A.2d 338 (1970).
30. *Seattle-First National Bank v. Crown Life Insurance Company*, 365 F.2d 280 (9th Cir. 1966).
31. *Franklin v. John Hancock Mutual Life Insurance Company*, 298 N.Y. 81, 80 N.E. 2d 746 (1948).
32. See *Wynglass v. Prudential Life Insurance Company of America*, 68 Mich. App. 514, 242 N.W. 2d 824 (1976).
33. *Smith v. Equitable Life Assurance Society*, 614 F.2d 720, 723 (10th Cir. 1908).
34. See for example, Christopher B. Daly, "Sexual Abuse Cases Taking a Rising Toll on Catholic Church," *Philadelphia Inquirer*, Nov. 6, 1944, D3.
35. 1994 Ky. App. LEXIS 127 (Ky. Ct. App. Oct. 21, 1994).
36. Id.
37. 445 S.E. 2d 618 (N.C.Ct.App.1994).
38. 520 N.W. 2d 675 (Mich.Ct.App. 1994).
39. 33 F.3d 189 (3rd Cir. 1994).
40. Jennifer H. Arlen, "Compensation Systems and Efficient Deterrence," 52 *Maryland Law Rev.* 1093 (1993).
41. See *Mutual of Enumclaw Insurance Company v. Wiscomb*, 95 Wn.2d 373, 622 P. 2d 1234 (1980).
42. Alan L. Widiss, "Uninsured Motorist Coverage: Observations on Litigating Over When a Claimant is 'Legally Entitled to Recover,' " 68 *Iowa Law Rev.* 397(1983).
43. Robert E. Keeton and Jeffery O'Connell, *Basic Protection for the Traffic Victim*, (Little Brown and Company, Boston) 1965.
44. Michael J. Trebilcock, "Incentive Issues in the Design of 'No-Fault' Compensation Systems," 39 *Univ. Toronto L.J.* 19 (1989).
45. See *American States Ins. v. Borbor*, 826 F.2d 888 (9th Cir. 1987) which held there was coverage under a CGL policy for the wife of the perpetrator who allegedly molested children at their daycare center based on a theory of negligence on the part of the wife for failing to investigate the husband's actions.
46. 842 F.Supp. 1151 (W.D.Ark. 1994).
47. 26 F.3rd 1359 (5th Cir. 1994).
48. 870 P2d 745 (N.M. 1994).
49. 545 P.2d 225 (Cal. 1976).
50. *Marinez v. Workers' Compensation Appeals Board*, 544 P.2d 1350 (Cal 1976).
51. *Beauchamp v. Dow Chemical Co.*, 398 N.W.2d 882 (Mich. 1986).

16

CONSTITUTIONAL AND CIVIL RIGHTS OF VICTIMS

Chapter Outline

Section 1983 Actions
Introduction
Requirement of State Action
Scope of Liability

1983 Theories of Liability
Denial of Equal Protection
Failure to Act

Violence Against Women Act
Background
Gender-Based Civil Rights

Injunctions
Background and Use of Restraining Orders
Advantages and Disadvantages

Defenses
Absolute Immunity
Qualified Immunity

Summary

Key Terms

Discussion Questions

Suggested Readings

Learning Objectives

After reading this chapter, you should be able to:

- Distinguish between the various theories upon which liability may be imposed on tortfeasors
- Explain the history and significance of 42 U.S.C. Section 1983
- Discuss the ramifications of the Violence Against Women Act and how it affects the field of victimology
- Understand the use of injunctions
- Distinguish between absolute and qualified immunity

Up to this point, the text deals with situations in which victims have been injured by individuals acting alone or in concert with other perpetrators. In these situations, victims turn to those employed by the criminal justice system to assist them in punishing these persons. However, occasionally there are instances when those who work in the criminal justice system harm or contribute to the harm suffered by persons. These offenders may face criminal penalties as well as civil damages. In addition to pursuing recovery based on theories of negligence and/or intentional torts, the law provides victims with an additional set of rights which should always be considered when evaluating alternatives dealing with monetary recovery or other efforts to make these victims whole.

Section 1983 Actions

Introduction

It must be stressed that the great majority of those who work in the criminal justice system are honest, caring professionals. However, there are those who intentionally or negligently injure citizens. When those in the criminal justice system commit acts that injure others, they may be charged with a violation of either a state or federal criminal statute. If the offender's actions violate a person's federal civil rights, two criminal statutes may offer that individual redress. These statutes require action by the federal prosecutor and do not permit the victim to sue wrongdoers.[1]

Much confusion surrounds the historical evolution of the present-day civil rights acts. This is not a history text; however, understanding the background and evolution of these laws assists professionals in explaining their scope and function to victims. The first law passed by Congress was the Civil Rights Act of 1866.[2] This law declared that all persons born in the United States were citizens regardless of race or prior conditions of servitude. The act made it a crime for any person under color of law to deprive a person of any right secured or protected by the Constitution or the laws of the United States. This law failed to stop the continuing racial strife in the southern states and after race riots in Memphis and New Orleans, Congress enacted the Enforcement Act of 1870.[3] This law was intended to guarantee the right to vote without regard to color, race, or previous conditions of servitude. The Enforcement Act made it a crime for a state official to prohibit a person the right to vote. The historical roots of the present-day federal civil rights criminal codes are found in the Civil Rights Act of 1866 (18 U.S.C 242) and in the Enforcement Act of 1870 (18 U.S.C. 241). In response to continuing violence against Blacks, Congress enacted the Ku Klux Klan Act of 1871.[4] This act is best known for its primary civil enforcement mechanism—the ability to file a federal lawsuit for acts under color of law that violate a person's federal civil rights—and was the forerunner of the present-day law allowing such suits (42 U.S.C. 1983). However, when originally enacted it was viewed as a federal criminal sanction for those that engaged in violence against Blacks, specifically members of the Ku Klux Klan.

Title 18 of the United States Code Section 241 prohibits conspiracies to deprive a person of his or her civil rights.[5] Section 242 prohibits civil rights violations by persons acting under color of law. The government must prove four elements to establish a violation of Section 242: (1) the victim was an inhabitant of a state, district, or territory of the United States; (2) the defendant acted under color of law; (3) the conduct deprived the victim of a right guaranteed by the United States Constitution; and (4) the defendant acted with a specific intent to violate the protected right.[6]

In addition to the criminal sanctions facing those who violate a person's federal civil rights, Congress has provided an additional remedy in the form of civil damages. Title 42 of the United States Code Section 1983 provides in part:

> *Every person who, under color of any statute, ordinance, regulation, custom, or usage of any State or Territory, subjects, or causes to be subjected, any citizen of the United States or any other person within the jurisdiction thereof to the deprivation of any rights, privileges, or immunities secured by the Constitution and laws, shall be liable to the party injured in an action at law, suit in equity, or other proper proceedings for redress. . . .*[7]

This quote has been the basis for thousands of lawsuits against those employed in the criminal justice system. It is an important legal tool for victims who have been injured by police officers and others in positions of authority. As will be discussed, Title 42 has several advantages over the intentional torts already discussed in other chapters.

Requirement of State Action

The United States Supreme Court addressed the scope of the Civil Rights Act of 1871 when it interpreted the phrase "under color of state law" in its decision of *United States v. Classic.*[8] The court reversed the dismissal of criminal charges brought against election officials who had engaged in fraudulent activities during a primary election. The court stated that "misuse of power, possessed by virtue of state law and made possible only because the wrongdoer is clothed with the authority of the state, is action taken 'under color' of state law."[9]

The Supreme Court further expanded this definition four years later in 1945 when it decided *Screws v. United States.* The court held that a sheriff's fatal beating of a Black prisoner was conduct "under color" of law.[10] Therefore, in criminal cases, conduct *under color of law* involves unauthorized, unlawful conduct of an official when the pretense of authority under which the officer acted furthered or assisted that officer in violating a person's constitutional rights in any way. *Screws* and *Classic* established the availability of criminal actions by persons who were victims of law enforcement misconduct. However, from 1945 until 1961, Section 1983 was virtually ignored by those who were wronged by illegal conduct by agents of the government.

Scope of Liability

The gradual expansion of the due process clause incorporating the Bill of Rights and the growth of the equal protection and due process concepts allowed victims of official misconduct greater latitude in filing of lawsuits. In 1961, the Supreme Court decided *Monroe v. Pape* and established the framework for future use of Section 1983 by those who were victims of illegal governmental activity.[11] In *Monroe,* the plaintiff and his family filed a civil lawsuit, instead of criminal action using Section 1983 against thirteen Chicago police officers and the city of Chicago, alleging that the officers broke into their home without a warrant, forced them out of bed, and made them stand naked while the officers searched the house. The police then took the plaintiff to the police station and held him incommunicado for ten hours before releasing him without filing any charges. The plaintiff claimed that the police acted "under color of law" and deprived them of their constitutional protection against unreasonable searches and seizures. The Supreme Court held that color of law had the same meaning in a civil case as it did in a criminal case and concluded that because Section 1983 provided for a civil action, the plaintiffs need not prove that the defendants acted with a specific intent to deprive a person of a federal right. However, the court dismissed the city of Chicago, holding that municipalities were immune from liability under the statute.

In 1978, the law surrounding civil rights violations expanded even further with the Supreme Court decision in *Monell v. Department of Social Services.*[12] In *Monell,* the plaintiffs were a class of female employees who alleged that the board of education of the city of New York and the New York Department of Social Services were forcing pregnant employees to take unpaid leaves of absence before those leaves were medically necessary. The lawsuit sought injunctive relief and back pay for the unlawful forced leaves. The defendants included the mayor, the city of New York, the commissioner of the board of education and the board itself, and the Department of Social Services and its chancellor. In allowing the lawsuit to go forward the court held that Section 1983 was violated whenever:

1. a person was deprived of a right, privilege, or immunity guaranteed under the Constitution and federal laws, and
2. such a deprivation resulted from the official policy or custom of a local governmental entity.

The Supreme Court decision was to have a tremendous impact of the desirability of suing individuals employed by municipalities. Victims of illegal action by agents of municipalities now had a deep pocket that they could reach. It must be stressed that *Monell* addressed the liability of local governmental agencies and not individual states.

Monell also overruled *Monroe* by holding that municipalities were "persons" and therefore not completely immune from suit under Section 1983. However, *Monell* did not address whether local governments, although not entitled to absolute immunity, could claim limited immunity in some situations. This question was answered in *Owens v. City of Independence* which held that the city was entitled to limited immunity from lawsuit based on the good faith of its officials.[13]

These and other decisions have given victims of illegal local governmental activity an option that should always be considered when local government actions injure them. Using either "due process" or "equal protection," almost any intentional tort committed by a state or local official can be converted into a constitutional violation and thereby made the subject of a Section 1983 action. Additionally, if the plaintiff prevails in these actions, that person is entitled to an award of attorney's fees in addition to any equable or money relief.[14] This provision allowing attorney's fees encourages attorneys to take on lawsuits that indicate they have the potential for success.[15]

1983 Theories of Liability

A number of theories of liability under Section 1983 hold individual officials and in many instances their local agency liable for injury to victims. A discussion of these theories is beyond the scope of this text; however, several theories of liability should be discussed because of the nature of the acts committed by agents of municipalities.

Denial of Equal Protection

One famous case in the victim's movement involving a denial of equal protection concerned a police department's response to calls for help by a battered spouse. Starting in October 1982 and continuing until June 1983, Tracey Thurman repeatedly contacted the police department in Torrington, Connecticut, begging for protection from her estranged husband, Buck. Tracey signed several sworn complaints against Buck; however, the police department considered the incidents a family matter and did not respond to them in the same manner as they did to "stranger assaults."

On the day of the final beating, Buck stabbed Tracey repeatedly. A police officer arrived and asked Buck for the knife, but did not arrest or restrain him in any manner. Buck gave the officer the knife and then proceeded to stomp on Tracey's head in front of the officer. He then went inside the house and returned with their son and cursed and kicked Tracey in the head. This series of blows left her partially paralyzed. Other officers arrived and they did not arrest Buck until he tried to assault Tracey as she lay on the ambulance stretcher.

Tracey filed suit in federal court against the city of Torrington, its police department, and all twenty-four officers that she had contacted over the years about Buck's assaultive acts. She alleged that the police department and its officers had been negligent in responding to her and further that they had violated her constitutional rights to equal protection under the law by treating her differently than they would persons who were assaulted by strangers.[16]

The jury awarded Tracey $2.3 million in damages and although the city's insurance company paid the judgment, it indicated that it might not pay any future awards of any police department that refused or failed to educate their officers about domestic violence.[17]

In recent years, victims of family violence have turned to the courts in an attempt to require law enforcement departments to provide effective intervention and protection against spousal assault. *Balistreri v. City of Pacifica* involved a spouse who obtained a restraining order against her husband. He violated this order numerous times and even after serious physical injuries and a firebomb being thrown through her window, the police refused her request to arrest the husband. The federal court dismissed a portion of her complaint, but allowed the allegation that the police had violated her equal protection rights in that she had shown that the officers may have treated her differently from other crime victims because she was a battered woman.[18]

Czachorowski v. Degenhart was a New York Superior Court case in which several battered women sued the police department for failing to comply with a state law requiring officers to advise victims of domestic violence of their rights and available services. The case was settled for a change in policy where the police agreed to hand out informational material, train officers in domestic violence, and institute a complaint procedure for victims of spousal abuse.[19]

In *Watson v. City of Kansas City* a federal court ruled that the victim could proceed with her suit against the police department. Nancy Watson was married to a Kansas City police officer who abused her and her son on numerous occasions. When she requested assistance from the police, they refused to help and threatened to take her child away and arrest her. After being raped and battered by her husband, she escaped and he committed suicide. She sued the police department for a denial of equal protection.[20]

As the discussion illustrates, victims of spousal abuse have turned to the courts in an attempt to force police departments to arrest the perpetrators of this form of family violence. Increasingly, courts have begun to listen and rule in their favor both on constitutional and tort grounds.

Failure to Act

In certain situations, local agencies may be liable for injuries to citizens that have occurred because of the agencies' failure to act. These failures may involve lack of proper training, lack of proper supervision, or lack of protection on the part of law enforcement officers. It should be stressed that many times plaintiffs will allege a violation of their civil rights based on all these theories.

Failure to Train

Billings v. Vernal City involved a rookie police officer who had been on the force for less than two weeks when he broke the plaintiff's arm while trying to arrest him.[21] The arrest was illegal because the officer did not have probable cause to place the plaintiff under arrest. The officer was on duty prior to completing the basic training required of all law enforcement officers in the state of Utah. The city argued that such a procedure was proper in that state law allows a police officer to receive formal training "within eighteen months" after beginning duty. The court held that to allow such a police officer on duty for "one minute" was grossly negligent. The plaintiff was awarded $23,500 in damages, $12,000 in court costs, and $25,000 in attorney's fees.

In 1989, the Supreme Court held that municipalities can be held liable under Section 1983 for failure to train their police officers if such failure amounts to "deliberate indifference."[22] In *City of Canton v. Harris*, the court stated that deliberate indifference occurs when ". . . in light of the duties assigned to specific officers or employees the need for more or different training is so obvious, and the inadequacy so likely to result in [a] violation of constitutional rights, that the policymakers of the city can reasonably be said to have been deliberately indifferent to the need."[23] The Court stated that the failure to train the officer must be closely related to the ultimate injury.

Failure to Supervise

In many private sector situations, supervisors are often sued for actions of their employees based on the common law theory of ***respondeat superior,*** which is latin for "let the master answer." Under this doctrine, the master (employer or supervisor) is responsible for the acts or omissions of his servant (employee) toward those to whom the master owes a duty of care. Liability normally attaches if the servant (employee) fails to use due care during the course of employment. This doctrine does not apply to public employment because police chiefs are not the masters of their employees. Both the chief and the officers work for a common master—the city. However, the doctrine applies to sheriffs because under common law deputies serve at the pleasure of the sheriff and therefore act for the sheriff in the course of employment.

However, in certain situations local police supervisors have been held liable for failure to properly supervise their officers. In *Dewell v. Lawson*, the chief of police was held liable for failing to establish procedures for the diagnosis and treatment of jail inmates.[24] The plaintiff was arrested and detained for public intoxication. He experienced a diabetic reaction that resulted in a coma, stroke, and ultimate death when the jailer failed to recognize the medical condition and therefore did not provide proper medical care. In *Grandstaff v. City of Borger*, the police chief was held liable for acts of his officers when they shot an innocent man during an apprehension of a suspect.[25] The officers opened fire on a pickup driven by the victim when he entered the area to offer assistance after seeing police activity near his house.

In *Parrish v. Luckie*, the city was liable for an officer's sexual assault of a woman, because the city had knowledge of the officer's propensity for violence and failed to take any corrective action.[26] The officer was investigated on two prior occasions for child abuse and criminally charged in one of those incidents. The department had also received complaints from other citizens that the officer had solicited sexual favors from several store clerks. However, the police chief failed to take any action and investigators discouraged citizens from filing complaints. The jury awarded damages in the amount of $200,000 against both the officer and the chief of police and because it was alleged that they acted in their official capacity, the city was responsible for paying the judgment.

Failure to Protect

In other situations, officers will be held liable for failing to follow up on actions they initiated. *Fundiller v. City of Cooper* involved a drug transaction with an undercover officer that resulted in the plaintiff being shot five times.[27] Other officers arrived at the scene and dragged Fundiller from his car and handcuffed him causing further injury. The appellate court stated that the city and its officials may be liable under Section 1983. The court established the standard for determining liability of agencies and their officers for practices that have become a custom or policy, stating that the custom must be created by an individual who represents the official policy of the agency and a causal link must exist between the act and the custom. In the area of liability for failure to protect, the court held that supervisors may be liable if a causal link exists between the employee's acts and the acts of the supervisor. The court further ruled that mere presence at the scene of the incident with a failure to act to protect the victim is sufficient for liability.

In *Raucci v. Town of Rotterdam*, a federal court ruled that the municipality owed a battered woman a special duty to protect her from her estranged husband because of actions by the police department which had assured her of protection. In spite of these assurances, the husband killed their six-year-old son and wounded the wife. The court upheld a jury verdict awarding the wife damages.[28]

Smith v. Wade involved a federal civil rights lawsuit by an inmate against a correctional officer who placed inmates with known dangerous propensities in a cell with the victim.[29] The Supreme Court upheld the award of compensatory and punitive damages against the officer stating that such damages are permitted when the conduct is shown to be motivated by evil intent or when it involves reckless or callous indifference to the federally protected rights of others.

Violence Against Women Act

Background

In August 1994, Congress passed and President Clinton signed the controversial Crime Bill.[30] While this act caused much debate and controversy, one act from the Crime Bill received support from both parties: the Violence Against Women Act (VAWA) of 1994.[31] The VAWA contains one of the Crime Bill's largest crime prevention programs that attempts to respond to the national problem of gender-based violence. The Violence Against Women Act makes crimes committed against women similar to those that are motivated by religious, racial, or political bias.

The act addresses gender-based violence in five areas: Title I, Safe Streets for Women, increases sentences for repeat offenders who continue to commit crimes against women; Title II, Safe Homes for Women, focuses on domestic violence; Title III, Civil Rights for Women, creates the first civil rights remedy for gender-based violence; Title IV, Safe Campuses, funds research on problems facing women on college campus; and Title V, Equal Justice for Women in the Courts, provides training for judges to address the problem of gender bias within the legal system. Although all sections of this law are important, of particular significance in this chapter is Title III which establishes civil rights violations for gender-based acts of violence.

Gender-Based Civil Rights

The creation of this federal civil rights law recognizes that gender-based violence against women should be accorded the same dignity as a violation of an individual's constitutional rights. The victim of this type of discrimination may recover compensatory and punitive damages and obtain an injunction to prevent future acts of violence.

The Title III of the act contains three major goals: First, it is intended to demonstrate that violence against women cannot be perceived as only a "family" problem, a "private" matter, or a sexual "miscommunication."[32] Second, the law treats gender-motivated violence the same as other bias-motivated attacks. Third, and perhaps most important, the law provides federal remedy for victims of gender-based violence that is not presently available in state courts.

Title III contains four major sections:

1. Section 302 subsection (b) states that every person has the right to be free from crime of violence motivated by gender.
2. Section 302 subsection (c) states that all persons, including those who act under color of any statute, ordinance, regulation, custom, or usage of any state, who commit a gender-motivated crime of violence are liable for compensatory and punitive damages as well as injunction, declaratory relief, and other such relief as a court may deem appropriate.
3. Section 302 subsection (d) defines a crime of gender-motivated violence as an act or series of acts that would constitute a felony against the person or that would constitute a felony against property if the conduct presents a serious risk of physical injury to another and that would come within the meaning of state or federal offenses described in Title 18 of the United States Code.[33] Such crime of violence is considered to be motivated by gender if it is committed because of the gender or on the basis of gender and is due at least in part to the animus (prejudice, spiteful or ill will) based on the victim's gender.
4. Section 302 subsection (e) states that nothing in this section entitles a person to relief based on random acts of violence unrelated to gender.

By establishing a civil rights cause of action for gender-based acts of violence, Congress has placed gender at the same level as race and religion. The VAWA and its new civil rights must await interpretation by the courts to determine its full scope and extent; however, there is every reason to believe that it will be accorded the same type of reception that other civil rights laws have received and therefore in the future female victims of violence will have a new legal weapon at their disposal.

Injunctions

Injunctions are restraining orders or protective orders which are court orders that prohibit the offender from having any contact with the victim.[34] They are civil versus criminal in nature and require a judge to rule on sufficient evidence to support the issuance of such an order. These orders are now available in forty-eight states and the District of Columbia. They offer the option of preventing contact such as harassment or threats which might ordinarily lead to an escalation of emotions and future violence.

The state of Massachusetts is one of the leaders in collecting data regarding the effectiveness of restraining orders.[35] In the fall of 1992, efforts by victim services advocacy groups and others resulted in changes to the state justice delivery system. Massachusetts created a Registry of Civil Restraining Orders designed to provide police and the courts with accurate and reliable information necessary to respond appropriately to victims' needs. It was the first statewide database of restraining order information in the nation.

For the program to be effective, a number of criminal justice professionals had to be able to access the database. The Office of the Commissioner of Probation established a statewide users community (see Figure 16.1). In Massachusetts, the agencies shown have access to the registry.

The program was designed for use on computers. Because of the importance of the data stored in the system, the computer program had to be easy to use and simple to learn. Massachusetts developed the program in COBOL on a Unisys mainframe. At the center of the restraining order program was the data entry screen (see Figure 16.2). This screen is used to enter, display, and update restraining order information. Quality control monitoring was utilized to ensure timeliness, accuracy, and completeness of all information. Since 1992, other states have followed Massachusetts lead and have adopted statewide restraining order registries. A computerized database is an important goal in responding to victims of crime and specifically to spousal abuse; however, certain geographical areas in the United States still do not use restraining orders. As the following discussion indicates, the debate continues regarding the effectiveness of this unique tool in preventing spousal abuse.

Background and Use of Restraining Orders

In the past, problems with the use of restraining orders stemmed from lack of clarity in the law and many police officers' unfamiliarity with this civil sanction. In 1983, only seventeen states provided protection against abuse from individuals who were living together but not married. However, by 1988, twenty-two states had added such protection to their statutes authorizing restraining orders.

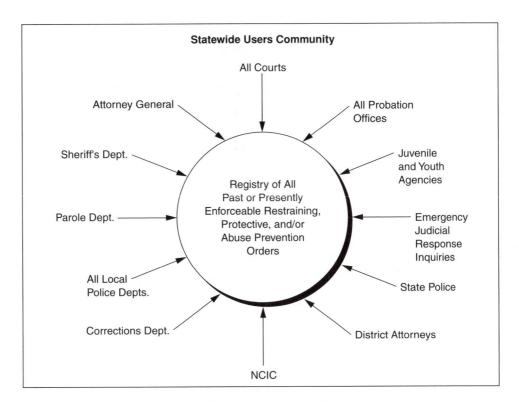

FIGURE 16.1   State of Massachusetts Accessing Restraining Orders

The use and nature of restraining orders vary from state to state. Most states now authorize persons who are married, related by blood, or cohabitants to request the issuance of such an order. The six types of behavior that may be prohibited by a restraining order are:

1. Protection against physical assault
2. Threatened physical abuse
3. Attempted physical abuse
4. Sexual assault of an adult
5. Sexual assault of a child
6. Damage to the personal property of the victim

As the list indicates, restraining orders may be issued for a wide variety of acts committed by the offender. However, simply having the order issued does not solve the problem. Due process requires that the offender be served with a copy of the order for it to be effective.

A majority of states provide for the issuance of temporary or emergency restraining orders. These orders are issued by the judge and usually require the threat of immediate injury to the victim. The United States Supreme Court upheld the issuance of these ex parte type of orders if (1) the request includes specific facts

---

CIVIL RESTRAINING ORDER SCREEN

DEFENDANT
PRIMARY NAME: DOE, JOHN   **DOB:** 03/09/65   **PROBATION**
                                                                CENTRAL FILE #: 123457CV

                                      P. O. B.: SOMERVILLE, MA

SEX: M   **SS#:** 012–22–2222   **MOTHER:** JANE JONES
                                                  FATHER: JOHN

ALIAS NAME: MOE, JOHN   6/9/65
                DOE, J.W.   3/9/65
                LEO, JOHN   3/9/65

PLAINTIFF
NAME: SMITH, JANE
          2022 MAIN ST.
          ANYTOWN, USA

DOCKET #: _____

TYPE OF
ORDER: MASS GENERAL LAWS: _____ ;   SECTION: _____

ORDER DATE: ____/____/____   **EXPIRATION DATE:** ____/____/____   **STATUS:**
                                                                           [ ] OPEN
                                                                           [ ] CLOSED

                    COURT ORDERS:
                        [ ] REFRAIN FROM ABUSE
                        [ ] NO CONTACT
                        [ ] VACATE/STAY AWAY (RESIDENCE)
                        [ ] ADDRESS IMPOUNDED
                        [ ] STAY AWAY (WORKPLACE)
                        [ ] SURRENDER CUSTODY
                        [ ] SUPPORT PAYMENTS
                        [ ] COMPENSATION
                        [ ] VISITATION RIGHTS: SEE ORDER
                        [ ] OTHER: SEE ORDER

FIGURE 16.2   State of Massachusetts Computer Screen

that justify the relief, (2) the notice and opportunity for a full hearing are given as soon as practicable, and (3) the order is issued by a judge.[36]

In most jurisdictions, police officers or process servers are responsible for serving restraining orders. The five basic methods of service of a temporary or emergency restraining order are (1) personal service, (2) informing the offender of the existence of the order, (3) leaving a copy with the victim so that she can serve the offender, (4) posting the notice and order at the residence of the victim, and (5) mailing a copy of the order via certified mail to the offender.

Some police departments have established procedures in which officers can contact judges while they are at the scene of a domestic dispute and have the judge authorize the issuance of such an order via the telephone. The officer then serves the suspect at the scene and requires him to leave the premise. Once a temporary order is issued, it becomes effective immediately and is valid until a formal hearing can be held at which time the abuser has a right to contest the allegations made by the victim. However, the issuance of the temporary order precludes the offender from having any contact with the victim until the formal hearing.

Restraining orders may provide different forms of relief for the victim of spousal assault. The traditional and most common form of relief is a no-contact order that prevents the offender from having any form of contact with the victim either at her residence, work, or anywhere else. This no-contact order includes telephone, written, and physical contacts. Many orders will set forth specific conditions regarding the visitation of any children that may be involved in the situation. Some will designate certain locations for the visit and others will require that the offender not consume any alcohol or drugs prior to the visit. A majority of the statutes authorize the court to require counseling for both parties. Even if the counseling does not solve the immediate problem, it is a visible sign of the authority of the court and should serve as a constant reminder to the offender of the power that the court now has over his existence.

In the event the abuser violates the restraining order, many statutes authorize charging the offender with civil contempt, criminal contempt, or a misdemeanor violation of a court order. Although police officers cannot normally arrest a person charged with civil contempt, the court may order that the offender pay a fine and serve a period of incarceration. Criminal contempt, if authorized by the state statute, would allow officers to arrest the offender if they found him in violation of the order. Criminal contempt in many jurisdictions is treated as a misdemeanor; however, many restraining order statutes allow officers to make warrantless arrests in these situations. If the violation of the order is considered a misdemeanor, many statutes also authorize the warrantless arrest of the offender. As the next section discusses, the use of this form of sanction still poses many problems.

Advantages and Disadvantages

Restraining orders provide the victim with another option in lieu of arrest. There are several advantages to the use of restraining orders.[37] Most arrests result in the offender being released in a matter of hours or within a few days at the most. A restraining order can be valid for up to a year in most cases.

Arrests may result in the loss of employment which might increase the tension that already exists in the relationship. Restraining orders do not preclude the offender from continuing with his employment, but at the same time they prevent him from living with the victim.

Restraining orders carry the weight and majesty of a judicial edict and some offenders may think twice before violating a court order. Although some offenders may have had numerous contacts with police and even the judicial system, most have not been involved with a direct order from a judge stating that they will not engage in certain conduct. The specter of facing a judge after violating an order may act as a deterrent for some abusers.

Just as there are advantages in this form of protection, so are there serious potential disadvantages in relying solely on the use of restraining orders in this area of family violence. The most obvious and threatening disadvantage is that the offender may simply ignore the order with the resulting injury to the victim. A restraining order is merely a piece of paper that carries only as much force and effect as the offender attaches to it. If the offender chooses to ignore it, there is no protection for the victim, unless she can contact the police and they can arrive and intercede before the abuser attacks and harms her.

There are additional disadvantages to the use of restraining orders. Many of these weaknesses are written into the very statutes that were enacted to protect the victim. Some statutes require the payment of a filing fee prior to issuance of a restraining order. Although most jurisdictions allow for the waiver of the fee if the victim cannot afford to pay it, some include the income of the abuser in determining if the fee can be waived. The payment of such fees acts as a deterrent to requesting a restraining order.

Some statutes require court or county clerks to assist the victim in filling out the forms requesting the restraining order. However, no state-provided funds or mandated special training is available for these clerks in this sensitive function. A great majority of spousal assault occurs in the evening or on the weekend after the courts are closed. Only twenty-three states provide for the issuance of emergency orders after normal working hours. Thus during the victim's greatest time of need, there is no alternative available to obtain these orders.

Most states require personal service of the order for them to become effective. However, many offenders are difficult to locate and therefore the victim is not protected until the abuser has been served. There is a lack of monitoring of the compliance with restraining orders. If the offender can convince or threaten the victim to remain silent, neither law enforcement officers nor the court will be aware that the offender has violated the order. Although the use of restraining orders presents some serious problems, they do provide some victims of spousal assault with an option that may protect them.

DEFENSES

Simply establishing that a person has violated the victim's civil rights does not end the inquiry. The law provides a number of defenses for both individuals and agencies accused of violating another's civil rights. There are two types of defenses: substantive and procedural. *Substantive defenses* are those that claim one of the elements of a civil rights action has not been met. For example, the defendant may argue that no constitutional right was violated by the officer. *Procedural defenses* challenge the validity of the lawsuit based on issues such as lack of jurisdiction (federal courts have specific jurisdictional requirements that must be satisfied to sue in federal court), statute of limitations, and other procedural requirements.[38]

Two common forms of defense raised in civil rights cases are *absolute immunity* and *qualified immunity.* Both of these defenses are considered "official immunity." At English common law the concept of sovereign immunity developed based on the assumption that kings were divine and therefore could do no wrong. Thus, the king's subjects could not sue the king. Early American court decisions relied on this rationale to support the position that the United States could not be sued without its permission. As a result, in 1946 Congress passed the Federal Tort Claims Act that allowed citizens under certain circumstances to sue the government and its agents or employees.[39]

The historical rationale for official immunity is based on the concept that a government can only act through its agents or officials and official immunity protects those who carry out these actions. Another justification for official immunity was set forth by the Supreme Court when it held:

> *The public interest requires decisions and action to enforce laws for the protection of the public. . . . Implicit in the idea that officials have some immunity—absolute or qualified—for their acts, is a recognition that they may err. The concept of immunity assumes this and goes on to assume that it is better to risk some error and possible injury from such error than not to decide or act at all.*[40]

The courts have consistently used the common law doctrine of immunity when dealing with Section 1983 cases. As will be discussed, the distinction between absolute and qualified immunity has on occasion become blurred and confusing.

Absolute Immunity

Absolute immunity is a complete shield in a lawsuit and involves a determination that there is no liability for any damages that the victim may have suffered as a result of the actor's conduct. Therefore, when a defendant has absolute immunity, any civil lawsuit will be dismissed by the court without ever considering the plaintiff's claim for damages. However, this defense is not automatic—it must be pled and proved by the defendant before the court will act to dismiss the lawsuit.

The concept of absolute immunity is to encourage a decision-making process without fear of reprisals no matter how unpopular such a decision may be for a particular person or group of persons. For absolute immunity to apply, persons must be acting within the broad general scope of their duties.[41] Additionally, absolute immunity applies even if it is determined that the person acted with malice or other evil intentions. A grant or absolute immunity prevents any civil lawsuits from going forward.

Society has determined that certain individuals and situations should be accorded the shield of absolute immunity. Judges when acting in their judicial capacity are afforded absolute immunity as are witnesses when they are testifying in court. Prosecutors depending on their role and function in the judicial system may have either absolute or qualified immunity.[42] If a prosecutor is acting as an advocate, his or her actions are absolutely immune; however, if the prosecutor is acting in a nonadvocatory role such as investigating cases or administering the office, he or she is afforded only qualified immunity.

Qualified Immunity

Qualified immunity is also known as the *good faith defense*. It is a defense that has grown and evolved during the last hundred years. The present-day defense of qualified immunity has its basis in the U.S. Supreme Court decision of *Anderson v. Creighton*.[43] In *Anderson*, an FBI agent and several local law enforcement officers conducted a warrantless search of the victim's home under the mistaken belief that a bank robbery suspect was in the home. According to the Creightons, the officers brandished shotguns, assaulted their daughter, and knocked Mr. Creighton to the ground. They arrested him and placed him in jail overnight before releasing him without filing any charges. The Creightons filed a Section 1983 action alleging that the officers violated their Fourth Amendment right to be free from unreasonable searches. The officers claimed they were immune from such lawsuit based on the defense of qualified immunity. The Supreme Court held that individuals would be entitled to qualified immunity if it was determined that the action was the type which a reasonable person could have believed was lawful in light of clearly established law and the information available to that individual at the time of the decision.

The immunity defenses provide those that work in the criminal justice system a shield against meritless lawsuits and at the same time allow a person who has been wronged by those perpetrators to pursue a lawsuit to recover damages for injuries. The laws dealing with the immunity defenses are complex and constantly changing and therefore it is essential that professionals working with victims refer them to attorneys for a complete explanation of their rights in this area.

Summary

This chapter should not be taken as an indictment of law enforcement officers or others who work in the criminal justice system. The overwhelming majority of personnel in this field are caring professionals who obey the law. However, a small percentage of those in the criminal justice system, either because of negligence or intentional acts, injure private citizens. When this occurs, many victims are hesitant to report such injury because of the mistaken belief that they have no recourse against those in power.

Victim service providers need to understand the history and evolution of the present-day laws that hold those in the criminal justice profession liable for injuries to others. Title 42 United States Code Section 1983 is an invaluable tool to use in these situations. It requires that the tortfeasor act under *color of law*. This is a key element in any 1983 action.

The Violence Against Women Act of 1994 has established a new gender-based civil right for women. It provides victims of gender-based crimes with an important legal remedy and states that crimes based on gender will be considered as serious as crimes based on other protected classifications.

Injunctions are a critical aspect of the civil rights of victims of crime. These legal tools are normally used against persons known to the victim, most commonly against former spouses or boyfriends. The effectiveness of injunctions is still being studied. However, some states have automated their records and now law enforcement agencies can access these records from statewide databases.

Simply knowing that the victim has been injured by someone acting under color of law is only the first step in this process. Victim service providers must be aware of the various types of defenses available to those in the criminal justice system. By understanding these defenses, professionals can better advise victims of their constitutional and civil rights.

Key Terms

Under color of law involves unauthorized, unlawful conduct of an official when the pretense of authority under which the officer acted furthered or assisted them in violating a person's constitutional rights in any way.

Respondeat superior is latin for "let the master answer." Under this doctrine, the master (employer or supervisor) is responsible for the acts or omissions of his servant (employee) toward those to whom the master owes a duty of care.

Injunctions are restraining orders or protective orders which are court orders that prohibit the offender from having any contact with the victim.

Discussion Questions

1. Does the potential of civil liability affect how police respond to victims of crime?

2. Should local agencies be held liable for failing to train their officers, if the officers acted in good faith?

3. Why is the requirement of state action important in 1983 lawsuits?

4. Is a gender-based civil rights law necessary?

5. Are temporary restraining orders a useful tool in responding to domestic violence? List those situations in which you would recommend issuance of a TRO and those situations in which a TRO would not be appropriate.

6. Should absolute immunity exist? Why? Why not?

Suggested Readings

Peter Finn & Sarah Colson, *Civil Protection Orders: Legislation, Current Court Practice and Enforce-* *ment,* (National Institute of Justice, Washington, D.C.) March 1990.

Endnotes

1. See *Powers v. Karen* 768 F. Supp. 46 (E.D. N.Y. 1991).
2. Civil Rights Act (Enforcement Act) of 1866, ch. 31, 14 Stat. 27.
3. Enforcement Act of 1870 (Act of May 31, 1870), ch. 114, 16 Stat. 140, amended by Act of Feb. 28, 1871, ch. 99, 16 Stat. 433.
4. Ku Klux Klan (Anti-lynching) Act, ch. 22, 17 Stat. 13 (1971).
5. 18 U.S.C. Section 241 (1988).
6. 18 U.S.C. Section 242 (1988).
7. 42 U.S.C. Section 1983 (1981, West Supp. 1985).
8. 313 U.S. 299 (1941).
9. 313 U.S. at 326.
10. 325 U.S. 91 (1945).
11. 325 U.S. 167 (1961).
12. 436 U.S. 658 (1978).
13. 455 U.S. 622 (1980).
14. See The Civil Rights Attorneys Fees Awards Act of 1976, 42 U.S.C. Section 1988 (1981, West Supp. 1994).
15. *Hensley v. Eckerhart,* 461 U.S. 423 (1983); and *Farrar v. Hobby,* 113 S.Ct. 566 (1992).
16. *Thurman v. City of Torrington,* 595 F. Supp. 1521 (Conn. 1984).
17. M. Buddy & K. Taylor, "Please Somebody Help Me," *20/20 News* (January 23, 1986). The judgment was later reduced to $1.9 million.
18. 855 F. 2d 1421 (1990).
19. New York Superior Court of Erie County, Case Number 07961 (1988).
20. 520 N.Y.S. 2d 352 (1987).
21. U.S. Dist. Utah, C77-0295 (1982).
22. *City of Canton v. Harris,* 489 U.S. 378 (1989).
23. Id.
24. 489 F.2d 877 (10th Cir. 1974).
25. 767 F.2d 161 (5th Cir. 19875).
26. 963 F.2d 201 (8th Cir. 1992).
27. 777 F.2d 1436 (11th Cir. 1985).
28. 902 F.2d 1050 (1990).
29. 103 S. Ct. 1625 (1983).
30. Pub. L. No. 103-322, 108 Stat. 1796. The Crime Bill contains over $30 billion for punishment and prevention programs.
31. Pub. L. No. 103-322, Title IV, 108 Stat. 1902–1955. Codified in various sections of 8 U.S.C. and 42 U.S.C.
32. See S. Rep. No. 197, 102d Cong., 1st Session 41 (1991).
33. 18 U.S.C. contains two possible crimes of violence: The first is an offense that has an element of use or attempted use or threatened use of physical force against the person or property of another. The second is any other offense that is a felony and by its nature involves a substantial risk that physical force may be used against the person or property of another in the course of committing the offense.
34. This section has been adapted from Peter Finn & Sarah Colson, *Civil Protection Orders: Legislation, Current Court Practice and Enforcement,* (National Institute of Justice, Washington, D.C.) March 1990.
35. Donald Cochran, "Project History of the Massachusetts Statewide Automated Restraining Order Registry," *Office of the Commissioner of Probation, Massachusetts Trial Court,* (Boston) July 1994.
36. *Mitchell v. W. T. Grant Co.,* 416 U.S. 600 (1974).
37. For an excellent discussion of the advantages to using restraining orders, see Elizabeth Topliffe, "Why Civil Protection Orders Are Effective Remedies for Domestic Violence But Mutual Protective Orders Are Not," 67 *Indiana Law Journal* 1039 (Fall 1992).
38. There are other technical defenses that are of more interest to lawyers instead of victim service providers. These include collateral

estoppel and double jeopardy, laches, and the Younger Doctrine.

39. 28 U.S.C. Section 1346 et al.

40. *Scheuer v. Rhodes,* 416 U.S. 232, 241–242 (1974).

41. See for example *Stump v. Sparkman,* 435 U.S. 349 (1978) where the Supreme Court held that a judge who ordered a fifteen-year-old girl sterilized without notice to her and based on a simple request of her mother was absolutely immune from a civil lawsuit even though the judge had no express statutory authority for the acts he did.

42. Brian P. Barrow, *"Buckley v. Fitzsimmons:* Tradition Pays a Price for the Reduction of Prosecutorial Misconduct" 16 *Whittier L. Rev.* 301 (1995).

43. 483 U.S. 635 (1987).

17

COMPENSATION AND RESTITUTION OF VICTIMS

Chapter Outline

Compensation
    Introduction
    Program Operation
    Eligibility
    Benefits

Restitution
    Introduction
    History
    Types of Restitution
    Problems with Restitution
    Methods of Collecting Restitution

Summary

Key Terms

Discussion Questions

Suggested Readings

Learning Objectives

After reading this chapter, you should be able to:

- Distinguish between compensation and restitution
- Understand the rationale behind funding of compensation programs

- List the justification for denying benefits to certain types of victims
- Explain the philosophy underlying the concept of restitution
- Distinguish between the various types of restitution available to victims

Compensation

Introduction

Victims often suffer physical injury, emotional and mental trauma, and financial loss as a result of a crime.[1] The financial loss to crime victims can cause additional stress as they worry about hospital and doctor bills being paid, physical recovery from their injuries, and their ability to return to work. Crime victim compensation programs exist to provide financial assistance to crime victims and hopefully reduce some of these stressors. These programs exist in all fifty states, plus the District of Columbia and many will pay for medical care, mental health counseling, lost wages, and in the case of homicides, funeral costs and loss of support.[2] Although no amount of money can replace the use of an arm or the loss of a loved one, it can help victims preserve their financial stability and dignity and thereby assist in the recovery process.

As discussed in Chapter 1, in 1984 Congress enacted the Victims of Crime Act (VOCA) which established a Crime Victims Fund, supported by revenues from federal offenders. This revenue was based on fines, penalty assessments, and forfeited appearance bonds. When VOCA was enacted in 1984, the fund ceiling or amount that could be allocated to the fund was $100 million. Amendments to VOCA occurred in 1986, 1988, 1990, and in 1992 when Congress removed the ceiling. Although deposits fluctuate yearly, the total amount deposited in the fund from its inception to 1994 was over $1.2 billion.[3]

Some of this money is used to improve the investigation and prosecution of child abuse cases including those child abuse acts committed against Native Americans. However, most of the money in the fund is used to support state victim compensation and victim assistance service programs. *Victim compensation* is a direct payment to, or on behalf of, a crime victim for crime-related expenses such as unpaid medical bills, mental health counseling, funeral costs, and lost wages.[4] *Victim*

FOCUS: Compensation and Restitution

Victim's Perspectives[5]

"The state paid for both the defense and the prosecution. I had to find a way to pay the $12,000 this crime cost us."

—a victim addressing the issue of compensation

"I think if the criminals who do these things are caught they should have to pay for the damage they do, even if takes them years. My family and I will be trying to recover from this for the rest of our lives."

—a victim addressing the issue of restitution

assistance includes services such as crisis intervention, counseling, emergency transportation to court, temporary housing, advocacy, and criminal justice support.[6]

VOCA also established special assessments for individual crimes which are levied on every conviction. Additionally, VOCA has a "Son of Sam" provision that requires royalties from the sale of literary rights or any other profits derived from a crime, to be deposited in the Crime Victims Fund and held for five years to satisfy any civil judgment a victim may obtain. If no judgments are filed, these funds become part of the general Crime Victims Fund.[7] Most states also have their own "Son of Sam" laws that cover state crimes.

Victim assistance programs and services have been discussed in previous chapters. These include organizations that provide a variety of services to victims of state and federal crimes. There are over 8000 agencies or organizations that provide services to victims and nearly 3000 of those organizations received some VOCA funding.[8]

Program Operation

California established the first compensation program in 1965, and within three years five other states created similar programs. California is still the largest program in the nation, with payout at about one-third the total benefits paid by all programs combined.[9] The median annual payout per state is approximately $2 million. (One-half of the states pay less and one-half pay more.)

Every state administers a crime victim compensation program through a central agency. (In two states, Arizona and Colorado, operation of the program has been delegated to counties and districts.)[10] These agencies are organized and funded on a statewide basis with administration, claims investigation, and decision making handled at that statewide headquarters. Debate continues among those in the field regarding centralization versus decentralization of compensation services.[11]

Most victim compensation programs are small agencies employing only a handful of staff. The lack of personnel creates delays in processing claims, prevents training of groups regarding their right to compensation, and does not allow for specialized services such as bilingual staff. Some agencies are using student interns or volunteers to carry out staff functions.

These programs provide assistance to victims of both federal and state crimes. Although each state compensation program is independently run, most programs have similar eligibility requirements and offer the same types of benefits. The maximum state award generally ranges between $10,000 and $25,000.[12]

Victims applying for compensation must comply with certain requirements including reporting the crime and filing claims by certain deadlines. In most states, the victim service professional provides compensation applications and information to the victim. The victim then contacts the agency. Program staff then mail an application to the victim who fills it out and returns it to the compensation agency. Once the claim form is received, it is processed by an investigator or claims specialist. These employees do not go into the field to obtain their information, rather they collect data using letters, telephone calls, and other techniques. These investigations must verify a variety of information including the fact that the crime was reported to the proper law enforcement agency, that there is appropriate documentation of medical expenses, that they obtain data regarding funds paid by insurance companies, and that they determine the amount, if any, of lost wages.

Once all pertinent information is gathered, the victim compensation agency will decide whether to make an award, and the monetary value of that award to the victim. In most states, victims may appeal a denial of benefits. These appeals are heard by a different panel than the one who made the original determination. Some states require that the appeal be heard by a judge.

The various state compensation programs are represented by the National Association of Crime Victim Compensation Boards (NACVCB). This is a national organization that provides advocacy, training, and communication among the state boards. Occasionally the NACVCB communicates with Congress and federal agencies on all matters affecting the state compensation programs.

Eligibility

Not all victims of every crime are eligible for state compensation. In general, the majority of states limit compensation to victims who suffered injuries as a result of the criminal conduct of another and to survivors of homicides. Additionally, there is a wide disparity between eligibility requirements in these programs with some states mandating that the victim suffer some sort of physical injury and others allowing for physical or mental injuries. Most states allow the parents of deceased victims to collect compensation.

A majority of states disallow some classes of persons from eligibility. Some states preclude firefighters and police officers from victim compensation awards. The rationale for this exclusion is that if their injuries are job related they are eligible for other state program—workers' compensation. Some states exclude convicted prisoners from filing claims while they are in jail or prison, or serving probation or parole. VOCA has required states to provide compensation to nonresidents victimized within a state as well as persons who are subject to federal jurisdiction, such as Native Americans. Additionally, state residents who are victimized in another state are eligible in their home state if the state where the crime occurred does not have a victim compensation program to which they can apply. If the claim is denied, the victim usually has no recourse, because the crime did not occur in the state of residence. Only if the state where the crime occurred has no program—or does not extend eligibility to the non-resident is the victim allowed to file in the state of residence. However, a few states provide that as long as the victim files where the crime occurred, they may also file in their home state.

Historically, drunk driving was not considered a violent crime that entitled the victim to state-funded compensation. In 1983, only five states classified drunk driving crimes as compensable.[13] As a result of a nationwide public awareness program, as well as successful lobbying by MADD, drunk driving cases are now included as compensable offenses in all states that participate in the VOCA program. Dealing with two or more insurance companies and several lawyers who represent the various parties tends to increase the length of time from filing a claim to receiving an award.[14]

Two key issues are common in drunk driving cases: contributory misconduct and subrogation. Contributory misconduct, which will be discussed in more detail later in this chapter, is an eligibility requirement that applies to all crime victim compensation decisions and takes on special significance in drunk driving cases because of the social environment that accompanies many drinking and driving situations. Many people may go to a bar and have a few drinks and then drive home and believe that they are fit to accomplish that task. Additionally, unlike the majority of crimes, some victims of drunk drivers know the perpetrator and may have been in the same car as the drunk driver when the offense occurred. Some states deny awards if the victim was a willing passenger of a known drunk driver driver, other states reduce payments if the victim voluntarily rode with a known drunk and some states do not consider such activity as misconduct. *Subrogation* is the process in which third parties are asked to reimburse the state for compensation payments previously made to the victim. Generally speaking, the state pays any award to which the victim is entitled under the state compensation laws and then attempts to recoup that payment from any insurance companies that are involved in the incident.

In the past, domestic violence victims were summarily denied compensation. Many states denied these claims because of the belief that the victim contributed to her own injuries by staying in the relationship or that any award would benefit the wrongdoer if he was still living with the victim. Similar to the change in attitudes toward victims of drunk driving, our perception of domestic violence victims has resulted in a change in policy in all states. All states now include domestic violence as a compensable crime.

Some state compensation programs have very few domestic violence claims. The staffs of these programs believe it is because victims underreport this form of violence. Additionally, cultural barriers may prevent certain minority groups from reporting because exposing male offenders to public attention violates cultural norms.

Contributory misconduct occurs when victims participate in the crime or otherwise contribute to their injuries by their own conduct. All states have laws or regulations designed to exclude such parties from receiving compensation. This is one of the most frequent issues facing compensation staff today. The concept of victim participation is a complex and emotional subject that does not have a clear bright line delineating innocent victims from those that caused their own injuries.

In deciding the existence of contributory misconduct, many compensation programs rely on police reports, witness statements, the prosecuting attorney's opinion, the results of any trial, and the oral or written statements of the victim. In most states, if there is an issue of misconduct, the victim is given an opportunity to rebut such a conclusion prior to any final decision resulting in a denial of the claim. Many states do not have hard and fast rules regarding contributory misconduct and end up judging each case on its own merits.

Most states require that the victim promptly report the crime to the police. Generally, states require that a police report be filed within seventy-two hours of the discovery of the crime. Additionally, all states require that the victim cooperate in any

---

PRACTICUM: Contributory Misconduct—Who Is at Fault?[16]

Practicum 1:

The victim was shot by her husband after she had a protection order amended to let him visit their children in her apartment. Did the victim contribute to her injuries?
Holding: Absent other facts, most programs would find no contributory misconduct on the part of the victim.

Practicum 2:

The victim was robbed and shot after accepting a ride from a stranger on a city street at 3 A.M.
Holding: Most programs would find no misconduct.

Query: What if the victim was a prostitute and engaged in her work at the time she accepted the ride?

Practicum 3:

The victim was wounded in a drive-by shooting while talking to a third party.
Holding: Most states would find no misconduct.
Query: What if the third party was a drug dealer and the defendant was attempting to make a purchase of drugs? What if the shooting was part of an ongoing gang war for control of the city's drug markets?

---

subsequent investigation or court proceedings. Though a number of states can make an exception when the victim's life or safety is at risk. Apprehension or conviction of the perpetrator is not a requirement of receiving compensation.[17]

Eligibility issues pose complex and emotional problems for victims. Victim service professionals should understand the rationale and basis for these requirements so they can explain them to victims. Being unjustly denied a compensation claim can have severe financial and mental consequences for a victim.

Benefits

Once a victim has qualified for compensation, the next step in the process is determining what type of benefits are available. Many factors are involved in determining the type and amount of benefits available to victims. Some states have a small deductible amount ($50–$100) that must be reached before they will pay compensation. All states pay for only nonreimbursed expenses. In other words, if a victim has private health insurance that covers the cost of medical treatment, the state compensation award will not pay for those expenses.

Collateral financial sources are any payments received by the victim for costs reimbursed by other sources such as private insurance, workers' compensation, restitution, or disability payments. This policy prevents victims from recovering losses for the same injury twice and thus enriching themselves. Although most states attempt to use subrogation in an attempt to recoup money paid to victims, program staffs have reported frustration with the low amounts recovered.[18]

A majority of states compensate victims for a variety of crime-related costs including dental care, plastic surgery, vocational rehabilitation (education), home care, and moving expenses. Most states also pay for mental health counseling. However, deciding who is a qualified mental health provider and determining the appropriate forms of treatment are complex issues facing many compensation staff members. Although some states require mental health professionals to be licensed, other states allow "counseling" to be done by a variety of persons including those without advanced degrees. Additionally, the type and extent of the treatment may be difficult to control because some mental health providers may decide to prolong treatment beyond what is necessary to increase the victim's bill.

A majority of states allow payment for a portion of any attorney's fees incurred by the victim in processing the compensation claim. The amount awarded does not decrease the victim's award, rather it is a separate payment to the attorney. Many compensation staff members feel it is in the victim's best interest to be represented by an attorney when appealing a denial of compensation benefits.

In some states, compensation claims dramatically increased during the period between 1895 and 1992. Several factors contributed to this increase including higher visibility of compensation programs, more awareness and advocacy on the part of victim service providers, and new laws mandating greater compensation of victims. This increase in claims and awards reflects the fact that victim's have an increased awareness that they should receive the financial help they need.

Compensation is only one financial remedy available to victims of crime. Another remedy looks to the offender to make the victim whole. The topic of restitution will be discussed in the next section.

Restitution

The facts contained in this Focus box are not drawn from some historical account detailing the early days of restitution. They come from a 1995 newspaper article examining the present-day structure of restitution in Los Angeles.[19]

Introduction

The 1982 *Final Report of the President's Task Force on Victims of Crime* included several key points regarding restitution.[20] The report recommended that legislation be

---

FOCUS: Who Is Responsible for Collecting Restitution?

Each year, the Los Angeles Municipal Court orders hundreds of defendants convicted of crimes to pay hundreds of thousands of dollars in restitution to their victims. Yet, in the majority of these cases, no branch of the criminal justice system is designated as responsible for collecting the restitution and disbursing it to the victims. Collecting restitution is left as the defendant's responsibility.

The city attorney's office is charged with the responsibility of ensuring that the defendant pays the ordered amount to the victim. In the event restitution is not paid, the city attorney's office then asks the court to find the defendant in violation of probation.

enacted requiring judges to order restitution for property loss and personal injury in all cases unless the judge explicitly finds that restitution is not appropriate. However, the report also stated that although restitution is a proper goal to be pursued, it has limitations. The report noted that restitution cannot be ordered unless the perpetrator is caught and convicted. Even if it is ordered, the offender often has no resources with which to make any payments. Finally, those perpetrators who can make payments may take many years to finally pay off the balance. In the interim, the victim is left to bear the cost of the crime.[21]

As a result of this report and other factors influencing the victims' movement over the last decade, a number of laws have been enacted addressing the issue of restitution. Hillenbrand reports that one reason these laws may have been enacted is the change in perception regarding restitution. She states that society began to view restitution not as a way to punish or rehabilitate the offender, but as a method of bringing justice to victims.[22] Other authorities argue that laws mandating restitution have been passed as "politically correct" with little or no thought given to their effect. This has resulted in a system that does not deliver its promise of making victims whole. Consequently, victims become more disillusioned with the criminal justice system when they learn that the court order mandating the offender to pay restitution carries no weight or authority.[23]

Even the definition of restitution causes conflict. It represents many things to many people. Whereas the victim may view restitution as a way to regain financial loss and to punish the offender, the court may see it as a method of instilling responsibility in the offender. The agency charged with collecting restitution may view it as simply one more task for an already overburdened department. Traditionally, *restitution* is a court-ordered sanction that involves payment of compensation by the defendant to the victim for injuries suffered as a result of the defendant's criminal act.

As the following Practicum illustrates, the definition of restitution, and who should pay, raises troubling issues. What is fair and just to a victim may seem outlandish to a judge or the perpetrator. The following sections will examine how we happened to arrive at this juncture in our development of victims' rights. Also, the problems in collecting restitution and some innovative methods that address these issues will also be examined.

History

The concept of making a victim whole is not new.[24] As indicated in Chapter 1, the Code of Hammurabi in the eighteenth century included provisions for payment of money to the victim or the victim's family.[25] In Saxton, England, a legal system developed which provided for restitution to the victim's family for the injury incurred by the victim and restitution to the king for violating the king's peace. As discussed earlier, this system eventually evolved into one in which the wrong was perpetrated against the state and not the victim. The victim and the victim's rights became secondary to the pursuit of justice.[26]

Modern restitution as we know it today can be traced to the criminal laws that authorized suspended sentences and the use of probation. By the late 1930s, several states had laws that allowed judges to order restitution as a condition of

---

PRACTICUM: How Much Restitution Should Be Ordered?

The victim is a forty-two-year-old executive who was robbed in New York's Central Park while on a business trip. The offender took the victim's wallet, which contained a picture of his deceased wife, several credit cards, and $400 in cash. The perpetrator also demanded the victim's Rolex watch. The victim explained that the watch was a gift from his deceased wife, but the assailant tore it off his wrist and then proceeded to pistol-whip him.

The perpetrator was caught and convicted and the court held a hearing to determine the amount of restitution that should be ordered. The defense attorney argued that his client was homeless and had not worked for three years

because of a drinking and drug problem. The prosecutor asked for funds to reimburse the victim for the $400 and the value of the lost Rolex, as well as any medical bills that were not covered either by the state compensation program or the victim's health insurance.

The victim stated that his wife bought him the Rolex twenty-one years ago and it cost her $500; however, today the fair market value of the Rolex was $5000. The victim wants to replace the watch and is asking for $5000. He also wants $400 for the lost cash and is asking $10,000 for the lost picture of his wife, stating that he has no other pictures of her. How much restitution should the judge order?

---

granting probation.[27] This process viewed restitution as part of the correctional process. In the late 1970s and 1980s, the victims' movement began to argue that restitution show be viewed as protecting victims from suffering financial hardship rather than punishing or rehabilitating the offender.

The modern concept of restitution in the criminal justice system serves a variety of purposes in the administration of justice. Restitution attempts to establish a relationship between the perpetrator and the victim in an effort to make the offender aware of the financial consequences suffered by the victim as a result of the offender's acts. Another purpose of restitution is to advance the concept of personal responsibility and accountability to the victim. A third idea regarding restitution holds that although it cannot undo the wrong, it can assist the victim financially and emotionally and at the same time educate the offender. Finally, restitution serves to punish the offender. The funds used to pay restitution must come from the offender's pocketbook and thus have a continuing impact on that offender.[28]

Types of Restitution

Restitution can now be ordered for a variety of criminal acts including sex crimes, child sexual abuse, telemarketing fraud, and domestic violence.[29] Restitution can also be ordered to pay for lost wages, child care, and other expenses involved in attending court hearings.[30] Additionally, there are several different types of restitution.[31]

The most common form of restitution is financial, which requires the offender to make payments directly to the actual victim of the crime. Financial–community restitution requires the offender to make payments to a community agency such as a restitution center, which then pays the victim. Individual service restitution requires the offender to perform a service for the actual victim. For example, the offender might be required to repair or replace property damaged during the commission of the crime. Community service restitution requires the offender to perform some beneficial service to the community. In this type of restitution, society serves as the symbolic victim and this is sometimes referred to as "symbolic restitution." Finally, some states authorize restitution fines. Restitution fines differ from actual restitution in that they are collected and deposited in the state's crime victim compensation fund. These monies then become part of the fund's operating expenses.

Restitution may be tied to different aspects of a defendant's sentence and is frequently imposed at the earliest possible time in the criminal process. Additionally, many plea agreements call for restitution. Imposing payment as a condition of probation is the most common method of collecting restitution. A court order may also follow the defendant to the correctional institution. Many states are now imposing the requirement that inmates work while incarcerated and while working in prison, they normally only receive a minimal amount of money (usually far less than the minimal wage). Several states have passed laws requiring that a portion of that amount, no matter how small, be set aside for payment as restitution to the victim. More states are implementing policies that require restitution to be established as a condition of any parole. Additionally, states are passing laws that provide that any restitution order in a criminal case will also be considered as a civil order for remuneration from the defendant to the victim and may be processed in civil courts.

Problems with Restitution

Restitution is a complex process that involves a number of different professionals working in the criminal justice system. Unfortunately, these professionals are usually overworked and under budgeted. As indicated in the article featured in the Focus box at the beginning of this section, many of these professionals claim that collecting and disbursing restitution is someone else's job.[32] This leads to poor communication and diminished accountability among agencies inside the criminal justice system. This, in turn, causes poor consultation and communication with victims. Because there may be no agency controlling or coordinating restitution, judges may impose insufficient or excessive restitution orders.

Many victims feel dissatisfied with the restitution process. They may believe that the amount imposed in the court order was insufficient. Other victims feel powerless as they search for answers to their questions only to be directed from one agency to another.[33]

Occasionally, a crime involves multiple perpetrators against a single victim. If the prosecution grants one perpetrator immunity to testify against the others, the victim will not be able to receive a court order of restitution against that defendant. By the same token, in crimes involving single perpetrators and multiple victims, deciding which victim should receive the limited funds of the perpetrator can create great difficulties.

Another obvious problem with restitution is the socioeconomic status of the perpetrator. In a majority of cases, the offenders are poor and unlikely to earn the funds necessary to make full restitution. Additionally, juvenile offenders are often incapable of obtaining or holding onto jobs that might provide them with the funds necessary to pay the court-ordered restitution.

Methods of Collecting Restitution

Control or monitoring of restitution orders is critical. The American Bar Association (ABA) conducted a survey of restitution directors and recommended that higher compliance rates occur when: (1) efforts are made to monitor payments, and (2) consistent action is taken to respond to delinquencies.[34] Respondents in the survey reported that the highest delinquency rates occurred at the time of the first payment and at mid-sentence. They stated that delinquency seldom occurred at the end of the offender's sentence. This study suggests that early and effective responses to delinquency can successfully interrupt a pattern of nonpayment.

The ABA study also suggests that compliance rates were higher in jurisdictions where the judge made an effort to determine if the offender had the ability to pay before the amount of restitution was set. When judges order restitution at a level so high as to be unreachable, it can result in noncompliance because the offender takes the attitude of why even try to meet this impossible goal. This noncompliance frustrates both the victim and the official charged with collecting restitution.[35]

Finally, the ABA study suggests the implementation of a policy within the criminal justice system that establishes a priority of collecting and disbursing fines, forfeitures, fees, and other assessments. This policy is necessary because oftentimes the offender is not only ordered to pay restitution, but also may have fines and other fees imposed such as repaying the court for the services of the public defender. These competing court-ordered financial obligations may affect the offender's ability to pay restitution to the victim.[36] Other recommendations that may make the restitution process more effective include specializing in the collection of restitution, employing automation, and using other nontraditional methods to collect restitution.

The Los Angeles criminal justice system is a large and sprawling bureaucratic system that seems impervious to change and the Los Angeles Probation Department is one of the largest in the nation. The adult probation department in Los Angeles tested a process of assigning specialized restitution caseloads to some of their officers. Their sole duty is to monitor and collect the court-ordered restitution. This procedure has proved to be so successful that the department has assigned probation officers to each of its offices in Los Angeles, whose primary duty is to collect restitution.[37]

Automation of records and bookkeeping can assist in collecting restitution. An investment in computer systems and software dedicated to the collection and disbursement of restitution sends a message to offenders that this is a high priority. Automation frees staff from performing routine repetitive tasks and can result in allowing them to work more closely with victims. Additionally, it can free up time to send letters informing victims of the restitution process by simply typing in their name and address and hitting the print key. Warning letters to offenders who are delinquent can also be generated quickly without much staff time. Finally, computerization gives staff the ability to collect data and develop statistics regarding restitution.[38]

A number of other innovative methods for collecting restitution are in use across the nation. These include filing civil law suits and obtaining judgments based on the restitution order. In states that allow this process, once the default is placed on the judgment, the victim can garnish the offender's wages, file liens on real property, and attach other assets. One department in Phoenix, Arizona, requires offenders to turn over their uncashed paychecks to the department. The department then cashes the check, deducts the amount owed for restitution, and writes the offender another check for the balance. Some states are using restitution centers which house offenders for six months to a year while they work in the community. Their checks are given to the center which deducts its expenses, other fines, and restitution before paying the balance to the perpetrator.[39] The Office for Victims of Crime continues to fund research in this area by calling for promising practices and policies in the field that address the issue of collection of restitution.

Summary

Crime victim compensation funds can pay for unreimbursed expenses suffered by victims of violent crimes. These state programs are funded by federally imposed fines, forfeitures, and other moneys taken from federal offenders. Each state receives a portion of these funds to compensate victims. More victims are filing claims and although some program managers are concerned over the financial drain caused by these increased claims, most see this as a positive development within the victims' rights movement.

In the last twenty years, restitution has reemerged within the criminal justice system as a valuable method of assisting victims of crime. Victim advocates continue to call for more efficient methods of monitoring and collecting restitution. As a result, professionals within the criminal justice system are reevaluating existing programs and policies in an attempt to meet the demand that restitution make the victim whole. Victim service providers need to be aware of the pros and cons of the restitution process and be prepared to offer suggestions to those who have the power to make necessary changes that will benefit victims of crime.

Key Terms

Victim compensation is a direct payment to, or on behalf of, a crime victim for crime-related expenses such as unpaid medical bills, mental health counseling, funeral costs, and lost wages.

Victim assistance includes services such as crisis intervention, counseling, emergency transportation to court, temporary housing, advocacy, and criminal justice support.

Subrogation is the process in which third parties are asked to reimburse the state for compensation payments previously made to the victim.

Contributory misconduct occurs when victims participate in the crime or otherwise contribute to their injuries by their own conduct.

Restitution is a court-ordered sanction that involves payment of compensation by the defendant to the victim for injuries suffered as a result of the defendant's criminal act.

Discussion Questions

1. Explain how a typical compensation program is funded and operated.

2. Understand the various eligibility requirements for receiving compensation.

3. List the various benefits victims of crime may receive under a state compensation program.

4. Explain why the historical perspective of restitution is important in understanding today's models.

5. Can you list reasons why an incarcerated prisoner should not have to make restitution to a victim? Assume you are the prisoner's advocate and must convince a judge of your position.

Suggested Readings

Crime Victim Compensation: A Fact Sheet and Crime Victim Compensation: An Overview, (National Association of Crime Victim Compensation Boards, Alexandria, Va.) July 1, 1994.

Dale G. Parent, Barbara Auerbach, & Kenneth E. Carlson, *Compensating Crime Victims: A Summary of Policies and Practices,* Office of Justice Programs, (U.S. Department of Justice, Washington, D.C.) January 1992.

Focus on the Future: A Systems Approach to Prosecution and Victim Assistance, National Victim Center, MADD, and American Prosecutors Research Institute, (U.S. Department of Justice, Washington, D.C.) no date.

Daniel McGillis & Patricia Smith, *Compensating Victims of Crime: An Analysis of American Programs,* (National Institute of Justice, Washington, D.C.) 1983.

A. J. Lurigio, W. G. Skogan, & R. C. Davis, (eds.), *Victims of Crime: Problems, Policies, and Programs,* (Sage, Newbury Park, Calif.) 1990.

B. Gateway & J. Hudson, (eds.), *Criminal Justice, Restitution, and Reconciliation,* (Willow Tree Press, Inc., Monsey, N.Y.) 1990.

National Victim Assistance Academy Text, (Office for Victims of Crime, Washington, D.C.) 1996.

A. R. Roberts, *Helping Crime Victims,* (Sage, Newbury Park, Calif.) 1990.

Barbara E. Smith, Robert C. Davis, & Susan W. Hillenbrand, *Enforcement of Court-Ordered Restitution: Executive Summary,* (American Bar Association, Chicago) 1989.

D. Beatty, L. Frank, A. J. Lurigio, A. Seymour, M. Paparozzi, B. Macgargle, *A Guide to Enhancing Victim Services Within Probation and Parole,* (American Bar Association, Chicago) 1994.

Endnotes

1. Much of the material that appears in this section has been adapted from various federally funded projects including NACVCB's *Crime Victim Compensation: A Fact Sheet and Crime Victim Compensation: An Overview,* (National Association of Crime Victim Compensation Boards,

Alexandria, Va.) July 1, 1994; hereinafter *Crime Victim Compensation*, Dale G. Parent, Barbara Auerbach, & Kenneth E. Carlson, *Compensating Crime Victims: A Summary of Policies and Practices*, Office of Justice Programs, (US Department of Justice, January 1992); hereinafter *Compensating Crime Victims* and *Focus on the Future: A Systems Approach to Prosecution and Victim Assistance*, National Victim Center, MADD, and American Prosecutors Research Institute, (US Department of Justice, Washington, D.C.) no date; hereinafter *Focus on the Future*.

2. *Crime Victim Compensation*.
3. "Victims of Crime Act Crime Victims Fund," *OVC Fact Sheet*, (Office for Victims of Crime, Washington, D.C.) no date.
4. Id.
5. *Final Report, President's Task Force on Victims of Crime*, (GPO, Washington, D.C.) December 1982.
6. Id.
7. *Compensating Crime Victims*, p. 2.
8. Id.
9. *Crime Victim Compensation*, p. 2.
10. Id.
11. *Compensating Crime Victims*, p. 7.
12. "Victims of Crime Act Crime Victims Fund," *OVC Fact Sheet*, (Office for Victims of Crime, Washington, D.C.) no date.
13. Daniel McGillis & Patricia Smith, *Compensating Victims of Crime: An Analysis of American Programs*, (National Institute of Justice, Washington, D.C.) 1983.
14. *Compensating Crime Victims*, p. 20.
15. *Compensating Crime Victims*, p. 21.
16. Adapted from scenarios presented in *Compensating Crime Victims*, pp. 24–25.
17. *Crime Victim Compensation*, p. 3.
18. *Compensating Crime Victims*, p. 30.
19. Michael D. Harris, "No One Wants Responsibility for Restitution," *Los Angeles Daily Transcript*, p. A-1 (January 6, 1995).
20. *Final Report, President's Task Force on Victims of Crime*, (GPO, Washington, D.C.) December 1982.
21. Id. at 38.
22. Susan Hillenbrand, "Restitution and Victim Rights in the 1980s," in A. J. Lurigio, W. G. Skogan, and R. C. Davis, (eds.), *Victims of Crime: Problems, Policies, and Programs*, (Sage, Newbury Park, Calif.) 1990.
23. Carol Shapiro, "Is Restitution Legislation the Chameleon of the Victims' Movement?" in B. Gateway and J. Hudson, (eds.), *Criminal Justice, Restitution, and Reconciliation*, (Willow Tree Press, Inc., Monsey, N.Y.) 1990.
24. This section has been adapted from Sterling O'Ran, "Restitution," *National Victim Assistance Academy Test*, (Office for Victims of Crime, Washington, D.C.) 1996; hereinafter *National Victim Assistance Academy Test*.
25. See for example, Gordon, *Hammurabi's Code: Quaint or Forward Looking*, (Rinehart, New York) 1957; and S. A. Cook, *The Laws of Moses and the Code of Hammurabi*, (Adam and Charles Black, London) 1903.
26. Cathryn Jo Rosen & Allen T. Harland, "Restitution to Crime Victims as a Presumptive Requirement in Criminal Cases," in A. R. Roberts, *Helping Crime Victims*, (Sage, Newbury Park, Calif.) 1990.
27. L. F. Frank, "The Collection of Restitution: An Overlooked Service to Crime Victims," 8 *St. John's Journal of Legal Commentary*, 107 (1992).
28. *National Victim Assistance Academy Text*, pp. 21–10–5.
29. *Attorney General Guidelines for Victim and Witness Assistance*, (U.S. Department of Justice, Washington, D.C.) 1995.
30. 18 U.S.C. Section 3663(b) as amended by Section 40504 of P.L. 103–322 (1994).
31. *National Victim Assistance Academy Text*, pp. 21–10–8 through 11.
32. Michael D. Harris, "No One Wants Responsibility for Restitution," *Los Angeles Daily Transcript*, p. A-1. (January 6, 1995).
33. *National Victim Assistance Academy Text*, pp. 21–10–7.
34. Barbara E. Smith, Robert C. Davis, & Susan W. Hillenbrand, *Enforcement of Court-Ordered Restitution: Executive Summary*, (American Bar Association, Chicago) 1989.
35. Id.
36. Id.
37. D. Beatty, L. Frank, A. J. Lurigio, A. Seymour, M. Paparozzi, & B. Macgargle, *A Guide to Enhancing Victim Services within Probation and Parole*, (American Bar Association, Chicago) 1994.
38. Id.
39. Id.

18

VICTIM IMPACT STATEMENTS

Chapter Outline

History of Victim Impact Statements
Purpose
Constitutional Issues

Use of Victim Impact Statements
Law Enforcement
Prosecutors
Judiciary

Effect of Victim Impact Statements
Victim Satisfaction
Sentencing

Victim Impact Panels
Introduction
Procedure

Summary

Key Terms

Discussion Questions

Suggested Readings

Learning Objectives

After reading this chapter, you should be able to:

- Explain the constitutional evolution of victim impact statements
- Understand fundamental fairness and how it relates to victim impact statements

- Distinguish between law enforcement and prosecutorial-based victim assistance programs
- Explain how victims view the affect of victim impact statements and compare this with how judges view this process
- Distinguish between victim impact statements and victim impact panels

History of Victim Impact Statements

A new series of rights are emerging in our judicial system.[1] These rights confer upon the victim, or the relatives of deceased victims, the opportunity to speak out or be heard during various phases of the criminal justice process. As with many rights that converge on a single point, an actual or potential conflict results. How we handle this conflict is a reflection of the morals and ethics of our society. This section will review the history of these various rights and examine the rationale behind the current status of the law as it relates to victim impact statements.

Purpose

One controversial "right" bestowed upon victims is known as the *victim impact statement.* This statement presents the victim's point of view to the sentencing authority. Providing the sentencing authority with all relevant information is not a new phenomenon in the criminal justice system. For many years courts have accepted information regarding the defendant prior to the imposition of a sentence.

Traditionally, presentence reports have been utilized by judges to determine the proper punishment for criminal defendants. The report, which is normally prepared by a probation officer, details the defendant's background, education, and prior criminal record. Many of these reports also include information concerning the victim of the crime.[2]

Victim impact evidence is now admitted in sentencing for a variety of criminal acts, including those that fall within the realm of family violence. However, the law on admissibility and use of victim impact statements is based on use of this evidence during death penalty cases. To understand the nature of victim impact statements it is necessary to review how this evidence is used in the most serious type of criminal case—those involving capital punishment.

The use of victim impact evidence during the sentencing phase of a criminal crime raises serious constitutional issues. The right to confront witnesses comes head-to-head with the right to have all relevant evidence placed before the sentencing authority. Intense feelings have been aroused in the Supreme Court when it addressed this issue.

Constitutional Issues

In *Booth v. Maryland,* the Supreme Court initially addressed the issue of using victim impact statements in a sentencing jury's determination.[3] In 1983, John Booth and Willie Reed bound and gagged an elderly couple. Believing the couple might be able to identify them, Booth stabbed them numerous times with a kitchen knife. The trial judge in *Booth* allowed the jury to consider a victim impact statement, which detailed the family and community's respect and admiration for the victims as well as the impact of the murder on the victim's family.[4]

The Supreme Court, in reversing the death sentence, held that it was impermissible to allow the jury access to such evidence in the sentencing phase of a death penalty proceeding.[5] The Court listed three factors which precluded the prosecution from introducing evidence of the homicide's impact on the victim's family.

First, in holding that the victim impact statement (VIS) impermissibly allows the jury to focus on the victim rather than the defendant, the Court stated:

> When the full range of foreseeable consequences of a defendant's actions may be relevant in other criminal and civil contexts, we cannot agree that it is relevant in the unique circumstances of a capital sentencing hearing. In such a case, it is the function of the sentencing jury to "express the conscience of the community on the ultimate question of life or death." When carrying out this task the jury is required to focus on the defendant as a "uniquely individual bein[g]." The focus of a VIS, however, is not on the defendant, but on the character and reputation of the victim and the effect on his family. These factors may be wholly unrelated to the blameworthiness of a particular defendant.[6]

The Court was particularly moved by the fact that the capital defendant does not typically choose his victim and, in fixing the punishment, there should be no correlation between the murder and the grief experienced by the victim's family.

Second, the Court held that the sentence of death should not turn on the characteristics of the victim and the victim's family. Specifically, the Court recognized that the imposition of the death penalty should not be determined on the basis of the ability of the victim's family to articulate their anguish and bereavement, regardless if the victim left behind a family, or on the fact that the victim was a stellar member of the community.[7] These factors focus attention on the victim and away from the central inquiry of whether the defendant's characteristics and background are such that the death sentence is warranted.[8]

Finally, the Court stated that because a VIS contains the subjective perceptions and feelings of family members, the defendant has limited rebuttal opportunity.[9] Further, to the extent the defendant is given an opportunity to rebut such information, "[t]he prospects of a 'mini-trial' on the victim's character is more than simply unappealing, it could well direct the sentencing jury from its constitutionally required task—determining whether the death penalty is appropriate in light of . . . the crime."[10]

In summing up the Court's holding that introduction of the VIS violates the Eighth Amendment's prohibition against cruel and unusual punishment, Justice Powell commented:

> One can understand the grief and anger of the family caused by the brutal murders in this case, and there is no doubt that jurors generally are aware of these

feelings. But the formal presentation of this information by the State can serve no other purpose than to inflame the jury and divert it from deciding the case on the relevant evidence concerning the crimes and the defendant. As we have noted, any decision to impose the death sentence must "be, and appear to be, based on reason rather than caprice or emotion." The admission of these emotionally charged opinions as to what conclusions the jury should draw from the evidence clearly is inconsistent with the reasoned decision making we require in capital cases.[11]

It should be apparent that at the time of the decision in *Booth v. Maryland,* the relevant considerations at the sentencing phase of a murder trial were those aspects of a defendant's background, or character, or those circumstances which extenuate or mitigate the defendant's culpability.

South Carolina v. Gathers followed the rationale of *Booth* and held unconstitutional the imposition of a death penalty based on prosecutorial remarks that were considered inflammatory.[12] Demetrius Gather and three companions sexually assaulted and killed Richard Haynes, a man they encountered in a park. During the incident, the perpetrators ransacked a bag the victim was carrying. The bag contained several articles pertaining to religion, including a religious tract entitled, "Game Guy's Prayer." During the sentencing phase of the trial, the prosecutor's argument included references to Haynes's personal qualities and included a reading of the "Game Guy's Prayer." The Supreme Court reversed the sentence stating that such references to the qualities of the victim were similar to the *Booth* holding, which prohibited victim impact statements. The court determined that such evidence was likely to inflame the jury and thus violate the defendant's Eighth Amendment rights. In a well-reasoned and logical dissent, Justice O'Conner stated, "Nothing in the Eighth Amendment precludes the community from considering its loss in assessing punishment nor requires that the victim remain a faceless stranger at the penalty phase of a capital case." The dissent by Justice O'Conner was a signal that the winds of judicial temperament might be changing.

In *Payne v. Tennessee,* the court completely reversed itself and allowed the imposition of a death sentence to stand, based in part on evidence contained in a victim impact statement. In 1987, Pervis Tyrone Payne entered the apartment of Charisse Christopher and her two children. Payne stabbed Charisse and the two children numerous times with a butcher knife. Charisse and her daughter died; however, three-year-old Nicholas survived.

Payne was caught and convicted for the murders. During the penalty phase, four witnesses testified regarding the defendant's background, reputation, and mental state. These witnesses urged the jury to not impose the death penalty. In rebuttal, the prosecution called the maternal grandmother who was caring for Nicholas. She was allowed to testify, over the defendant's objection, that Nicholas continued to cry out calling for his dead mother and sister. The witness was also allowed to testify regarding her personal grief over the loss of her loved ones.

During the closing argument, the prosecutor hammered on the pain and suffering that Nicholas and his deceased family had endured stating:

But we do know that Nicholas was alive. And Nicholas was in the same room. Nicholas was still conscious. His eyes were open. He responded to the paramedics. He was able to follow their directions. He was able to hold his intestines in as he was carried to the ambulance. So he knew what happened to his mother and baby sister.

There is nothing you can do to ease the pain of any of the families involved in this case. There is nothing you can do to ease the pain of Bernice or Carl Payne, and that's a tragedy. There is nothing you can do basically to ease the pain of Mr. and Mrs. Zvolanek, and that's a tragedy. They will have to live with it for the rest of their lives. There is obviously nothing you can do for Charisse and Lacie Jo. But there is something you can do for Nicholas.

Somewhere down the road Nicholas is going to grow up, hopefully. He's going to want to know what happened. And he is going to know what happened to his baby sister and his mother. He is going to want to know what kind of justice was done. He is going to want to know what happened. With your verdict, you will provide the answer."[13]

The jury sentenced Payne to death and the case was appealed to the U.S. Supreme Court. Payne contended that the trial court erred when it allowed the maternal grandmother to testify. Relying on *Booth* and *Gathers*, Payne argued that such evidence was a violation of his Eighth Amendment rights.

After reviewing the principles that have guided criminal sentencing over the ages, the Court stated that the consideration of the harm caused by the crime has been an important factor in the existence of the exercise of judicial discretion. The majority opinion went on to state that neither *Booth* nor *Gathers* even suggested that a defendant, entitled as he is to individualized consideration, is to receive that consideration wholly apart from the crime which he has committed.

In setting forth the groundwork for overruling *Booth* and *Gathers*, the Court stated:

Under our constitutional system, the primary responsibility for defining crimes against state law, fixing punishments for the commission of those crimes, and establishing procedures for criminal trials rests with the States. The state laws respecting crimes, punishments, and criminal procedures are of course subject to the overriding provisions of the United States Constitution. Where the State imposes the death penalty for a particular crime, we have held that the Eight Amendment imposes special limitations upon that process.

The States remain free, in capital cases, as well as others, to devise new procedures and new remedies to meet felt needs. Victim impact evidence is simply another form or method of informing the sentencing authority about the specific harm caused by the crime in question, evidence of a general type long considered by sentencing authorities. We think the Booth *Court was wrong in stating that this kind of evidence leads to the arbitrary imposition of the death penalty. In the majority of cases, and in this case, victim impact evidence serves entirely legitimate purposes.*[14]

Thus the Supreme Court overruled *Booth* and *Gathers* to the extent that they prohibited introduction of evidence or argument regarding the impact of the crime on the victim, families, and the community. In addition, the Court's decision clearly stated that the decision regarding the admission of such evidence was the prerogative of the individual states. The Court ruled it would not intervene unless the evidence introduced was so unduly prejudicial that it renders the trial fundamentally unfair.[15] If this occurred the court reasoned, the due process clause of the Fourteenth Amendment provides a mechanism for relief.

The decision was not without heated dissent. In a dissenting opinion, Justices Marshall and Blackmun uttered a quote that will ring in the halls of justice and law school classrooms forever: "Power, not reason, is the new currency of this Court's decision making."[16] Justices Marshall and Blackmun went on to point out that the court was disregarding the accepted judicial principle of stare decisis. In a well-reasoned, but emotional conclusion, the justices stated:

> *Today's decision charts an unmistakable course. If the majority's radical recon-struction of the rules for overturning this Court's decisions is to be taken at face value—and the majority offers us no reason why it should not—then the over-ruling of* Booth *and* Gathers *is but a preview of an even broader and more far-reaching assault upon this Court's precedents. Cast aside today are those con-demned to face society's ultimate penalty. Tomorrow's victims may be minorities, women, or the indigent. Inevitably, this campaign to resurrect yesterday's "spir-ited dissents" will squander the authority and the legitimacy of this Court as a protector of the powerless.*[17]

The decision also generated controversy in the academic world when a series of articles appeared condemning the court for both allowing victim impact evi-dence and appearing to repudiate its acceptance of stare decisis.[18] Although the dissent and certain individuals within the academic community may condemn the majority's opinion, it is now clearly the law of the land. In addition, the Supreme Court's decision enhances the victims' rights movement in the United States. It allows individual states to determine what is relevant evidence in the death penalty phase of a capital crime.

Some would argue that the decision in *Payne* leaves prosecutors and defense attorneys scrambling to determine what type of evidence is admissible under the guise of victim impact statements. The answer is simply that evidence which does not result in rendering a trial fundamentally unfair is proper. This concept of fun-damental fairness is not a new, untested, or ill-defined doctrine.

There is a long history defining acts by the state that are classified as funda-mentally unfair. The doctrine of fundamental fairness has its roots in two early cases. In *Powell v. Alabama* several black youths were accused of repeatedly raping two young white girls. They were caught, tried, and convicted. Their conviction was overturned on the ground that the failure of the trial court to appoint counsel until the day of the trial was a violation of the defendants' due process.[19] In *Brown v. Mississippi,* a sheriff hung the defendant from a tree and whipped him until he confessed to the murder of a white man. The Supreme Court held that such actions are revolting to the sense of justice and the confession was suppressed.[20]

The *doctrine of fundamental fairness* accepts the concept that due process is a generalized command that requires states to provide the defendant with a fair trial. If the admission of the victim impact evidence "revolts the sense of justice" or "shocks the conscience" of the court, such admission would be erroneous under the due process clause.

Victim impact evidence is now an accepted part of the judicial process. The ability of a victim of family violence to inform the court of the impact of the offender's acts on her life can only benefit the victim and continue to educate the public regarding the dynamics of violence.

Use of Victim Impact Statements

Law Enforcement

Law enforcement officers should understand the victim impact process for a number of reasons: (1) many departmental policy manuals require that they inform victims of this right, (2) the officer can demonstrate concern by explaining the process to the victim, and (3) educating victims about their rights ensures that others within the criminal justice system will understand the impact of crime on the victims.[21] Once any crime has been reported, law enforcement officers should inform the victims of their rights early in the investigation process. They should offer assistance and encourage victims to keep a record or diary of their feelings, emotions and hardships. This record should also track expenses so that the impact statements accurately reflect the appropriate amount of restitution. After an offender's arrest, victims should be encouraged to talk with the local victim—witness coordinator and the prosecutor regarding their feelings about the crime and any plea bargain.

Law enforcement officers do not stop participating in the process simply because they have arrested the perpetrator. Nor should they stop their involvement with the victims of crime. They should "share ownership of the case"

FOCUS: Acceptance of Victim Impact Statements

A particular segment of society believes that victims should not be allowed to speak out at a defendant's sentencing. In February 1995, at the sentencing hearing of Long Island Railroad gunman Colin Ferguson, who shot, wounded, and killed several Long Island commuters, victims spoke out about their anguish and feelings. The *Wall Street Journal*, the *New York Times*, and the *Washington Post* all responded by endorsing the use of victim impact statements.

The *New Republic*, however, argued that the use of such statements might inflame the judge or jury.[22] It stated that one of the most basic requirements of the rule of law is that judges and juries be impartial. Further, the editorial stated that victim impact evidence guarantees "that the trials will degenerate into lawless emotionalism."[23]

by working with and keeping victims informed of their rights. The officer should encourage victims to participate in the process and explain that their information may make a difference. Officers should inform victims of the procedures and policies regarding victim impact statements in their jurisdiction. Do they send a letter to the judge? Do they fill out a form? Where do they get this form? Can they talk with the probation officer? A number of questions need to be answered and law enforcement officers are in the best position to answer these questions for victims.[24]

The debate continues in the criminal justice profession regarding the extent of law enforcement's role in the victim impact statement process. Supporters of an active role by law enforcement argue that this process provides victims of crime with information about their rights and thus allows them to participate in the justice process almost from the beginning. Supporters also explain that such a process allows victims to begin to document their feelings and financial losses early in the process. Opponents argue that forcing law enforcement officers to give information regarding victims' rights early in the process leads victims to assume that the offender will be identified, arrested, and convicted. Statistically, a number of crimes occur in which the perpetrator is never caught. Opponents also argue that most victims are not familiar with the criminal justice system and officers will have to spend valuable time educating them about the system when, in fact, the perpetrator may never be caught.[25]

In recent years, many law enforcement agencies have established police-based victim assistance programs. These programs have the ability to provide services to crime victims who might otherwise have been excluded from receiving such services because some of these programs focus on those victims whose cases have formally entered the criminal justice system. For example, a police-based victim assistance program might inform victims of their right to state compensation funds.[26] As the previous chapter explained, these funds are available even if the perpetrator is not apprehended. As these programs gain popularity, victim service providers must be ready to assist law enforcement agencies in setting up their own program and working with these agencies to ensure that victims of crime are informed of their rights.

Prosecutors

The duties of prosecutors and law enforcement officers often overlap within the criminal justice process. Police make arrests, conduct investigations, interrogate suspects, and file cases with the district attorney's office. Many times prosecutors accompany police on raids, sit in on interrogations, and conduct their own follow-up investigations. Just as these two principles in the criminal justice system work together to attain a conviction of the perpetrator, so must they coordinate their efforts in working with victims and their interaction with the criminal justice system. In no place is this more important than during the sentencing phase of any trial.

Our criminal justice system is slowly beginning to recognize that its failure to grant victims an active role in the dispensation of justice is shortsighted because the continued successful functioning of the prosecutor's office depends on the cooperation and assistance of victims. Traditionally, prosecutor's offices have been assigned the role of creating and administrating victim assistance programs.

This role was viewed as necessary in that prosecutors have a vested interest in facilitating victim participation in the system.[27]

Placing victim assistance programs in prosecutors' offices provide them with a number of advantages: they have instant access to information about the victim's physical, emotional, and financial status which can assist in charging or deposition of cases; they will lessen the chances that an adversarial relationship will develop between the victim and the prosecutor; and they can favorably influence the victim's decision regarding any proposed plea bargain.[28]

Prosecutors should establish policies and procedures that assign agency responsibility for the distribution and collection of victim impact statements. These guidelines should address the issue of coordination between the various agencies in the criminal justice system. This coordination is necessary so that victims are not filling out two, three, or more impact forms and more importantly, so that victims are not overlooked in the system.

Prosecutors should also ensure that victims are informed of the policies and procedures surrounding the victim impact statement including the following: the purpose and use of the impact statement; who is eligible to submit a statement; how it should be submitted (written, oral, video, etc.); how the court will use the statement; and how to request assistance with filling out the statement. This information will not only assist the prosecutor in arguing for an appropriate sentence, but will also make the victim feel part of the system. Working with crime victims and helping them to prepare a victim impact statement offers a prosecutor a chance to become more responsive to the needs of victims, and thereby improve the nature of the criminal justice system.

Some prosecutors may resist this active involvement with victims. Some may argue that this infringes on the discretion vested in prosecutors, whereas others will claim that victims do not understand the system, and they as prosecutors do not have the time to explain it to them. Just as some prosecutors resisted working with the staffs of rape crisis centers, others may resist this participation by victims of crimes. Victim service providers must be the advocates for these types of change. They are knowledgeable, and experienced, and they understand the system and can work with reluctant prosecutors to overcome any fears or concerns about working with victims of crime.

Judiciary

Crime is an extremely personal phenomenon and therefore no two victims will experience the same emotional, physical, or financial impact. It is imperative that judges have access to all pertinent information prior to sentencing so that they can balance society's needs, the defendant's needs, and the victim's needs. One method of balancing these needs is through the use of victim impact statements.

The *President's Task Force on Victims of Crime* addressed the issue of victim participation at sentencing by stating:

> *Victims, no less than defendants, are entitled to their day in court. Victims, no less than defendants, are entitled to have their views considered. A judge cannot*

evaluate the seriousness of a defendant's conduct without knowing how the crime has burdened the victim. A judge cannot reach an informed determination of the danger posed by a defendant without hearing from the person he has victimized.[29]

Judges should participate in this victim impact process by ensuring that victims are made aware of the opportunity to present their views prior to sentencing. This presentation of their position should be facilitated by judges, and victims should be allowed to present victim impact evidence in a variety of methods including orally, in writing, by video, or via any other method that accurately presents the victim's feelings to the court.

Americans have always believed that the ultimate responsibility for how the judicial system operates rests with judges. Judges should ensure that victims participate at the sentencing hearing which, with the exception of parole hearings, is the last opportunity that they have to influence the fate of the offender. Allowing victims to be part of this hearing can reaffirm their beliefs in the judicial system.

Effect of Victim Impact Statements

Victim Satisfaction

The effect of victim impact statements is still being studied and debated. One area being studied carefully is victim satisfaction with victim impact statements. Some authorities believe impact statements help the victim emotionally deal with the consequences of the crime. Others believe victims are more satisfied with the criminal justice system if they participate by being allowed to express their feelings in a victim impact statement. This section will briefly examine these and other aspects of victim satisfaction and victim impact statements.

In 1981, a National Institute of Justice study revealed that victims' satisfaction with the criminal justice system increased if they believed that they had influenced the process, regardless of whether they really had. For example, victims who had been able to speak to prosecutors and judges were more satisfied with the system than those who believed they were not able to speak.[30] In 1982, another study indicated that a sense of participation was more critical to victims' satisfaction with the criminal justice process than how severely the defendant was punished.[31] In 1984, another study revealed that victims wanted more information

---

FOCUS: Feelings Regarding Victim Impact Statements

"My victim impact statement was the last opportunity I had to let anyone know about my daughter."

—a victim

"I want you to go over each victim impact statement. . . . You have to live with the stu-

pidity of your behavior for the rest of your life, but you also have to understand what these families have to live with as well. . . .

—Judge to a defendant at time of sentencing[32]

about their case and the opportunity to tell the prosecutor and judge how the case affected them.[33]

In 1989, Dean Kilpatrick reported the results of his research which indicated that victim participation not only affected potential cooperation within the criminal justice system, but that it was also critical in promoting victims' recovery from the aftermath of crime by helping them to reassert a sense of control over their lives.[34] Kilpatrick states that a criminal justice system which denies victims a chance to participate fosters a sense of helplessness and lack of control. He points out that there is a great danger in promising victims participation in the system and then failing to follow through with that promise, because it results in further victimization.

Robert Wells, another noted authority, states that victim impact statements may promote the psychological recovery of victims. Just as talking about what happened promotes healing, writing about it may also assist victims to emotionally deal with the crime. Allowing victims to tell how they were affected by the crime sends a supportive message that the criminal justice system cares about what happened.[35]

However, other experts claim the mental and emotional benefits of victim impact statements and victim participation are overrated. In a 1985 study carried out in Brooklyn, Davis compared the outcome of two court experiments in which victims gave impact statements in one court, and where no statements were allowed in another court. He found no evidence that victims in the court that mandated impact statements felt a greater sense of participation or increased satisfaction.[36] Davis followed this research with a 1989 study in the Bronx Supreme Court in New York.[37] The study analyzed 293 victims of robbery, nonsexual assault, and burglary. Each victim was assigned to one of three classifications: (1) some victims were interviewed and a victim impact statement written and distributed, (2) other victims were interviewed, but no impact statement was prepared, and (3) only the name and address of the victim was recorded. A series of interviews was conducted with each victim. The results of this study indicated that victim impact statements are not an effective means of promoting victim satisfaction within the criminal justice system. There were no data to support the theory that victim impact statements led to greater feelings of involvement, greater satisfaction with the criminal justice system, or greater satisfaction with the sentences imposed on the offenders. Davis concluded that more research is necessary regarding the effect of impact statements on victim satisfaction with the system.

As this discussion indicates, controversy continues over the effect of victim impact statements on victim satisfaction. However, there is sufficient individual and anecdotal evidence of victim approval of the use of impact statements that we should continue using them until definitive studies can be conducted. The next section will examine whether victim impact statements affect the outcome of sentencing.

Sentencing

There is limited research on the effect that victim impact statements have on judges. Superficially, it would appear that such evidence can only assist the court in rendering its decision and therefore should be readily accepted and consistently used by the judicial system. However, judges, like every other member of the criminal justice system, are understaffed and overworked. Does additional information really help or does the process simply take more time? Are judges swayed by the emotional appeal of a citizen or are they bound to render impartial justice to the defendant?

Early research indicates that state trial court judges found financial information contained in a victim impact statement useful in determining appropriate sentences and restitution orders.[38] Of those judges interviewed, 70 percent found the information useful and another 20 percent found it useful in regard to restitution orders. Although this research indicates victim impact evidence is useful to judges, this "usefulness" appears limited to the area of restitution and financial issues, and not to other aspects of sentencing the defendant.

In 1990, Erez and Tontodonato produced an important study involving 500 Ohio felony cases and found that the cases in which a victim impact statement was taken were more likely than those without a statement to result in the offender going to prison rather than receiving probation.[39] This research has been cited by a number of victim impact statement proponents as authority for the position that such statements have an effect on sentencing. Although this study was significant, it had several flaws including a wide disparity in offense seriousness between cases that had impact statements. Additionally, the authors acknowledged that further research needed to be conducted in this area.

Davis and Smith also researched the effect of impact statements on sentencing. In the same 1989 study that examined victim satisfaction, Davis and his associate evaluated the significance of impact statements on judicial sentencing.[40] They concluded that victim impact statements did not produce sentences that reflect the effects of crime on the victims. Nor did they find that sentencing decisions were affected by impact statements once the charge and the defendant's prior record were considered by the court. They did find that the severity of the charges is a high predictor of sentences. Whereas judges professed to be interested in impact statements, prosecutors believed that judges only occasionally considered this information when imposing sentences. Conversely, prosecutors claimed that victims should be consulted on a regular basis, but judges stated that prosecutors rarely related impact evidence to them.

Clearly more research is also needed in this area. Additionally, such research must find a way to get around the "political correctness" of advocating the use of victim impact statements. As Davis's study points out, judges claim they endorse impact statements, but prosecutors don't believe them. On the other hand, the same prosecutors claim they use impact statements, but the judges don't see them. Realistically, few elected or appointed officials in today's climate within the criminal justice system will admit to anything less than wholehearted endorsement of victim impact statements. What is needed is an in-depth study to determine the impact of such evidence outside the realm of political correctness. Until such research is done, we can only speculate on its real effect.

Victim Impact Panels

Introduction

Victim impact panels (VIPs) differ significantly from victim impact statements. However, because they involve victims discussing the impact of the offense on their lives, they are included in this chapter rather than elsewhere in this text. MADD established victim impact panels as a method of dealing with the problem of drunk driving.[41] MADD does not believe that victim impact panels should replace traditional criminal sanctions for driving under the influence. They are offered to enhance and supplement such sentencing by placing offenders face to face with victims of drunk driving whose lives have been changed by someone who drank and then got behind the wheel of a car.

Procedure

MADD or other victim groups select a panel of three to four victims to speak briefly about the drunk driving crashes in which they were injured or a loved one was killed, and what the event has meant to them. They do not blame or judge the attendees. A victim impact panel coordinator moderates the panel, and victims are never allowed to speak at groups in which their own offender is present. The attendees are convicted drunk drivers who are required to attend a panel as an element of their sentences. A probation officer or other agent of the court attends each panel to monitor attendance. Any person who fails to appear for a panel is required to return to court for appropriate action.[42]

Victims who have served on these panels find that telling their stories lightens their personal pain and assists in the healing process. Victims also report that they have experienced something positive from a previously devastating event and they believe that by telling their stories they may be preventing some other family from suffering a similar fate.[43]

The goals of the victim impact panel are to enhance the emotional healing of victims by offering them an opportunity to speak out about the incident. These panels also enable attendees to understand drunk driving from the victim's perspective. Hopefully these stories will curtail the attendees' decisions to drink and drive.

Victim impact panels are different than victim impact statements. However, they both serve to allow victims to express their feelings regarding the consequences of a crime. The opportunity to express feelings regarding the event can be a valuable healing process. Although victim impact panels are relatively new within the criminal justice system, they offer another sentencing option to judges.

Summary

Victim impact statements are now accepted as a constitutionally firm mechanism that may be used in criminal cases, whether these cases are simple assaults or death penalty cases. The use of these statements is governed by the principle of fundamental fairness which requires courts to ensure that the defendant receives a fair trial. A properly conducted victim impact statement does not violate this mandate.

To be effective, the victim impact statement must be accepted by all parties within the criminal justice system. Law enforcement officers should be aware of it and be prepared to inform victims of its availability. Prosecutors are the logical choices to coordinate victim impact statements and should take the lead. Judges are looked upon as the final authority within the criminal justice system and they should demand that the victim have an opportunity to speak at sentencing.

Controversy continues regarding the effectiveness of victim impact statements. More research needs to be conducted on both the issue of victim satisfaction and the effect of impact statements on sentencing. However, victim impact statements should continue to be used because some evidence supports the fact that victims believe the statements are an important right to which they should be afforded.

Victim impact panels are a new technique that offer victims of drunk driving the opportunity to express their feelings. They are similar to victim impact statements in that victims believe they serve a useful function. We must continue to explore alternative mechanisms that assist victims of crime in overcoming the consequences of the criminal act.

Key Terms

Victim impact statement presents the victim's point of view to the sentencing authority.

Doctrine of fundamental fairness accepts the concept that due process is a generalized command that requires states to provide the defendant with a fair trial.

Discussion Questions

1. Explain and give concrete examples of fundamental fairness. Can you list ways in which a victim impact statement would violate this constitutional standard?

2. Should law enforcement officers inform the victim of a crime about victim impact statements? Prepare a form that should be given to victims outlining their rights.

3. How are we ever going to determine if victim impact statements serve a valid purpose in the criminal justice system? How would you structure such a study? What are the pitfalls inherent in these types of studies?

4. Should a drunk driver be mandated to attend a victim impact panel? Why? Justify your answer.

Suggested Readings

Robert Wells, "Victim Impact Statements," *Crime Victim and Witness Assistance Training Project*, (Federal Law Enforcement Training Center, Glyno, Georgia) 1990.

Ellen K. Alexander & Janice H. Lord, *Impact Statements: A Victim's Right to Speak—A Nation's*

Responsibility to Listen, (National Victims Center, Arlington, Va.) 1992.

Janice H. Lord, *Victim Impact Panels: A Creative Sentencing Opportunity*, (Mothers Against Drunk Driving, Dallas) 1990.

Endnotes

1. This section has been adapted from H. Wallace, *Family Violence: Legal Medical and Social Perspectives*, (Allyn & Bacon, Boston) 1996.
2. See Phillip A. Talbert, "The Relevance of Victim Impact Statements to the Criminal Sentencing Decision," 36 *UCLA L Rev* 199, 202–211 (1988); and Maureen McLeod, "Victim Participation at Sentencing," 22 *Crim L. Bull.* 501, 505–511 (1986).
3. *Booth v. Maryland*, 482 U.S. 496 (1987).
4. Id. at 500–01.
5. Id. at 509. The Court did, however, carefully note that information typically contained in a victim's statement is generally admissible in noncapital cases and may be considered in capital cases if directly related to the circumstances of the crime. Id. at 508 n. 10. For example, the Court noted that the prosecution may produce evidence as to the characteristics of the victim to rebut an argument made by the defendant (e.g., victim's peaceable nature to rebut claim of self-defense.) Id.
6. Id. at 507–07 (citations omitted).
7. Id. at 505–07.
8. Id. at 507–08.
9. Id.
10. Id.
11. Id.
12. 490 U.S. 805 (1989).
13. 115 L.ED. 728–729.
14. 115 L.Ed. 734–735.
15. 115 L.Ed. 2d 735.
16. 115 L.Ed. 748.
17. 115 L.Ed. 756.
18. See Jimmie O. Clements, Jr., *Casenote, Criminal Law—Victim Impact Evidence—The Scope of the Eight Amendment Does Not Include a Per Se Bar to the Use of Victim Impact Evidence in the Sentencing Phase of a Capital Trial Payne v. Tennessee*. 23 St. Mary's L. J. 517 (1991); Aida Alaka, *Note, Victim Impact Evidence, Arbitrariness and the Death Penalty: The Supreme Court Flipflops in Payne v. Tennessee*, 23 Loy. U. Chi. L.J. 581 (1992); K. Elizabeth Whitehead, *Case Note, Mourning Becomes Electric: Payne v. Tennessee's Allowance of Victim Impact Statements During Capital Proceedings*, 45 Ark. L. Rev. 531 (1992).
19. *Powell v. Alabama*, 287 U.S. 45, 53 S.C. 55, 77 L.Ed. 158(1932).
20. 297 U.S. 278, 56 S.Ct. 461, 80 L.Ed. 682 (1936).
21. This section has been adapted from Robert Wells, "Victim Impact Statements," *Crime Victim and Witness Assistance Training Project*, (Federal Law Enforcement Training Center, Glyno, Georgia) 1990, hereinafter *Crime Victim and Witness Assistance*.
22. *The New Republic*, p. 9 (April 17, 1995).
23. Id.
24. *Crime Victim and Witness Assistance*.
25. Ellen K. Alexander & Janice H. Lord, *Impact Statements: A Victim's Right to Speak—A Nation's Responsibility to Listen*, (National Victim Center, Arlington, Va.) 1992, hereinafter *Impact Statements*.
26. Id. at p. 10.
27. Id. at p. 14.
28. Id.
29. *President's Task Force on Victims of Crime: Final Report*, (GPO, Washington, D.C.) 1982, p. 77.
30. Barbara Smith & Susan Hillanbrand, *Non-Stranger Violence: The Criminal Courts*

Responses, (National Institute of Justice, Washington, D.C.) 1981.

31. Deborah P. Kelly, "Delivering Legal Services to Victims: An Evaluation and Prescription," 9 *Justice System Journal,* 62 (1982).

32. *Impact Statements* pp. 10, 17.

33. J. Hernon & B. Forst, "The Criminal Justice Response to Victim Harm," *Research Report,* (National Institute of Justice, Washington, D.C.) 1984.

34. Dean Kilpatrick & Randy K. Otto, "Constitutionally Guaranteed Participation in Criminal Proceedings for Victims: Potential Effects on Psychological Functioning," 34 *The Wayne State Law Review,* 17 (1989).

35. Robert Wells, "Victim Impact: How Much Consideration Is It Really Given?" *The Police Chief,* p. 44 (February 1991).

36. Robert C. Davis, *First Year Evaluation of the Victim Impact Demonstration Project,* (Victim Services Agency, New York) 1985.

37. Robert C. Davis & Barbara E. Smith, "Victim Impact Statements and Victim Satisfaction: An Unfulfilled Promise," 22 *Journal of Criminal Justice,* 1 (1994).

38. Susan Hillenbrand, *Victim Rights Legislation: An Assessment of Its Impact on the Criminal Justice System,* (American Bar Association, Chicago) 1987.

39. E. Erez & P. Tontodonato, "The Effect of Victim Participation in Sentencing on Sentence Outcomes," 28 *Criminology,* 451 (1990).

40. Robert C. Davis & Barbara E. Smith, "The Effects of Victim Impact Statements on Sentencing Decisions: A Test in an Urban Setting," 11/3 *Justice Quarterly,* 453 (September 1994).

41. This section has been adapted from Janice H. Lord, *Victim Impact Panels: A Creative Sentencing Opportunity,* (Mothers Against Drunk Driving, Dallas) 1990. Used with permission of MADD.

42. Id. at p. 6.

43. Id. at p. 10.

Epilogue

EMERGING TRENDS

Many current and emerging issues concerning victimology are addressed in the main body of this text. However, this should not imply that all issues dealing with victims, offenders, or society's reactions to crime have been included. Some of the more traditional subjects have received extensive coverage, whereas other newer topics have only been briefly discussed. These are issues facing professionals and researchers in the field today, or they are potential problems that may need to be addressed in the near future.

Although not included in the text, additional issues warrant mention in this epilogue. These topics are a combination of subjects that are discussed at academic and professional conferences. They are important issues and will take on more significance in time. Rather than ignore these topics, I have included a brief discussion of them in the hopes of stimulating further discussion.

Campus Crime

Campus crime until recently was another form of victimization that was not discussed publicly. It became a topic of discussion and research when, in the mid-1980s, survivors of homicide and other crime victims filed civil lawsuits against universities for failing to protect students on their campuses. As a result of these lawsuits and public lobbying, several laws were passed that mandated that colleges and universities make public any crime which occurred on their campus.

These laws included the Campus Security Act of 1990 which requires that institutions publish and distribute an annual report which describes security and law enforcement policies, crime prevention activities, and campus crime statistics. A year later Congress enacted the Campus Sexual Assault Victims Bill of Rights. This law requires that institutions enact and publish policies regarding prevention and awareness of sex offenses. The law requires that universities inform students of their rights and provide clear information on how to report sex offenses.

University campuses have a certain attraction for many people. They are places of learning, debate, and sports. It is hard to think of violent predators lurking within the grounds of these institutions, but facts are beginning to surface that indicate rape and other crimes occur in university settings. The existence of campus crime is now acknowledged and universities are beginning to respond to this form of victimization.

Stalking

Stalking has been described as the crime of the nineties. One media report indicates that as of 1990, there were more than 200,000 stalkers in the United States.[1] Many articles dealing with stalking rely on news reports and television shows for their data. This relative lack of hard scientific data has contributed to the misunderstanding and confusion that surrounds the crime of stalking.

The stalking and subsequent death in 1989 of Rebecca Shaeffer, the costar of the television series *My Sister Sam*, was the impetus behind the adoption of the nation's first stalking law. California enacted that law in 1990 and all but two states have followed with their own stalking laws.[2] The remaining two states, Arizona and Maine, utilize their harassment and terrorizing statutes to combat stalking.[3] States continue to amend their statutes to provide more protection to victims of stalking and various state statutes prohibit certain acts. Some states prohibit telephone contacts and other states punish threatening acts toward family members.

The Los Angeles Police Department formed the first Threat Management Unit in the nation. Its purpose was to specialize in stalker profiling, arrest, and prosecution of these offenders. Zona, Sharma, and Lane have conducted an in-depth review of stalkers in the Los Angeles area.[4] Utilizing the files of the Threat Management Unit of the Los Angeles Police Department, Zona and his associates were able to establish a database of seventy-four subjects that had engaged in stalking behavior. Their profile classified stalkers as erotomanic, love obsessional, simple obsessional, and having false victimization syndrome.

Erotomanic. The erotomanic stalker has a delusional disorder in which the predominant theme of the delusion is that a person, usually of higher status and opposite gender, is in love with the subject. The victim does not know the stalker and many times will be a public figure or celebrity. Stalkers are convinced that their victims love them and would return the affection if not for some external influence. The duration of stalking and delusion usually lasts one to four months.

Love Obsessional. The love obsessional stalker is similar to the erotomanic in many ways. The subject does not know the chosen victim except through the media. This stalker may also suffer from delusions; however, the subject has a primary psychiatric diagnosis. These individuals often believe that if the victim would simply acknowledge their existence then the victim would fall in love with them. These subjects usually engage in a campaign to make their existence known to the victim by writing, telephoning, or otherwise attempting to contact the victim. This behavior lasts approximately 146 months.

Simple Obsessional. Unlike the two previous categories, the simple obsessional stalker had a prior relationship with the intended victim. This relationship may have been that of a former spouse, employer, or neighbor, and in all cases the stalking began after the relationship had soured, or there was a perception by the subject of mistreatment. The stalking, which in duration averages 5.1 months, is an attempt to rectify the problem or seek revenge.

False Victimization Syndrome. The false victimization syndrome is the rarest category that includes stalkers. Such individuals have a desire to be placed in the victim's role. By insisting that someone is stalking them, they become the victim. A similarity seems to exist between this classification and Munchausen syndrome by proxy discussed earlier in this text. Although this is not truly a "stalker," Zona and his associates included it for purposes of comparison and understanding of the stalking process.

There have been other classifications of stalkers, however, no single typology has been accepted by all the professionals in this area.[5] There is still much to be learned about stalkers and their behavior, and how to respond to stalking. Victim service providers need to understand that this is an evolving area in the field of criminal law and although several convicted stalkers have been interviewed by medical professionals, much information is lacking as to why certain individuals engage in this type of behavior.

Workplace Violence

Newspapers, magazines, and the electronic media bombard us daily with the danger and violence that await us when we arrive at work. Numerous books have suddenly appeared in the marketplace dealing with workplace violence. This reaction to the phenomenon of workplace violence is not limited to the popular press. Prominent legal journals have recently published articles stating, "Workplace violence, often perpetrated by disgruntled employees, has reached epidemic proportions in the United States."[6]

One major problem in this emerging area is the lack of a unanimous definition of either violence or what constitutes the workplace. The workplace can and does take many shapes, forms, and varieties. It may be a skyscraper in New York, a packing shed in California, or even an eighteen-wheeler traveling down the interstate. In essence, a workplace is any location in which a person carries out work-related functions. The Department of Labor does not include in its definition fatalities that occur when a person is commuting to or from work. It should be noted that this definition is broader than those used by other federal and state agencies administering specific laws or regulations. This definition does not require that the injured person be the one conducting work-related functions. As will be seen, individuals who are innocent bystanders at a work location can also become victims.

Another controversial issue is the definition of violence within the workplace. The section entitled "Violence and Victims" in this epilogue provides a definition of *violence,* which is the threatened or actual use of force or power against another person, against oneself, or against a group or community that either results in or has a likelihood of resulting in injury, death, or deprivation. Violence in the workplace must also include sexual harassment.

Although the popular view of sexual harassment is that women are always the victim, this perception is not correct. Men have been victims of sexual harassment by women and even by other men. Therefore, *workplace violence* is any form of nonconsensual verbal or physical actions carried out by one person or persons upon another within the working environment.

In 1993, Northwestern National Life Insurance conducted a survey on workplace violence.[7] The survey was based on telephone interviews with 600 full-time civilian workers excluding business owners and sole proprietorships. Northwestern National did not specifically establish a definition for workplace violence, however, it provided three criteria used to establish violence at the job site: harassment, threats, and physical attacks. They used common lay terms rather than technical legal terms in establishing these definitions. Northwestern National found that violence in the workplace is common. Using its survey of 600 workers to project results for the entire working population of the United States, Northwestern National reported that in one year, over 2 million workers were victims of physical attacks; another 6 million workers were threatened and 16 million were harassed.[8]

In August 1993, the Center for Disease Control issued its *National Profile: Fatal Injuries to Workers in the United States, 1980–1989: A Decade of Surveillance.* The National Traumatic Occupational Fatalities (NTOF) surveillance system was developed by the National Institute for Occupational Safety and Health (NIOSH). The purpose of this system was to provide information regarding work-related injury deaths in the United States. Information in the NTOF system was taken directly from death certificates filed in the fifty states, New York City, and the District of Columbia for workers sixteen years and older who died as a result of an injury at work. Some scholars have criticized using only death certificates as a means of measuring injury or death while at work, because motor vehicle crashes and homicides are external causes of death that may be missed when using death certificates to establish occupational injuries.

The leading causes of death in the workplace in the United States were motor vehicle crashes (23 percent), machine-related incidents (14 percent), and homicides (12 percent). Homicides accounted for the highest fatality rate per 100,000 workers in the occupation divisions of sales (1.4 percent), service (1.1 percent), and executives/administrators/managers (0.9 percent). The rates for homicide are three times as high for men compared with women, but women are more likely to be killed as a result of a homicide in the workplace than from any other cause. The Center for Disease Control ended its report with the startling fact that more than seventeen workers die each day from an injury at work.

It appears that no location within the workplace is absolutely safe. One of every seven fatal incidents occurred in a building open to the public, such as a grocery store or other retail store, restaurant, office building, or school. Of the approximately 200 deaths that occurred in a parking lot or garage, about 50 percent were homicides.

Men are more likely than women to be attacked by a stranger, although women are more likely to be attacked by someone they know. Five percent of women attacked in the workplace were assaulted by a husband, an ex-husband, boyfriend, or ex-boyfriend. Sixty percent of all women attacked in the workplace knew the assailant.

According to the federal government, an average of fifteen people are murdered at work each week in this country.[9] Have we become a more violent society in the workplace? At first glance, it may appear as if the workplace has become a war zone. However, by adding other figures, workplace violence takes on another perspective. Surprisingly, the statistics from NTOF show a dramatic lowering in the number of deaths over the last ten years. During the last decade, the number of fatal injuries decreased from a high of 7405 in 1980 to 5714 in 1989. This represents a 23 percent decrease in deaths over a ten-year period.

The United States Department of Labor estimates the total national workforce to be 121 million people. Based on the National Census of Fatal Injuries figure of 1063 homicides, which further indicated that approximately 14 percent of all those homicides were committed by a co-worker or personal associate, approximately 149 workers died at the hands of someone they knew or with whom they worked. Using these figures, the odds of being killed by someone you know or with whom you work are approximately 1 in 812,080. The National Weather Service projects the odds of being struck by lightning at 1 in 600,000.

The fact that workplace homicide is considerably less prevalent than the media and some consultants would have us believe does not diminish the tragedy of preventable death in the workplace. Employers and those charged with the safety of their company's job site still need to be alert to possible incidents of violence.

Gang Violence

Drive-by shootings, automatic weapons, and gunfire on our intercity streets have all become too common with many of these acts being related to gang violence. The nature and behavior of gangs have changed since they were first studied. They have become more violent and more dangerous. Communities in all fifty states reported that approximately 652,000 gang members are part of 25,000 gangs nationwide. Gang problems are reportedly worsening in 48 percent of these communities.[10]

FOCUS: Characteristics of Victims and Witnesses of Gang Violence

There are certain characteristics that are unique to victims and witnesses of gang violence:

Victims and witnesses generally live with and/or among the perpetrators of their crimes. Victims and witnesses may have to face an entire gang, as opposed to a single perpetrator, even at funerals.

Victims and survivors are often seen as contributors to the crime. Many victims and survivors find a lack of sympathy and services from the criminal justice system because they are seen as having contributed to the crime in some way.

Victims are frequently afraid and unable to exercise their rights. Because of intimidation, fear of retaliation, or due to poverty or culture, many victims of gang violence do not exercise their right to be notified, attend, and be heard at court proceedings.

Source: Adapted from *Victims of Gang Violence: A New Frontier in Victim Services,* U.S. Department of Justice (Washington, D.C.: October 25, 1996).

The term *gangs* has been defined by various scholars and researchers. One common definition of a gang is "an ongoing, organized association of three or more persons, whether formal or informal, who have a common name or common signs, colors or symbols, and members or associates who individually or collectively engage in or have engaged in criminal activity."[11] Although no one scholar can point to reasons why young people join gangs, two common factors appear to be the breakdown of the family and desperate poverty.

Membership in gangs can severely affect a youth's future. Gang members usually socialize only with other gang members, thereby reinforcing their limited point of view of life. They often drop out of school, which limits their chances for higher education and employment. They frequently establish life long habits and a pattern of involvement with law enforcement agencies. They may commit serious crimes, which leads to long criminal incarcerations. They may be killed or maimed as a result of gang violence.

Gang activity is a study in violent crime. A perpetual cycle of violence has been established within the street gangs. Gang rivalries dating back years continue to ignite violence. Many times the victims of this violence are other rival gang members. As new generations of gang members enter the mainstream, they are taught to hate the rivals. Individual gang members do not look at this continuing violence against their rivals as wrong; they view it as a legitimate endeavor.

There will continue to be ongoing studies of gangs and their membership and this trend toward violence. Gang violence and its victimization present to victim service providers unique problems that will require innovative approaches in the future.

Rural Crime Victims

Although rural crime rates have traditionally been lower than urban crime rates, patterns of rural crime now indicate that some urban problems are moving to rural areas, whereas some problems are already unique to rural areas.[12] Although far less research has been conducted about rural crime than crime in urban areas, the National Institute of Justice, in the publication *Rural Crime and Rural Policing,* indicates the following characteristics and dimensions of rural versus urban crime:

- Recent studies indicate that children in rural communities are as likely, and possibly more likely, to be abused or neglected than children in cities.
- Crimes such as homicide, rape, and assault are more likely to occur among acquaintances in rural areas than is true in urban areas.
- Although limited surveys of the level of rural domestic violence have been conducted, an Ohio study found that the highest rates for domestic violence disputes were in the least populated jurisdictions.
- Violent crime occurs more often in urban areas, however, property crime rates are much closer. Larceny is the most common property crime and motor vehicle theft the least common crime in both areas.
- The greatest difference between rural and urban crime is robbery, which occurs fifty-four times more often per 100,000 citizens in urban areas.
- Certain crimes are unique to rural areas, such as agricultural crimes—thefts of crops and timber, and wildlife crimes.
- Although rural families face the same drug, alcohol, poverty, and stress problems as do families who live in a metropolitan area, rural communities typically have fewer resources.

Crime in urban America is spreading to rural communities at an increasing rate. For example, urban drug trafficking is seen as the driving force behind the spread of drug use and the increase in gangs in rural areas. Emerging crime facing rural citizens includes:

- Criminal drug trafficking organizations in rural areas
- Increased use of drugs, including crack in rural areas
- Increasing rates of hate crimes
- The spread of gangs into rural America
- Rest-stop crimes and crimes tied to the presence of interstate highways

Many rural counties have very low populations. Currently, one of three rural counties (850) have fewer than 10,000 residents. This presents a challenge to establishing even basic services for crime victims such as counseling for child abuse victims and shelters for battered women.[13] Many rural domestic violence victims face the additional problem of not only having to leave their home to find safety, but also having to leave their community. Often, the nearest shelter may be several communities and many miles away. Not only are these victims forced to leave whatever support network was available, but their children must be taken out of school for them to reach safety.

Federal crime victims who reside in rural areas face serious problems. Many victims must travel long distances to a U.S. courthouse. Often, these victims face similar attitudinal problems that other victims face—lack of understanding of the impact of distance and lack of support services. In addition, rural federal crime victims are skeptical about seeking assistance from the U.S. attorney, feeling the federal official is really not "one of the locals." This feeling may arise because the U.S. attorney is not elected by the populace, as are most county attorneys.

Violence on tribal lands is one of the most pressing issues in modern society. Feelings of alienation and rage are common among members of various tribes. Victims of crime on tribal lands face unique problems that are not duplicated elsewhere in the United States. In addition, confusing jurisdictional boundaries between state, federal, and tribal law is no where more evident than in victims' rights. For example, in a statewide survey of Wyoming's victim services, domestic violence victims who received orders of protection on the reservation had to file for similar protection orders in the local county to be protected from their abusers when they left the reservation. Often, their batterers would wait until the victims left the reservation to shop at the grocery store to intimidate, threaten, and harm them.

Although a tremendous amount of research is being funded and conducted in this area, and excellent support provided from the Office for Victims of Crime to local tribal victim assistance programs, few of these projects have adopted a multi-systems approach to researching and understanding tribal victims of crime issues.

Historically, high rates of poverty have been associated with high crime rates. Although poverty has been a common problem, crime has been less frequent in rural areas. However, economic problems facing rural areas increasingly affect the nature and extent of crime. The impact on the resources available to communities to respond to crime and to assist victims cannot be underestimated. In sentencing offenders, often the only option for judges to select is jail, because few community sentencing programs exist in rural areas.

Several crimes are specific to rural settings and impact those who live there in unique ways. For example, agricultural crimes impact not only small and large farmers, but also the country as a whole through escalating food and insurance prices. Recent incidents of agricultural crimes include $1 million in annual thefts of avocado, lime, and mango fruit in Florida, $1 million in annual losses to timber thieves and vandals in western Washington, and $30 million a year lost to theft from California farmers. Wildlife crimes, especially poaching, have become a major concern of conservation police officers. The trauma associated with these types of rural crimes should not be underestimated. When livelihoods depend on big harvests, stealing crops is tantamount to robbery in urban America.

The effects of geography alone pose serious problems for rural victims. Distance affects the response time and the speed in which law enforcement and emergency services respond to victims' calls for assistance. Whereas urban areas judge emergency response time in minutes, access to medical treatment in rural areas takes longer, resulting in higher death rates for rural victims suffering the same injuries as those living in urban environments. In addition, rural law enforcement waits longer for backup, forcing decisions of responding to dangerous situations alone or the delay of critical emergency responses—such as on domestic violence reports.

For many rural crime victims, simply traveling to the local police station to make a report takes on special significance because of the distance, lack of transportation, and time involved in making such a trip. Transportation issues are especially critical for elderly victims and children going to therapy sessions. Travel to criminal justice agencies is exacerbated for tribal crime victims that participate in the federal justice system. Many tribal crime victims have to travel hundreds of miles to participate in the criminal justice process. One crime victim from the Wind River Reservation in Wyoming had to travel over 500 miles to present a victim impact statement at the federal courthouse—and was told of the sentencing hearing the day before!

In addition, aspects of the rural culture may affect crime victims' willingness to report crime and to participate in the criminal justice system. One study found that shoplifting and employee theft were rarely reported to the police. Rather, the cases were handled informally. One criminal justice official said "I simply can't get people to tell me things. I hear about them two or three weeks later, and when I ask them why they didn't come to see me about it, they say, 'Oh, I took care of it myself.' We simply can't get people to take advantage of the services of this office."[14]

Overall, the issues of rural crime and rural justice have not received national attention in the development of policies and protocol for law enforcement or other areas of the criminal justice system. For example, in the 447-page book *Local Government Police Management*, considered by most law enforcement officers to be the definitive reference on municipal police administration, the distinction between rural and urban policing is covered in a brief one-page section. Moreover, this one-page overview does not even appear in updated editions.[15] Rural crime victimization is an important topic that warrants further study.

Violence and Victims

There is a continuing concern in America that violence has increased and is becoming more random. As discussed in the text, violence is not new to our species. It is embedded in our history and mores, and in fact has become woven into our very emotional makeup. However, the current surge of juvenile violence and violent acts committed by those under the age of twenty-five is a new phenomenon that many people believe will significantly increase over time.

Even addressing this issue is controversial because there are a number of different definitions for the word *violence*. However, most authorities accept the definition from the Center for Disease Control, which states that violence is "the threatened or actual use of force or power against another person, against oneself, or against a group or community that either results in or has a likelihood of resulting in, injury, death, or deprivation."[16]

The impact of violence has been discussed in various chapters in this text. It affects victims, relatives, friends, and the community. It has emotional and financial impacts on all of these parties. Criminal violence has absolutely no redeeming qualities.

No single factor or factors have been identified as the cause of violence. Some authorities believe that four major catalysts are present or contribute to violence in our society: the media, firearms, alcohol, and corporate promotion of violence. Poverty, hopelessness and isolation, and the decline of our educational system are social contributions that can also lead to violence. Additionally, mental health problems and other disorders arising from childhood traumatization are significant indicators of a propensity for violence. Finally, the devaluing of life, including racism, sexism, and other forms of discrimination, were values associated with escalating violence.[17]

Violence—its causes, effect, and remediation—must continue to be the subject of research. Different theories must be tested and evaluated. Violence and its impact on victims of crime must also be studied and treated as it will continue to be a major concern of our society for the foreseeable future.

Technology

More and more people are discovering the Internet. It is a tremendous asset for learning and gathering information that can be utilized in the continuing study of victimology. Computers, e-mail, electronic conferencing, and other technological advances allow us to respond to issues much more quickly than in the past. However, this in turn can lead to an overload of information that will have to be addressed. How do we sift the necessary knowledge from the useless? Technology, with all its exciting possibilities, needs to be carefully and appropriately applied. This will be the challenge of the next decade.

Professionalism versus Academia

As indicated in Chapter 1, a number of national organizations have provided invaluable assistance to both victims of crime and victim service providers. These organizations provide professional training for individuals working within the field, but they are neither structured nor do they have the long-range financial resources to carry out extensive research in the area of victims, offenders, and their interactions.

Universities, on the other hand, have traditionally been the location and source of science-based research that benefits society. A number of universities have conducted research in areas pertaining to victims. Many research institutions continue to study the effects of crime on victims, others examine offenders reactions to crime, and still others attempt to find the cause of crime.

These two important institutions, professional organizations and academia, have not yet joined forces to combine and share their respective knowledge and skills. We must first acknowledge that victimology involves both perspectives. Then we must begin the process of sharing the information and skills of individuals in both of these institutions. The first step may be issuing "calls for papers" for both institution's annual conferences. Panels made up of researchers and professionals in the field may lead to interesting discussions and liaisons that would benefit both sides.

The Study of Victimology

Criminology is now accepted by most researchers as a valid academic subject. However, a number of individuals still believe it is more vocational than scientific in nature. Others claim that it is more of a profession than a true academic discipline. These statements and perceptions also apply to the study of victimology. Because victimology combines several existing disciplines, it is in danger of being ignored by all of them. At present, only one university in the nation offers a bachelor of science degree in victimology. However, more community colleges and universities are offering courses entitled "Victimology," or courses that include issues within the definition of victimology. This is a new and evolving discipline that will take years to take shape. In the meantime, we must continue to search for knowledge and appropriate responses to victims of crime.

Endnotes

1. Maria Puente, "Legislators Tackling the Terror of Stalking," *USA Today*, July 21, 1992.
2. See Kelli L. Attinello, "Anti-Stalking Legislation: A Comparison of Traditional Remedies Available for Victims of Harassment Versus California Penal Code Section 646.9," 24 *Pac. L. J.*, 945 (1993).
3. For an excellent review of stalking statutes, see Karen S. Morin, "The Phenomenon of Stalking: Do Existing State Statutes Provide Adequate Protection," 1 *San Diego Just. J.*, 123 (1993).
4. Michael A. Zona, et al., "A Comparative Study of Erotomanic and Obsessional Subjects in a Forensic Sample," 38 *J Forensic Sci*, 894 (July 1993).
5. In one of the earliest studies of stalking, Dietz and his associates in 1991 examined stalkers of celebrities and political officials. They examined threatening letters and other inappropriate material sent to celebrities and political officials, and subsequently developed a concept of patronage which classified the level of attachment the stalker had for the

victim. See Park E. Dietz, et al., "Threatening and Otherwise Inappropriate Letters to Hollywood Celebrities," 36 *J. Forensic Sci*, 185 (January 1991); and Park E. Dietz, et al., "Threatening and Otherwise Inappropriate Letters to Members of the United States Congress," 36 *J. Forensic Sci*, 1445 (September 1991). These levels of attachment were termed minimal, moderate, or maximal patronage.

Holmes established six distinct types of stalkers based on the type of victim that was stalked. This classification included the following forms or types of stalkers: the celebrity stalker, the lust stalker, the hit stalker, the love-scorned stalker, the domestic stalker, and the political stalker. See Ronald M. Holmes, "Stalking in America: Types and Methods of Criminal Stalkers, 9/4 *J. Contemp. Crim. Just.*, 317 (December 1993); and Holmes, "Stalking in America," *Law and Order,*" 88 (May 1994).

Gavin de Becker, a consultant in personal security measures, established four categories of stalkers based on the relationship between the pursuer and the victim: (1) pursuit of public figures by the mentally ill with no prior relationship, (2) pursuit of public figures by healthy persons with no prior relationship, (3) pursuit of regular citizens with no prior relationship, and (4) pursuit of regular citizens with some prior interpersonal relationship. See Gavin de Becker, "Intervention Decisions—The Value of Flexibility," paper presented at the 4th Annual Threat Management Conference, Disneyland Hotel, Anaheim, California, June 29, 1994.

McAnaney, Curliss, and Abeyta-Price reviewed the literature in this evolving field and established four classifications of stalkers: erotomania and de Clerambault's syndrome, borderline erotomania, former intimate, and sociopathic stalkers, K. G.

McAnaney, L. A. Curliss, C. E Abeyta-Price, "From Imprudence to Crime: Anti-Stalking Laws," 68 *Notre Dame Law Review,* 819 (1993).

6. George Barford and Kaiwen Tseng, "Psychological Tests and Workplace Violence—A Review," 68 *Florida Bar Journal,* 76 (March 1994).
7. *Fear and Violence in the Workplace,* (Northwestern National Life, Chicago) 1993.
8. Executive Summary, *Fear and Violence in the Workplace,* (Northwestern National Life, Chicago) 1993, p. 2.
9. *Fatal Injuries to Workers in the United States, 1980–1989: A Decade of Surveillance,* (U.S. Department of Health and Human Services, Washington, D.C.) 1993.
10. *1995 National Youth Gang Survey,* National Youth Gang Center, (Office of Juvenile Justice and Prevention, Washington, D.C.) June 20, 1996.
11. C. Conly, *Street Gangs: Current Knowledge and Strategies,* (National Institute of Justice, Washington, D.C.) 1993.
12. Ralph A. Weisheit, et al., *Rural Crime and Rural Policing,* Research in Brief, (National Institute of Justice, Washington, D.C.) October 1994.
13. Victor Veith, "A Strategy for Confronting Child Abuse in Rural Communities," 28 *Prosecutor,* 15 (September/October 1994).
14. Ralph A. Weisheit, et al., *Rural Crime and Rural Policing,* Research in Brief, (National Institute of Justice, Washington, D.C.) October 1994.
15. Id.
16. Mark Rosenberg, "Violence Prevention: Integrating Public Health and Criminal Justice," presentation at the United States Attorneys' Conference, Washington, D.C., January 20, 1994.
17. *Final Report, Violence Prevention: A Vision of Hope,* (California Attorney General, Sacramento) August 1995.

A p p e n d i x

CRITICAL DATES IN THE VICTIMS' RIGHTS MOVEMENT

1972

- The first three victim assistance programs are created:
  —Aid for Victims of Crime in St. Louis, Missouri;
  —Bay Area Women Against Rape in San Francisco, California; and
  —Rape Crisis Center in Washington, D.C.

1974

- The Federal Law Enforcement Assistance Administration (LEAA) funds the first victim–witness programs in the Brooklyn and Milwaukee District Attorneys' offices, plus seven others through a grant to the National District Attorneys Association, to create model programs of assistance for victims, encourage victim cooperation, and improve prosecution.
- The first law enforcement-based victim assistance programs are established in Fort Lauderdale, Florida, and Indianapolis, Indiana.
- The U.S. Congress passes the Child Abuse Prevention and Treatment Act which establishes the National Center on Child Abuse and Neglect (NCCAN). The new Center creates an information clearinghouse and provides technical assistance and model programs.

1975

- The first "Victims' Rights Week" is organized by the Philadelphia District Attorney.

- Citizen activists from across the country unite to expand victim services and increase recognition of victims' rights through the formation of the National Organization for Victim Assistance (NOVA).

1976

- The National Organization for Women forms a task force to examine the problem of battering. It demands research into the problem, along with money for battered women's shelters.
- Nebraska becomes the first state to abolish the marital rape exemption.
- The first national conference on battered women is sponsored by the Milwaukee Task Force on Women in Milwaukee, Wisconsin.
- In Fresno County, California, Chief Probation Officer James Rowland creates the first victim impact statement to provide the judiciary with an objective inventory of victim injuries and losses prior to sentencing.
- Women's advocates in St. Paul, Minnesota starts the first hotline for battered women. Women's Advocates and Haven House in Pasadena, California, establish the first shelters for battered women.

1977

- Oregon becomes the first state to enact mandatory arrest in domestic violence cases.

1978

- The National Coalition Against Sexual Assault (NCASA) is formed to combat sexual violence and promote services for rape victims.
- The National Coalition Against Domestic Violence (NCADV) is organized as a voice for the battered women's movement on a national level. NCADV initiates the introduction of the Family Violence Prevention and Services Act in the U.S. Congress.
- Parents of Murdered Children (POMC), a self-help support group, is founded in Cincinnati, Ohio.
- Minnesota becomes the first state to allow probable cause (warrantless) arrest in cases of domestic assault, regardless of whether a protection order had been issued.

1979

- Frank G. Carrington, considered by many to be "the father of the victims' rights movement," founds the Crime Victims' Legal Advocacy Institute, Inc., to promote the rights of crime victims in the civil and criminal justice systems. The nonprofit organization was renamed VALOR, the Victims' Assistance Legal Organization, Inc., in 1981.

- The Office on Domestic Violence is established in the U.S. Department of Health and Human Services, but is later closed in 1981.

- The U.S. Congress fails to enact the Federal Law Enforcement Assistance Administration (LEAA) and federal funding for victims' programs is phased out. Many grassroots and "system-based" programs close.

1980

- Mothers Against Drunk Driving (MADD) is founded after the death of thirteen-year-old Cari Lightner, who was killed by a repeat offender drunk driver. The first two MADD chapters are created in Sacramento, California, and Annapolis, Maryland.

- The U.S. Congress passes the Parental Kidnapping Prevention Act of 1980.

- Wisconsin passes the first "Crime Victims' Bill of Rights."

- The First National Day of Unity in October is established by NCADV to mourn battered women who have died, celebrate women who have survived the violence, and honor all who have worked to defeat domestic violence. This Day becomes Domestic Violence Awareness Week and, in 1987, expands to a month of awareness activities each October.

- NCADV holds its first national conference in Washington, D.C., which gains federal recognition of critical issues facing battered women, and sees the birth of several state coalitions.

- The first Victim Impact Panel is sponsored by Remove Intoxicated Drivers (RID) in Oswego County, New York.

1981

- Ronald Reagan becomes the first President to proclaim "Crime Victims' Rights Week" in April.

- The disappearance and murder of missing child Adam Walsh prompts a national campaign to raise public awareness about child abduction and enact laws to better protect children.

- The Attorney General's Task Force on Violent Crime recommends that a separate Task Force be created to consider victims' issues.

1982

- In a Rose Garden ceremony, President Reagan appoints the Task Force on Victims of Crime, which holds public hearings in six cities across the nation to create a greatly needed national focus on the needs of crime victims. The Task Force *Final Report* offers 68 recommendations that become the framework for the advancement of new programs and policies.

- The Federal Victim and Witness Protection Act of 1982 brings "fair treatment standards" to victims and witnesses in the federal criminal justice system.
- California voters overwhelmingly pass Proposition 8, which guarantees restitution and other statutory reforms to crime victims.
- The passage of the Missing Children's Act of 1982 helps parents guarantee that identifying information of their missing child is promptly entered into the FBI National Crime Information Center (NCIC) computer system.
- The first Victim Impact Panel sponsored by MADD, which educates drunk drivers about the devastating impact of their criminal acts, is organized in Rutland, Massachusetts.

1983

- The Office for Victims of Crime (OVC) is created by the U.S. Department of Justice within the Office of Justice Programs to implement recommendations from the President's Task Force on Victims of Crime.
- The U.S. Attorney General establishes a Task Force on Family Violence, which holds six public hearings across the United States.
- The U.S. Attorney General issues guidelines for federal victim and witness assistance.
- In April, President Reagan honors crime victims in a White House Rose Garden ceremony.
- The First National Conference of the Judiciary on Victims of Crime is held at the National Judicial College in Reno, Nevada.
- President Reagan proclaims the first National Missing Children's Day in observance of the disappearance of missing child Etan Patz.
- The International Association of Chiefs of Police Board of Governors adopts a Crime Victims' Bill of Rights and establishes a victims' rights committee to bring about renewed emphasis on the needs of crime victims by law enforcement officials nationwide.

1984

- The passage of the Victims Of Crime Act (VOCA) establishes the Crime Victims Fund, made up of federal criminal fines, penalties and bond forfeitures, to support state victim compensation and local victim service programs.
- President Reagan signs the Justice Assistance Act, which establishes a financial assistance program for state and local government and funds 200 new victim service programs.

- The National Minimum Drinking Age Act of 1984 is enacted, providing strong incentives to states without "21" laws to raise the minimum age for drinking, saving thousands of young lives in years to come.

- The National Center for Missing and Exploited Children (NCMEC) is created as the national resource for missing children. Passage of the Missing Children's Assistance Act provides a Congressional mandate for the Center.

- The Spiritual Dimension in Victim Services is founded to involve the religious community in violence prevention and victim assistance.

- The U.S. Congress passes the Family Violence Prevention and Services Act, which earmarks federal funding for programs serving victims of domestic violence.

- Concerns of Police Survivors (COPS) is organized at the first police survivors' seminar held in Washington, D.C., by 100 relatives of officers killed in the line of duty.

- The first National Symposium on Sexual Assault is co-sponsored by the Office of Justice Programs and the Federal Bureau of Investigation.

- A victim–witness notification system is established within the Federal Bureau of Prisons.

- The Office for Victims of Crime hosts the first national symposium on child molestation.

- Victim–Witness Coordinator positions are established in the U.S. Attorneys' offices within the U.S. Department of Justice.

- California State University, Fresno, initiates the first Victim Services Certificate Program offered for academic credit by a university.

- Remove Intoxicated Drivers (RID) calls for a comprehensive Sane National Alcohol Policy (SNAP) to curb aggressive promotions aimed at youth.

1985

- The Federal Crime Victims' Fund deposits total $68 million.

- The National Victim Center is founded in honor of Sunny von Bulow to promote the rights and needs of crime victims, and to educate Americans about the devastating effect of crime on our society.

- The United Nations General Assembly passes the International Declaration on the Rights of Victims of Crime and the Abuse of Power.

- President Reagan announces a Child Safety Partnership with 26 members. Its mission is to enhance private sector efforts to promote child safety, to clarify information about child victimization, and to increase public awareness of child abuse.

- The U.S. Surgeon General issues a report identifying domestic violence as a major public health problem.

1986

- The Office for Victims of Crime awards the first grants to support state victim compensation and assistance programs.
- Rhode Island passes a constitutional amendment granting victims the right to restitution, to submit victim impact statements, and to be treated with dignity and respect.
- MADD's "Red Ribbon Campaign" enlists motorists to display a red ribbon on their automobiles, pledging to drive safe and sober during the holidays. This national public awareness effort has since become an annual campaign.

1987

- The Victims' Constitutional Amendment Network (VCAN) and Steering Committee is formed at a meeting hosted by the National Victim Center.
- Security on Campus, Inc. (SOC) is established by Howard and Connie Clery, following the tragic robbery, rape, and murder of their daughter Jeanne at Lehigh University in Pennsylvania. SOC raises national awareness about the hidden epidemic of violence on our nation's campuses.
- The American Correctional Association establishes a Task Force on Victims of Crime.
- NCADV establishes the first national toll-free domestic violence hotline.

1988

- The National Aging Resource Center on Elder Abuse (NARCEA) is established in a cooperative agreement among the American Public Welfare Association, the National Association of State Units on Aging, and the University of Delaware. Renamed the National Center on Elder Abuse, it continues to provide information and statistics.
- *State v. Ciskie* is the first case to allow the use of expert testimony to explain the behavior and mental state of an adult rape victim. The testimony is used to show why a victim of repeated physical and sexual assaults by her intimate partner would not immediately call the police or take action. The jury convicts the defendant on four counts of rape.
- The Federal Drunk Driving Prevention Act is passed, and states raise the minimum drinking age to 21.
- Constitutional amendments are introduced in Arizona, California, Connecticut, Delaware, Michigan, South Carolina and Washington. Florida's amendment is placed on the November ballot where it passes with 90 percent of the vote. Michigan's constitutional amendment passes with over 80 percent of the vote.

- The first "Indian Nations: Justice for Victims of Crime" conference is sponsored by the Office for Victims of Crime in Rapid City, South Dakota.
- VOCA amendments legislatively establish the Office for Victims of Crime, elevate the position of Director by making Senate confirmation necessary for appointment, and induce state compensation programs to cover victims of homicide and drunk driving.

1989

- The legislatures in Texas and Washington pass their respective constitutional amendments, which are both ratified by voters in November.

1990

- The Federal Crime Victims' Fund deposits total over $146 million.
- The U.S. Congress passes the Hate Crime Statistics Act requiring the U.S. Attorney General to collect data of incidence of certain crimes motivated by prejudice based on race, religion, sexual orientation, or ethnicity.
- The Student Right-to-Know and Campus Security Act, requiring institutions of higher education to disclose murder, rape, robbery, and other crimes on campus, is signed into law by President Bush.
- The Child Protection Act of 1990, which features reforms to make the federal criminal justice system less traumatic for child victims and witnesses, is passed by the U.S. Congress.
- The first National Incidence Study on Missing, Abducted, Runaway, and Throwaway Children in America shows that over one million children fall victim to abduction annually.
- The National Child Search Assistance Act requires law enforcement to enter reports of missing children and unidentified persons in the NCIC computer.

1991

- U.S. Representative Ilena Ros-Lehtinen (R-FL) files the first Congressional Joint Resolution to place victims' rights in the U.S. Constitution.
- The Violence Against Women Act of 1991 is considered by the U.S. Congress.
- California State University, Fresno, approves the first Bachelors Degree Program in Victimology in the nation.
- The Campus Sexual Assault Victims' Bill of Rights Act is introduced in the U.S. Congress.
- The results of the first national public opinion poll to examine citizens' attitudes about violence and victimization, *America Speaks Out*, are released by the National Victim Center during National Crime Victims' Rights Week.

- The U.S. Attorney General issues new comprehensive guidelines that establish procedures for the federal criminal justice system to respond to the needs of crime victims.

- The first national conference that addresses crime victims' rights and needs in corrections is sponsored by the Office for Victims of Crime in California.

- The first International Conference on Campus Sexual Assault is held in Orlando, Florida.

- The American Probation and Parole Association (APPA) establishes a Victim Issues Committee to examine victims' issues and concerns related to community corrections.

- The International Parental Child Kidnapping Act makes the act of unlawfully removing a child outside the United States a federal felony.

- The Spiritual Dimension in Victim Services facilitates a conference of leaders of thirteen religious denominations to plan ways in which these large religious bodies can increase awareness of crime victims' needs and provide appropriate services.

- The New Jersey legislature passes victims' rights constitutional amendment, which is ratified by voters in November.

- Colorado legislators introduce a constitutional amendment on the first day of National Crime Victims' Rights Week. Fifteen days later, the bill is unanimously passed by both Houses to be placed on the ballot in 1992.

- In an 8–0 decision, the U.S. Supreme Court ruled in *Simon & Schuster v. New York Crime Victims Board* that New York's notoriety-for-profit statute was overly broad and, in the final analysis, unconstitutional.

1992

- *Rape in America: A Report to the Nation,* clarifies the scope and devastating effect of rape in this nation, including the fact that 683,000 women are raped annually in the United States.

- The Association of Paroling Authorities, International establishes a Victim Issues Committee to examine victims' needs, rights, and services in parole processes.

- The U.S. Congress reauthorizes the Higher Education Bill which includes the Campus Sexual Assault Victims' Bill of Rights.

- The Battered Women's Testimony Act, which urges states to accept expert testimony in criminal cases involving battered women, is passed by Congress and signed into law by President Bush.

- In a unanimous decision, the U.S. Supreme Court—in *R.A.V. vs. City of St. Paul*—struck down a local hate crimes ordinance in Minnesota.

- Five states—Colorado, Kansas, Illinois, Missouri, and New Mexico—ratify constitutional amendments for victims' rights.

- Twenty-eight states pass anti-stalking legislation.
- Massachusetts passes a landmark bill creating a statewide computerized domestic violence registry and requires judges to check the registry when handling such cases.

1993

- Wisconsin ratifies its constitutional amendment for victims' rights, bringing the total number of states with these amendments to 14.
- President Clinton signs the "Brady Bill" requiring a waiting period for the purchase of handguns.
- Congress passes the Child Sexual Abuse Registry Act establishing a national repository for information on child sex offenders.
- Twenty-two states pass stalking statutes, bringing the total number of states with stalking laws to 50, plus the District of Columbia.

1994

- The American Correctional Association Victims Committee publishes the landmark *Report and Recommendations on Victims of Juvenile Crime,* which offers guidelines for improving victims' rights and services when the offender is a juvenile.
- Six additional states pass constitutional amendments for victims' rights—the largest number ever in a single year—bringing the total number of states with amendments to 20. States with new amendments include: Alabama, Alaska, Idaho, Maryland, Ohio, and Utah.
- President Clinton signs a comprehensive package of federal victims' rights legislation as part of the Violent Crime Control and Law Enforcement Act. The Act includes:
  —Violence Against Women Act, which authorizes more than $1 billion in funding for programs to combat violence against women.
  —Enhanced VOCA funding provisions.
  —Establishment of a National Child Sex Offender Registry.
  —Enhanced sentences for drunk drivers with child passengers.

1995

- The Federal Crime Victims' Fund deposits total $233,907,256.
- The Crime Victims' Rights Act of 1995 is introduced in the U.S. Congress.
- Legislatures in three states—Indiana, Nebraska, and North Carolina—pass constitutional amendments which will be placed on the ballot in 1996.
- The National Victims' Constitutional Amendment Network proposes the first draft of language for a federal constitutional amendment for victims' rights.

- The U.S. Department of Justice convenes a national conference to encourage implementation of the Violence Against Women Act.
- The first class graduates from the National Victim Assistance Academy in Washington, D.C. Supported by the Office for Victims of Crime, the university-based Academy provides an academically credited 45-hour curriculum on victimology, victims' rights, and a myriad other topics.

1996

- Federal Victims' Rights Constitutional Amendments are introduced in both houses of Congress with bipartisan support.
- Both presidential candidates and the Attorney General endorse the concept of a Victims' Rights Constitutional Amendment.
- The Federal Crime Victims' Fund reaches an historic high with deposits totaling over $500 million.
- Eight states ratify the passage of constitutional amendments for victims' rights—raising the total number of state constitutional amendments to 29 nationwide.
- The Community Notification Act, known as "Megan's Law," provides for notifying communities of the location of convicted sex offenders by amendment to the national Child Sexual Abuse Registry legislation.
- President Clinton signs the Antiterrorism Act providing one million dollars in funding to strengthen antiterrorism efforts, making restitution mandatory in violent crime cases, and expanding the compensation and assistance services for victims of terrorism both at home and abroad, including victims in the military.
- The National Domestic Violence Hotline is established to provide crisis intervention information and referrals to victims of domestic violence and their friends and family.
- To fully recognize the sovereignty of Indian Nations, OVC for the first time provides all grants in Indian Country directly to the tribes.
- OVC launches a number of international crime victim initiatives including working to foster worldwide implementation of a United Nations declaration on victims' rights and working to better assist Americans who are victimized abroad.

Source: Adapted and modified from material compiled by the National Victim Center with the support and assistance of the U.S. Department of Justice Office for Victims of Crime, Victims' Assistance Legal Organization, Inc. (VALOR), and the many national, state and local victim service providers who offered documentation of their key victims' rights landmark activities.

INDEX

ABC. *See* American Broadcasting Corporation

Absolute immunity, 297–98, 301n. 41

Academia versus professionalism, 341–42

Accessory liability, 253–54

Accidental injuries and child abuse, 169

Accidental or intentional death, 272–73

Accidental loss versus intentional acts, 70–71

Accomplice liability, 253–54

Accountability in restorative justice, 69

Acquaintance crimes, 22, 108
child abuse, 174, 182
rape, 129, 132–34, 142

Acquittals, 44, 45

Active neglect of elderly, 197

Actual damages versus nominal damages, 247, 248

Acute primary infection of HIV, 224. *See also* HIV/AIDS

Acute stress disorder (ASD), 80, 88

Adjudication, 47, 54

Adjudicatory hearings in juvenile court dependency procedures, 66–67, 71

Administrative law, 6, 16

Admissibility of victim impact statements, 317

Adult Protective Services, 200

Adult status of juveniles, 41

Adventitious disabilities, 231

Advocacy for victims in legislation, 99–100

Aetna Life & Casualty Co. v. Barthelemy, 274

Affirmative defenses in filing a response, 62, 71

African-Americans, 208
hate crimes against, 207, 212, 217
violence against, 285

Against Our Will (Brownmiller), 7

Age of Aquarius, 186

Agency on Aging, 200

Aggravated assault in crime index, 21

Aggression
and child abuse, 176–77
and cycle of violence theory, 176–77

Aggressive assaults, 7

Agricultural crimes, 338, 339

AIDS, 223, 224. *See also* HIV/AIDS

Aid for Victims of Crime in St. Louis, 344

Airlines, 267

Alabama passes victims' rights amendment, 352

Alaska passes victims' rights amendment, 352

Alcohol and spousal abuse, 154

Aldrete, Sarah "Witch," 111

Aliens, undocumented, 216, 217

American Association for Protecting Children, 172

American Bar Association, 312
General Standards of Conduct, 45

American Broadcasting Corporation (ABC), 93

American Burn Association, 76

American Civil Liberties Union (ACLU), 141

American Correctional Association, *Report and Recommendations on Victims of Juvenile Crime*, 352

American Correctional Association, Task Force on Victims of Crime, 349

American court system
dual nature of, 37
specialization of, 37
supervision of, 37
See also Courts; Federal court system; State court system

American law, 5, 6, 36

American Medical Association, 134

American Probation and Parole Association (APPA), Victim Issues Committee, 351

Americans with Disabilities Act of 1990, 231

American Sociological Association, 184

American States Ins. v. Borbor, 282n. 45

America Speaks Out, National
    Victim Center, 350
Amnesty International, 151
Anal intercouse. *See* Rectal
    intercourse
Anderson v. Creighton, 298
Anger, 79
Anger rapes, 125–26
Animals, cruelty to, 172
Animal sacrifices, 187, 188
*Ann M. v. Pacific Plaza Shopping
    Center,* 266
Annual report on gay and lesbian
    violence, National Gay and
    Lesbian Task Force Policy
    Institute, 235
Answer in filing a response, 62, 71
Antiterrorism Act, 353
AP. *See* Associated Press
Appellate courts, 39
Appellate jurisdiction, 39
Apportionment, 65, 254–55, 261n. 24
Appropriations committees, 98, 105
Aquinas, Thomas, 234
Argersinger v. Hamilin, U.S.
    Supreme Court, 45
Aristotle, 172
Arizona passes victims' rights
    amendment, 349
Arraignment in criminal justice
    procedures, 49–50
Arrest, 48, 54
    citizen's, 158, 259
    definition of, 158, 164
    of spousal abusers, 158–63
    statutory limits on, 158
    warrantless, 259, 295, 345
    warrants for, 48, 259
Arson
    of African-American
        churches, 212
    of churches, 220n. 10
    in crime index, 21
    and fire insurance, 271
    statistics on, 20
Aryan race, 217
*Asahi Metal Industry Co. v. Superior
    Court,* 72n. 6
ASD. *See* Acute stress disorder
Asher, Richard, 185
Asians, hate crimes against, 217
Assault
    definition of, 260
    statistics on, 20, 23

Assault and battery, 250–51
Assigned defense counsel, 45
Associated Press (AP), 93
Association of Paroling
    Authorities, International,
    Victim Issues Committee, 351
Asymptomatic incubation period
    of HIV, 224. *See also*
    HIV/AIDS
Asymptomatic phase of HIV, 224.
    See also HIV/AIDS
Atamina v. Supermarkets Gen. Corp.,
    269–70
Attempted homicides, 108
Attorney
    competency of, 46
    right to, 8
Attorney General's Task Force on
    Violent Crime, 346
Attractive nuisance doctrine, 268
Augustus, John, 46–47
Authority of law, 259
Automation in collecting
    restitution, 312–13
Automobile insurance, 275–77

Bailey, F. Lee, 46
Bail hearings, 48
Bail schedules, 48
Bail setting, 38, 48–49
Baker v. Wade, 239
Balistreri v. City of Pacifica, 288
Ballew v. Georgia, 56n. 23
Ballistics, 75
Babylon, 4
Bankruptcy courts, 37
Barmore v. Elmore, 268
Barnes v. Costle, 139
Basic Protection for the Traffic Victim
    (Keeton and O'Connell),
    277
Battered Child Syndrome (Helfer and
    Kempe), 175
"Battered Elder Syndrome: An
    Exploratory Study, The"
    (Block and Sinnott), 195
"Battered Husband Syndrome,
    The" (Steinmetz), 149
Battered woman syndrome,
    150–52, 163–64
Battered women's movement,
    345, 346
Battered women's shelters, 8, 149,
    228, 238, 339, 345

Battered Women's Testimony
    Act, 351
Battering rapes, 136
Battery, definition of, 158, 164, 260
Battery and assault, 250–51
Bay Area Women Against Rape in
    San Francisco, 344
Benedict, Ruth, 218
Beneficiaries in life insurance,
    272–73
Benton v. Maryland, 261n. 3
Beyond a reasonable doubt. *See*
    Reasonable doubt
Bias crimes, definition of, 214, 219.
    See also Hate crimes
Bierezynski v. Rogers, 261n. 24
Billings v. Vernal City, 289
Bill managers, 100
Bill of Rights, U.S. Constitution, 43,
    47, 48, 286
Bills, how a bill becomes a law, 97,
    106n. 3
Biological factors as theory of
    sexual violence, 125
Birth control, 186
Birth defects, 172
Blackmun, Harry A., 321
Black's Law Dictionary, 128
Blackstone, 135
Block, M.R. and J.D. Sinnott, "The
    Battered Elder Syndrome: An
    Exploratory Study," 195
Blood alcohol level, 113–14
Blood feuds, 3, 4
Booking, 43, 54
Boot camps, 46
Booth v. Maryland, U.S. Supreme
    Court, 317–19, 320–21
Bowers v. Hardwick, 239
"Brady Bill," 352
Brainwashing prisoners
    of war, 151
Breast feeding and HIV, 225. *See
    also* HIV/AIDS
Brownmiller, S., *Against Our Will,* 7
Brown, Nicole, 247
Brown v. Mississippi, 321–22
Buckey, Peggy McMartin, 187
Buckey, Raymond, 187
Building a Solution (Susman and
    Vittert), 82
Bundy, Ted, 109
Burch v. Louisiana, 56n. 23
Burden of proof, 47, 52, 65, 246

Bureau of Justice Statistics, *The Costs of Crime to the Victim*, 87
Burglary
  in crime index, 21
  of elderly, 202
Burns, 76–77
Bush, George, 350, 351
Business visitors, 267–68
Bus lines, 267

California
  first compensation program in, 304
  passes victims' rights amendment, 349
  Proposition 8, 347
California State University at Fresno, 17n. 1
  bachelors degree program in victimology, 350
  Victim Services Certificate Program, 348
California State University (Hayward), 207
California Supreme Court, 266, 269
Call screening, 158, 164
"Calls for papers," 342
Campus
  crime on, 332–33, 349
  sexual harassment on, 140–41
  sexual violence on, 7
Campus Security Act of 1990, U.S. Congress, 332
Campus Sexual Assault Victims' Bill of Rights, U.S. Congress, 332, 350, 351
Canaanite excavations, 171–72
Canada, Victim–Offender Reconciliation Program, 69–70
Capital punishment and victim impact statements, 317–21, 330n. 5
Caretakers in elder abuse, 196, 198
Carnal knowledge, 128
Carrington, Frank G., 345
CASAS. *See* Court-appointed special advocates
Case-in-chief in criminal justice procedures, 51
Case management agencies, 232, 233
Casualty insurance, 273
Causes of actions, 60
Census Bureau, 23

Center for Disease Control, 224, 226, 228, 341
  National Profile: Fatal Injuries to Workers in the U.S., 335–36
Cestui que vie (insured), 272
CGL. *See* Commercial general liability (CGL) policy
Challenging jurors, 50
Character-trait model of child abuse, 178
Charlotte Experiment, 161, 162
Child, definition of, 184, 190
Child abuse, 303, 338
  and aggression, 176–77
  classification of offenders, 174
  in daycare centers, 187–88
  decline in, 29–30
  definition of, 169
  and disabilities, 232
  extent of problem, 171–73
  family member as offender, 174, 182
  gender differences in victims, 181
  juvenile court dependency procedures for, 66–68
  legislation on, 172
  and masturbation, 180
  Munchausen Syndrome by proxy, 185–86
  and police workloads, 27
  programs for, 103
  rationalizations for, 180
  ritual abuse, 186–88
  in schools, 172
  sexual, 171
  and sexual fantasies, 180
  sibling abuse, 183–85
  statistics on, 20
  by stepfathers, 182
  stereotypes of abusers, 180
  theories of, 174–79
  types of, 169–74
  See also Child neglect; Physical child abuse; Sexual child abuse
Child Abuse Prevention and Treatment Act of 1974, 191n. 4, 344
Child custody, 38, 58
Child neglect, 66, 170–71, 189, 338
  continuum of, 170
  extent of problem, 173
  juvenile court dependency procedures for, 66–68

  and poverty, 179
  theories of, 179–80
  See also Child abuse; Sexual child abuse
Child pornography, 181
Child Protection Act of 1990, U.S. Congress, 350
Children
  best interests of, 67
  definition of, 184, 190
  dependent, 66–68
  murder of, 115
  needs of, 42
  rights of in juvenile court dependency procedures, 67–68
  as survivors of homicide victims, 117
  as victims, 93–168
Child Safety Partnership, 348
Child sexual abuse. *See* Sexual child abuse
Child Sexual Abuse Registry Act, U.S. Congress, 352, 353
Christian conservatism and hate crimes, 217
Christopher, Charisse, 319–20
Christopher, Nicholas, 319–20
Church arsons, 212, 220n. 10
Churchill, Winston, 135
Church of Satan, 187
Circuit courts, 38
Citation, 43, 54
Citizens arrest, 158, 259
City of Canton v. Harris, 289
Civil conspiracy, 254, 260
Civil contempt and injunctions, 295
Civil courts, 37
Civil justice system, 57–72
  civil procedures, 58–65
  juvenile court dependency procedures, 66–68
  restorative justice, 68–70
Civil law, 5
Civil litigation, 9, 43, 50
  and intentional torts, 246–47
  and restitution, 311, 313
Civil procedures, 58–65
  filing a complaint, 59–61
  filing a response, 62
  judgment, 65
  jurisdiction, 59
  pretrial activities, 62–64
  trial, 64–65
  verdict, 65

Civil rights, 58
  defenses for violations of, 296–98
  gender-based, 291–92
Civil Rights Act of 1866, 284, 285
Civil Rights Act of 1871, 285–86
Civil Rights Act of 1964
  and disabled persons, 231
  and employment discrimination,
    138, 139
Civil rights laws, 8
Civil rights of victims, 283–301
Clery, Howard and Connie, 349
Clery, Jeanne, 349
Clinical studies on domestic
    violence, 30
Clinton, Bill, 13–14, 96, 290, 352, 353
Closing arguments in criminal
    justice procedures, 52
Cochran, Johnny, 46
Coconut Grove fire in Boston, 78
Code of ethics for victim advocates
    in the media, 92
Code of Hammurabi, 4, 309
Code of Ur-Nammu, 3
Cohabiting couples, 155
Collateral financial sources, 307
Colleges
  duty to protect students, 268,
    332–33
  and grants, 104
  sexual harassment at, 140–41
  sexual violence at, 7
  See also Campus crime
Collision coverage, 275, 281
Colorado passes victims' rights
    amendment, 351
Colorado Springs Experiment, 161
Comas, 77
Commercial crime, 23
Commercial general liability (CGL)
    policy, 277–78, 282n. 45
Commission on Uniform Crime
    Reports, 20–21
Common carriers, 267
Common law, 5, 6, 39
  aiding and abetting, 253
  and releases, 255
  respondeat superior theory,
    289, 299
  and spousal abuse, 155
  and wrongful death, 249
Commonwealth attorneys, 44
Community involvement in elder
    victimization, 200

Community Notification Act, 353
Community policing, 28–29
Community protection in
    restorative justice, 69
Community service, 69, 311
Community support systems, 216
Commuting, 334
Compensation, 247, 302–8, 353
  benefits of, 307–8
  definition of, 303, 313
  eligibility for, 305–7
  program operation of, 304–5
Compensatory damages, 61, 71
Competency of attorneys, 46
Competency in restorative
    justice, 69
Complaints, 60, 70–71
Comprehensive coverage, 275, 281
Comprehensive general liability
    insurance, 277, 281
Computers, 341
  in collecting restitution, 312–13
  restraining orders on, 292,
    293, 294
Concerns of Police Survivors
    (COPS), 348
Condoms, 130
Conduct requirement in mental
    distress, 252–53
Conferences in pretrial
    activities, 64
Confessions to crimes, 43, 55n. 9
Confidentiality
  and HIV/AIDS, 226
  in juvenile court system, 40, 41
  and the media, 95
  in research studies, 126
Confinement requirement in false
    imprisonment, 251–52
Conflict Tactics Scale (CTS), 29
Congenital disabilities, 231
Connecticut passes victims' rights
    amendment, 349
Consent, 257
  duress causing, 258
  exceeding scope of, 258
  lack of capacity to, 258
Consequences of victimization,
    73–89
Conservatism and crime, 8–9
Conservative groups, 218
Conspiracy, civil, 254, 260
Constant A. v. Paul C.A., 238
Constitutional law, 6

Constitutional rights of victims,
    283–301
Consumer goods and services
    frauds, 31
Contact versus fear, 250–51
Continuing education, 15
Contract defense services, 45
Contract law, 58
Contributory misconduct, 306,
    307, 314
Control of women's sexuality, 7
Corporal punishment, 169
Corporate clients, 44
Correctional officers, 46, 47, 54
Correctional system in criminal
    justice system, 46–47
Costs associated with crime, 85
Costs of Crime to the Victim, The,
    Bureau of Justice Statistics, 87
Counterclaim in filing
    a response, 62
County attorneys, 44
County courts, 38
County of Riverside v. McLaughlin,
    U.S. Supreme Court, 48
Court-appointed special advocates
    (CASAS) in juvenile court
    dependency procedures, 67
Court reporters, 64, 98
Courts
  of appeals, 39
  of Chancery, 39
  of common pleas, 38
  in criminal justice system, 46
  geographic organization of, 37
  of last resort, 39
  See also American court system;
    Federal court system; State
    court system
*Cramer v. Balcor Property
    Management,* 265
Credentials and certifications in
    victimology, 15
Crime
  acquaintance, 22, 108
  agricultural, 338, 339
  campus, 332–33, 349
  and child abuse, 176–77
  confessions to, 43, 55n. 9
  and conservatism, 8–9
  costs associated with, 85
  economic, 30, 31
  extent of, 20
  gang, 336–37

measurement of, 19–34
non-reporting of, 22
official reports on, 20–29
profiting from, 250, 304, 351
property, 30, 338
rural, 335–40
stranger, 22, 108
white-collar, 23, 30–31
workplace, 334–36
See also Fraud; Research; Violent
crimes; specific kinds of crime
Crime Bill of 1994, 290–92
Crime Control Act of 1990, 41
Crime index, 21
Crime Victims' Bill of Rights
first in Wisconsin, 346
International Association of
Chiefs of Police Board of
Governors, 347
Crime Victims Fund, 15, 103, 303,
304, 347
Crime Victims' Legal Advocacy
Institute, Inc., 245
Crime Victims' Rights Act of 1995,
U.S. Congress, 352
Criminal acts
and comparable intentional
torts, 246
and life insurance benefits, 272
of third parties, 265
Criminal codes, 128
Criminal contempt and
injunctions, 295
Criminal court system, 36–42
Criminal and His Victim, The (von
Hentig), 10–11
Criminal justice procedures, 47–53
arraignment, 49–50
case-in-chief, 51
closing arguments, 52
defendant's evidence, 51
deliberation and verdict, 52
first appearance, 48–49
grand jury hearing, 49
jury selection, 50–51
opening statement, 51
preliminary hearing, 49
pretrial activities, 48
sentencing, 52–53
Criminal justice system, 35–56
court system of, 36–42
justice procedures in, 47–53
parties in, 42–47
and spousal abuse, 156–63

and survivors of homicide
victims, 116, 117
Criminal law, 5
Criminal sanctions versus
restorative justice, 68, 69
Criminal trials, fairness during, 8
Criminology, 12, 342
definition of, 3, 16
as a science, 17n. 2
Crisis
definition of, 78, 88
impact stage of, 79
recoil stage of, 79–80
reorganization stage of, 80
Cross-complaint in filing a
response, 62
Cross-examinations, 51
Crowley, Aleister, *Magick in Theory
and Practice,* 186
Cruelty to animals, 172
CTS. *See* Conflict Tactics Scale
Cultural awareness, 207–11
case study, 219–20
definition of, 208, 219
training for, 209–11
Cultural differences and hate
crimes, 214
Cultures
diversity of, 29
and patriarchy, 7
and reporting domestic
violence, 306
and sexuality, 7
violence in, 136–37
Culture of violence as theory of
sexual violence, 125
Cycle of violence theory, 150–52,
163, 189
and aggression, 176–77
in child abuse, 174–75
and domestic violence, 175–76
in elder abuse, 197
See also Physical child abuse
Czachorowski v. Degenhart, 288

*Damaged Parents: An Anatomy of
Child Neglect* (Polansky), 179
Darrow, Clarence, 52
Darwin's theory of evolution, 52
Databases
of restraining orders, 292,
293, 294
state, 16
Daycare centers, 187–88, 282n. 45

Deadly force versus nondeadly
force in self-defense, 256
Death penalty cases, 38
and victim impact statements,
317–21, 330n. 5
Default judgments, 51
Defendent's evidence in criminal
justice procedures, 51
Defense attorneys in criminal
justice system, 45–46
Defense of others, 257
Defense of property, 257
Defenses to intentional torts,
156–59
Defenses for violations of civil
rights, 296–98, 300n. 38
Delaware passes victims' rights
amendment, 349
Deliberation and verdict in
criminal justice procedures, 52
Dementia in HIV, 225
Demographics, changing, 29
Demurrer in filing a response,
62, 71
Denial, 79
Dependant children, 66–68
Dependency theory of spousal
abuse, 153–54
Depositions in discovery, 63, 64, 71
Depression, 82
in elderly, 201–2
Dershowitz, Alan, 46
Detention hearings in juvenile
court dependency procedures,
66, 71
Deterrance, 52, 54
Dewell v. Lawson, 289
*Diagnostic and Statistical Manual of
Mental Disorders,* 4th edition
(DSM-IV), 80
Disability as cost of crime, 86
Disabled persons
communicating with, 230
definitions of, 212, 219, 231, 240
emerging issues, 232–33
hate crimes against, 207, 212
institutional abuse of, 233
and legal issues, 231–33
risk reduction and prevention
for, 233
statistics on, 231
types of victimization, 231–32
as victims, 229–33
Discovery, 60, 63–64

Disinhibition theory, 154
Dispositional hearings in juvenile
    court dependency procedures,
    67–68, 71
District attorneys, 44
District courts, 38
Diversity of populations, 29
Divorces, 38, 58
DNA samples, 130
Doctrine of fundamental fairness.
    See Fundamental fairness
    doctrine
Domestic violence, 6, 136
    clinical studies on, 30
    compensation for victims
        of, 306
    and cycle of violence theory,
        175–76
    educating public about, 8
    as "family matters," 157, 158
    and hereditary
        predisposition, 175
    and HIV/AIDS, 225, 228
    as major public health
        problem, 348
    mandatory arrest in, 245
    national toll-free hotline for, 349
    and police workloads, 27
    probable cause arrests in, 345
    restraining orders in, 61
    right of victims in, 9
    See also Family violence; Marital
        rape; Spousal abuse
Domestic Violence Awareness
    Week, 346
Domestic Violence Factoids
    (Gelles), 147
Double indemnity clauses, 272
Double jeopardy, 246, 261n. 3
"Dream Team," 46
Drinking age, 113, 348, 349
Drive-by shootings, 336
Driving under the influence (DUI),
    113. *See also* Drunk driving
Drugs
    and crime, 27
    and HIV/AIDS, 225, 228
    and juveniles, 41
    in ritual child abuse, 186
    in rural areas, 338
Drunk driving, 77, 346
    with child passengers, 352
    and compensation, 305–6, 350
    statistics on, 20

and victim impact panels,
    328, 347
See also Mothers Against Drunk
    Driving; Vehicular homicide
DSM-III-R, 234
DSM-IV. *See Diagnostic and
    Statistical Manual of Mental
    Disorders,* 4th edition
Due process, 59, 70, 286, 287, 321
DUI. *See* Driving under the
    influence
Duress causing consent, 258
Duty of care, 267
Duty to protect, 264–66

Ecological theory of child neglect,
    179, 189
Economic crime, 30, 31
Economic dependency, 153
Economics and marital rape, 136
Economic theory of child neglect,
    179, 189
Education
    continuing, 15
    on domestic violence, 8
    on victims' rights movement,
        14–15
Edward the Confessor, King of
    England, 5–6
EEOC. *See* Equal Employment
    Opportunity Commission
Egypt, 171
Eighth Amendment, U.S.
    Constitution, 48, 55n. 8,
    319, 320
Elder abuse, 194–205
    areas of, 197
    caretakers in, 196, 198
    definition of, 196–97, 203
    extent of the problem, 195–96
    research on, 196
    theories of, 197–99
Elder victims, 4, 194–205
    burglary of, 202
    and fraud, 201–2
    loss of life savings of, 292
    sexual assault of, 200–201
    and violent crimes, 201
Electronic conferencing, 341
E-mail, 341
Emergency removal of child, 66
Emotional trauma of victims, 43
Employees, workers'
    compensation for, 278–80

Employers of victims, 43
Employment-based sexual
    harassment, 137–41
Empowerment of victims, 90–106
Enforcement Act of 1870, 284–85
England
    Magna Carta of, 6
    Roman rule of, 5
English common law, 5, 39,
    135, 297
Entering a plea, 49–50
Environmental–sociological–
    cultural model of child abuse,
    178, 189
Environmental stress model of
    child abuse, 178
Equal Employment Opportunity
    Commission (EEOC), 129
Equal protection, 286, 287–88
Equity, 39, 54
Equity power, 38–39, 61
*Erichsen v. No-Frills Supermarkets of
    Omaha, Inc.,* 266
Erotomanic stalkers, 333
Estate law, 58
Ethical (professional) conduct, 46
Ethnic differences and hate
    crimes, 214
Ethnicity, crime motivated by, 22
Exclusive remedy in workers'
    compensation, 279–80
Expert witnesses, 64, 66, 248
Extrafamilial sexual abuse, 171, 189

Failure of local agencies
    to act, 288–90
    to protect, 290
    to supervise, 289–20
    to train, 289
False imprisonment, intentional
    tort of, 251–52, 260
False-positive factors in
    identification of hate crimes,
    215–16
False victimization syndrome in
    stalking, 334
Families
    nontraditional, 236, 240
    of victims, 43
Family Bereavement Center
    (Detroit), 121n. 26
Family law, 37, 58
Family relationships and homicide
    victims, 114–16

Family stress theory in elder abuse, 198, 203
Family systems, 152
Family violence, definitions of, 237, 240. *See also* Domestic violence
Family Violence Prevention and Services Act, U.S. Congress, 345,348
Fantasies, sexual, 180
Fatal crimes, statistics on, 20
Fatal injuries in intangible losses, 87
Fault-based insurance, 276, 277
FBI, 21, 22, 23
    definition of white-collar crime, 31
    National Crime Information Center (NCIC) computer system, 347, 350
    National Symposium on Sexual Assault, 348
Fear versus contact, 250–51
Federal agencies, research-based studies by, 15–16. *See also* Governmental agencies
Federal Bureau of Investigation. *See* FBI
Federal Bureau of Prisons, victim–witness notification system, 348
Federal circuit courts, 40
Federal court juvenile system, 41
Federal court system, 36, 39–40
    circuit courts, 40
    district courts, 40
    U.S. Supreme Court, 40
    See also American court system; Courts; State court system
Federal Crime Victims' Fund, 348, 350, 352, 353
Federal district courts, 40
Federal Drunk Driving Prevention Act, 349
Federal grants, 103–4
Federalism, 36
Federalist Papers (Hamilton), 40
Federal Tort Claims Act, 297
Federal Victim and Witness Protection Act of 1982, 347
Feder v. Banker's Trust Co., 270
Felonies, 37, 45, 49
    definition of, 158, 164
    and juveniles, 41
Female infanticide, 172

Females as victims, 122–45. *See also* Women
Feminist movement, 6–8, 135, 186. *See also* Women
Ferguson, Colin, 322
Fifth Amendment, U.S. Constitution, 55n. 8, 65, 246–47
Filing a complaint
    in civil procedures, 59–61
    in criminal procedures, 48
Filing a response in civil processes, 62
Final Report of the President's Task Force on Victims of Crime, 308–9
Final summation, 52
Financial advice frauds, 31
Financial consequences
    and survivors of homicide victims, 116
    of victimization, 82–88
Financial independence of elderly, 202
Financial restitution, 310
Fingerprinting, 48
Firearms
    and crime, 27, 28
    gunshot wounds from, 74, 74–76
    handguns, 352
    and homicides, 109
    in the United States, 75
Fire insurance, 273, 281
Fire Insurance Exchange v. Diehi, 274
First Amendment, U.S. Constitution, 6, 213
First appearance in criminal justice procedures, 48–49
First National Conference of the Judiciary on Victims of Crime, National Judicial College, 347
First National Day of Unity, 346
First-party insurance, 276, 277
Fixed incomes of elderly, 202
Flag burning, 6
Florida passes victims' rights amendment, 349
Force-only rapes, 136
Foreseeability, 248, 269, 281
Formal pleading, 66
Foundation grants, 103, 104
Four preconditions model of sexual abuse, 180–81, 189
Fourteenth Amendment, U.S. Constitution, 321

Francis, Connie, 267
Fraud, 30
    definition and types of, 31
    and elderly, 201–2
Fraudulent lawsuits, 276
Freedom of expression, 6, 213
Freedom of the press, 92
Fresno County, California, first victim impact statement in, 345
Fresno Valley Medical Center, 89n. 1
Friends of victims, 43
Fundamental fairness doctrine, 321–22, 329
Fundiller v. City of Cooper, 290
Fundraising, 103–5
Future harm versus imminent harm, 252

"Game Guy's Prayer," 319
Gang killings, juvenile, 109
Gang violence, 336–37
    in rural areas, 338
Garnishing wages, 313
Gather, Demetrius, 319
Gays, 207, 213
    closeted, 216
    definition of, 240
    and HIV-related violence, 229
    as victims, 233–39
    See also Homosexuals
Gelles, R.J., *Domestic Violence Factoids,* 147
Gender
    in child abuse victims, 181
    and hate crimes, 213, 214
    and violence, 291
General jurisdiction, 38–39, 54
General Standards of Conduct, American Bar Association, 45
Genocide, 217
Genovese, Kitty, 264
Gideon v. Wainwright, U.S. Supreme Court, 45
Glass ceiling, 153
Goldman, Ronald, 247
Goldsmith v. Physicians Insurance Company, 273–74
Governmental agencies, 6. *See also* Federal agencies
Grand jury hearing in criminal justice procedures, 49
Grandstaff v. City of Borger, 289
Grants
    definition of, 103–4, 106

to Indian Nations, 353
to support victims, 349
Violence Against Women Act
(VAWA), 15–16
Greece, 234
Green River Killer, 111
Grieving process, 78
Griffin, S., "Rape: The All
American Crime," 7
Gross inaction in child neglect, 170
Guest statutes, 276
Guilt of survivors of homicide
victims, 115
Guilty plea, 40
Gunshot wounds, 74, 75–76

Habeas corpus appeals, 40
Hale, Sir Matthew, 135
Hamilton, Alexander, *Federalist
Papers*, 40
Hammurabi, Code of, 4, 309
Handguns, 352. *See also* Firearms
Harris v. Forklift Systems, Inc., U.S.
Supreme Court, 129
*Haser v. Maryland Casualty
Company*, 271
Hate crimes, 206–21, 351
and cultural awareness, 207–11
and HIV positive persons, 213,
216, 229
homosexuals as victims of,
235–36
identification of, 214–16
legal aspects of, 213–14
in rural areas, 338
statistics on, 212
symbols of, 207, 213, 215, 216
typology of, 216–18
See also Bias crimes
Hate Crime Statistics Act of 1990,
U.S. Congress, 22, 211, 214, 350
Haynes, Richard, 319
Head Start program for cultural
awareness training, 210–11
Head trauma, 77
Healing process, 79–90
Hearing-impaired women as
victims, 232
Hedonistic serial killers, 111–12
Helfer, R. and C.H. Kempe, *The
Battered Child Syndrome*, 175
Helplessness of victims, 91
Hereditary predisposition and
domestic violence, 175

Herod, King, 171
Higher diety and hate crimes, 217
Hillside Strangler, 111
Hinckley, John, 252
Hispanics, hate crimes against,
207, 217
Historical perspecives and marital
rape, 135–36
HIV/AIDS, 75, 78, 130, 223–29
dementia in, 226
and hate crimes, 213, 216, 229
and homosexuals, 237
involuntary testing for, 227
phases of, 224
specific victim populations,
227–29
transmission of, 224–25
victim service issues in, 226–27
See also AIDS; Sexually
transmitted disease
*HIV/AIDS and Victim Services: A
Critical Concern of the 90s*,
Office for Victims of Crime,
214n. 1
Homeowner's insurance, 273–75
Homicides, 23
compensation for, 350
sibling, 184
statistics on, 108–9
theories and types of, 109–12
vehicular, 112–14
See also Homicide victims;
Murder; Survivors of
homicide victims
Homicide victims, 107–21
and family relationships, 114–16
statistics on, 108–9
See also Murder; Survivors of
homicide victims
Homosexuals
closeted, 216
definitions of, 234, 240
extent of domestic violence by,
237–38
hate crimes against, 207, 213,
235–36
historical perspectives of, 234
and HIV/AIDS, 237
and HIV-related violence,
229, 235
intimate violence by, 235–37
and legal aspects, 238–39
outing of, 237–38
rights of, 236

sodomy statutes, 239
support services for, 238
as victims, 233–39
See also Gays; Lesbians
Hostile environment sexual
harassment, 138, 139
Hotlines, national toll-free
domestic violence, 349, 353
Household burglary, statistics
on, 23
Household crimes, reporting of, 22
Household theft, statistics on, 23
House Select Committee
on Aging, 196
Howard Johnson Motel, 267
Huberty, James O., 110
Hullinger, Charlotte, 13
Hullinger, Robert, 13
Hung juries, 52
Huratado v. California, 55n. 8

IACP. *See* International Association
of Chiefs of Police
Idaho militia groups, 218
Idaho passes victims' rights
amendment, 352
Illegal aliens, hate crimes against,
216, 217
Illinois Juvenile Court Act, 41
Illinois passes victims' rights
amendment, 351
Immediate injuries that heal
leaving no trace, 75
Immigrants, 207, 217
Imminent harm versus future
harm, 252
Immunity doctrine, 297
Impact statements. *See* Victim
impact statements
Impeachment, 55n. 9, 64
Imperfect self-defense, 256
Incapacitation, 52–53, 54
Incest, 183
Indepencence of elderly, 202
Indiana passes victims' rights
amendment, 352
"Indian Nations: Justice for Victims
of Crime" conference, Rapid
City, South Dakota, 350
Indian Nations, 353. *See also* Native
Americans
Individual service restitution, 310
Industrial Revolution, 172
Infanticide, 171–72

Inferred intent rule, 273–74, 281
Information clearinghouses, 344
Information filing, 41
Information overload, 341
Infraction cases, 48
Injunctions, 38, 292–96, 299
    advantages and disadvantages
        of, 295–96, 300n. 37
    in civil processes, 61
    effectiveness of, 292, 295–96
    temporary restraining orders,
        39, 61
    use of, 292–95
    violations of, 295, 296
Injuries in physical consequences
    of victimization, 74–75
Injuries that leave visible scars, 75
In-kind retaliation, 3
Innkeepers, 267
Innocence presumption, 51
In personam personal jurisdiction,
    59, 70
In rem personal jurisdiction, 59, 70
Insanity plea, 40
Institutional abuse
    of disabled persons, 233
    of elders, 197
Insurance companies
    automobile insurance, 275–77
    casualty insurance, 273, 281
    claims as cost of crime, 86
    fire insurance, 273, 281
    homeowner's insurance, 273–75
    liability insurance, 277–78
    life insurance, 271–73, 281
    scams of, 31
    settling with, 248–49
    as third-party codefendants, 87
    unlawful activity of, 270–71
    and victim compensation and
        restitution, 307
    workers' compensation, 278–80
Insured, 272
Insurer, 271
Intangible losses, 82, 84, 85, 87
Integrated theoretical models, 154
Intentional or accidental death,
    272–73
Intentional acts versus accidental
    loss, 70–71
Intentional torts, 245–47, 249–61
    and comparable criminal
        acts, 246
    defenses to, 156–57

and Section 1983 actions,
    284, 287
transferred intent, 246
Intent requirement in mental
    distress, 252
Interactional model of child abuse,
    178, 189
Intercourse, types of, 126, 171
Intergenerational transmission of
    violence theory, 175, 176. *See
    also* Cycle of violence
Intermediate appellate courts, 39
Intermittent reinforcement, 152
Internal Revenue Service and
    nonprofit organizations,
    99–100
International Association of Chiefs
    of Police Board of Governors,
    Crime Victim's Bill of
    Rights, 347
International Association of Chiefs
    of Police (IACP), 20–21
International Conference on
    Campus Sexual Assault, 351
International Declaration on the
    Rights of Victims of Crime,
    United Nations, 348
International Parental Child
    Kidnapping Act, 351
*International Shoe Co. v. State of
    Washington,* 59
Internet, 341
Interrogatories in discovery, 63,
    64, 71
Interspousal immunity in
    insurance claims, 276
Interstate highways and crime, 338
Interviews, 95–96
Intrafamilial immunity in
    insurance claims, 276
Intrafamilial killers, 250
Intrafamilial sexual abuse, 171, 189
Invitees, 267
Isle of Lesbos, 234
Isolation
    and child abuse, 182
    of elderly, 202
    and spousal abuse, 155
Israeli tribes, 4

Jack the Ripper, 111
Jails, 46, 54
Jesus, 171
Jews, hate crimes against, 212, 217

Job discrimination and HIV/AIDS,
    229. *See also* HIV/AIDS
Joint and several liability, 254–55
Joint tortfeasors, 253–55
*Journal of the American Medical
    Association,* 134
*Journal of Marriage and the
    Family,* 157
Judeo-Christian morality, 4–5
Judges and victim impact
    statements, 324–25, 326–27
Judgment in civil procedures, 65
Judgment proof, 65
Judiciary Act of 1789, 39
Juries, 39, 44
    number of members on, 56n. 23,
        65
    selection of in criminal justice
        procedures, 50–51
Jurisdiction
    appellate, 39
    concurrent, 37
    definition of, 37, 54, 70
    general, 38–39
    limited, 38
    personal, 59
    of the subject matter, 59
    and venue, 59
Jurisdictional hearings in juvenile
    court dependency procedures,
    66–67, 71
Justice Assistance Act, 347
Justice courts, 38
Justifiable homicides, 108
Justinian Code, 5
Juvenile adjudication, 41
Juvenile court dependency
    procedures, 66–68
    adjudicatory hearing, 66–67
    detention hearing, 66
    dispositional hearing, 67–68
    jurisdictional hearing, 66–67
Juvenile court system, 37, 38, 40–42
Juvenile crime
    and firearms, 28
    and gangs, 109, 337
    increase in, 340
    and neutralization theory, 199
    See also Youth
Juveniles, definition of, 41

Kansas passes victims' rights
    amendment, 351
Karmen's Theory of Victimology, 12

Keeton, Robert E. and Jeffery O'Connell, *Basic Protection for the Traffic Victim*, 277
Kelly, L., *Surviving Sexual Violence*, 7
Kidnapping, 252, 346
Kilpatrick, D. G., *Rape in America*, 81, 127, 128, 132, 174, 351
Kinetic energy, 75
King, Martin Luther, Jr., 215
Kline v. Massachusetts Avenue Apartment Corporation, 264–65
Ku Klux Klan, 207, 217–18
Ku Klux Klan Act of 1871, 285

Lamb, Laura, 113
Landlords, 264–65
Larceny-theft, 21, 338
La Vey, Anton, *The Satanic Bible*, 187
Law enforcement
    in criminal justice system, 43–44
    and the media, 92, 94, 106n. 1
    reports from, 20, 21
    responses to spousal abuse, 157–59, 167n. 51
    and victim impact statements, 322–23
Law Enforcement Assistance Administration (LEAA), 13, 103, 344, 346
Law and order movement, 8–9
Laws
    development of, 3–6
    how a bill becomes a law, 97, 106n. 3
LEAA. *See* Law Enforcement Assistance Administration
Learned helplessness, 151
Learning theory, 152
Legal cause of injury, 248
Legal expenses as cost of crime, 86
Legal immigrants, hate crimes against, 217
Legal precedents, 5–6
Legislation, 96–100
Lehigh University, 349
Leonard v. Jones, 61
Lepine, Marc, 217
Lesbians, 207, 213
    battering by, 236, 237
    closeted, 216
    definition of, 240
    and HIV-related violence, 229
    as victims, 233–39
    See also Homosexuals

Liability
    theories of, 269–70
    theories under United States Code Section 1983 actions, 287–90
Liability insurance, 277–78
Licensees, 268, 281
Life insurance, 271–73, 281
Lighter, Candy, 13
Lightner, Cari, 113, 346
Limited duty rule, 269, 281
Limited jurisdiction, 38, 54
Lincoln, Abraham, 137
Literary rights and profits from crime, 304
L.M.S. v. Angeles Corporation, 265
Lobbying, 99–100, 106
Local courts, 38
Local Government Police Management, 340
Local serial killers, 112
Long Island Railroad gunman, 322
Long-term care institutions, 197
Long-term catastrophic injuries, 75
Long-term crisis reaction, 81, 88
Lopez v. New Mexico Public Schools Insurance Authority, 278
Lopez v. Southern California Regional Transit, 267
Los Angeles Police Department, Threat Management Unit, 333
Los Angeles Probation Department, 312
Love obsessional stalkers, 333–34

Machoism as theory of sexual violence, 124
MADD. *See* Mothers Against Drunk Driving
Magick in Theory and Practice (Crowley), 186
Magistrate courts, 38
Magna Carta, 6
Major life activities, 212
Mandatory testing for HIV/AIDS, 227. *See also* HIV/AIDS
Manslaughter in crime index, 21
Marbury v. Madison, 40
Marital dependency, 153, 164
Marital rape, 123, 134–37, 142
    factors contributing to, 135–37
    historical perspective of, 135–36
    Nebraska abolishes exemption, 345

Marriage
    and spousal abuse, 155
    and survivors of homicide victims, 116–17
Marshall, Thurgood, 321
Maryland passes victims' rights amendment, 352
Massachusetts Registry of Civil Restraining Orders, 292, 352
Mass murderers, 110, 119
Masturbation and child abuse, 180
Material harm in elder abuse, 197, 203
Measurement of crime, 19–34. *See also* Research
Mechanical devices in defense of property, 257
Media, 91–96
    and morals in America, 218
    and survivors of homicide victims, 117
    and victims' rights, 14
Mediation, victim–offender, 69–70
Medical aspects in physical consequences of victimization, 75–78
Medical care as cost of crime, 86
Medical payment coverage, 275, 281
"Megan's Law," 353
Mendelsohn, Benjamin, "father of victimology," 9–10
Mendelsohn's theory of victimization, 9–10
Menendez brothers, 110, 256
Mental consequences of victimization, 78–82
Mental disabilities, 231
Mental distress, intentional tort of, 252–53, 260
Mental health care as cost of crime, 86
Mental illness model of child abuse, 177–78
Meritor Savings Bank v. Vinson, U.S. Supreme Court, 129
Message crimes, 216
Metro-Dade (Miami) Experiment, 161
Michelle Remembers (Pazder and Smith), 187
Michigan passes victims' rights amendment, 349
Middle Ages, 5
Militia movement, 207, 218

Milk, Harvey, 213
Millett, K., *Sexual Politics,* 7
Milwaukee Experiment, 161
Milwaukee Task Force on
Women, 345
Mincey v. Arizona, 55n. 9
Minimum contacts in the state, 59,
72n. 6
Minneapolis Domestic Violence
Experiment, 159–63
Minneapolis Police
Department, 159
Minnesota, first state to allow
probable cause arrest, 345
Minorities, hate crimes against,
207, 212. *See also* specific
minorities
Misdemeanors, 37, 45, 47, 48
definition of, 158, 164
and injuctions, 295
Misfeasance, 264
Missing Children's Act of 1982, 347
Missing Children's Assistance Act,
U.S. Congress, 348
Mission-oriented offenders in hate
crimes, 217
Mission-oriented serial killers, 111
Mississippi Burning (film), 213
Missouri passes victims' rights
amendment, 351
Mistrials, 52
Mitchell, Todd, 213
Model Penal Code (MPC), 128–29
Momentary inattention in child
neglect, 170
*Monell v. Department of Social
Services,* U.S. Supreme Court,
286–87
Monroe v. Pape, 286, 287
Montana militia groups, 218
Mood swings, 79
Mosaic Code, 4–5
Moscone, George, 213
Moses, 171
Mothers Against Drunk Driving
(MADD)
and compensation, 305
first Victim Impact Panel, 347
founding of, 13, 113, 346
mystical experiences study, 117
"Red Ribbon Campaign," 340
and victim impact panels, 328
Mother-to-child transmission of
HIV, 225. *See also* HIV/AIDS

Motions in pretrial activities, 63
Motion to strike in filing a
response, 62
Motor vehicle theft
in crime index, 21
statistics on, 23, 338
MPC. *See* Model Penal Code
Multiculturalism, 207. *See also*
Cultural awareness; Cultures
Munchausen Syndrome by proxy,
185–86, 190, 334
Municiple courts, 38
Murder
in crime index, 21
definition of, 108, 119
See also Homicide
My Sister Sam (TV show), 333
Mystical experiences of survivors
of homicide victims, 117–18

NACVCB. *See* National Association
of Crime Victim
Compensation Boards
NAP. *See* National Assessment
Program (NAP) survey
National Aging Resource Center
on Elder Abuse (NARCEA),
349
National Assessment Program
(NAP) survey, 27–29, 32
National Association of Crime
Victim Compensation Boards
(NACVCB), 305
*National Bias Crimes Training
Manual,* Office for Victims of
Crime, 220n. 6
National Broadcasting Corporation
(NBC), 93
National Census of Fatal
Injuries, 336
National Center on Child Abuse
and Neglect (NCCAN),
172, 344
National Center of Elder Abuse,
349
National Center for Missing and
Exploited Children
(NCMEC), 348
National Center for the Prevention
and Control of Rape, 8
National Child Search Assistance
Act, 350
National Child Sex Offender
Registry, 352

National Coalition Against
Domestic Violence (NCADV),
345, 346, 349
National Coalition Against Sexual
Assault (NCASA), 13, 345
National Crime Information Center
(NCIC) computer system, FBI,
347, 350
National Crime Victimization
Survey (NCVS), 13, 23–27,
32
compared with Uniform Crime
Reports, 28
National Crime Victims' Rights
Week, 344, 346, 350, 351
National District Attorneys
Association, 344
National Domestic Violence
Hotline, 349, 353
National Family Violence Surveys,
29–30, 154, 155
National Gay and Lesbian Task
Force Policy Institute, annual
report on gay and lesbian
violence, 235
National identity and racial
identity, 217
National Incidence Study on
Missing, Abducted, Runaway,
and Throwaway Children in
America, 250
National Incident-Based Reporting
System (NIBRS), 23
National Insitute of Justice, and
Minneapolis Domestic
Violence Experiment, 159
National Institute of Justice,
15–16, 27
*Rural Crime and Rural
Policing,* 338
*Victim Costs and Consequences: A
New Look,* 82
National Institute for Occupational
Safety and Health
(NIOSH), 335
National Judicial College, First
National Conference of the
Judiciary on Victims of
Crime, 347
National Minimum Drinking Age
Act of 1984, 348
National Missing Children's
Day, 347
National organizations, 341

National Organization for Victim Assistance (NOVA), 13, 15, 81, 345

National Organization for Women, 345

National Profile: Fatal Injuries to Workers in the U.S., Center for Disease Control, 335–36

National symposium on child molestation, Office for Victims of Crime (OVC), 348

National Symposium on Sexual Assault, 348

National Traumatic Occupational Fatalities (NTOF), 335, 336

National Victim Assistance Academy, victimology curriculum at, 353

National Victim Center, 348, 349, 353

America Speaks Out, 350

National Victims' Constitutional Amendment Network, 352

"National Women's Study, The," 127

Nationwide Mutual Insurance Co. v. Abernathey, 274

Native Americans, 303, 305, 339, 340, 353

Natural/biological model of sexual harassment, 140

NBC. *See* National Broadcasting Corporation

NCADV. *See* National Coalition Against Domestic Violence

NCCAN. *See* National Center on Child Abuse and Neglect

NCIC. *See* National Crime Information Center (NCIC) computer system

NCVS. *See* National Crime Victimization Survey

Nebraska abolishes marital rape exemption, 345

Nebraska passes victims' rights amendment, 352

Nebraska Supreme Court, 266

Necessity defense, 258–59

Necessity in self-defense, 256

Neglect, child. *See* Child neglect

Negligence, 245, 247–49, 260

Neighborhood Watch, 202

Neutralization theory in elder abuse, 199, 203

New Jersey passes victims' rights amendment, 351

New Mexico passes victims' rights amendment, 351

New Republic, 322

Newspapers, 98

New York City Gay and Lesbian AntiViolence Project, 239

New York Police Department, 172

New York Times, 322

NIBRS. *See* National Incident-Based Reporting System

NIOSH. *See* National Institute for Occupational Safety and Health

Nix v. Whiteside, 46

No-contact order in injunctions, 295

No-fault insurance, 276–77

Nolo contendere plea, 40, 54

Nominal damages, 246, 260

Nominal damages versus actual damages, 247, 248

Noncapital cases, 330n. 5

Non-Christians, hate crimes against, 217

Nondeadly force versus deadly force in self-defense, 256

Nonfatal injuries in intangible losses, 87

Nonfeasance, 264

Nonprofit organizations and Internal Revenue Service, 99–100

Nonprogressive long-term survivors, 224

Non-reporting of crime, 22

Nontraditional families, 236, 240

Norman Conquest, 5

North Carolina Court of Appeals, 274

North Carolina passes victims' rights amendment, 352

Northwestern National Life Insurance, 335

Not guilty plea, 40

Notification of survivors of homicide victims, 118–19

NOVA. *See* National Organization for Victim Assistance

NTOF. *See* National Traumatic Occupational Fatalities

Nursing homes and elder abuse, 197. *See also* Institutional abuse

Oath, 64

Obscene movies, 171

Obsessive rapes, 136

O'Conner, Sandra Day, 319

Office of the Commissioner of Probation, 292

Office on Domestic Violence, U.S. Health and Human Services Department, 346

Office for Victims of Crime (OVC), 14, 15, 214, 313

formation of, 347

grants to Indian Nations, 353

grants to support victims, 349

HIV/AIDS and Victim Services, 214n.1

National Bias Crimes Training Manual, 220n.6

national symposium on child molestation, 348

National Symposium on Sexual Assault, 348

and tribal victims, 339

Official immunity, U.S. Supreme Court, 297

Official reports on crime, 20–29

O'Hara v. Western Seven Trees Corporation, 265

Ohio passes victims' rights amendment, 352

Omaha Experiment, 161, 162

Ombudsperson programs for disabled persons, 233

Opening statement in criminal justice procedures, 51

Oral sex, 126, 171, 225

Organizational model of sexual harassment, 140

Ortell v. Spencer Co., 269

Oswego County, New York, first Victim Impact Panel, 346

Outing of homosexuals, 237–38, 240

Owens v. City of Independence, 287

Pain and suffering as cost of crime, 86, 87

PAO. *See* Public affairs officer

Parens patrea, 42

Parental Kidnapping Prevention Act of 1980, U.S. Congress, 346

Parents
  in juvenile court dependency
    procedures, 66, 67, 68
  and murder of child, 115
  murder of, 115
Parents of Murdered Children
  (POMC), 13, 116, 345
Parole, 311, 325
  definition of, 47, 54
Parole officers, 46, 47
Parricides, 110, 110
Parrish v. Luckie, 289–90
Parties in the criminal justice
  system, 42–47
Pasadena, Women's Advocates and
  Haven House, 345
Passengers on common
  carriers, 267
Passive neglect of elderly, 197
Patriarchy, 7, 140
Patz, Etan, 347
Payne v. Tennessee, U.S. Supreme
  Court, 319–20
Pazder, Lawrence and Michelle
  Smith, *Michelle Remembers*, 187
Penile–vaginal penetration, 128
"People of the State," 43
Pepper, Claude, 196
Pepper Commission, 196
Peremptory challenges, 50, 54
Perjury, 46
Perpetrators in criminal justice
  system, 43
Personal injury protection (PIP),
  276–77
Personalistic theory of child
  neglect, 179, 189
Personal safety plan for disabled
  persons, 233
Personal theft
  reporting of, 22
  statistics on, 23
*Peterson v. San Francisco Community
  College District*, 268
Petition in juvenile court
  dependency procedures, 66
Physical abuse of elderly, 197
Physical child abuse, 66, 169, 189
  extent of problem, 171–73
  theories of, 177–79
  See also Child abuse; Cycle of
    violence theory
Physical consequences of
  victimization, 74–78

Physical disabilities, 231
Physical injuries in child
  abuse, 169
Physical trauma of victims, 43
PIP. *See* Personal injury protection
Plato, 172
  Symposium, 234
Plea bargaining, 44
  and restitution, 311
  and victim impact statements,
    322, 324
Pleadings, 60
Pleas, 49–50
Ploof v. Putnam, 261n. 29
Polansky, N., *Damaged Parents: An
  Anatomy of Child Neglect*, 179
Police. *See* Law enforcement
Police and fire services as cost of
  crime, 86
Police Foundation, 159
Police reporters, 98
Policing, community, 28–29
Policy committees, 98, 105
Policy owner, 271–72
Political action committees, 99
Polls, *America Speaks Out*, 350
POMC. *See* Parents of Murdered
  Children
Pornographic movies, 171
Pornography, child, 181
Posttraumatic stress disorder
  (PTSD), 80–81, 88, 117
Poverty and child neglect, 179
Powell, Lewis F., Jr., 318–19
Powell v. Alabama, 321
*Powell v. New York Life Insurance
  Company*, 272
Power
  definition of, 164
  imbalances in, 152
  and sexual harassment, 140
  in sexual violence, 7
Power/control-oriented serial
  killers, 112
Power rapes, 125
Power theory of spousal abuse, 153
"Prayer," 61, 62
Pregnancy
  in rape, 78
  and spousal abuse, 154–55
Pregnancy Discrimination Act of
  1978, 138
Preliminary hearing in criminal
  justice procedures, 49

Preponderance of the evidence,
  246–47
Presentencing reports, 53, 317
Press liaisons, 100
Presumption of innocence, 51
Pretrial activities
  in civil procedures, 62–64
  in criminal procedures, 48
Primitive law, 3, 16
Prior similar incidents rule,
  269–70, 281
Prisoners of war, 151
Prisons, 46, 54
  research in, 235
  in United States, 68
Private citizen arrests, 44, 158, 259
Private defense counsel, 45–46
Private laws, 5
Private necessity, 258–59, 261n. 29
Private process servers, 51
Private protective services, 44
Private wrong, 58
Probable cause, 158, 164, 345
Probate matters, 37, 38, 58
Probation, 309–10, 311, 327, 328
  definition of, 47, 54
Probation officers, 46–47, 317
Procedural defenses, 297
Process servers, 51
Productivity as cost of crime, 86
Professional (ethical) conduct, 46
Professionalism
  increased, 15
  and training, 13, 341
  versus academia, 341–42
Professional organizations, 342
Profits from crime, 250, 304, 351
Proof, two levels of, 246–47
Proof beyond a reasonable doubt,
  65, 246–47
Property
  damage and loss as cost of
    crime, 86
  defense of, 257
  persons entering upon, 266–69
Property crime, 30, 338
Property law, 58
Proportionality in self-defense, 256
Proposition 8, California, 347
Prosecutors
  in criminal justice system, 44–45
  and victim impact statements,
    323–24
Protective orders. *See* Injunctions

Proximate cause of injury, 248
Psychodynamic model of child
    abuse, 177, 189
Psychological abuse of elderly,
    197, 203
Psychological factors as theory of
    sexual violence, 125
Psychopathological model of child
    abuse, 177–78
Psychopathology theory in elder
    abuse, 198
Psychosis and hate crimes, 217
Psychosocial systems model of
    child abuse, 178
PTSD. *See* Posttraumatic stress
    disorder
Public affairs officer (PAO), 94
Public awareness
    of domestic violence, 8
    of victims' rights, 14–15
Public defenders, 45
Public laws, 5
Public necessity, 258–59
Public speaking, 100–102
Public wrong, 58
Puente, Dorothea, 111
Punitive damages, 61, 71, 246
Purdy, Patrick Edward, 110–11

Qualified immunity, 298
Quality of life, 82, 84, 85, 87
Quid pro quo sexual harassment,
    138, 141

Race riots, 284
Racial identity and national
    identity, 217
Racism
    and church arsons, 220n. 10
    crime motivated by, 22
    definition of, 218
    and hate crimes, 214
    See also Hate crimes
Radio, 93
Rage, 79
Railroads, 267
"Rape: The All American Crime"
    (Griffin), 7
Rape
    acquaintance, 129, 132–34, 142
    in crime index, 21
    crisis counselors for victims, 77
    definitional issues in, 126
    definition of, 142

of elderly, 200–201
and HIV/AIDS, 225, 226, 228
legal aspects of, 130–31
male, 235
marital, 123, 134–37, 142
medical examination of victims,
    77–78
myths about, 128
nature of, 7
and posttraumatic stress
    disorder, 81
and sexual child abuse, 171, 182
startling facts about, 123
State v. Ciskie, 349
statistics on, 20, 23, 81, 123,
    127–28
stranger, 128–32
typologies of, 125–26
victim selection in, 131–32
See also Sexual assault; Sexual
    child abuse; Sexual
    violence
Rape in America (Kilpatrick), 81,
    127, 128, 132, 174, 351
Rape crisis centers, 8, 324
Rape Crisis Center in Washington,
    D.C., 344
Rape shield laws, 131, 142
Rapid City, South Dakota, "Indian
    Nations: Justice for Victims of
    Crime" conference, 350
Rationalizations for child
    abuse, 180
Raucci v. Town of Rotterdam, 290
R.A.V. v. City of St. Paul, U.S.
    Supreme Court, 351
Reactive offenders in hate
    crimes, 217
Reagan, Ronald, 14, 103, 252, 346,
    347, 348
Reasonable doubt, 65, 246–47
Rebuttal evidence, 51
Rectal intercourse, 126, 171, 225
Redirect examinations, 51
Reed, Willy, 318
Refugees, 207, 217
Registry of Civil Restraining
    Orders, Massachusetts,
    292, 352
Rehabilitation, 52, 54
    and juvenile court system,
    40, 42
Release, 255, 260
Relief, forms of, 61
Religion, crime motivated by, 22

Religious faith and survivors of
    homicide victims, 117
Religious groups, hate crimes
    against, 212
Remove Intoxicated Drivers (RID),
    346, 348
Requests for production of
    documents in discovery, 63, 64
Research, 341, 342
    on crime, 30–31
    on elder abuse, 196
    in gay and lesbian communities,
    234, 235, 237
    need for, 20
    in prison populations, 235
    on sexual assault, 126–28
    of spousal assault, 166n. 35
    Violence Against Women Act
    (VAWA), 15–16
    See also Measurement of crime
Reservation of rights, 255
Respondeat superior, 289, 299
Responsibility and victims, 11–12
Restatement of Torts, 250, 252, 253
Restitution, 70, 303, 308–13, 353
    definition of, 309, 314
    fines for, 311
    history of, 309–10
    methods of collecting, 312–13
    problems with, 311–12
    types of, 310–11
    and victim impact statements,
    322, 327
Restorative justice, 68–70
Restraining orders. *See* Injunctions
Rest-stop crimes, 338
Retribution, 52, 54, 69
Reunification efforts in juvenile
    court dependency procedures,
    67, 68
Revenge, 3, 79
Reynolds, Mike, 91
Rhode Island passes victims' rights
    amendments, 349
Rights of child in juvenile court
    dependency procedures, 67–68
Rights of victims. *See* Victims' rights
Right to an attorney, 8, 45, 56n. 15
Right to a jury trial, 50
Right to vote, 285
Ritual child abuse, 186–88, 190
Robbery
    in crime index, 21
    statistics on, 23, 338

Roman law, 4, 52, 172
Ros-Lehtinen, Ilena, 350
Rowland, James, 345
Royal judges, 5
Royalties and profits from
  crime, 304
Rules committees, 98, 105
Rules of evidence, 64
Rural crime, 338–40
  compared with urban crime, 338
  and geography, 340
  services for victims, 338–39
Rural Crime and Rural Policing,
  National Institute of
  Justice, 338
Rural populations, 2

Sacrifices of animals, 187, 188
Sadism rapes, 126
St. Augustine, 234
St. Paul, first hotline for battered
  women, 345
"Salyer's Rules or Statutes," 250
Sane National Alcohol Policy
  (SNAP), 348
Satanic Bible, The (La Vey), 187
Satanic cults, 186–88
Schafer, S., *The Victim and His
  Criminal,* 111–12
Scopes Trial, 52
Screws v. United States, 286
Search and seizure, 8
Security on Campus, Inc.
  (SOC), 349
Security-related services, 44
Select committees, 98, 106
Self-defense, 256–57
Self-incrimination, 65
Semen, 130
Senior centers, 200
Senior citizens, 200. *See also* Elder
  abuse; Elder victims
Seniors and Lawmen Together
  (SALT), 200
Sensitivity training, 209–11
Sentencing
  in criminal justice procedures,
    52–53
  and victim impact panels, 328
  and victim impact statements,
    317, 318, 324, 325, 326–27
Serial murderers, 111–12, 119
Serving the defendant, 61
Settlement of case, 64

Sexual assault, 123–28
  consent in, 257
  definitional issues in, 126
  definition of, 123–24
  of elderly, 200–201
  and HIV, 225
  and homeowner's insurance,
    273–75
  programs for, 103
  See also Rape; Sexual
    discrimination; Sexual
    harassment; Sexual violence
Sexual child abuse, 66, 171, 189
  extent of problem, 173–74
  extrafamilial, 171
  and HIV/AIDS, 228
  intrafamilial, 171
  stages of, 182–83
  theories of, 180–83
  See also Child abuse; Child
    neglect; Rape
Sexual control of women, 7
Sexual discrimination, 124. *See also*
  Sexual harassment
Sexual fantasies and child
  abuse, 180
Sexual harassment, 6, 124, 137–41,
  142, 335. *See also* Sexual
  discrimination
Sexuality in sexual violence, 7
Sexually transmitted diseases
  (STDs), 75, 78, 227. *See also*
  HIV/AIDS
Sexual motivation as theory of
  sexual violence, 124
Sexual mutilation, 112
Sexual orientation
  closeted homosexuals, 216
  crime motivated by, 22, 207, 213,
    235–36
  and HIV-related
    violence, 229
  and victims, 233–39
  See also Homosexuals
Sexual Politics (Millett), 7
Sexual transmission of HIV, 225.
  See also HIV/AIDS
Sexual violence
  on campus, 7
  definition of, 124, 142
  extent of the problem, 126–28
  Kelly's conceptualization of, 7
  research studies on, 126–28
  theories of, 124–25

See also Domestic violence; Rape;
  Sexual assault; Sexual child
  abuse
Shaeffer, Rebecca, 333
Shelters for women, 8, 149, 228,
  238, 339, 345
Sherman, Lawrence, 159
Shield laws, 95
Shock, 79
Shotgun wounds, 76
Sibling abuse, 183–85, 189
Sidebar stories, 93, 105
Silence of the Lambs, The (film), 111
*Silverball Amusement, Inc. v. Utah
  Home Fire Insurance
  Company,* 277
*Simon & Schuster v. New York Crime
  Victims Board,* U.S. Supreme
  Court, 351
Simple obsessional stalkers, 334
Simpson, Nicole Brown, 247
Simpson, O.J., 46, 65, 247
Sixth Amendment, U.S.
  Constitution, 45, 46
Slaves, 137
Smith, Michelle, 187
Smith v. Wade, d, 290
Snell v. O'Halloran, Inc., 265
Social control in sexual violence, 7
Social control of women, 7
Social exchange theory in elder
  abuse, 198, 203
Social forces in victimology, 6–9
Social guests, 268
Socialization as theory of sexual
  violence, 124
Social learning and deviance
  disavowal theory, 154
Social learning model of child
  abuse, 178
Social psychological model of child
  abuse, 178
Social stress theory of spousal
  abuse, 152–53
Society for the Prevention of
  Cruelty to Children, 172
*Society of the Roman Catholic Church
  of Diocese of Lafayette v.
  Interstate Fire & Casualty,*
  277–78
Sociocultural model of sexual
  harassment, 140
Sociology and criminology, 3
Sodomy statutes, 239

"Son of Sam" provision in
VOCA, 304
SOP. *See* Standard operating
procedure
South Carolina passes victims'
rights amendment, 349
South Carolina v. Gathers, U.S.
Supreme Court, 318, 320–21
Southern Poverty Law Center, 207
Sovereign immunity, 297
Spanking and child abuse, 169
Sparta, 172
Special victim populations, 222–43
Special verdict forms, 65
Spectrum disease, 224
Spiritual Dimension in Victim
Services, 348, 351
Spousal abuse
and alcohol, 154
and criminal justice system,
156–63
definition of, 148, 163
dynamics of, 150–52
extent of problem, 149–50
and isolation, 155
legislation on, 157
and marriage, 155
police response to, 157–59
and pregnancy, 154–55
programs for, 103
and self-defense, 256
theories of, 152–55
See also Domestic violence;
Spousal assualt
Spousal assault
definition of, 156, 164
homicides, 108, 110, 115, 119
research of, 166n. 35
Thurman v. City of Torrington,
156, 287–88
See also Domestic violence;
Spousal abuse
Spousal immunity and marital
rape, 136
Spouses as victims, 146–67
Spree killers, 111, 119
Spring guns in defense
of property, 257
Stabbing wounds, 76
Stalking, 30, 61, 250–51, 333–34,
342–43n. 5
laws on, 98, 352
Standard operating procedure
(SOP), 94

Standing committees, 98, 105
Stare decisis, 5, 16, 321
State court juvenile system, 41
State court system, 37–39
appellate courts, 39
supreme courts, 39
trial courts, 38–39
See also American court system;
Courts; Federal court system
State criminal codes, 21
State databases, 16
State grants, 104
States, automony of, 36
State v. Ciskie, 349
Statistical data on crime, 19–34
Status offenders, 66
Statutory laws, 6
STDs. *See* Sexually transmitted
diseases
Steed v. Imperial Airlines, 261n. 6
Steinmetz, Suzanne, "The Battered
Husband Syndrome," 149
Stepchildren, 261n.6
Stepfathers and child abuse, 182
Stereotypes
of child abusers, 180
of child abuse victims, 181, 182
and hate crimes, 208, 212
Stipulations, 64
Stockholm syndrome, 151, 164
Stockton School Yard
Massacre, 111
Stranger crimes, 22, 108
child abuse, 174, 182
rape, 128–32
Student Right to Know and
Campus Security Act, 350
Stump v. Sparkman, 301n. 41
Subrogation, 306, 307, 313
Substance abuse, 82
Substantive defenses, 297
Suicide and life insurance
benefits, 272
Summary judgments in pretrial
activities, 63
Superior courts, 38
Support groups and HIV/AIDS,
229. *See also* HIV/AIDS
Support systems, 216
Supreme courts, 39
Surrebuttal, 51
Survival groups, 218
Survival statutes, 249, 260
Surviving Sexual Violence (Kelly), 7

Survivors of homicide victims, 108
definition of, 119
and family relationships, 114–16
guilt of, 115, 116, 117
mental and emotional responses
of, 116–18
notification of, 118–19
Susman, Jarjorie and Carol Holt
Vittert, *Building a Solution,* 82
Suspended sentences, 309–10
Symbolic restitution, 311
Symbols in hate crimes, 207, 213,
215, 216
Symposium, Plato, 234
Symptomatic phase of HIV, 224

Tangible losses, 84, 85–86
Task Force on Family
Violence, 347
Task Force on Victims of Crime, 14,
103, 324–25, 346–47
American Correctional
Association, 349
Technology, 341
Telemarketing frauds, 31
Television, 93–94
Temporary restraining orders. *See*
Injunctions
Tenants, 264–65
Ten Commandments, 4
Texas passes victims' rights
amendment, 350
Third-party codefendants, 87
Third-party insurance, 277
Third-party liability and insurance,
262–82
Third-party liability insurance, 281
Threat Management Unit, Los
Angeles Police Department,
333
"Three Strikes and You're Out,"
53, 91
Thrill-seeking offenders in hate
crimes, 216–17
Thurman v. City of Torrington, 156,
287–88
Token damages, 246
Tort law, 58, 245, 247, 264, 268
Torture in rape, 126
Totality of circumstances rule,
270, 281
Traffic tickets, 38, 48
Training and professionalism,
13, 15

Transferred intent doctrine, definition of, 246, 252, 260
Transmission of HIV, 224–25. *See also* HIV/AIDS
Transportation issues in rural areas, 340
Traumatic bonding theory, 151–52, 164
Trauma to the head, 77
Traveling serial killers, 112
Treason, 6
Trespassers, 258–69
Triads in elder victimization, 200
Trial courts, 38–39, 54
Trials
  in civil procedures, 64–65
  differences in civil and criminal, 65
Tribal lands, 339, 340. *See also* Native Americans
Tribes of Israel, 4
Turner System, 93
Twelve Tables, 5, 172

Unanimous verdict, 65
"Under color of law," U.S. Supreme Court, 285–86, 299
Underinsured motor insurance, 276
Undocumented aliens, 216
Uniform Crime Reports, 20–23, 32
  and child abuse, 172
  compared with National Crime Victimization Survey, 28
  on rapes, 127–28
Uninsured motorist insurance, 276
United Nations, International Declaration on the Rights of Victims of Crime, 348, 353
United Press International (UPI), 93
U.S. attorneys, 44
United States Code Section 1983 actions, 284–87
  theories of liability under, 287–90
U.S. Congress
  Campus Sexual Assault Victims' Bill of Rights, 332, 350, 351
  Child Protection Act of 1990, 350
  Child Sexual Abuse Registry Act, 352, 353
  Crime Victims' Rights Act of 1995, 352
  Family Violence Prevention and Services Act, 345, 348

Hate Crime Statistics Act, 22, 211
  legislation, 96–100
  Missing Children's Assistance Act, 348
  Parental Kidnapping Prevention Act of 1980, 346
  Victims' Bill of Rights, 13
  Victims of Crime Act (VOCA), 15, 103, 303–4, 347
  and victims' rights, 350
  Victims' Rights Constitutional Amendments, 353
  Violence Against Women Act (VAWA), 15–16, 290
  Violent Crime Control and Law Enforcement Act, 15, 352
  See also Civil rights acts
U.S. Constitution, 6
  Bill of Rights, 43, 47, 48, 286
  and freedom of the press, 92
  interpretation of, 8
  and militia groups, 218
  and U.S. Supreme Court, 40
  Victims' Rights Constitutional Amendment, 13–14, 96
  See also First, Fifth, Sixth, Eighth, and Fourteenth Amendments
U.S. Health and Human Services Department, 8
  Office on Domestic Violence, 346
U.S. Justice Department, 22
  and National Crime Victimization Survey, 23
  Office for Victims of Crime (OVC), 14, 15
  and Violence Against Women Act, 353
United States Merit System Protection Board, 137, 140
U.S. Supreme Court, 6, 40
  Argersinger v. Hamilin, 45
  Booth v. Maryland, 317–19, 320–21
  civil rights decisions of, 8
  County of Riverside v. McLaughlin, 48
  Gideon v. Wainwright, 45
  Harris v. Forklift Systems, Inc., 129
  on hate crimes, 213–14
  Meritor Savings Bank v. Vinson, 129
  Monell v. Department of Social Services, 286–87
  on official immunity, 297
  Payne v. Tennessee, 319–20

R.A.V. v. City of St. Paul, 351
Simon & Schuster v. New York Crime Victims Board, 351
South Carolina v. Gathers, 318, 320–21
  and supervision, 37
  "under color of law," 285–86, 299
  on unlawful activities of insurance companies, 270
  and victim impact statements, 317–22
Williams v. Florida, 50
  women justices on, 153
U.S. Surgeon General, 348
United States v. Classic, 285
Universities
  duty to protect students, 268, 332–33
  and grants, 104
  sexual harassment at, 140–41
  sexual violence at, 7
  See also Campus crime
University of Montreal, 217
University of New Hampshire, 29
Univesity of Virginia Faculty Senate, 141
Unjust enrichment doctrine, 249–50
Unknown long-term physical injuries, 75
Unlawful activity of insurance companies, 270–71
UPI. *See* United Press International
Urban populations, 27
Ur-Nammu, Code of, 4
Utah passes victims' rights amendment, 352

Vaginal intercourse, 126, 225
Vehicle accidents, 77
Vehicular homicide, 112–14
  statistics on, 113
  See also Drunk driving
Venue and jurisdiction, 59
Verdict, 52, 65
Victim assistance programs, 303–4, 313, 344. *See also* Victim services
Victim compensation. *See* Compensation
Victim Costs and Consequences: A New Look, National Institute of Justice, 82
Victim and His Criminal, The (Schafer), 111–12

Victim impact panels, 328, 346, 347
Victim impact statements, 53,
    316–31, 329
  acceptance of, 322
  constitutional issues of, 317–22
  and death penalty cases, 317–21,
    330n. 5
  first one in Fresno County,
    California, 345
  purpose of, 317
  and U.S. Supreme Court, 317–22
  and victim satisfaction, 325–26
Victim Issues Committee
  American Probation and Parole
    Association (APPA), 351
  Association of Paroling
    Authorities, International, 351
Victimization
  consequences of, 73–89
  financial consequences of, 82–88
  mental consequences of, 78–82
  physical consequences of, 74–78
Victim–offender mediation, 69–70
Victim–Offender Reconciliation
    Program (VORP), 69–70
Victimology
  academic courses in, 2, 17n.
    1, 342
  academic and professional
    conferences, 332
  bachelors degree program
    in, 350
  courses at National Victim
    Assistance Academy, 353
  credentials and certifications
    in, 15
  and criminology, 3
  definition of, 3, 16
  emerging trends, 332–42
  history of, 2–18
  multidisciplinary perspective of,
    12, 15
  social forces in, 6–9
  study of, 342
  and technology, 341
  theories of, 9–12
  See also specific laws and acts;
    U.S. Congress
Victims
  advocacy in legislation, 99–100
  children as, 73–168
  civil rights of, 283–301
  constitutional rights of, 283–301
  and correctional system, 45–47

  costs of crime for, 82–88
  in criminal justice system, 42–43
  disabled persons as, 229–33
  elder, 194–205
  emotional trauma of, 43
  employers of, 43
  empowerment of, 90–106
  families of, 43
  females as, 122–45
  of gang violence, 337
  hearing-impaired victims as, 232
  helplessness of, 91
  of homicide, 107–21
  homosexuals as, 233–39
  physical trauma of, 43
  reactions to various crimes, 82,
    83–84
  and responsibility, 11–12
  and restorative justice, 68–70
  special populations of, 222–43
  spouses as, 146–47
  typologies of, 9–11
  and violence, 340–41
  as witnesses, 44
Victims' Assistance Legal
    Organization, Inc. (VALOR),
    346, 353
Victims' Bill of Rights, U.S.
    Congress, 13
Victims' Constitutional
    Amendment Network
    (VCAN), 349
Victims of Crime Act (VOCA), U.S.
    Congress, 15, 103, 303, 303–4,
    347, 350
Victim services, 91, 304, 345
  as cost of crime, 86
  for disabled persons, 229–30, 231
  in HIV/AIDS, 226–27
  volunteering for, 13
  See also Victim assistance
    programs
Victim Services Certificate
    Program, Calfornia State
    University at Fresno, 348
Victims' rights, 4, 9, 43
  first statute on, 4
  and media, 14
  to privacy, 43
  and U.S. Congress, 350
Victims' Rights Constitutional
    Amendment
  U.S. Congress, 353
  U.S. Constitution, 13–14, 96

Victims' rights movement, 2,
    8–9, 309
  critical dates in, 344–53
  development of, 12–16
  father of, 345
  and public awareness, 14–15
Victim–Witness Coordinator
    positions, 348
Victim–witness notification system,
    Federal Bureau of Prisons, 348
Victim–witness programs, 13, 344
Violence
  cause of, 341
  in culture and marital rape,
    136–37
  definition of, 29, 341
  gang, 336–37
  gender-based, 291
  and victims, 340–41
  workplace, 334–36
Violence Against Women Act
    (VAWA)
  U.S. Congress, 15, 190–91,
    350, 352
  U.S. Justice Department, 353
Violent Crime Control and Law
    Enforcement Act, U.S.
    Congress, 15, 352
Violent crimes, 6
  fear of, 8
  reporting of, 22
  in U.S. Code, 300n. 33
Virginia McMartin Preschool, 187
Visionary serial killers, 111
VOCA. *See* Victims of Crime Act
Voir dire, 50, 54
Volunteering for victim assistance
    programs, 13
Von Bulow, Sunny, 348
Von Hentig, Hans, *The Criminal and
    His Victim*, 10–11
Von Hentig's Theory of
    Victimization, 10–11
VORP. *See* Victim–Offender
    Reconciliation Program
Voyeurism, 171

Walker, Lenore E., 150–52
Wall Street Journal, 322
Walsh, Adam, 346
Warrant of arrest, 48, 259. *See also*
    Arrest
Warrantless arrest, 259, 295, 345.
    See also Arrest

Washington passes victims' rights amendment, 349, 350
Washington Post, 322
Watson v. City of Kansas City, 288
Western legal theory, 5
White-collar crime, 23, 30–31
White supremacist groups, 207, 217–18
Whitman, Charles, 111
Widows, 4
Wildlife crime, 338, 339
William the Conqueror, 5
Williams v. Florida, U.S. Supreme Court, 50
Wills and estates. *See* Probate matters
Wilson, Mary Ellen, 172
Wilson v. Workers' Compensation Appeals Board, 279
Wind River Reservation, 340
Wire services, 98

Wisconsin
  first Crime Victims' Bill of Rights, 346
  passes victims' rights amendment, 352
Wisconsin v. Mitchell, 213
Witnesses
  in criminal justice system, 42–43
  in depositions, 64
  expert, 64, 66, 248
  of gang violence, 337
  right to confront, 317
Women
  civil rights for, 291–92
  control of, 7
  control of sexuality of, 7
  dependency of, 153
  as equals, 134, 141, 153
  hate crimes against, 213
  hearing-impaired as victims, 232

  historical perspectives on, 123, 135–36
  shelters for, 8, 149, 228, 238, 339, 345
  as victims, 122–45
  See also Battered women syndrome; Feminist movement; Lesbians
Women's Advocates and Haven House, Pasadena, 345
Workers' compensation, 278–80
Workplace sexual harassment, 137–41
Workplace violence, 334–36
Writ of Certiorari, 40, 54
Wrongful death, 249–50
Wrongful death statutes, 260

Yale University, 237
Young v. Huntsville, 265
Youth and crime, 27, 28, 337. *See also* Juvenile crime